NARRATIVE, RELIGION AND SCIENCE

An increasing number of contemporary scientists, philosophers and theologians downplay their professional authority and describe their work as simply 'telling stories about the world'. If this is so, Stephen Prickett argues, literary criticism can (and should) be applied to all these fields.

Such new-found modesty is not necessarily postmodernist scepticism towards all grand narratives, but it often conceals a widespread confusion and naïvety about what 'telling stories', 'description' or 'narrative' actually involve. While postmodernists define 'narrative' in opposition to the experimental 'knowledge' of science (Lyotard), some scientists insist that science is itself story-telling (Gould); certain philosophers and theologians even see all knowledge simply as stories created by language (Rorty; Cupitt). Yet story-telling is neither innocent nor empty-handed. Register, rhetoric and imagery all manipulate in their own ways; above all, irony emerges as the natural mode of our modern fragmented culture. Prickett argues that since the eighteenth century there have been only two possible ways of understanding the world: the fundamentalist, and the ironic.

STEPHEN PRICKETT is Regius Professor Emeritus of English at Glasgow University. He has published one novel, thirteen monographs, and some seventy-five articles on Romanticism, Victorian Studies and related topics, especially on literature and theology. His books include *Coleridge and Wordsworth* (1970), *Romanticism and Religion* (1976), *Words and the Word* (1986), *The Bible* (Landmarks of World Literature, 1991), and *Origins of Narrative: The Romantic Appropriation of the Bible* (1996), all published by Cambridge University Press.

D0228063

Acknowledgements

This book was largely written during a year's leave as a visiting scholar in the English Department of the Australian National University in Canberra, and later, for a shorter period, in the National University of Singapore. To Livio Dobrez and David Parker, successively Heads of Department at the ANU, I owe thanks not merely for sympathetic encouragement, but also for practical suggestions and many lent books. Similarly, in Singapore, Robbie Goh and Ban Kah Choon made me more than welcome, providing the time and conditions to complete my research.

A number of Glasgow colleagues have given generously of their own time to read parts or all of this work as it developed, and their comments have been invaluable. In particular I owe an enormous debt to Richard Cronin, Bob Grant and Donald Mackenzie. At a greater distance, to Kevin Hart, I owe no less profound thanks, as I do also to Patsy Erskine-Hill, whose close critical reading has saved me from many unseen ambiguities and even more infelicities. Special thanks must also go to Simon Haines who went beyond all canons of hospitality, lending me not only his own unfinished manuscripts, but also his extensive library, together with the room that held it.

Others, in Canberra, Glasgow and Singapore, such as Susan Ang, Robert Barnes, Terence Dawson, Clifford Siskin, Rajeev Patke and Rex Whitehead, will probably be unaware of the ideas I gleaned from casual remarks or conversations, but they too have played an important part in the genesis of this work. Finally, I have to thank Jeanette Sky for running to earth in the Royal Library of Copenhagen the anonymous print of *The Tomb of Napoleon* which had so inspired Kierkegaard, but which seems to have eluded many of his subsequent commentators. I acknowledge that Library's kindness in granting permission to reproduce it as cover and frontispiece to this book.

At an institutional level I am grateful first and foremost to the British Academy for the Research Leave Award that enabled me to write the bulk of this book, to the Australian National University for its hospitality, and to Glasgow University for its generosity in granting me the leave, both paid and unpaid, to complete the work. I would like also to thank the English Department at the National University of Singapore where I was invited to give a series of lectures based on my work for this book. For that invitation and for the subsequent debate that raged on by e-mail for days, I am deeply grateful. It was my first experience of electronic collegiality, and I shall never forget it.

Arthur Dent, Screwtape and the mysteries of story-telling

In Douglas Adams' novel, *Mostly Harmless*, which appears as volume five of his increasingly inaccurately named trilogy, *The Hitch-Hiker's Guide to the Galaxy*, we find the following gnomic conversation between our nearest equivalent to a hero, Arthur Dent, and a mysterious old man who appears to be pole-squatting in another dimension on the planet Hawalius, on the outer Eastern Rim of the Galaxy. It is a planet inhabited almost entirely by oracles, seers and soothsayers – together with an inordinate number of take-away pizza shops, because most of these mystics were quite incapable of cooking for themselves. Here Arthur encounters a village composed entirely of extremely high poles surmounted by platforms. The majority turn out to be unoccupied, except for a liberal sprinkling of bird-droppings, but from one of them Arthur sees an old man on a neighbouring pole who, after a little persuasion, offers this explanation of nearly everything:

'You cannot see what I see because you see what you see. You cannot know what I know because you know what you know. What I see and what I know cannot be added to what you see and what you know because they are not of the same kind. Neither can it replace what you see and what you know, because that would be to replace yourself.'

'Hang on, can I write this down?' said Arthur, excitedly fumbling in his pocket for a pencil.

'You can pick up a copy at the spaceport,' said the old man. 'They've got racks of the stuff.'

'Oh,' said Arthur, disappointed. 'Well, isn't there anything that's perhaps a bit more specific to me?'

'Everything you see or hear or experience in any way at all is specific to you. You create a universe by perceiving it, so everything in the universe you perceive is specific to you.'

Arthur looked at him doubtfully. 'Can I get that at the spaceport, too?' he said.

'Check it out,' said the old man.[1]

---

[1] Douglas Adams, *Mostly Harmless*, Heinemann, 1992, p. 83.

Though this may be standard stuff to the inhabitants of the mystic planet, it appears to be news to our everyman hero, Arthur Dent, who is clearly not well up in German Idealist philosophy.

We live in a society inundated by self-confessed story-tellers. Whereas 100, or even 50 years ago those who told the grand narratives about the world – scientists, historians and theologians – were anxious to impress us with the accuracy and authority of their knowledge, today they seem to be clamouring to be recognized as something nearer to that of village elders, the story-tellers of the tribe. Physics, declared Niels Bohr, father of the 'Copenhagen' interpretation of quantum theory in the 1920s and 1930s, tells us not about what is, but what we can *say* to each other concerning the world. There is no 'scientific method' writes Jean-François Lyotard, a scientist is before anything else a person 'who tells stories'.[2] This description of the scientist is echoed by John Gribbin, the physics writer, who recently commented at the end of a lengthy discussion of quantum theory, 'I do not claim that it is anything more than just a fiction; all scientific models are simply Kiplingesque "just-so" stories that give us a feeling that we understand what is going on.'[3] Startling as this might seem to the non-scientist, within their profession such views from Bohr or Gribbin are no longer controversial. Gribbin seems in fact, consciously or unconsciously, to be echoing the American biologist Stephen Jay Gould, who had used precisely the same phrase, 'just-so stories' – but without mentioning Kipling – in an essay in 1991.[4] Science, Gould claimed, was best thought of as a series of interpretative or 'adaptive stories' to explain certain phenomena.

Even more explicit is the philosopher and evolutionary sociobiologist, Daniel Dennett, one of Gould's fiercest critics:

I have to tell you a story. You don't want to be swayed by a story? Well, I *know* you won't be swayed by a formal argument; you won't even *listen* to a formal argument for my conclusion, so I start where I have to start.[5]

Nor are scientists the only ones now aspiring to a status only a few years ago abandoned to the poets, novelists and the other composers of fictions whom Plato saw as the first people who ought to be expelled from his ideal Republic. Historians, who have in truth as much right as modern-day poets to see themselves as the direct descendants of ancient bards, have

[2] *The Ghost in the Atom* eds. P.C.W. Davies and J.R. Brown, Cambridge University Press, 1986, p. 11.
[3] John Gribbin, *Schrödinger's Kittens, and the Search for Reality*, Weidenfeld and Nicolson, 1995, p. 222.
[4] Stephen Jay Gould, 'Not Necessarily a Wing' in *Bully for Brontosaurus: Reflections in Natural History*, Hutchinson Radius, 1991, p. 144.
[5] Daniel Dennett, *Darwin's Dangerous Idea: Evolution and the Meanings of Life*, Harmondsworth: Penguin, 1996, p. 21.

long been aware that they are really only telling stories about the past – hence, no doubt, their embarrassment at the wilder fantasies of their craft, such as *Braveheart*. Philosophers such as Jacques Derrida (yes – he *is* a professional philosopher!) have echoed the German Romantic Friedrich Schlegel in calling for philosophy to aspire to the status of literature.[6] More surprising is the way in which those one-time purveyors of divine truth, theologians and biblical scholars, now scramble to get aboard the story-tellers' bandwagon. A recent, and very interesting, study of the New Testament was beguilingly entitled *The New Testament as True Fiction*.[7] Writing in 1996, Nicholas Lash, then Norris Hulse Professor of Divinity at the University of Cambridge, similarly takes it for granted that the primary function of both science and philosophy is to tell stories.

> I am not arguing that human beings are incapable of metaphysics, or that they 'only' tell stories . . . It would be more accurate to say that the narrative comes first, and that the formal systems we construct – whether in philosophy or science – are coloured, shaped, determined, by the story-telling soil from which they spring.[8]

Teachers of literature like myself, accustomed to being sharply reminded, ever since Plato, that we are in the only discipline to deal with fictions as a matter of course, can be forgiven for feeling overwhelmed by the sudden popularity of our field. But it is difficult to avoid the suspicion that this new enthusiasm of other disciplines to be part of the story stems less from an innate love of literature than from a widespread belief that it might solve problems of their own – in particular the twin twentieth-century problems of subjectivity and pluralism.

At every level, our modern world is riven with conflicting descriptions and contradictory explanations. Historians differ fiercely from one another in their interpretations of the past, and, quite apart from the fact that we cannot check every fact they assert, we know that there is in the end no authoritative and final version against which they can be measured. Scientists investigating the material and biological structure of matter are swayed by historical paradigms of which they may be only partially conscious,[9] but they rarely address the questions of the Kantian

---

[6] Which, of course, is not the same as *equating* the two. See Derrida's 'Remarks on Deconstruction and Pragmatism', in *Deconstruction and Pragmatism*, ed. Chantal Mouffe, Routledge, 1996, pp. 79–80.

[7] Douglas Templeton, *The New Testament as True Fiction*, Sheffield Academic Press, 1999. For those who wish to know more about this book, see my review of it in *The Times Literary Supplement*, March 3, 2000, p. 30.

[8] Nicholas Lash, *The Beginning and End of Religion*, Cambridge University Press, 1996, p. 18.

[9] The term comes, of course, from Thomas Kuhn's *The Structure of Scientific Revolutions*, University of Chicago Press, 1962.

philosopher as to how far we can ever know things-in-themselves in the first place. The world described by cosmologists or quantum physicists is in any case so bizarre as scarcely to relate to the world we experience at all. Sociologists are as likely to interpret any scientific theory in terms of the social structure of the society that produced it, as they are to acknowledge its accuracy in describing the material world.[10] The dialectical materialist believes that material conditions and the means of production shape society; the Freudian believes, on the contrary, that we unconsciously shape our external conditions to suit internal needs. Environmentalists take a very different view of our world from any of these.

Moreover, it is just over 200 years since Kant changed the whole course of Western philosophy by arguing that time and space are internal constructs of the mind. For him, not merely were things in themselves ultimately unknowable but, in effect, our knowledge of the world is shaped – and limited – by our own mental capacities. Whatever modifications have since been proposed to his arguments, no one has decisively refuted him. Yet over that same period modern science has made spectacular developments by assuming, at least at an 'instrumental' level, that reality is both objective and knowable. The current ('big bang') cosmological theory of the origins of the universe predicates that space and time are indivisibly woven into the fabric of things. According to this view, there *was no time* before that moment – that 'singularity' – some fifteen billion years ago.

As we shall see, there have been a number of very interesting attempts to reconcile these apparently totally contradictory views of the world, but there is as yet certainly no consensus about their success. To a degree that few of us (even professional philosophers and scientists) comprehend, our philosophy and our science remain at odds. How then can we approach any common reality beneath such seething diversity? To many, I suspect, the idea that we are simply telling stories about the world appeals because it appears to solve what would otherwise be an enormous epistemological problem.

This may well be so, but as Lash comments, narrative is not itself a neutral medium. In C. S. Lewis' *Screwtape Letters*, which I first read as a child, I remember a passage where Screwtape, a senior devil, writes to his nephew, a junior devil called Wormwood, about the mental condition of modern human beings. 'Your man has been accustomed, ever since he

---

[10] See, for instance, Joseph Carroll's review of three recent biographies of Darwin, by Adrian Desmond and James Moore, by Janet Browne, and by John Bowlby, in *Times Literary Supplement*, February 20, 1998, pp. 7–8.

was a boy, to have a dozen incompatible philosophies dancing about together inside his head. He doesn't think of doctrines as primarily "true" or "false", but as "academic" or "practical", "outworn" or "contemporary", "conventional" or "ruthless". Jargon, not argument, is your best ally . . . '[11]

As an adult, not to mention a professor of literature concerned with modern intellectual history, I have long been uncomfortably aware that Screwtape was guilty of gravely understating his case. He was by no means the first, and was certainly not the last to notice that we live in a culture dominated by stereotypes, illusions, copies, imitations, sound-bites and fantasies. Not merely do our clichéd labels invoke ready-made emotions, but also most contemporary humans have *many more* than half a dozen such incompatible ideas floating around inside their heads. Moreover, as we have seen, their incompatibility is not simply a matter of different beliefs or even just of jargon.

As Arthur Dent discovered, our perspectives on the world will depend, not least, on how we see ourselves – of the kinds of story we tell ourselves about who we are. The pattern shifts with every change in viewpoint, whether personal or historical. Our perspectives will also depend on where we come from and our historical circumstances at the time. In 1954 Lewis described himself in a famous lecture as a 'dinosaur'.[12] He was referring, only partly with self-deprecating irony, to his lack of sympathy with certain aspects of modern culture, but (even without the prompting of Freud) we might well suspect that the wry humour of declaring oneself an extinct monster might mask very real fears that it could be true.

Let's look again at Screwtape's advice to Wormwood. If we are to understand it at all, we need first of all to remember the context in which it was written – a context which is, in some ways, easier for us to reconstruct with hindsight, than it would have been for many of those actually living through the terrifying and dramatic events engulfing Britain in 1942. It would be easy, for example, to forget the huge shifts in popular awareness between the early 1940s, when Lewis was writing *Screwtape*, and the 1950s when Lewis was attempting to sum up his own intellectual development. In 1942, in a world at war, with ideologies seemingly polarized between Hitler's Fascism and Stalinist Communism, the possibilities for unconscious rhetorical pluralism of the kind Screwtape is hopefully wishing on Wormwood's 'patient', though they were certainly widespread, were

---

[11] C.S. Lewis, *The Screwtape Letters*, Geoffrey Bles, 1942, p. 11.
[12] 'De Descriptione Temporum', *They Asked for a Paper*, Geoffrey Bles, 1962.

simply fewer than in the 1950s. Certainly they were many fewer than in the 1990s, a decade after the French sociologist Lyotard's proclamation of the 'end of grand narratives' had ushered in postmodernism,[13] and following the American historian Fukuyama's famous – or notorious – vision that we had reached 'the end of history'.[14] If the former announced a joyful incoherence of all things, the latter's much-misunderstood claim referred in Hegelian terms to the apparent cessation of ideological conflict in the Western world after the fall of communism. But whether true or not (and Fukuyama's own title had a carefully placed question mark after it) what it would be safer to call the present 'ideological lull' has simply made room for a succession of 'minor' conflicts, usually in the name of incompatible nationalisms, in which religion is often a significant factor. At the same time even the most stable and homogeneous societies have discovered that they already incorporate a degree of ontological pluralism that would have been difficult for Lewis (or even Screwtape) to foresee.

'Pluralism' is a relatively new word for a relatively new condition. It was first used in a strictly material sense in the early nineteenth century to describe the practice of well-placed clergy drawing salaries from several churches at the same time – often without residing at any of them. It was only just over 100 years ago, in 1887, that it was first applied, presumably as a metaphor from the corruptions of Anglicanism, to the holding of fundamentally different and incompatible ideas – perhaps originally with the implication that, like the *rentier* clergy, any such mental 'pluralist' would in the end 'reside' in none of them. In practice, however, it quickly came to refer less to individual people than to the kind of society whose inhabitants held widely differing views about themselves and about how that society should operate. The first such society had been seventeenth-century England, which, unlike any other countries in Europe, had experienced within the span of a single century officially condoned clergy from across the whole spectrum of Christianity, from the Catholic priesthood through to Puritan ministers.[15] Even a disastrous Civil War had failed to produce a viable or enforceable consensus, and over the next 100 years or so, the English had slowly had to come to terms with the fact that there was no going back to any traditional world of common beliefs and aspirations.

---

[13] Jean-François Lyotard, *The Postmodern Condition: A Report on Knowledge*, trs Geoff Bennington and Brian Massumi, foreword by Fredric Jameson, Manchester University Press, 1984.

[14] Francis Fukuyama, 'The End of History?', *The National Interest*, Summer, 1989, pp. 3–18.

[15] See Peter Harrison, 'If the time of the appearance of this new interpretative framework was the late seventeenth and early eighteenth centuries, then the place was England.' *'Religion' and the Religions in the English Enlightenment*, Cambridge University Press, 1990, pp. 3; 84.

As a result, one of the commonest modern meanings of 'pluralism' refers to the agreed stand-off between once rival Christian Churches. In modern democratic countries, theories of the state, of justice, and of what constitutes the 'good life' in general are essentially pluralistic in outlook – not just in religion, but in every form of social, political and economic life.[16] Thus we take it for granted that conservatives and socialists may differ profoundly about the means to their political goals, but they do so within a democratic framework. John Stuart Mill's now classic idea of liberty – the freedom to act in so far as it does not impinge upon the freedom of others – has elevated pluralism from being a necessary evil of the seventeenth century into a common good of the twentieth.

But there is a fundamental difference between those who merely hold differing views within an accepted framework, and those whose personal stories allow no such framework in common. Such 'ontological pluralism' adds a whole new dimension and presents a whole new dilemma. As the name suggests, ontological conflicts concern the very nature of *being* itself. In theory – and all too often in practice – they permit no other way of seeing things. Though a theist is likely to regard the world in a quite different way from an atheist, it is fortunate that, at least since the seventeenth century, many forms of theism (including nowadays most – but not all – forms of Christianity) make peaceful co-existence with non-believers an explicit part of their faith. But a minority of Muslims believe that, as a complete ideology and way of life, Islam cannot so-cially co-exist with any other kind of society, and can only properly be practised within an Islamic state governed by the Sharia. Similarly, some Orthodox Jews see an ontological difference between themselves and non-Jews (or even liberal and secularized Jews) so great that they would prefer to see Israel as a religious state all of whose citizens were governed solely by Hebrew Law. Like these religious orthodoxies, some forms of nationalism permit no compromise with opposing beliefs – let alone op-posing nationalisms. Massacres in Northern Ireland, Bosnia and Ruanda bear witness to such conflicting ontologies. Others, although not (at the moment) violent, represent differences of being so great as to make the

---

[16] See, among others, Isaiah Berlin, *Four Essays on Liberty*, Oxford University Press, 1969; Stuart Hampshire, *Morality and Conflict*, Harvard University Press, 1983, and *Innocence and Experience*, Harvard University Press, 1989; John Kekes, *The Morality of Pluralism*, Princeton University Press, 1993; Martha Nussbaum, *The Fragility of Goodness*, Cambridge University Press, 1986; Michael Oakeshott, *Rationalism in Politics*, Methuen, 1962, and *On Human Conduct*, Oxford: Clarendon Press, 1975; John Rawls, *A Theory of Justice*, Harvard University Press, 1971; Peter Strawson, 'Social Morality and Individual Ideal', in *Freedom and Resentment*, Methuen, 1974; Charles Taylor, *Sources of the Self*, Cambridge University Press, 1989, and *Multiculturalism*, Princeton University Press, 1994; and Bernard Williams, *Ethics and the Limits of Philosophy*, Fontana, 1985.

prospect of any reconciliation very difficult to imagine. At a different level of militancy, for instance, some Australian aboriginal peoples have an attitude to their ancestral land which is quite incompatible with modern Western conceptions of 'ownership', which assume the right to change, improve, or exploit property according to circumstances. In such a context, disputes about land are less concerned with legal title than with two incommensurable scales of value.

All this, however, serves not to diminish the force of Screwtape's advice to Wormwood, but, if anything, to strengthen it. If he was mistaken at all, it was in not foreseeing just how fundamentally pluralistic the twentieth century was to become. But, as the ending of the book makes clear, though God may be presumed to have foreknowledge, devils evidently do not. In advising his inexperienced nephew on how to draw his 'patient' into the ever-expectant arms of 'our Father below', Screwtape, it now appears, was prophetic in his insight and wrote better than he knew. But, of course, this is only half the picture. Screwtape is not a real person, he is a character in a story – the fictional creation of C.S. Lewis. Does the fact that it is 'only a story' make any difference to all of the above? Can we say, for instance, that Lewis, in giving those words to Screwtape, also 'wrote better than he knew'?

This poses a much more difficult question. It obviously does not alter the increasing pluralism of the late twentieth-century world, but it does sharply affect our reading of it. Screwtape, after all, is a *devil*. Though it nowhere says so, the whole novella is based on a premise of ironic inversion, in which everything that Screwtape recommends or advises is self-evidently evil, and everything he disapproves of, denigrates or hates is to be seen as valuable, worthwhile and good. The fact that every reader perceives this within a very few lines, and has no difficulty coping with such an inverted narrative, is a tribute both to Lewis' considerable literary skill and to the fact that the historical development of our literary culture has increasingly trained us to cope with narrative irony. Was this growth of twentieth-century pluralism, not to mention the rank undergrowth of jargon that has accompanied it, accurately foreseen by Lewis as being in reality an unmitigated disaster?

Certainly there is some evidence for this. It is clear both from *The Screwtape Letters*, and from his other, more serious and academic writings, that Lewis thought there *had* to be what we would now call a 'meta-narrative', that is, a single over-arching description of things that made sense of the world. The interesting thing is that though for most of his adult life he was a committed Christian, he seems to have taken it for granted that this was *not* a partisan Christian position. It is true that he would have assumed that it had to be the Christian viewpoint, but not, I think, because it was specifically Christian, but simply because it was obviously right. Any intelligent and logically minded person, whether a classical pagan philosopher, a Church Father, or a modern scientific rationalist, would have had to have agreed on this point, at least. If there were two conflicting accounts of reality, in the end one of them must turn out to be wrong. For him, as a matter of logic rather than belief, there could only be one Truth. We might well be ignorant of it, but, in so far as we did have evidence, and in so far as we could reason about that evidence, we could only arrive in the end, as he himself by his own account had done, at one final master-narrative. For him, only a grand narrative was properly habitable. On the whole, he had greater sympathy with those who inhabited a different grand narrative from himself, than with those who tried to camp out without any at all.[17]

Is this perhaps one of the things he meant by calling himself a 'dinosaur'? Of the four arguments he produces in that lecture to show the gulf between himself and the 'modern' world, one of the most telling is his lack of sympathy with the idea that there might be more than one correct (as distinct from simply mistaken) 'meaning' to a poem. Moreover, there is no doubt that later in life Lewis came to view himself as the self-appointed guardian of what he saw as an essentially monistic tradition. It included not merely historical Christianity, but the other peoples of 'the book', Judaism and Islam, as well as the other great world religions which follow what he called loosely 'the Way' – a conception of life and a system of morality, which whether based upon divine inspiration, or simply humanistic ideals, would have included a stream of historical figures as diverse as Socrates and Plato, the Stoics, and Buddha, Jesus and St Paul, not to mention George Eliot, John Stuart Mill and Gandhi. For them it made sense to speak, in the singular, of the 'Truth' – and to base their lives upon the search for it. Opposed to this would be the consummation devoutly wished on us by Screwtape and his fellow devils, where jargon and labels fragment reality, and people would unconsciously or consciously apply different and unrelated criteria to different parts of their experience – giving us, in effect, whether we like it or not, our modern world.

---

[17] A theme of his early satire on opposing intellectual systems, *Pilgrim's Regress*, Geoffrey Bles, 1943.

And this is our problem in a nutshell. Lewis, with the best will in the world, seems not merely wrong in his expectation of the eventual triumph of truth and common sense, but his most feverish nightmares appear to have come to pass. His satiric creation, Screwtape, with, literally, the *worst* will in the world, seems from the very first chapter to have been right after all. This is certainly not the first example in history of satire becoming literal truth, but it is the more disconcerting in that it affects not just politics, or fashion, or or some other essentially ephemeral human activity, but the very bedrock and stability of our world. Either there is a single, over-riding truth about things (whether we know it or not) or there isn't. This is a problem more immediately obvious in ostensibly theocratic or monistic states, such as Taliban Afghanistan or former communist countries, than in western liberal democracies, simply because in the latter ('the modern world') we are embedded in a tacit procedural agreement that is essentially capitalistic in its pluralism. Experience has shown us that it is preferable to throw a large number of solutions at a given problem in the hope that one or more might succeed, and not to start from *a priori* first principles. We rarely, if ever, discuss questions of absolute truth, and when on the rare occasions that Church leaders do so, they are greeted with embarrassed silence by their allies, and abuse from their opponents.

It is tempting, of course, to put the whole problem down to our ignorance; to argue that things will appear different when we know more. This may be so. The trouble is that history and experience point the other way. Until the beginning of the eighteenth century it was still possible for people to believe that the steady progress of science and learning in general would eventually prove the great truths of the Christian religion. It was possible to believe in the convergence of all knowledge. But what happened was not convergence, but divergence on a hitherto unimaginable scale. We are today living through the greatest explosion of information the world has ever seen. Every area of human knowledge seems to have undergone at least one radical revision in the last half-century. We now know infinitely more about our universe, our history, our pre-history, even our biology than our parents did. And what is the result? Despite Edward O. Wilson's belief in consilience, an increasingly coherent world-picture, we most of us discover a vastly greater and in many ways more mysterious fragmentation of knowledge than ever before.

As so often, Douglas Adams parodies the problem very neatly. In the first volume of *The Hitch-Hiker's Guide* we are told the 'Answer': it is forty-two. The real problem, of course, is the *Question* to which that is supposedly the Answer. Many readers have assumed that forty-two is a figure Adams just plucked out of the air. This may, of course, be so. But perhaps we should give Adams the credit for knowing that there is in fact a very real scientific mystery attached to that number. It concerns the fundamental forces that bind the electrons of an atom together. Electrons repel each other inversely as the square of the distance due to electricity, and attract each other inversely as the square of the distance due to gravitation. The actual equation can be expressed as follows:

$$\frac{\text{Gravitational Attraction}}{\text{Electrical Repulsion}} = \frac{1}{4.17 \times 10^{42}}$$

That is, the ratio of gravitational to electrical force is the number given above followed by forty-two zeros. That is an amazing enough number, and it is only equalled by the ratio of the diameter of another fundamental particle, a proton, to the diameter of the universe, which is also a number followed with forty-two digits.[18] But, of course, if the universe is really expanding at the rate astronomers at present calculate, that is presumably a temporary coincidence, rather than a constant. Nevertheless, the coincidence is extraordinary enough to whet our appetite for mysterious numerological parallels, and, as Adams saw, it suggests the makings of a good story.

But stories, like the words that compose them, are slippery things. Though the philosophers of the past wrote of 'Truth' with a capital 'T', that does not necessarily mean they all meant the same thing by it. The 'truth' of a work of fiction is not necessarily the same as the 'truth' of philosophy, or the 'truth' of a mathematical theorem. As we have said, Screwtape is neither a real person, nor even a real devil (supposing such to exist!) but part of a fictional narrative. His story may only be a fragment, resting on a set of metaphysical assumptions (Heaven and Hell; guardian angels and personal devils; etc.) not necessarily shared by all members of our pluralistic society, but granted its premises, which are clearly to be recognized as an ironic literary device, it conforms to the pattern of all such stories in that it interprets and makes sense of the events it purports to describe within its given framework. This may not be 'truth' as a physicist would understand the word, but, as we shall see, there can be other definitions. It has been said of Shakespeare, for instance, that

---

[18] Richard Feynman, *The Character of Physical Law*, BBC, 1965, pp. 30–2.

he allows us to see aspects of reality that we could not see without him. Such praise should properly be reserved only for the greatest writers, but we can surely say of Lewis that at least he *reminds* us of aspects of reality all too easily forgotten.

The Screwtape Letters begin with the 'grave news' that Wormwood's unnamed 'patient' has become a Christian. Since this is a correspondence between devils, the truth or falsehood of Christianity itself is not an issue: it represents the Enemy, and must be fought with every weapon available. The ending, the death of the 'patient' in an air-raid, is, paradoxically, victory for the powers of Good, since he is thus taken for ever beyond the reach of the bungling Wormwood. In the best Stalinist tradition, such failure merits liquidation – in this case the poor devil is eventually to be consumed, we gather, by no less an appetite than the voracious Screwtape himself. The theological symbolism is obvious: the forces of Hell (and their earthly totalitarian equivalents) are self-defeating and in the end self-consuming.

Even such a potted summary reminds us that the problem of pluralism with which Lewis began was not simply a philosophical one, but was embedded in a particular narrative. As it was presented to us, it was not just an intellectual problem, but a matter of life and death – or, more precisely, Eternal Life or Eternal Damnation. This is, in the most literal sense, a narrative of God. Whether or not it is great literature in the Shakespearean sense, showing us new realities unavailable before, it partakes of the grandest narrative of all in our society: that of the Fall and Redemption of humanity; of Heaven and Hell. As we have seen, there are other competing narratives in our pluralistic society, some of which, like the narratives told by Darwin and Freud, may today command even wider assent, but in choosing to assert, however symbolically and ironically, the supremacy of his chosen grand narrative, Lewis could have adopted no more powerful medium to express his theme.

As in the parallel form of allegory, the fact that the story itself is essentially unrealistic does not detract from the reality of the issues at stake. Readers of Orwell's *Animal Farm* are in no doubt they are reading a fable. That doesn't stop them hating Snowball and Napoleon, or being furious at Boxer's fate when he is carted off in the knackers' van. Similarly, the fact that pluralism is introduced in the narrative with Screwtape's hopeful endorsement changes the way we are disposed to read it. Instead of seeing it as a difficult but interesting cultural problem, we are instantly inclined – as Lewis intended we should be – to see in it something insidious, sinister and even perverse. We have, in short, been manipulated not by argument, nor even by labels, but by something more powerful and compelling than either: literary narrative.

Clearly, if we are to consider further the problems driving so many modern disciplines towards 'story-telling', we must start by trying to understand a little more about narrative itself.

CHAPTER I

Postmodernism, grand narratives and just-so stories

POSTMODERNISM AND GRAND NARRATIVES

We have so far been using the word 'narrative' as if it had a clear and agreed meaning, but this is, of course, not so. For the French philosopher Jean-François Lyotard, for example, narrative not merely tells a story, but, of itself, constitutes a kind of 'knowledge' – a particular way of understanding the world.

> Scientific knowledge does not represent the totality of knowledge; it has always existed in addition to, and in competition and conflict with, another kind of knowledge, which I will call narrative in the interests of simplicity . . . I do not mean to say that narrative knowledge can prevail over science, but its model is related to ideas of internal equilibrium and conviviality next to which contemporary scientific knowledge cuts a poor figure, especially if it is to undergo an exteriorization with respect to the 'knower' and an alienation from its user even greater than has previously been the case.[1]

In contrast with the kind of 'objective' knowledge of the material world supposedly provided by science, for Lyotard, narrative provides an essentially subjective and personal view of things. We have within us all a personal 'story' which we tell ourselves, and which we constantly modify and alter in the light of experience. Indeed it has been argued that our very mental health and stability depends upon the kind of internal narrative we construct.[2] A fractured and incoherent self-construction can be both symptom and cause of profound psychic dislocation.[3] But it is more than just a personal story-telling. Lyotard has borrowed from Ivan Illich

---

[1] Jean-François Lyotard, *The Postmodern Condition: A Report on Knowledge*, pp. 7–8.
[2] See, for instance, C.G. Jung, *Collected Works*, ed. H. Read, M. Fordham and G. Adler, Routledge, 1953–78, Vol. XVI, para. 135. For comments on this view see Anthony Stevens, *Private Myths: Dreams and Dreaming*, Penguin, 1996, p. 108.
[3] For practical therapeutic applications see, for instance, Murray Cox and Alice Theilgaard, *Mutative Metaphors in Psychotherapy: The Aeolian Mode*, Tavistock, 1987.

the term 'conviviality' to imply the *communal* nature of narrative. Originally, we must presume, public narratives (as distinct from our 'private' ones) were a matter of reciting aloud to an audience. Homer's originally oral epics were an essential part of the classical Greek sense of 'identity' – a word whose Latin root, *idem*, we recall, meant not individuality, but 'sameness'. Through Homer, all Greeks could feel their common heritage, and experience the 'sameness' that differentiated them from the surrounding barbarians. Roman, Norse, Teutonic and Anglo-Saxon mythology and epics served a similar purpose. Even more recently, the stories of the founders of the United States of America, Washington, Jefferson, Paul Revere, John Paul Jones, Daniel Boone and Davey Crockett, are used to create a common feeling of 'Americanness' among an immigrant population most of whose genetic ancestors were in quite other parts of the world in the late eighteenth and early nineteenth centuries when these heroes supposedly shaped their nation.

Nor was this 'conviviality' necessarily destroyed or even weakened by literacy and the popularity of private reading. Protestantism, with its stress on individual study of the Bible, was a product of the printing-press. Yet if we stress the tendency of those first Protestant and later Puritan communities to split into rancorous and disputatious sects, we miss the corresponding sense of community, equally fostered by individual Bible study, that bound the members of those sects tightly together. Even reading novels, which since the eighteenth century has been almost invariably a silent and solitary activity, has done little to dampen the inherent conviviality of narrative – as any literary society or fan-club will testify. Sterne, Fanny Burney and Byron were mobbed by admirers. Dickens found inexhaustible audiences for his readings from his own work – and wept with them over the death of little Nell. Kipling's short story, 'The Janeites', hinges on the comradeship, even the sense of an 'inner ring',[4] created on the First World War battlefield by a number of quite different individuals, from officers to nurses, on discovering their common love of Jane Austen.

For Lyotard (who naturally does not use such illustrations) narratives have their place – and it is an important one. But whether personal or communal, that place is essentially subjective and limited. What is at stake is the nature of what he calls 'grand narratives'. The physical

[4] For C.S. Lewis, the term is unambiguously bad, signifying invisible corruption (see his essay 'The Inner Ring' (1944) in *They Asked for a Paper*). Kipling is more subtle and ambiguous, giving us both the very real shock of pleasure and surprise in the characters involved, but not missing the material advantages it gives the wounded private who is the narrator.

sciences have traditionally sought to explain the world in terms of fixed natural laws which permitted, in theory at least, mathematically predictable workings and outcomes. The so-called 'social sciences', despite the notorious slipperiness of their material, were set up more recently to imitate the model of precision presented by the older sciences, and looked for similar 'natural laws' governing human behaviour in economics, the distribution of wealth, criminology and more recently in sociobiology. Classical Marxism, for instance, had claimed that economics provided universal 'laws' of human behaviour. But by the mid-years of the twentieth century the uncertainties created, in particular in physics, by the seemingly inexplicable behaviour of particles in quantum theory began to cast doubts on this model of science. Responding as ever to trends in the physical sciences, some social scientists expressed serious doubts about what their own discipline could achieve. Others were questioning not merely the possibility but even the desirability of such over-arching theories as total explanations of everything. In 1959 an American sociologist, C. Wright Mills, criticized the whole idea of 'Grand Theory', arguing that the belief that the social disciplines should be aiming to construct 'a systematic theory of "the nature of man and society"' was actually impeding any real progress.[5] Though only repeating what was by then quite a widespread view,[6] this critique was unusual in that it attacked the pretensions of Grand Theory in the name of imagination rather than science. Other criticisms quickly followed, among the most telling being Thomas Kuhn's argument that there were no facts independent of our theories about them, and that consequently there was, and could be, no one way of viewing, classifying and explaining the world which all rational persons were logically obliged to accept.[7] Such theories, it was suggested, were better seen not in terms of natural law but 'fictions', *stories* which we constructed to explain events. 'Grand Theory' was better described as 'grand narrative'.

It was not, however, until the debate about postmodernism began in earnest in the late 1970s that the controversy over the possibilities of grand narratives spilled over and began to affect literature and aesthetics.

As with any other fashionable term, 'postmodernism' has recently attracted a wide variety of sometimes conflicting usages. It was actually

---

[5] C. Wright Mills, *The Sociological Imagination*, N.Y.: Oxford University Press, 1959, p. 23.

[6] See Quentin Skinner's 'Introduction' to *The Return of Grand Theory in the Human Sciences*, ed. Quentin Skinner, Cambridge University Press, 1985.

[7] Thomas Kuhn, *The Structure of Scientific Revolutions*, University of Chicago Press, 1962, pp. 140 ff.

first used by the historian, Arnold Toynbee, who, as part of his attempt to write a Christian interpretation of world history in 1939, used the term to mean an unrealized moment in the future when history and humanity might be redeemed.[8] Not least, perhaps, owing to his unfortunate timing, the word did not catch on. But even that false start showed it uncomfortably straddling the divide between two very different kinds of meaning. On the one hand, it suggested a definable historical period – in its current usage always taken to include the present moment – while on the other it implied a collection of related theories, a movement, or even just a mood which somehow looks to the future to redeem, or at least, explain the present. Though it often seems to mean very different things in art, architecture, literature and philosophy, a common thread running through most of these fields is the fact that it wholeheartedly embraces rather than deplores pluralism. Postmodernism luxuriates in meanings, rather than meaning.

Thus in *The Postmodern Condition*, Lyotard argues that what *he* called 'postmodernism' is actually to be *defined* in terms of its resistance to any kind of grand narrative:

> I will use the term *modern* to designate any science that legitimates itself with reference to a metadisclosure . . . making an explicit appeal to some grand narrative, such as the dialectics of meaning, the emancipation of the rational or working subject, or the creation of wealth . . . . I define *postmodern* as incredulity toward metanarratives. This incredulity is undoubtedly a product of progress in the sciences: but that progress in turn presupposes it.[9]

This critique of 'grand' or 'meta-narratives' borrowed from the earlier Anglo-American debate over the place of theory in the social sciences. Lyotard, however, added to that brew the iconoclastic ideas of his fellow Frenchman, the social historian Michel Foucault, whose avowed objective was to expose the way modern societies control and discipline their populations through the knowledge-claims and practices of the human sciences, such as medicine, psychiatry, criminology and sociology. Foucault's self-declared concern was not with the meaning of particular statements, but with the often concealed social and intellectual rules that permit them to be made in the first place. What he was really interested in was the nature and exercise of power. For him, 'truth', so far from having any absolute validity, was simply an effect of certain kinds

---

[8] Thomas Docherty, 'Postmodernism: An Introduction', in *Postmodernism: A Reader*, ed. Thomas Docherty, Harvester Wheatsheaf, 1993.
[9] Lyotard, *Postmodern Condition*, pp. xxiii–xxiv.

of language. 'Truth', he writes, 'is a thing of this world: it is produced only by multiple forms of constraint. And it induces the regular effects of power.'[10] (As Bertrand Russell had remarked a generation earlier, 'truth is what you tell the police'!)

But if grand narratives are the stories we tell ourselves to explain the world we live in, such 'explanations' inevitably reach beyond verifiable knowledge into the realm of myth. The word 'myth' is essentially a description not of content but of function. Myths are the stories we tell ourselves to make sense of the disparate and fragmented state of knowledge. It is not their truth but their task that is important. Whether stories of aboriginal rainbow-serpents, Greek gods and heroes, the events of the New Testament, great national figures like Napoleon, or the conquest of disease by an ever-advancing medical science, such stories seek to explain why the world is as it is. A myth is a just-so story.

For Lyotard this makes them essentially a delusion. For him, narratives must always be plural, always in competition with one another. Not merely the great narratives, of the kind provided by Christianity, Darwinism or Freudianism, but, as we have just seen, even the great moral abstractions that have moved mankind in the past, such as 'Justice' or 'Truth', are simply the constructs of whatever group exercised social control at the time. They have no validity beyond that.[11] For us, in contemporary post-industrial postmodern society, Lyotard insists, 'the grand narrative has lost its credibility'.[12] (To say 'truth' at this juncture, of course, would be to use a word from just such a discredited grand narrative. 'Credibility', on the other hand, is satisfactorily provisional and subjective.) Indeed, Lyotard's distinction between 'modernity' and 'postmodernity' depends on rejection of all such narratives.

But Lyotard's alternative, scientific knowledge, has its own problems. Whereas narrative (whether personal or collective) is internalized, science is external, objective, and, Lyotard claims, liable to alienate the knower, who cannot feel a part of such knowledge, or make it 'personal' in any way. Nevertheless, as scientific knowledge increases, we become increasingly sceptical of the other grand 'meta-narratives' that once underpinned our world. These include not merely 'Justice' and 'Truth', or the emancipation of the rational and the creation of wealth, but even the meta-narrative of science itself.

[10] Michel Foucault, *Power/Knowledge: Selected Interviews and Other Writings 1972–1977*, ed. Colin Gordon, Harvester, 1980, p. 131.
[11] The ultimate victory for Thrasymachus in Plato's *Republic*.
[12] *Postmodern Condition*, p. 37.

Here, however, the argument takes an interesting turn. By the meta-narrative of science, Lyotard, we discover, does *not* mean what one might expect: the idea that were we eventually to know everything to be known about the physical world, it would all add up, perhaps even fall into place as 'the grand Theory of Everything', or 'superforce', spoken of hopefully by certain cosmologists, such as Stephen Hawking and Paul Davies.[13] He is, it seems, not interested in science in this sense at all, but in the sociology of science, and in the way scientists, when, for instance, they were interviewed by the media, resorted to an implied 'epic of knowledge' in order to gain funding.[14] This is a myth with which the state is happy to collude, he argues, here following Foucault, because this, in turn, can be used for its own end – power. 'The state spends large amounts of money to enable science to pass itself off as an epic: the State's own credibility is based on that epic, which it uses to obtain the public consent its decision makers need.'[15] For this purpose the more elitist and therefore more mysterious science becomes, the better. But for Lyotard, of course, such a 'legitimation' of science by what amounts to its antithesis, narrative, is utterly *illegitimate* (though where such an idea as 'legitimacy' comes from in the first place is far from clear):

A science that has not legitimated itself is not a true science; if the discourse that was meant to legitimate it seems to belong to a prescientific form of knowledge, like a 'vulgar' narrative, it is demoted to the lowest rank, that of an ideology or instrument of power.[16]

But in the course of this argument, something rather odd has happened to the terminology (and this is not a matter of translation). As it is presented to us here, 'narrative' is a necessary, but somehow more primitive, form of knowledge than that represented by 'science'. It was introduced originally, we recall, as a salutary reminder that 'scientific knowledge does not represent the totality of knowledge', and that human 'equilibrium and conviviality', those basic emotional needs, were still important. But it is rooted in tradition, rather than in new discovery. 'Narration', writes Lyotard, 'is the quintessential form of customary knowledge.'[17] Our tribal stories, whether conveyed through classical epics, Shakespearean drama, nineteenth-century novels, or even the twentieth-century cinema, have in the past always given us a sense of who we are, where we ultimately belong. But whereas it was once our principle way of knowing, in the postmodern Lyotardian vision this is no longer true.

---

[13] See Paul Davies, *Superforce*, Heinemann, 1984.　　[14] Lyotard, *Postmodern Condition*, p. 27.
[15] Ibid. p. 28.　　[16] Ibid. p. 38.　　[17] Ibid. p. 19.

It is therefore impossible to judge the existence or validity of narrative knowledge on the basis of scientific knowledge and vice versa: the relevant criteria are different . . . Lamenting the 'loss of meaning' in postmodernity boils down to mourning the fact that knowledge is no longer principally narrative.[18]

Such a sense of loss is, however, ephemeral. We soon get used to the absence of the big structuring narratives. Their loss is more a matter of a change of habit than a central cultural collapse.

That is what the postmodern world is all about. Most people have lost the nostalgia for the lost narrative. It in no way follows that they are reduced to barbarity. What saves them from it is their own linguistic practice and communicational interaction.[19]

An attentive reader might also remark that if this is so, one reason could well be that whether or not it is correct that knowledge is as fragmented as this would suggest, at least in structural terms, Lyotard has merely replaced positive grand narratives by a negative one. To insist that in contemporary post-industrial postmodern society all grand narratives have lost credibility is not, of course, an empirical statement at all, but a grand epistemological, or even metaphysical, generalization.[20] To refute it, presumably all one would have to do would be to find *one* grand narrative that had survived somewhere within a 'post-industrial post-modern society', and the thesis would collapse. One might cite, for example, estimates of the number of Fundamentalist Christians in the United States – defining 'fundamentalist' here in strictly 'narratological' terms of a declared belief in the literal truth of the Genesis account of Creation. These, we are told, amount to as much as forty-eight per cent of the population, or over a hundred and ten million – rather more than twice the entire population of Lyotard's France.[21] But to look for actual examples of this kind is to reveal how logically slippery Lyotard's generalizations

---

[18] Ibid. p. 26.   [19] Ibid. p. 41.

[20] Their vulnerability to the charge of covert metaphysics has made both Lyotard and Foucault understandably sensitive to the word. Here, for instance, is Foucault's reply to a question from Paul Rabinow about 'intention' as a 'fundamental determining factor': 'Nothing is fundamental. That is what is interesting in the analysis of society. That is why nothing irritates me as much as these inquiries – which are by definition metaphysical – on the foundations of power in a society or the self-institution of a society, etc. These are only reciprocal relations, and the perpetual gaps between intentions in relation to one another.' Interview with Paul Rabinow: 'Space, Knowledge, and Power', trs Christian Hubert, in *The Foucault Reader*, ed. Paul Rabinow, N.Y.: Pantheon Books, 1984, p. 247.

[21] Dennett, *Darwin's Dangerous Idea*, p. 516; even the more modest estimate by Margaret Talbot would still put the number above sixty million ('A Mighty Fortress', *New York Times Sunday Magazine*, February 27, 2000, p. 36).

are. One suspects that for him, by definition, Bible-belt American Fundamentalists, however first-world they might be in their living standards, however much they might be employed in service and communications rather than manufacturing industry, and however much they might surf the Internet in their spare time, would not qualify as 'post-industrial postmodern' people. More significantly, perhaps, even were one to produce a substantial body of working biologists throughout the world who believed in Darwinism and natural selection as the grand narrative that explained all life on earth as well as the actions and interactions of human societies, they would not count either. Lyotard's argument here is better seen as itself a 'grand narrative' than as any kind of testable hypothesis. We cannot treat it with any rigour as a verifiable fact. It is rather a story we tell ourselves to make sense of the disparate and fragmented state of modern knowledge. It is, in short, a myth.

We can see this, for instance, even more clearly in his formula for the 'science' of the future:

Postmodern science – by concerning itself with such things as undecidables, the limits of precise control, conflicts characterized by incomplete information, 'fracta', catastrophes, and pragmatic paradoxes – is theorizing its own evolution as discontinuous, catastrophic, nonrectifiable, and paradoxical. It is changing the meaning of the word knowledge, while expressing how such a change can take place . . . And it suggests a model of legitimation that has nothing to do with maximized performance, but has as its basis difference understood as paralogy.[22]

We will deal with that curious word 'paralogy' in a moment, but we need first to address this Lyotardian notion of what should constitute 'postmodern science'. While there is indeed an increasing trend towards the study of discontinuities and 'catastrophe theory' in some areas of contemporary science, to suggest that *most* science is concerned with such problems – or even that its future lies in that direction (note how postmodernism typically uses an unknown future to legitimize a theorized present) – once again leaps from an observable trend to a blanket generalization. This is in fact 'meta-narrative' on the grand scale: nothing less than a predictive theory of theories. Legitimate observation of detail becomes covert grand narrative.

And this brings us to a second feature of the Lyotardian idea of 'narrative'. Nature, as ever, abhors a vacuum. If the dismissal of grand narratives functions, despite its author's declared intentions, as itself a kind of grand narrative, then perhaps narrative, even in this limited and

---

[22] Lyotard, *Postmodern Condition*, p. 60.

even 'primitive' sense, is more important than the argument would at first sight suggest. The Lyotardian idea of 'paralogy' is a key term in this transformation, and it takes us right to the heart of the problems inherent in a postmodern world of ontological pluralism. 'Paralogy' is not a new word in either English or French – the *Oxford English Dictionary* (*OED*) cites the first use in 1599 – but Lyotard gives it a wholly new connotation. The original meaning is 'to reason falsely' – usually from an unconscious logical error. For Lyotard, however, such 'breaks' in logic serve to reveal not the falsity of the reasoning, but rather the falsity of the expectation that things shall cohere at all. So far from breakdown, for him such errors often provide a breakthrough. He writes:

Paralogy must be distinguished from innovation: the latter is under the command of the system, or at least used by it to improve its efficiency; the former is a move (the importance of which is often not recognised until later) played in the pragmatics of knowledge. The fact that it is in reality frequently, but not necessarily, the case that one is transformed into the other presents no difficulties for the hypothesis.[23]

The fact that such paralogical 'leaps' may not cohere with each other or with the larger picture is not merely unimportant, it may be a positive advantage, since it is our expectation of universal coherence that must be jettisoned. As Fredric Jameson argues, Lyotard's ultimate vision of science and knowledge today is as a search

not for consensus, but very precisely for 'instabilities', as a practice of *paralogism*, in which the point is not to reach agreement but to undermine from within the very framework in which the previous 'normal science' had been conducted.[24]

Once again, narrative rather than science is crucial. Quantum theory, or even big bang cosmology, have indeed destabilized much of traditional (if not 'normal') science, and both present narratives of a kind – though whether chemical engineering can be read as 'narrative' seems much more doubtful. But as we have seen, Lyotard is not actually interested in the content of scientific knowledge at all. He is interested in its structures – and these, even where they constitute 'instabilities', are essentially narrative. Thus grand narratives are contrasted with what he calls the 'little narratives' (*petits récits*) which, he argues, remain 'the quintessential form of imaginative invention, most particularly in science'.[25]

---

[23] Lyotard, *Postmodern Condition*, p. 61.   [24] Ibid. Foreword by Fredric Jameson, p. xix.
[25] Ibid. p. 60.

It is the words 'imaginative invention' that are the give-away here. As we shall see, they belong to what looks at first sight like a quite different associative set – that of nineteenth-century German Romanticism, which, following Kant, was perhaps the first intellectual movement to claim that science itself was an imaginative restructuring of the world in precisely the same way as a work of fiction, even if it obeyed different rules.[26] In case we should miss the point of his argument, Lyotard cites a passage from P. B. Medawar: '*having ideas* is the scientist's highest accomplishment', adding 'there is no "scientific method": a scientist is before anything else a person "who tells stories"'.[27] What Lyotard is admitting, in effect, here is that so far from science being a fundamentally different form of knowledge from narrative, the supposed 'objectivity' of science is in fact itself actually *composed* of a multitude of minor (and presumably 'subjective') narratives.

Such a reversal should not be that surprising. As in the case of Foucault, the problem with absolute relativism, of course, is that it results in the notorious 'Cretan paradox' – exemplified in the Greek story of the Cretan who says 'all Cretans are liars'. If the Cretan is telling the truth, then he himself must be lying . . . As one critic has put it: 'If what Foucault says is true, then truth is always relative to discourse; there cannot be any statements which are true in all discourses, nor can there be any statements which are true for all discourses – so that on Foucault's own account, what he says cannot be true!'[28] Lyotard's own arguments about narratives as power, based as they are not on internal evidence of the disciplines involved, but on his pre-conceptions about the nature of power in general, suffer from the same logical flaw.

JUST-SO STORIES

But if Lyotard's arguments appear to turn themselves inside out, his conclusion is not one that would surprise most practising, 'coal face' scientists, who, unlike him, are performing real experiments rather than theorizing about their sociological implications. In this sense, such narratives take their place among others that purport to explain aspects of experience. But even the telling of stories carries with it a hidden freight whose implications are far-reaching. As Daniel Dennett succinctly puts

---

[26] See below, pp. 62–71; 121–7.

[27] In fact, this is a position Medawar specifically disclaims. See P.B. Medawar, *The Art of the Soluble*, 6th edn, Methuen, 1967, p. 116. (Lyotard, *Postmodern Condition*, p. 60).

[28] Mark Philp, 'Michael Foucault', in Skinner (ed.), *The Return of Grand Theory*, p. 70.

it, 'there is no such thing as philosophy-free science; there is only science whose philosophical baggage is taken on board without examination'.[29]

The French physicist, Bernard D'Espagnat, for instance, so far from seeing science as providing an adequate account of the world, insists that such descriptions can never be more than partial – or in his terms 'veiled'. Like Gribbin and Gould he insists that we must never lose sight of the narrative impulse in science: even to put what are essentially mathematical concepts in language is to creative narratives – or in his terminology, to 'allegorize' them. 'Texts in which the early stages of the Universe are described in terms of thermal agitation of particles in collision, but with no indication that such language is purely and simply allegorical, are unacceptable', he insists, 'even when written by eminent physicists.'[30] Nor is he afraid to take this to its logical conclusion: 'I cannot see on what basis we could maintain that religion and myth are not themselves also 'models', giving us – in a manner equally indistinct and uncertain – access to *other* features of the real.'[31]

Gould has no problems in seeing science as one among several narrative forms describing the world, but he also recognizes that narrative is not a neutral medium, and may have its own agenda, allowing the intrusion of what he sees as 'unconscious literary assumptions' into his 'just-so stories'.

Astute scientists understand that political and cultural bias must impact their ideas, and they strive to recognise these inevitable influences. But we usually fail to acknowledge another source of error that might be called literary bias. So much of science proceeds by telling stories – and we are especially vulnerable to constraints of this medium because we so rarely recognise what we are doing. We think we are reading nature by applying rules of logic and laws of matter to our observations. But we are often telling stories – in the good sense, but stories nonetheless.[32]

For an example of just such a 'story', we need look no further than one of Gould's favourite topics: the evolution of the horse over the past fifty-five million years. This has been a favourite example of evolutionary 'progress' ever since it was first used in a lecture by T.H. Huxley in 1870. In a classic series of drawings made for that lecture by Othniel C. Marsh,

[29] Dennett, *Darwin's Dangerous Idea*, p. 21.
[30] Bernard D'Espagnat, *Reality and the Physicist: Knowledge, Duration and the Quantum World*, trs J.C. Whitehouse and Bernard D'Espagnat, Cambridge University Press, 1989, p. 127.
[31] Ibid. p. 189.
[32] Stephen Jay Gould, 'Literary Bias on the Slippery Slope', *Bully for Brontosaurus: Reflections in Natural History*, London: Hutchinson Radius, 1991, p. 251.

and widely reproduced since in works as diverse as biology textbooks and Arthur Mee's *Children's Encyclopedia*, we are shown the steady increase in size from the cat-sized *Hyracotherium* (or *eohippus*) to the modern *Equus*. The sequential pictures of the changes, such as the reduction of toes to a single hoof, for faster galloping, and the steady increase in the size of molars, as they became more specialized grass-eaters, combine to give a very clear impression of the evolutionary 'development' of the modern horse. The problem with this splendid narrative, as Gould points out, is that it gives a totally misleading picture of the many-branched evolutionary 'bush' from which it was drawn. So far from being a triumph of evolutionary success, the genus *Equidae* is in fact practically extinct. In Gould's ironic phrase, it is 'life's little joke' that 'we choose horses because their living species represent the endpoint of such an unsuccessful lineage'. Though it was once widespread, with dozens of species, across almost every continent of the world (with the exception of Australia), it died out of both North America (where ninety per cent of the known fossils have been found) and South America. All that is left is a number of relatively minor branches, including three zebras, four donkeys and asses, and the horse (*Equus caballus*) which, having evolved in North America, unaccountably survived only in the Old World. Because, and only because, it is the main survivor, however, *Equus caballus* had to be placed at the top of our narrative 'ladder' as the final supreme achievement of the genus.[33]

Gould's story of the creation of the 'story of the horse' is an excellent illustration of our capacity for apprehending a loose mass of data in terms of a narrative. Indeed, it is clear that for him our tendency to tell stories may be one of the *conditions* of consciousness and intelligence itself. It is, quite simply, the way the human mind works.

Any definition of this (human) uniqueness, embedded as it is in our possession of language, must involve our ability to frame the world as stories and to transmit these tales to others. If the propensity to grasp nature as story has distorted our perceptions, I shall accept this limit of mentality upon knowledge . . . [34]

Nor is this acceptance of the place of storytelling as a way of shaping our world confined to fiction, mythology and science. This is, for instance, clearly also theological ground, and theologians have not been slow to move in to the field now technically entitled 'narrative theology'.

---

[33] Stephen Jay Gould, 'Case Two: Life's Little Joke', *Life's Grandeur: The Spread of Excellence from Plato to Darwin*, Cape, 1996, pp. 57–73.
[34] Ibid. p. 252.

For theologians like scientists, Lyotard's distinction between the kinds of narrative created by science, and the kinds of internalized narrative that have always structured our individual and social lives, does not arise. Practising science is as much a matter of 'telling stories' as the plays of Shakespeare or the cycles of the Old Testament. They are simply different kinds of stories, not a different kind of knowledge. But for Nicholas Lash, for instance, though all our knowledge may be rooted in our 'story-telling soil', that is no reason to return to the grand narratives of the past:

> ... theologians engaged in the growth industry of 'narrative theology' ignore, at their peril, developments which reflect philosophically that declining confidence in the possibility of large-scale, purposive, 'plot-linear' narrative unity which has been one of the hallmarks of the story of the novel for nearly a hundred years. Our world is, in a phrase of Frank Kermode's, 'hopelessly plural', disconnected, disorientated, fragmentary. We work (as Gadamer would say) within 'horizons'. And though horizons may be expanded, we fool ourselves if we suppose them ever to extend very far.
>
> Cosmologists and theologians, however, not only tell stories, but have the impudence to tell stories of the *world*. And even if the cosmologists would claim that their stories are of set purpose, plotless, it seems to me that both groups could reflect with profit on the problem, not simply of what is meant by claiming that some particular story of the world is *true*, but rather of what *kind* of story a 'story of the world' might be. Who could tell it, what would it be announcing, and how would it be told?[35]

Unlike Lyotard who, as we have seen, is peculiarly uninterested in the actual content of science as distinct from its role as a form of social control, Lash is acutely concerned with the *content* of the narratives created by both science and theology. Though for him there is no essential difference between the narratives presented by the two disciplines *as narratives*, he is uncomfortably aware that to describe any explanation as being a 'story' raises almost as many problems as it solves. Though he is no postmodernist, Lash shares all the postmodern suspicion of grand narratives and unifying explanations.

In particular, he recognizes the degree to which our notion of narrative has been historically conditioned by the pre-eminent role of the novel, as an art-form, in the last 200 years. Some have questioned whether the nineteenth-century novel, with its omniscient narrator, and its tendency to explain and tie up all the loose ends in its denouement has conditioned us to expect a similar neatness from real life – which possesses no such order or 'conclusion'. Others have argued that only fictional heroines,

---

35 Lash, *The Beginning and End of Religion*, pp. 84–5.

such as Catherine Morland and Emma Bovary, have been so seduced. But even those who would agree with Humphrey Bogart, that 'Life writes lousy plots', might still note that to think of life in terms of plots at all, is to allow art to influence life.

But if both Gould and Lash are aware, in ways that neither Foucault nor Lyotard appear to be, that what we might call 'narrative perception' inevitably shapes the way in which we structure the world around us, none of these seem fully aware of the way in which language and culture influence not merely the way stories are told, but the way in which we read them. It is not entirely clear, for instance, how Gould, by any account one of the most 'literary' of contemporary science writers, is using the word 'literary' in the passage quoted earlier. Does he mean by it our innate desire to shape what he calls the 'bush' of facts into a coherent 'story'? Does he mean that the pressure to order science into a narrative automatically means that we will choose some kinds of words rather than others to tell his story? What exactly are these 'constraints of the medium' which he both values and fears? Similarly, what precisely does Lash mean by querying the 'kind of story' that a theologian – or a cosmologist – might tell about the world?

Again, the story of the horse is revealing. Though presumably neither Huxley nor Marsh would have endorsed the idea in so many words, the narrative of development told in Marsh's pictures is one of hierarchy and 'progress'. In other words, an idea of *purpose* has been illegitimately smuggled into a series of changes which should be seen as the products of strictly random variation coupled with enhanced survival and reproduction for a tiny number of those mutations – the process of 'natural selection'. The fact is that it is very difficult to talk about natural selection *without* using purposive language. Almost any evolutionary writing (including Gould's own) is full of purposive language and metaphors. I was myself guilty of it when I wrote above that the evolution of the hoof was 'for galloping faster'. It was, of course, 'for' no such thing. By strict Darwinian theory, each stage in the evolution of the hoof was the result of random mutations which had the entirely fortuitous result of allowing the possessor to move faster and for longer periods over open grassland, and so to escape potential predators, and so produce more similarly fleet-footed descendants. Now it is possible to argue, as some have done, that such 'purposive' language to describe evolution is merely a convenient shorthand. It enables us to make a point in three words rather than three carefully colourless sentences. This is very likely true, but to distinguish between mere 'shorthand' and a way of thinking that is irredeemably purposive is not easy. We like a story to have a point, a meaning, a moral – or, at the very least, an ending. Unlike 'the story of the story of the horse', as told by Gould, which, because it has a point to make, provides fascinating reading, 'the story of the horse', told in properly sober and correct Darwinian terminology, has none of these things. Strictly speaking, there is no 'meaning' to the sequence of events, merely a number of contingent influences that we can only guess at.

But that is not, of course, how the story gets told. Consider these statements from a recent and highly regarded book on sociobiology, Matt Ridley's *The Origins of Virtue* (all italics are mine):

> When a T cell starts to multiply it is conscious of nothing and it is certainly not motivated by some urge to kill the invader. But it is, in a sense, *driven by the need* to multiply: the immune system is a competitive world in which only those cells thrive that divide when they get the chance . . . So attacking the foreign invader is, for these cells, a by-product of the normal business of *striving to grow* and divide. The whole system *is beautifully designed* so that *the self-interested ambitions* of each cell can only be satisfied by each cell *doing its duty* for the body.
>
> In the early 1970s, a biologist rediscovered the Alchian-Williams lesson. John Maynard-Smith had never heard of the prisoner's dilemma. But he saw that biology could use game theory as profitably as economics. He argued that, just as rational individuals should adopt strategies like those predicated by game theory as the least worst in any circumstances, so *natural selection should design* animals to behave instinctively with similar strategies.
>
> *Natural selection has chosen it* to enable us to get more from social living.[36]

That Ridley does not mean us to take the italicized statements literally is made clear by the first sentence of the first extract. But from there on the anthropomorphic phrases flow thick and fast, and we are rapidly left floundering as to the exact boundary between metaphoric and literal. If, for instance, we feel on firm ground in recognizing that natural selection 'designing' or 'choosing' is metaphorical, what of those competitive T cells being 'driven by a need'? My point is not that Ridley is writing badly – quite the contrary. In fact, he makes his points vividly and clearly. His dilemma is a universal one. To illustrate the problem, try re-phrasing each of those passages in totally non-purposive, non-metaphorical language.

This is a point that Daniel Dennett, as a philosopher of science, is prepared to face and tackle head-on. For him, we use the language of intention and purpose in biology because such metaphors represent

---

[36] Matt Ridley, *The Origins of Virtue*, Viking, 1996, pp. 45–6; 59; 66.

something that is *really there*. It comes, however, not from God, or even from ourselves, but from the blind emergent forces of nature.

> ... intentionality doesn't come from on high; it percolates up from below, from the initially mindless and pointless algorithmic processes that gradually acquire meaning and intelligence as they develop. And, perfectly following the pattern of all Darwinian thinking, we see that the first meaning is not full-fledged meaning ... But you have to start somewhere, and the fact that the first step in the right direction is just barely discernible as a step towards meaning at all is just what we would expect.[37]

Dennett is a rigorously monistic evolutionist. Since, he insists, all values must come by the same evolutionary source from which we, and all life, ultimately sprang, there is nothing incongruous in reading back our own notions of purpose into the non-sentient and thoughtless mechanisms by which life developed. His metaphor for this is 'reverse engineering'. Just as rival car-makers may strip down one of their opponents' new models to see how it works, and question the purpose of every new piece of engineering they encounter, so biologists are similarly entitled to question the 'purpose' of each new genetic modification. Surprisingly, Dennett seems unaware of how close this argument is to that of one of his most despised opponents,[38] the French Jesuit, Teilhard de Chardin, who argued that mind was implicit (or, as Dennett would say, 'emergent') in matter.[39]

But for many of us, this attempt to read metaphors of purpose, not as *metaphors*, but *literally*, solves the problem only by blurring it. We shall be looking at Dennett's main arguments later, here I just need to put down a marker to the effect that his notions of blind 'purpose' and emergent 'meaning' involve using those words in a quite different way from that in which they are normally used. The word 'purpose', for instance, normally implies the *opposite* of chance, and is *not* a synonym for it. Such fundamental problems over the terminology of evolution have led one literary scholar, A.D. Nuttall, to offer his own, not entirely tongue-in-cheek, 'refutation' of Darwinism. It goes like this. There are actually *two* forms of Darwinism currently in circulation, a 'strong' form and a 'weak' one. The 'strong' form is the correct account we have just outlined. It is rigorously non-directional and purposeless, not to mention exhaustive in the sense that it claims to account for all living phenomena. The 'weak' pays lip-service to the 'strong' form, but quietly allows that

---

[37] Dennett, *Darwin's Dangerous Idea*, p. 205.   [38] Ibid. pp. 320–1.
[39] See, for instance, *The Phenomenon of Man*, trs Bernard Wall, Collins, 1959.

other factors might also have an effect. In practice it permits purposive language and imagery in its narrative, and is thus much more intelligible and easy to apply. As we see in the examples above, it is, in fact, the form in everyday use, not merely with the general public, but even among working biologists when off-guard. The problem with this 'weak' version is that it is not really Darwinism at all. It is a covertly purposive theory which depends on and is validated by the 'strong' theory which it actually undermines.

But it is important to stress that the problem highlighted by Dennett, Gould, Nuttall and Ridley is not part of a modern misuse of Darwin by journalists and popularizers. It originates from an ambiguity deep within Darwin's original thought. In order to deny a creative role to God, as conceived within the Protestantism he had been brought up with, he adopted a strict materialism which reduced the workings of nature to the operation of blind laws and chance. But this, in effect, denied his own basic intuitions of the living processes of nature.[40] Time and again a vitalistic language creeps back into his writing. With his usual candour, he struggles with the problem himself:

> The term 'natural selection' is in some respects a bad one, as it seems to imply conscious choice; but this will soon be disregarded after a little familiarity . . . For brevity's sake I sometimes speak of natural selection as an intelligent power . . . I have, also, often personified the word Nature; for I have found it difficult to avoid this ambiguity; but I mean by nature only the aggregate action and product of many natural laws – and by laws only the ascertained sequence of events. With a little familiarity such superficial objections will be forgotten.[41]

But they did not prove so easily forgettable, and no subsequent reworking of Darwinism has been able to eliminate them. Far from being superficial, they actually seems to be endemic to the whole argument, so that what looked like a minor linguistic problem has turned into something much more deep-rooted and central to the whole theory. Whether or not we regard it as a flaw in Darwinism, however, depends on how far we expect our scientific paradigms to be unambiguous and unironic. As we shall see in the next chapter, there seem to be good reasons to assume that they are neither.

Whether one accepts that this constitutes another example of what might be called 'the constraints of the medium' is another matter. But

---

[40] See Rupert Sheldrake, *The Presence of the Past: Morphic Resonance and the Habits of Nature*, Collins, 1988, p. 272.
[41] Darwin, *The Variation of Animals and Plants Under Domestication*, John Murray, 1875, pp. 7–8.

there are other factors at work conditioning our responses to narrative in ways in which it is now very difficult for us to be fully aware. In a provocative and stimulating essay, *Take Read*, the American theologian Wesley Kort has argued that our relationship to the written text (and therefore to 'narrative' in our present sense) goes back to the Calvinistic attitude to the written word.[42] In Calvin's *Institutes* the reader is urged to study the Scriptures with minute intensity, weighing and pondering the meaning of every word or phrase, for on discovering its inward meaning for him or her hung Salvation itself. For a world only just liberated into a minimal literacy by the printing press, such an attitude to the word was revolutionary. This intense self-searching and self-constructing relationship to the text, argues Kort, has shaped our world historically in that this very 'sacramental' relationship was subsequently transferred first to the 'book' of Nature (i.e. science), then to the idea of history, and finally to the reading of literature. For him, postmodernism, with its denial of the possibility of an inherently value-laden text, has thus broken a chain of implicit valorization of the word stretching back in effect almost to the dawn of literacy.

The detail of history is not, alas, always as neat as such a summary narrative might suggest, but if one sees this movement not as a matter of one stage of reading replacing another, but, as it were *augmenting* the stages that had gone before, the model is helpful. Certainly there was a concerted effort in the late seventeenth and early eighteenth centuries to produce a 'scientific' Christianity, giving it all the demonstrable certainty that Newton had apparently given to our knowledge of the cosmos. In 1668, John Wilkins, Dean of Ripon and a Fellow of the Royal Society, published an *Essay Towards a Real Character and a Philosophical Language* advocating a totally unambiguous scientific language of his own invention. In the course of what he nicely calls 'a disgression' he offers his own reconstruction of Noah's Ark, from the information given in Genesis Chs. 6–8, showing that it was fully seaworthy, and would hold all the animals then known as well as those discovered later, together with precisely the right amount of foodstuffs, including an appropriate surplus of 1,888 extra sheep to feed all the carnivores during the forty-day voyage. In 1699, John Craig, a mathematician and later prebendary of Salisbury, published his *Theologicae Christianae Principia Mathematica*, presenting the whole of Christian doctrine as a series of a priori mathematical propositions reasoned from first principles. As we shall see in the next

---

[42] Wesley A. Kort, *Take Read: Scripture, Textuality and Cultural Practice*, Pennsylvania State University Press, 1996.

chapter, there was nothing inconsistent with Newton about Craig's incorporating in his title that of Newton's most famous work. Arguments from design, proving the existence of God from the intricate structure of His Creation were common in the early years of the eighteenth century. A long tradition of apologetic by clergyman-scientists includes John Ray's *Wisdom of God in the Creation* (1701), William Derham's *Physico-Theology* (1713) and *Astro-Theology* (1715), culminating at the end of the century with William Paley's best-sellers *Evidences of Christianity* (1794) and *Natural Theology* (1802).

Similarly we can perhaps see in Hegel's philosophy a historicizing of religion, just as Darwinian science represents a historicizing of science. With yet another paradigm-shift, of which this book is clearly a part, the twentieth century has certainly seen a progressive aestheticizing of religion, science and history. Unfortunately the chronology of these moves refuses such neat periodization. Thus, as we shall see, the origins of this progressive aestheticizing of the grand narratives of religion, science and history lie in German Romanticism at the end of the eighteenth century – the very matrix that was also to produce such great historians as von Ranke and Niebuhr, who were to give Europe its new and dynamic sense of history. But there is little doubt that, whatever its causes, and however loosely we care to date it, through some such transference the Western tradition has acquired a peculiarly strong and resilient sense of narrative.

NARRATIVE AND IRONY

But before we accede to the suspicions which both Gould and Lash seem to hold about the pressures of narrative on human thought, it may be worth noting that it is precisely this narrative tendency that makes possible the kind of imaginative leap we most value in both science and the arts. However much he may disagree with Gould over the principles of Darwinism, Daniel Dennett is as clear as Gould that even before it is science, Darwinism is first and foremost a narrative – and a compelling, all-embracing narrative at that.[43] Similarly, as Gillian Beer writes in her stimulating study of evolutionary theory, *Darwin's Plots*, 'reading *The Origin* is an act which involves you in a narrative experience'.[44] Nor is this simply

---

[43] Dennett, *Darwin's Dangerous Idea*, p. 12.
[44] Gillian Beer, *Darwin's Plots: Evolutionary Narrative in Darwin, George Eliot and Nineteenth-Century Fiction*, Routledge & Kegan Paul, 1983, p. 5.

a matter of finding in science a narrative experience analogous to that of literature. There are, she argues, much closer and more direct links:

Lyell, . . . uses extensively the fifteenth book of Ovid's *Metamorphoses* in his account of proto-geology, Bernard cites Goethe repeatedly, and – as has often been remarked – Darwin's crucial insight into the mechanism of evolutionary change derived directly from his reading of Malthus's essay *On Population*. What has gone unremarked is that it derived also from his reading of the one book he never left behind during his expeditions from the Beagle: *The Poetical Works of John Milton*.

. . . the organisation of *The Origin of Species* seems to owe a good deal to the example of one of Darwin's most frequently read authors, Charles Dickens, with its apparently unruly superfluity of material gradually and retrospectively revealing itself as order, its superfecundity of instance serving as an argument which can reveal itself only *through* instance and relations.[45]

Not merely are there direct literary influences on both the structure and content of Darwin's ideas, but it is easy to miss that our whole way of 'reading' evolutionary theory is essentially literary. As the titles of Gould's books so often remind us, we are entering a world of dramatic contrasts, comic, ironic and sometimes occasionally tragic. Even to enter into its vastly superhuman time scales involves some kind of 'willing suspension of disbelief.' 'Evolutionary theory,' writes Beer, 'is first a form of imaginative history. It cannot be experimentally demonstrated sufficiently in any present moment. So it is closer to narrative than to drama . . . '[46]

Evolutionism has been so imaginatively powerful precisely because all its indications do not point one way. It is rich in contradictory elements which can serve as a metaphorical basis for more than one reading of experience: to give one summary example – the 'ascent' or the 'descent' of man may follow the same route but the terms suggest very diverse evaluations of the experience.[47]

It may be that these 'diverse evaluations' go some way to answering Lash's question about the kinds of story it is *possible* to tell about the world. On closer examination such stories do not apparently present the kind of monolithic grand narrative assumed, but never examined, by Lyotard. In reality they display much of the diversity, disjunctions, and contradictions favoured by postmodernists in their *petits récits*. A similar phenomenon is noticeable if we look at one of the most famous and influential attempts ever made to tell the story of the world: the Book of Genesis. Any reader coming to the text afresh, and taking it not as a series

---

[45] Ibid. pp. 7–8.   [46] Ibid. p. 8.   [47] Ibid. pp. 8–9.

of disconnected stories, but as a continuous narrative, quickly notices an almost postmodern disjunction. There are as many gaps and holes as there are explanations. Many constitute famous biblical conundrums: if Adam and Eve were the first couple, where did Seth's wife come from? Others, such as God's irascibility, unpredictability and unabashed favouritism, have long been signals for elaborate Christian or Jewish apologetic. But the fact remains that what has for centuries been taken as the archetypal 'grand narrative' shows, on examination, all the signs of the very incredulity towards grand narratives that for Lyotard is the hallmark of the postmodern.

The 'modern', or post-critical, explanation for this fragmented state of the text has been what is generally known as 'the documentary hypothesis'. This theory, epitomized in the monumental scholarship of the great German scholars, Julius Wellhausen and Gerhard von Rad, discovers from stylistic and linguistic evidence in the text that the material we now have is composed of a number of different sources. Enter now a whole cast of supposed anonymous authors, known to us only by the initial letter of their characteristic style. There is 'J', the 'Jahwist', so-called because of the centrality of 'Yahweh', the unspoken and unspeakable name of God, composed in the Hebrew only of consonants (Ywh). There is 'P', the 'priestly' source, more concerned with the cult and rituals that came to govern every aspect of Hebrew behaviour. For some there is also 'E', the 'Elohist', who characteristically refers to God in what may be a plural form: the 'Elohim'. Then there is 'R', the 'redactor', who supposedly some time after the return from the Babylonian captivity, 'wrote up' these various putative and now lost sources to produce our present text of Genesis. Of these 'J' is assumed to be the earliest and most 'primitive' – dating possibly from the time of David and Solomon, around 1000 BCE ('Before the Common Era', as those who object to having their calendar Christianized, now have it.)

Whether this dense mass of stylistic hypotheses is correct or not – and, as on the latest news on Black Holes from deep space, the layman can hardly have an opinion – there is no doubt that the parts of Genesis attributed to J include many of the best-known, and most popular, stories in the entire Bible. Starting from this undeniable point, the American Jewish critic and writer, Harold Bloom, has taken it upon himself, somewhat tongue-in-cheek, to write *The Book of J*, in which a new translation of the supposed 'J passages' of Genesis by the Hebrew scholar, David Rosenberg, is supplemented by a detailed and very entertaining commentary by himself. Bloom adds his own modest hypothesis to

von Rad's by claiming to find from internal stylistic evidence that J was
a woman:

> I am assuming that J lived at or nearby the court of Solomon's son and successor,
> King Rehoboam . . . My further assumption is that J was not a professional scribe
> but rather an immensely sophisticated, highly placed member of the Solomonic
> elite, enlightened and ironic. But my primary surmise is that J was a woman,
> and that she wrote for her contemporaries as a woman.[48]

Whether or not this flagrant and coat-trailing twentieth-century hypothesis is right we shall (presumably) never know, but many of Bloom's
other comments are interesting and thought-provoking. For Bloom,
J is one of the really great writers of all-time, to be ranked with Homer,
Dante, Chaucer, Shakespeare, Cervantes and Tolstoy. And many of the
qualities we most admire in the later European writers in that list, first
appear in the work of J. 'We have been so influenced by J and her
revisionists,' he writes, 'and by Shakespeare, that we are contained by
their texts more than we contain them.' Moreover, as Bloom reminds us,
Shakespeare had not merely read J, like all his age, he had been brought
up on endless repetition of her stories.

> Our ways of representing ourselves to others are founded upon J's and Shake-
> speare's way of representing character and personality. Since J's prime character
> is Yahweh, we ought to reflect that the West's major literary character is God,
> whose author was J.[49]

Above all, for Bloom, J was one of the great ironists, and we fail to
understand Genesis unless we can read it as one of the great ironic texts of
all time. But, as he himself recognizes, 'irony' is a difficult concept to pin
down.

> 'Irony' goes back to the Greek word *eiron*, 'dissembler', and our dictionaries still
> follow Greek tradition by defining irony first as Socratic: a feigned ignorance
> and humility designed to expose the inadequate assumptions of others, by way of
> skilled dialectical questioning. With this Platonic irony, J has no affinities, and we
> may put it aside here. Two broader senses of literary irony are also irrelevant to
> our reading of J: the use of language to express something other than supposedly
> literal meaning, particularly the opposite of such meaning, and also the contrast
> or gap between expectation and fulfilment. A touch closer to J is what we call
> dramatic irony or even tragic irony, which is the incongruity between what
> develops on adjacent words and actions that are more fully apprehended by the

---

[48] Harold Bloom, *The Book of J*, N.Y.: Vintage, 1991, p. 9.
[49] Ibid. p. 316.

audience or readers than by the characters. J is a master of such irony, yet it tends to be one of her minor modes. Her major ironic stance is very different and must be regarded as her own invention.[50]

Though Bloom never completely spells out here what exactly this 'unique' irony of J's consists of, we know from earlier work, especially on Kafka and Buber, that he finds it in clashes between totally incommensurate orders of reality[51] – a point he returns to here over and over again, with comparisons with Kafka and Thomas Mann (the 'most playful of dramatic and romantic ironists').

J's irony . . . is of a different and more sublime order. It is the irony of ultimates and incommensurates, the irony of Yahweh's love for David. Joseph, favoured to some degree as David was favoured, is himself an ironist, unlike David.[52]

But Bloom, of course, was not the first to discover irony at the heart of the Old Testament. That honour may well belong to Robert Lowth, the originator of the English Higher Criticism of the Bible. His Oxford lectures on *The Sacred Poetry of the Hebrews* (1753) were not intended in any way to be revolutionary. Much of his framework seems to be derived from the work of Richard Simon in France in the 1680s.[53] Lowth published, as he had lectured, in Latin, and he was not even translated into English until 1778. An able Hebrew scholar, he had been elected to the Professorship of Poetry at Oxford in May 1741, and since he was obliged to start lecturing almost at once without time to prepare by consulting the normal academic sources, he seems to have turned to his theme of the psalms almost by default.[54]

Hebrew poetry, Lowth claimed, worked not by the common European devices of rhyme, assonance, rhythm etc., but by what he called 'parallelism', where one phrase or sentence is amplified or contrasted with another, immediately juxtaposed with it. The origins of this parallelism, Lowth argued, like the origins of European poetry, lay in the previous oral tradition – in this case in the antiphonal chants and choruses we find mentioned at various points in the Old Testament. He cites, for instance, I Samuel 18: 7, where David returns victorious from a battle with the Philistines and chanting women greet him with the words 'Saul hath slain his thousands', to be answered with a second chorus with the

[50] Ibid. p. 25.
[51] See e.g. Bloom's *Anxiety of Influence*, N.Y.: Oxford University Press, 1973, p. 330.
[52] Ibid. p. 233.
[53] See Françoise Deconinck-Brossard, 'England and France in the Eighteenth Century', in Prickett (ed.) *Reading the Text*, Oxford: Blackwell, 1991, pp. 137–47.
[54] See Prickett, *Words and the Word*, Cambridge University Press, 1986, Ch. 3.

parallel, 'And David his ten thousands'.[55] Lowth distinguishes no less than eight different kinds of parallelism, ranging from simple repetition, to echo, variation, contrast and comparison – as in the particular case cited, where the implications were not lost on Saul, who promptly tried to have David assassinated.

In other words, for Lowth, irony – the contrast between explicit and implied meaning – lay right at the structural centre of Hebrew poetry. If before, dramatic irony in the Bible had apparently been confined to such obvious moments as Nathan's denunciation of David, it was now possible to see biblical poetry, and, as we shall see, much of biblical prose as well, in terms of dramatic and ironic narrative. Moreover, in linking Jesus's parables with the prophetic metaphors of the Old Testament, Lowth is further encouraging a sense of ironic and hidden meanings in the New Testament texts.

In retrospect, indeed, one of the most remarkable features of his whole project is his continual movement between the literal and figurative senses of the text. In the Preliminary Dissertation to his *New Translation of Isaiah*, written in 1778, some thirty years after his ground-breaking *Lectures*, Lowth insists that his quest for scholarly accuracy is grounded firmly in a sense of what he calls 'the deep and recondite' readings of scripture.

The first and principal business of a Translator is to give us the plain literal and grammatical sense of his author; the obvious meaning of his words, phrases, and sentences, and to express them in the language into which he translates, as far as may be, in equivalent words, phrases, and sentences . . . This is peculiarly so in subjects of high importance, such as the Holy Scriptures, in which so much depends on the phrase and expression; and particularly in the Prophetical books of scripture; where from the letter are often deduced deep and recondite senses, which must owe all their weight and solidity to the just and accurate interpretation of the words of the Prophecy. For whatever senses are supposed to be included in the Prophet's words, Spiritual, Mystical, Allegorical, Analogical, or the like, they must all entirely depend on the Literal Sense.[56]

This is not so much a stress on the literal sense for its own sake,[57] as a belief that all figurative interpretation must be grounded in an accurate text. In discussing Isaiah 35: 5–6 ('Then shall the eyes of the blind be opened, and the ears of the deaf shall be unstopped. Then shall the lame

---

[55] Robert Lowth, *The Sacred Poetry of the Hebrews*, trs G. Gregory, 1787, Vol. II, p. 53.

[56] Robert Lowth, *Isaiah: A New Translation*, 5th edn, 2 vols., Edinburgh, 1807, Vol. II, p. lxviii.

[57] A long tradition of Reformation divines had stressed the importance of the literal meaning: e.g. William Perkins: 'there is only one sense and that is the literal', *The Art of Prophecying*, 1592.

man leap as an hart, and the tongue of the dumb sing . . . ') Lowth is at pains to link it with its standard New Testament antetype: Matthew 9: 4–5 ('that the lame walked and the deaf heard'). Indeed, his commentary suggests more a typical mediaeval four-fold reading than simply the kind of two-level typology more common in eighteenth-century commentaries.

> To these [the word of Matthew] the strictly literal interpretation of the Prophet's words direct us . . . According to the allegorical interpretation they may have a further view: this part of the prophecy may run parallel with the former, and relate to the future advent of Christ; to the conversion of the Jews, and their restitution to their land; to the extension and purification of the Christian Faith; events predicted in the holy Scriptures as preparatory to it.[58]

Such apparent conservatism did not ring the kind of alarm bells or arouse the opposition in England that Simon had done in Catholic France, yet it is hard to think of any secular term except 'dramatic irony' for what Lowth has come to see as conventional biblical typology.

Whether or not the word irony is actually used, however, there is certainly nothing new in the idea that biblical narrative – and in particular the parts of Genesis attributed to the putative J – is fraught with unspoken and 'hidden' meaning. For many early biblical commentators it was evidence for secret, often figurative or allegorical, meanings to the text.[59] For later, Romantic and post-Romantic readers, such as Kierkegaard and Auerbach, who both wrote on the Akedah (J's account of Abraham's sacrifice of Isaac), it consists of a curiously concentrated and dense narrative, stripped of what Auerbach calls 'foreground' detail, and that for Kierkegaard resists all interpretation and re-telling.[60] Nor has the discovery of irony in biblical narrative been confined to critics; it was anticipated by many of the greatest literary ironists, including Chaucer, Shakespeare, Sterne, Jane Austen and Thomas Mann.[61]

But irony is not peculiar to the Bible. As we shall see repeatedly in the course of this investigation, it is endemic to narrative, and to the so-called grand narratives in particular. Like any other word, however, 'irony'

---

[58] *Isaiah*, Vol. II, p. 232.
[59] See Stephen Prickett (ed.), *Reading the Text: Biblical Criticism and Literary Theory*, Oxford: Blackwell, 1991.
[60] Søren Kierkegaard, *Fear and Trembling*, trs Walter Lowrie, Princeton University Press, 1941; Erich Auerbach, *Mimesis*, Princeton University Press, 1953.
[61] For the irony of Sterne, Austen and Mann, see Stephen Prickett, *Origins of Narrative: The Romantic Appropriation of the Bible*, Cambridge University Press, 1996.

comes to us with its own history of meaning. For much of the history of European literary criticism, dominated not by Socrates and Plato, but by Aristotle, irony was seen primarily as the characteristic of a particular personality-type, and only by extension as a rather laboured rhetorical device. As Bloom points out, for Aristotle, the *eiron* was the person who deliberately deprecates himself. Though better than the *alazon* (or 'imposter', who pretends to be more than he is), because (like Socrates) the *eiron* is more effective and dangerous; neither, Aristotle tells us in the *Ethics*, is to be particularly admired.[62] When, in the *Poetics*, he wrote specifically on critical theory, Aristotle was much more interested in *anagnorisis* ('recognition'), and the relationship between *anagnorisis* and *peripeteia* ('reversal') continued to be of greater concern to later critics than any discussion of what we would now call the underlying irony animating both dramatic devices[63] – or, indeed, the latent irony of attitude so prominent in the great European literary tradition: one thinks of writers as diverse as Dante, Boccaccio, Chaucer, Rabelais, Shakespeare, Dryden, Swift, Pope, Sterne and Austen.

If we look for the history of the English word, what we find from the *Oxford English Dictionary* (*OED*) is not so much a shift in meaning as a progressive shift in application. Thus up until the end of the eighteenth century the word is characteristically used to describe a specific rhetorical trope or figure of speech: 'an ironie'. By the nineteenth century, however, we find increasingly the notion of tragic irony is abstracted from the theatre (both classical Greek and Shakespearean) and being applied to the human condition as a whole.[64] At the same time, we find a corresponding movement away from irony as the deliberate construction of a specific author to an innate quality of circumstances in general – a move which reaches its limit with the title of Hardy's collection of short stories, *Life's Little Ironies* (1894).

---

[62] See Northrop Frye, *Anatomy of Criticism*, Princeton, 1957, pp. 40–1.

[63] L. J. Potts in his 1959 translation of the *Poetics* (Cambridge, 1959) translates *peripeteia* as in Chapter 6 as 'irony of events' (pp. 25; 81–2) but this is not the kind of irony of narrative attitude under discussion here. Irony, in this sense, as Terrence Cave has shown, is a relative latecomer in the history of European poetics, dominated for so long by the more flexible and conceptually more powerful model of recognition. See John Ashton, *Understanding the Fourth Gospel*, Oxford: Clarendon Press, 1991, p. 549, n. 53. See also Terrence Cave, *Recognitions: A Study in Poetics*, Oxford: Clarendon Press, 1988, esp. pp. 184–90.

[64] Thus we find cited Connop Thirlwall, the Cambridge historian and Bishop of St David's, a friend of Hare and Maurice, in an essay of 1833 on 'The Irony of Sophocles', that 'the contrast between man, with his hopes, fears, wishes, and undertakings, and a dark inflexible fate, affords abundant room for the exhibition of tragic irony'. Thirlwall, *Essays, Speeches and Sermons*, ed. Stewart Perowne, Bentley & Son, 1880, pp. 1–57.

Yet the tensions of growing pluralism in European society provided a natural matrix for irony. The Canadian philosopher, Charles Taylor, sees in the conflict between Descartes and Montaigne in seventeenth-century France a key point in the evolution of modern consciousness. 'The Cartesian', he writes, 'calls for a radical disengagement from ordinary experience; Montaigne requires a deeper engagement in our particularity. These two facets of modern identity have been at odds up to this day.'[65] What he does not note, however, is the conscious irony of Montaigne's statement of his own position:

The world lookes ever for-right (outwards), I turn my sight inward, there I fix it, there I amuse it. Every man lookes before himselfe, I looke within myselfe.[66]

The peculiarity of such a claim, of course, is that to write 'I look within' is a public, and even published, statement of what is billed as the most private and personal activity imaginable. This is like the hermit advertising in the press where he is to be found, or the graffito found on a wall in Pompei 'Everyone writes on the walls in Pompei except me.' But there is more to it than that. Introspection as a *public* act subtly shifts the nature of the introspection itself. It becomes something done for an audience – a future and invisible one perhaps, but an audience nonetheless. St Augustine, Montaigne's great predecessor on that inward road of the self, solves this problem by addressing his *Confessions* not to his readers, but to God, 'to whom all hearts are open, all desires known'. But he nevertheless published it. Montaigne, the Renaissance humanist, and one of the great ironists of all time, has no such recourse open to him – and is fully aware of the inherent irony of his situation. It is one shared by every Romantic, from Rousseau onwards who writes of the joys of solitude; poets and mystics who attempt to convey their ineffable experiences in writing; every travel writer who finds the 'totally unspoiled' destination. It is an irony beloved of postmodernists, but one that that has been part of our progressively internalized culture at least since the time of Montaigne and Shakespeare.

By the end of the eighteenth century, however, irony had already begun to be seen as an important rhetorical device in itself. The source was more often classical than biblical. 'That which can be made explicit

[65] Charles Taylor, *Sources of the Self: The Making of the Modern Identity*, Cambridge University Press, 1989, p. 182.
[66] *The Essays of Montaigne*, trs John Florio, N.Y.: Modern Library, 1933, p. 596.

to the idiot is not worth my care', wrote William Blake to his rather literal-minded patron, the Rev. Dr Trusler in 1799. 'The wisest of the ancients considered what is not too explicit as the fittest for instruction, because it rouses the faculties to act.'[67] The context, like the construction, gives no clue as to whether this was a singular or a plural invocation, but the common contemporary usage of such a phrase pointed almost invariably to Socrates. 'It is common knowledge', declared Søren Kierkegaard in 1841, 'that tradition has linked the word "irony" to the existence of Socrates, but it by no means follows that everyone knows what irony is.'[68] Needless to say after that preamble, Kierkegaard had his own ironic axe to grind, and, indeed, he is a key figure in the changing fortunes of the word.

Among the German Romantics irony rapidly became a key critical term. For Johann Gottlieb Fichte (1762–1814), Friedrich Schlegel (1772–1829), Ludwig Tieck (1773–1853) and Karl Wilhelm Solger (1780–1819) it constituted an attitude, a way of thinking that, better than any other, represented the intense self-consciousness of the modern world. For them, however, as for the ancient Greeks, irony was an essentially negative attitude, an implicit assertion of superiority by the ironist over his fellows – often a cult of affected boredom (by implication) typified by Byron's narrative persona in *Don Juan*. Kierkegaard's acid wit is only partly obscured by clumsy English translation:

That both Germany and France at this time have far too many such ironists and no longer need to be initiated into the secrets of boredom by some English lord, a travelling member of a spleen club, and that a few of the young breed in Young Germany and Young France would long ago have been dead of boredom if their respective governments had not been paternal enough to give them something to think about by having them arrested – surely no one will deny.[69]

It was not accidental that this growing interest in the theory of irony should have coincided with a revival of study (again beginning in Germany) of Plato's philosophy. Kierkegaard's doctoral thesis of 1841, *The Concept of Irony with Continual Reference to Socrates*, thus follows an increasingly complex debate over Plato's irony fuelled by such figures as Wilhelm Gottlieb Tennemann (1761–1819), Friedrich Schlegel, Hegel,

---

[67] William Blake, Letter to the Rev. Dr. Trusler, August 23, 1799. *Complete Writings of William Blake*, ed. Geoffrey Keynes, Oxford University Press, 1966, p. 793.

[68] *The Concept of Irony, with Continual Reference to Socrates* (1841), ed. and trs by Howard V. Hong and Edna H. Hong, Princeton University Press, 1989, p. 11.

[69] *The Concept of Irony*, p. 285.

Schleiermacher, and, not least, Kierkegaard's Danish mentor, Poul Martin Møller.[70] In a curious twist of the Aristotelian idea that irony was first and foremost a character-trait, according to this German Romantic view, irony was the inescapable product of the long historical process of human subjectivity. Socrates was thus important not least because he was one of the first in history to assert his subjective individuality. Solger, the aesthetician and chief exponent of Romantic irony, believed that by his own time irony had become the condition of every artistic work. The Romantic artist demonstrates his own superiority to his work by deliberately destroying or interrupting the illusion created by it – the obvious German example would be something like Schlegel's extremely turgid novel, *Lucinde*, widely denounced as 'obscene' by contemporary critics. Byron's *Don Juan*, however, would again not merely be a more familiar instance to English-language readers, but also to the vast majority of German (or Danish) ones, then as now. For Kierkegaard, such a claim to detachment from nature and such an overweening sense of personal superiority could only produce a deeper and deeper dissatisfaction. The sense of freedom gained by the fully individualized human was in the end a cruel illusion.[71] The ironist as 'poet', deracinated from real experience, was caught in a vicious spiral in which each such break to 'reality' was itself only a further aesthetic move, and was so further lost in his own world.[72] Typically, Kierkegaard seems to accept Møller's argument that the irony of Fichte and Schlegel leads to 'moral nihilism' in the individual,[73] but turns the conclusion unexpectedly on its head:

... the intention in asking questions can be twofold. That is, one can ask with the intention of receiving an answer containing the desired fullness, and hence the more one asks, the deeper and more significant becomes the answer; or one can ask without any interest in the answer except to suck out the apparent content by means of the question and thereby to leave an emptiness behind. The first method presupposes, of course, that there is a plenitude; the second that there is an emptiness. The first is the *speculative* method; the second is the *ironic*. Socrates in particular practised the latter method.[74]

But for all the critical scorn he pours on the German ironists, not to mention on Hegel's attack on them, Kierkegaard's whole argument is

---

[70] See George Pattison, *Kierkegaard: The Aesthetic and the Religious*, Macmillan, 1992, Ch. 2.

[71] *The Concept of Irony*, p. 284.   [72] Pattison, *Kierkegaard*, p. 242.

[73] Following what he sees as the drift of Fichte's and Schlegel's ideas, Møller argues that irony 'is a consequent development of the fruitless struggle to construct a self-enclosed ethical system from the standpoint of the individual. This method must necessarily end with the loss of all content, with moral nihilism.' Pattison, *Kierkegaard*, p. 28.

[74] Kierkegaard, *The Concept of Irony*, p. 36.

itself an exercise in (his own kind of) irony. Thus so far from finding in Socrates merely 'a feigned ignorance and humility designed to expose the inadequate assumptions of others', he proceeds to find in the ancient Greek what amounts to a prototype of the *via negativa*.

The more Socrates tunneled under existence, the more deeply and inevitably each single remark had to gravitate toward an ironic totality, a spiritual condition that was infinitely bottomless, invisible, and indivisible. Xenophon had no intimation whatever of this secret. Allow me to illustrate what I mean by a picture. There is a work that represents Napoleon's grave. Two tall trees shade the grave. There is nothing else to see in the work, and the unsophisticated observer sees nothing else. Between the two trees there is an empty space; as the eye follows the outline, suddenly Napoleon himself emerges from this nothing, and now it is impossible to have him disappear again. Once the eye has seen him, it goes on seeing him with almost alarming necessity. So also with Socrates' rejoinders. One hears his words in the same way one sees the trees; his words mean what they say, just as the trees are trees. There is not one single syllable that gives a hint of any other interpretation, just as there is not one single line that suggests Napoleon, and yet this empty space, this nothing, is what hides that which is most important.[75]

Though it, too, is not exhaustive, that image of the Napoleonic profile in the outline of the trees, like a children's puzzle-picture, hidden, yet once seen, quite unmistakable, re-shaping our reading of everything else in the frame, is one of the great metaphors of irony – and we shall be returning to it. Whereas Bloom was determined to keep Athens separate from Jerusalem, and to see Greek and Hebrew irony as essentially things apart; Kierkegaard, the post-Romantic Christian Hegelian, is toying with a metaphor almost as applicable to the Bible as to Plato. He is also, be it noted, telling us a story. Irony is a narrative art. The meaning of each piece is inseparable from the whole.

Kierkegaard's interest in Socratic irony is genuine enough, but the irony he is really in pursuit of is not of course Socratic at all. The Socrates of whom Xenophon had no real understanding,[76] who 'tunneled under existence' and whose remarks gravitated 'toward an ironic totality, a spiritual condition that was infinitely bottomless, invisible, and indivisible', is one that would have been equally unrecognizable to Plato. Indeed, what Kierkegaard calls the 'unalloyed Socrates' is avowedly *anti-* Platonic.

---

75 Ibid. p. 19.
76 Our only other source of information about Socrates – who himself, so far as we know, never wrote a word.

Like Samson, Socrates grasps the pillars that support knowledge and tumbles everything down into the nothingness of ignorance. That this is genuinely Socratic everyone will admit, but Platonic it will never become.[77]

For this reason also Kierkegaard declares at the outset little interest in the so-called 'constructive dialogues', such as *The Republic, Timaeus* and *Critias*, where the 'Socrates' figure is really little more than Plato's mouthpiece, and, he argues, contributes nothing to our understanding of the historical personage.[78] Kierkegaard's Socrates is a Kierkegaardian, post-Hegelian ironist of the nineteenth century. His constant questioning is at once designed to demonstrate ignorance, and, at the same time, to imply another kind of foundation that cannot be revealed – perhaps cannot even be articulated, even if the ironist so desired.

... there is in the ironist an *Urgrund* [primordial ground], an intrinsic value, but the coin he issues does not have the specified value but, like paper money, is nothing, and yet all his transactions with the world take place in this kind of money.[79]

Such an *Urgrund* is very different from the kind of aesthetic irony he finds in the German Romantics, where each uncovering of aesthetic artifice is only yet another level of illusion. Kierkegaard's final analogy is with the place of doubt in science.

In our age there has been much talk about the importance of doubt for science and scholarship, but what doubt is to science, irony is to personal life. Just as scientists maintain that there is no true science without doubt, so it may be maintained with the same right that no genuinely human life is possible without irony... Irony limits, finitizes, and circumscribes and thereby yields truth, actuality, content; it disciplines and punishes and thereby yields balance and consistency. Irony is a disciplinarian feared only by those who do not know it but loved by those who do. Anyone who does not understand irony at all, who has no ear for its whispering, lacks precisely thereby what could be called the absolute beginning of personal life.[80]

Here irony is returned to its roots in self-consciousness, but at a wholly different level from the starting-point of the debate – not so much a quality of mind leading to contempt for others, or an exposure of artifice, as a 'discipline', but a voice whose 'whispering' in the ear constitutes the 'beginning of personal life'. In keeping with the Romantic movement from

---

[77] *The Concept of Irony*, p. 41.   [78] Ibid. p. 54.   [79] Ibid. p. 51.   [80] Ibid. p. 326.

external to internal, what started as an enquiry into ancient Greek scepticism has concluded with a discussion not merely of self-consciousness, but of self-critical analysis. Irony, in other words, for Kierkegaard has become not a stance vis-à-vis the rest of the world, but a *self*-searching. Yet again, the gaze is not outward but inward.

As we might expect, this rapidly becomes a poetic metaphor of inner space – or depth. Thus W.H. Auden writes in his poem 'In Praise of Limestone':

> Dear, I know nothing of
> Either, but when I try to imagine a faultless love
> Or the life to come, what I hear is the murmur
> Of underground streams, what I see is a limestone landscape.
>
> (lines 91–4)

If such great beliefs have any reality, they are hidden like water beneath an arid limestone plateau. But even the awareness of such geology of the spirit gives an unspoken depth to our appreciation of the arid broken surface.

In Romantic and post-Romantic literature irony is often, as here, the product of a particular quality of self-consciousness. Following in the German Romantic tradition already mentioned, one twentieth-century critic, Paul de Man, has described it as a capacity to know, but not overcome, 'inauthenticity'[81] – even giving it, in the end, a quasi-transcendental status. We can all, I suspect, recognize the particular tone of a piece of writing or speech where the author wishes us to remain sceptical of the view being advanced, even as it is being put forward. Certainly de Man should have known what this was like. It was only after his death that the world at large became aware that this pillar of liberalism at Yale University, when a journalist in Belgium during the Second World War, had worked for a Nazi collaborationist journal.

Any narrative that, in Lash's words, sets out to tell the story of the world ends in the ironic recognition of its own gaps, lacunae and failures. Again, Gillian Beer on evolution:

Darwin . . . sought to appropriate and to recast inherited mythologies, discourses, and narrative orders. He was telling a new story, against the grain of the language available to tell it in. And as it was told, the story itself proved

---

[81] Paul de Man, 'The Rhetoric of Temporality', *Blindness and Insight: Essays on the Rhetoric of Contemporary Criticism* (1983), 2nd edn, Routledge, 1989, p. 222.

not to be single or simple. It was, rather, capable of being extended or reclaimed into a number of conflicting systems.[82]

A narrative conceived and executed in such terms could scarcely fail to be ironic, and, indeed, if we look the clues are all there. The great 'absence' from *The Origin*, as many critics have noted, is, of course, man. Darwin's desire to avoid what he saw as unnecessary battles with a public that was likely to be incredulous enough anyway, meant that he consistently failed to draw the obvious conclusions about the origins of his own species. The resulting modesty and unwillingness to leap to speculative answers gives the whole text a kind of restrained agnostic irony that is in some ways more revealing about Darwin's own state of mind at the period than a more explicit statement might have been.[83] When he did finally address the question of the origins of humanity in *The Descent of Man*, the ambiguities of that word 'descent' have left critics debating ever since. As we shall see, so far from Darwin's work constituting a special case in the history of science-writing, it would be more true to say that it typifies an irony that, consciously or unconsciously, has pervaded all post-Romantic science.

LANGUAGE, CULTURE AND REALITY

The change from regarding words as directly standing for things, to seeing that they form independent linguistic structures that may or may not describe some independent reality, was one of the most momentous in the history of human thought.[84] In Genesis Adam had been given the task of naming the animals, and for Protestant Christianity, especially in the Lutheran tradition, this was a guarantee of a divinely sanctioned correspondence between words and things. According to the seventeenth-century German mystic Jakob Boehme:

> Now, that Adam stood in the image of God and not that of the beasts is shown by the fact that he knew the property of all the creatures and gave names to all the creatures according to their essence, form, and property; he understood the language of nature as revealed and articulated word in all essence, for the name of each creature has its origin there.[85]

---

[82] *Darwin's Plots*, p. 5.

[83] See, for instance, Adrian Desmond and James Moore, *Charles Darwin*, Michael Joseph, 1991.

[84] See Prickett, *Words and the Word*, pp. 37–68.

[85] Jakob Boehme, *Mysterium Magnum: or An Exposition of the First Book of Moses Called Genesis*, 1623, Ch. 19, para. 22.

This assumption of its divine origin, with the natural consequence that words *ought*, at least, to correspond directly to things, was to cause endless problems in any thinking about the origins and nature of language. I wrote 'ought' in the previous sentence, because, of course, there was a further theological problem implicit in this belief: the Fall. Adam had still been entirely sinless when he named the animals, and so invented language. Unless he and Eve had improbably switched to a totally different language after their expulsion from Eden, the language of Adam remained, by definition, the perfect language, and a great deal of effort was devoted to trying to reconstruct what that language might have been before it was fatally disrupted first by Babel and then the Flood. For some it was clearly classical Hebrew itself. Other seventeenth-century figures, as different in outlook as Boehme and the French philosopher Leibniz, believed that the radical and primitive language of Adam underlay all known current languages.[86] In the eighteenth century the growth of Indian scholarship provided a new candidate in the form of Sanskrit, the most ancient language yet discovered. At the same time, new voyages of discovery, revealing both the extent and the diversity of world languages, made the idea of a single origin to all languages, within what was still a biblical time-scale of only 6,000 years, more and more difficult to accept. That did not, however, prevent one eighteenth-century Englishman, James Parsons, from writing a book, *The Remains of Japhet* (1767) to prove that the oldest and therefore most 'Adamic' languages were Irish and Welsh. According to him these, the original European languages from which all others were descended, were the sole remains of 'Japhetan', the original antediluvian language of Adam which had survived the Flood.

As long as it was believed that language should ideally, even if not in actual practice, provide an exact fit between words and things, there was little room for irony – or even for fiction. It was this kind of linguistic fundamentalism that Swift satirizes in the Third Voyage of *Gulliver's Travels*. The learned members of the Laputan Academy, who believe that all words correspond to real things, seek the ultimate unambiguous clarity of expression by carrying round with them all the objects they would otherwise speak about. But so closely were questions of the origin and structure of language bound up with the religious tradition of the Christian West that it was not until the eighteenth century, with such

---

[86] See Hans Aarsleff, 'Leibniz on Locke on Language', *From Locke to Saussure: Essays on the Study of Language and Intellectual History*, Minneapolis: University of Minnesota Press, 1982, pp. 58–60.

Enlightenment figures as Vico, Herder, von Humboldt and others, that linguistic questions could be posed in a more fruitful way, and even here the massive gravitational attraction of the older ways of thinking is still evident.[87] Thus Johann Gottfried Herder, in his influential 1772 Berlin Academy Prize Essay, *On the Origin of Language*, is careful explicitly to distance himself both from his more conservative contemporary Johann Peter Süssmilch, who still advanced the traditional view that language was the divine and miraculous gift of God, and from the more radical French views of Condillac and Rousseau that it had evolved from the noises of animals. Though Herder, in fact, follows Condillac quite closely in many places,[88] his real interest is in the *psychological* origins of language as a vehicle not so much for communication as for thought. The distinguishing quality of human language is that it creates the possibility of a continuous internal dialogue. We use language primarily to tell *ourselves* stories.

   Once freed from the bonds of a 'correspondence' theory of language, it was possible to see the degree to which our narratives had always depended as much on existing narratives as they had on the external world. In pre-literate societies, the tribal narratives are both a key to understanding the environment, and to self-understanding.[89] Bruce Chatwin's *The Songlines* describes how the traditional tribal songs of many nomadic Australian Aboriginal people contain vital topographical information for anyone trying to follow their often invisible trackways across the desert. If one ventures into the territory of a neighbouring tribe one has to 'learn their songs' – a gesture not merely that one comes in peace with good intentions, but also very often a necessary act for survival. Though much of Chatwin's thesis remains controversial, there is ample evidence to show that such songs exist among the nomadic tribes of the central deserts of Australia. Similarly, among literate peoples, 'metafiction', the way in which one story draws upon another, is not the product of modern critical theory, but is a constant and inescapable presence in the written word, constituting at once a revision of the past and a legitimation of

---

[87] See Hans Georg Gadamer, 'Man and Language' (1966), *Philosophical Hermeneutics*, trs and ed. David E. Linge, University of California Press, 1976, p. 60; Giambattista Vico, *The New Science* (1744), trs Thomas Goddard Bergin and Max Harrold Frisch, Ithaca, N.Y.: Cornell University Press, 1968; Johann Gottfried Herder, 'Essay on the Origin of Language' (1772) in *Herder on Social and Political Culture*, trs and ed. F.M. Barnard, Cambridge University Press, 1969; Wilhelm von Humboldt, *On Language* (1836), trs Peter Heath, introduction by Hans Aarsleff, Cambridge University Press, 1988.

[88] Aarsleff, 'The Tradition of Condillac: The Problem of the Origin of Language in the Eighteenth Century and the Debate in the Berlin Academy before Herder', in *Locke to Saussure*, pp. 146–99.

[89] See Walter J. Ong, *Orality and Literacy: The Technologising of the Word*, Routledge, 1982.

the present. Thus Virgil links the *Aeneid*, his great epic on the foundation
of Rome, to the earlier foundational Greek epics of Homer. Similarly,
Dante, writing in fourteenth-century Italy, actually incorporates Virgil
symbolically as a character in his narrative.[90] Throughout classical antiquity, it was a 'fundamental law of life' that all new creations should
refer back to the works from which they were derived: 'as the colony to
the mother city; the statue to the founder, the song to the Muses, the
copy to the original, and the work of art to the model'.[91]

Whatever the theory, however, the practice was not always so ordered
and hierarchical as this time-honoured principle might suggest. According to Manus O'Donnell's *Life of St Columba*, the original 'Battle of the
Books' concerned the ownership of a Psalter which Bishop Finnian of
Druin-Finn had loaned to the Irish saint. When Columba secretly had
a copy made, Finnian, hearing of it, demanded that it, too, should be
returned with the original. The matter was referred to the king, Diarmait
mac Cer-béil, who ruled that 'If I had loaned you my cow, and it had
calved while in your byre, would you not have returned both to me?'
In the ensuing battle of Cúl-Dremne, we are told, thousands perished,
and Columba, also under threat of excommunication from the Synod of
Tailtiu, was forced to flee (apparently still with Psalter) to Iona.[92] What
was claimed to be the disputed book was later adopted as the 'battler' of
the O'Donnells, and carried into war by them.

Such were the perils of unclear copyright laws. But whatever the historical truth behind the story of Columba's Psalter, it captures something of the massive hold of tradition in determining the transmission of
narratives. It is also, of course, a story of plural values: each side in the
dispute started from opposing premises, and, not surprisingly, reached
opposing conclusions. Perhaps unusually, however, here language was
not the problem. Yet once words had been detached from things, the
problem of linguistic difference took centre stage. Whereas most Enlightenment thinkers had assumed a high degree of correspondence between
one language and another, for Romantics like Herder language expresses
the distinctive experience of a particular people, and thus each language
will embody its own unique way of seeing the world. To think and speak
in words is to 'swim in an inherited stream of images' in which we come

[90] See Prickett, *Words and the Word*, pp. 149–73.
[91] Ernst Curtius, 'Virgil' in *Essays on European Literature*, trs Michael Kowal, Princeton University
Press, 1973, p. 7.
[92] See J.F. Kenny, *The Sources for the Early History of Ireland* (1929), reprinted, Irish University Press,
1968, pp. 391, 435, and 630.

to consciousness and which we accept on trust.[93] It follows that even the senses are culturally variable: 'The North American', wrote Herder, 'can trace his enemy by the smell... the shy Arab hears far in his silent desert... The shepherd beholds nature with different eyes from those of the fisherman.'[94]

For the Romantics, translation from one language to another is theoretically impossible. Because words in one language never have exact equivalents in another, even the simplest transference from one language to the next will not convey quite the same impression because words have different connotations, different historical flavours, different *nuances* (a French word, for instance, that has no exact English equivalent). Paradoxically, translation is nevertheless necessary, and we do it all the time. Samuel Taylor Coleridge, who argued most fiercely for its impossibility, himself made two classic translations of Schiller's plays from German into English. Nor should we regard this as even inconsistency. Since words do not correspond exactly to things, but make up a semi-independent system, there will always be some kind of gap between description and reality, or between one language and the next. For instance, to translate the relatively simple English phrase 'the pastoral function of the ministry' directly into French is impossible, because the French word for 'minister' is *pasteur* (shepherd). Since *la fonction pastorale du pastorat* simply sounds like a tautology, and has lost the English meaning, some elaborate paraphrase becomes essential. In his book on the history of translation, *After Babel*, George Steiner points out that the same problems that affect translation, affect the reading of *any* text.[95] To read words from another century requires a knowledge of the exact meaning of those words at that time, and in that context, which may be very different from how they are used today. But, he asks, can we even stop there? To read any author, to absorb any new idea, involves turning the unknown into the known, re-phrasing into our words, placing it within our own experience. And for that reason, simply because we are finite beings for whom there is no such thing as perspectiveless vision, or knowledge that is not from a particular standpoint, there will always be a gap, a residue, the possibility of a different interpretation. For Friedrich Schleiermacher, the father of

[93] See Isaiah Berlin, 'Herder and the Enlightenment', *Vico and Herder: Two Studies in the History of Ideas*, Hogarth Press, 1976, p. 168.

[94] Cited by Marshall Sahlins, *How 'Natives' Think: About Captain Cook, For Example*, University of Chicago Press, 1995. Extract in the *Times Literary Supplement*, June 2, 1995, p. 13.

[95] George Steiner, *After Babel: Aspects of Language and Translation*, Oxford University Press, 1976.

what is called 'hermeneutics', or the science of meaning, 'understanding is an unending task'.[96]

But, of course, it is precisely the perception of this inevitable gap between words and meaning, description and reality, that not merely makes irony possible, but almost inevitable in the writing of the last 200 years. Almost every post-Romantic writer, whether novelist, theologian or scientist is conscious of the fact that there is more to be said; that the last word will never be uttered; the definitive conclusion never reached; finality never attained; and this alone gives a quite different flavour to their discourse from that of, say, their Enlightenment predecessors. It also had a profound effect on the status of the novel, the central narrative form of the last three centuries.

As we shall see in the next chapter, what happened, in effect, was that one 'paradigm', that of linguistic equivalence, had been replaced by another, which perceived language not in terms of correspondence but of incommensurability. But such paradigm-shifts are driven not just by abstract notions of linguistics, but also by social and even political imperatives. Behind Herder's assertion of national distinctiveness was a new sense of German identity that was being shaped in defiance of the French cultural dominance of Enlightenment Europe. We can trace this conflict through the history of two words, 'civilization' and 'culture'.[97]

'Civilization', as the word came to be used in France from the 1750s stood for an ideal order of human society, involving the arts, learning and manners. In this sense it was used strictly in the singular; only with vanished societies of the past could one speak of 'civilizations'. The connotations, justifying both colonial expansion and European linguistic hegemony, were of the evident superiority of *la civilisation française*. French was the lingua franca throughout Europe: it was the language of diplomacy, of aristocrats and of the royal courts of many states in Germany and even Tsarist Russia. The new meaning of the word, though not necessarily with its innate French bias, was quickly taken up in England – but not without some resistance. The first example of this use of the word in the *OED* is Boswell's record of Johnson, in 1772, *refusing* to incorporate it in the Fourth Edition of his Dictionary. Almost a century later, Dean Church's 1868 lectures on 'The Gifts of Civilization' insist

---

[96] He did not invent the term, either in German or English. The earliest usage given in the *OED* is 1737.

[97] For much of what follows I am indebted to Marshall Sahlins, *How Natives Think*.

that the word has an essentially moral as well as technical connotation, covering 'all that man does, all that he discovers, all that he becomes, to fit himself most suitably for the life in which he finds himself here'.[98] While the gifts and benefits of Christian civilization manifestly outweigh those of pagan Rome, the same word nevertheless applies equally to both. By Church's time it had acquired much of its impetus from the way it could be used to differentiate the superior state of the colonizing power from the inferior state of the colonized. For him, India was still in 'a low state of civilization' while Egypt, China and Japan, though 'singularly ingenious' and 'industrious' have not yet reached a 'high' stage.[99]

In contrast, the word 'culture' (*Kultur*) had its origins in late eighteenth-century Germany, and was used by Herder and his fellow Romantics in defiance of the generalized and global pretensions of the Anglo-French 'civilization'. 'Culture' was specific, local and plural, describing not an ideal order of human society in general, but the distinctive modes of existence of different societies. For German bourgeois intellectuals, lacking power or even political unity, cultural differences became essential. Defending a national *Kultur* both against the rationalism of the *philosophes* and a Francophile Prussian court, Herder urged that different ways of life were valuable in themselves, and not to be seen as stages of development towards a common goal. Unlike 'civilization', which could be transferred between a more advanced and less advanced peoples – preferably by a beneficent imperialism – culture was what truly identified and differentiated a people. Culture came in kinds, not in degrees; in the plural, not the singular. Nor could there be any uncultured peoples, as there were uncivilized ones. 'Only a real misanthrope', Herder once ironically remarked, 'could regard European culture as the universal condition of our species.' Each people had its own appropriate kind of happiness based on the cultural legacy of their ancestral tradition, transmitted in the distinctive concepts of their language, and adapted to their specific life conditions. It is through this tradition, endowed also with the morality of the community and the emotions of the family, that experience is organized, since people do not simply discover the world, they are taught it. Moreover, they experience their world not merely in terms of ideas but values. We cannot speak of 'reasoning correctly' as if it were simply an objective activity, any more than we can of unmediated sensory perceptions. Reason is invested with feeling and bound to imagination.

[98] R.W. Church, *The Gifts of Civilization*, new edn, Macmillan, 1890, p. 150.
[99] Ibid. p. 152.

It is here, in the cultural theories of late eighteenth-century Germany, that we find the origins of the Lyotardian conflict between grand and little narratives. For the German Romantics, the little and local narratives, reflecting the divided social and political condition of their land, take precedence over the imperial grand narratives of France. No political 'explanation' of ideas is ever wholly satisfactory, but if we wanted to pursue this contrast between German and French modes of thought, we might observe how slow Lyotard is in acknowledging the roots of his argument, and how typically Gallic it is that even his *resistance* to totalizing theories is itself elevated into a universal principle.

One answer to Lash's question about what shape the story of the world might be, therefore, is that on inspection, what we have taken to be the grand narratives of the past turn out to be not quite what we took them for. Any story of the world, whether scientific, sociological, psychological or religious, will also inevitably be pluralistic, literary, ironic, tentative and multiplex. If our worlds are, in part, our own constructs, perhaps the difficulty is that we ourselves live in a plurality of worlds, inhabit several different time-schemes, and use several incompatible scales of reckoning. In the following chapters we shall be looking at the way some of these narratives have been constructed and reconstructed over the last 300 years. If the human world has altered dramatically in that time, the material world has not, but our descriptions of both have, not so much because we understand *them* better (though we undoubtedly do), but because we understand better the nature of our own descriptions.

CHAPTER 2

Newton and Kissinger: Science as irony?

SAID, KISSINGER AND NEWTON

In his book, *American Foreign Policy*, Henry Kissinger, Nixon's Secretary of State in the 1970s, compares what he sees as the Western attitude to the world with those of the developing countries. The West, he writes, 'is deeply committed to the notion that the real world is external to the observer, that knowledge consists of recording and classifying data – the more accurately the better'. Citing as an example the Newtonian revolution, which has not taken place in the developing world, Kissinger argues that 'Cultures which escaped the early impact of Newtonian thinking have retained the essentially pre-Newtonian view that the real world is almost completely *internal* to the observer.' Consequently, he adds, 'empirical reality has a much [sic] different significance for many of the new countries than for the West because in a certain sense they never went through the process of discovering it'.[1]

Edward Said, the Palestinian–American critic, quotes this passage in his book, *Orientalism*, an angry indictment of the way in which Europe (or, what the naturalized American, Kissinger, would call the 'West') has constructed its Eastern opposite: the 'Orient'. Said's book deservedly attracted a lot of critical attention when it was first published in 1978, but I do not recall any specific comment on this particular piece of intertextuality – which is a pity, because it is worthy of some scrutiny. To begin with, Kissinger evidently takes it for granted that we will agree with him that what we may loosely call modern Western thought differs from both pre-modern European thought, and non-Western thinking – the latter category one so all-inclusive as to be almost synonymous with Said's own grandly vague 'Oriental' – by the scientific revolution of the late seventeenth and early eighteenth centuries – for which Newton can

---

[1] Henry Kissinger, *American Foreign Policy*, N.Y.: Norton, 1974, pp. 48–9, cited by Edward Said, *Orientalism: Western Conceptions of the Orient*, Harmondsworth: Penguin, 1991, p. 46.

stand as a kind of shorthand. Nor is this a case of quoting out of context: an inspection of the original, Kissinger's *American Foreign Policy*, of 1974, confirms that though Said has in fact put together two quotations from different pages, he is being scrupulously fair to both content and tone of his source.

Said, however, is so incensed by what he sees as the obviously racialist conclusion to Kissinger's argument that he does not bother to look at, let alone question, whether Kissinger's argument is correct. Yet it is difficult to know which is the more remarkable: that an apparently sophisticated politician such as Kissinger should make a statement like this in the first place, or that Said, apparently a no-less sophisticated academic, should accept it at its face value – for both are, of course, fundamentally wrong, not merely about the 'Newtonian revolution' but also about its consequences. Yet Kissinger and Said are not alone. Indeed, it is hardly an exaggeration to say that this mis-reading of Newton and the consequent history of the Enlightenment has been responsible not merely for endless false dichotomies between different kinds of societies, but also for a fundamentally false conception of the present. And – in case one should doubt the importance of such academic mistakes in the real world – we may note that it was on such premises that the Vietnam War was conducted, and lost, by President Nixon's all-powerful secretary of state.

Though *The Postmodern Condition* was published a few years before *Orientalism*, Lyotard seems to be arguing a similar point when he claims that Western politics and ethics are legitimated by a particular 'objective' and 'scientific' perspective on the world. Contrariwise, of course, the agenda of science is heavily influenced by Western political and ethical assumptions.

there is a strict interlinkage between the kinds of language called science and the kind called ethics and politics: they both stem from the same perspective, the same 'choice' if you will – the choice called the Occident.[2]

For Kissinger, Lyotard and Said alike, the basic tenets of Western culture are seen as springing directly from a rational and scientific world-picture beginning in the early eighteenth century, and conveniently epitomized by the name of Sir Isaac Newton. Yet the first example of Newtonianism that Kissinger cites, that 'knowledge consists of recording and classifying data' is an almost direct quotation from the fifteenth-century Pythagorean, Nicholas of Cusa ('knowledge is always measurement') and

---

[2] *Postmodern Condition*, p. 8.

so far from being some forward-looking leap of the imagination, belongs totally to the world of mediaeval science that Kissinger imagined Newton to have replaced.[3]

Indeed, in so far as this picture of Newton lay at the centre of the Enlightenment idea of scientific objectivity, it was always a myth. Nor is the idea that our own twentieth-century scientific world is rooted in such Enlightenment assumptions any better founded. It would be more true to say that what dominated the imagination of subsequent generations was the *idea* that one person, symbolized by the name of Newton, could calculate and predict patterns of behaviour in the universe. Thus John Locke made it his ambition to be 'the Newton of the mind'; and Karl Marx, a century and a half later, working on the tacit assumption that all systems, like those of Newton, must have 'laws' governing their operation, sought to understand the '*laws of motion* of the economy' (my italics). Yet this image of Newton, the arch-materialist and pioneer of scientific rationality, in fact owes more to Locke's *Essay Concerning Human Understanding*, than it does to Newton himself. It may at first sight seem absurd to suggest that Locke could possibly have appropriated Newton, who was a full ten years younger – especially when we remember that, though the latter's *Principia Mathematica* had appeared in 1687, Locke's *Essay* (1690) was published fourteen years *before* Newton's *Opticks*, which did not come out until 1704. Yet we now know that Newton's experiments with a prism, and the discovery of the spectrum, had been known to Locke as early as 1690 when he re-drafted his *Essay* for publication.[4] Taking Newton's model of the eye as his organizing metaphor for the way the mind works, Locke manages at the same time to suggest a basic analogy between what Newton had achieved and what he was about to attempt: 'The understanding, like the eye, whilst it makes us see and perceive all other things, takes no notice of itself; and it requires art and pains to set it at a distance and make it its own object.'[5]

Though Locke could hardly appropriate Newton's *ideas*, he could, and did, appropriate what seemed to be his *conclusions* in such a way that it was very difficult to think of the world of mathematical quantities that Newton had revealed except in Lockean terms. Given the relative inaccessibility of Newton's work – especially the mathematics – it was difficult even for the educated public to resist the conclusion that Locke was simply drawing corollaries from Newton's theorems with all the logic

---

[3] E.A. Burtt, *Metaphysical Foundations of Modern Science*, Routledge, 1932, p. 42.
[4] See Marjorie Hope Nicolson, *Newton Demands the Muse*, Archon Books, 1963, p. 7.
[5] John Locke, *Essay Concerning Human Understanding*, Book I, Ch.1, para. 1.

of a syllogism. His theory of knowledge was all the more convincing for its modesty, and its insistence that there were severe limits on what *could* be known. Thus for most of the eighteenth century the distinction between 'primary' qualities that belonged to things, and 'secondary' qualities that were attributed to them by our brains, first advanced by Galileo[6] and taken up by Locke, *appeared* to have been proved by Newton's *Opticks*. Here Newton had, for instance, shown that colour was not a property of objects themselves, but of light and the human eye. His studies of the structure of the eye had shown that what we 'see' is conveyed to the brain through the optic nerve by means of an image on the retina. Whatever we might think we were perceiving of a concrete and three-dimensional world, the reality was no more than the equivalent of two tiny inverted cinema-screens inside the head. This Lockean version of what Newton's optics meant for perception and aesthetics was at once logical and bleak. As one twentieth-century historian of ideas has graphically put it:

The world that people had thought themselves living in – a world rich with colour and sound, redolent with fragrance, filled with gladness, love and beauty, speaking everywhere of purposive harmony and creative ideals – was crowded now into minute corners of the brains of scattered organic beings. The really important world outside was a world hard, cold, colourless, silent, and dead; a world of quantity, a world of mathematically computable motions in mechanical regularity.[7]

Such was the view of a whole post-Lockean generation of poets and writers: Addison, Akenside,[8] Sterne,[9] and Thomson[10] all in their own ways either deplored or celebrated it. Addison's essay on 'The Pleasures of the Imagination', for instance, captures perfectly the new ambivalence towards the natural world engendered by Locke's epistemology:

Things would make but a poor appearance to the eye, if we saw them only in their proper figures and motions. And what reason can we assign for their exciting in us many of those ideas which are different from anything that exists in the objects themselves (for such are light and colours), were it not to add supernumerary ornaments to the universe, and make it more agreeable to the imagination? We are everywhere entertained with pleasing shows and apparitions, we discover imaginary glories in the heavens, and in the earth, and see some of this visionary

[6] Burtt, *Metaphysical Foundations of Modern Science*, p. 75.
[7] Ibid. pp. 236–7.
[8] See, for instance, *Pleasures of the Imagination* (1744), Vol. II, pp. 103–20
[9] For the impact of Locke on Sterne, see A.D. Nuttall, *A Common Sky*, Sussex University Press, Chatto, 1974, Ch. 1.
[10] See, for instance, *The Seasons*, 'Spring', pp. 203–17.

beauty poured out over the whole creation; but what a rough and unsightly sketch of Nature should we be entertained with, did all her colouring disappear, and the several distinctions of light and shade vanish? In short, our souls are at present delightfully lost and bewildered in a pleasing delusion, and we walk about like the enchanted hero of a romance, who sees beautiful castles, woods, and meadows; but upon the finishing of some secret spell, the fantastic scene breaks up, and the disconsolate knight finds himself on a barren heath, or in a solitary desert.[11]

The tone of this forerunner of Keats' 'La Belle Dame Sans Merci' is one of an almost enforced cheerfulness, as if the only compensation for the loss of a naive enjoyment of the beauties of nature is a melancholy pleasure in the sophistication that knows itself undeceived. It is hardly surprising that the Romantics, such as Blake and Keats, should have reacted with such vehemence not just against Locke, who appeared merely to be applying the new scientific discoveries, but also against their supposed originator, Isaac Newton.

That Newton knew that his experiments proved no such thing, or that he was actually a platonic mystic who had spent as much time working on such posthumously published works as *The Chronology of the Ancient Kingdoms Amended* (1728) or *Observations on the Book of Daniel and St John* (1733), as he had on his scientific experiments,[12] was largely unknown to the eighteenth-century public, and would have been almost inconceivable to many of his later admirers. Locke's *Essay* had, in effect, provided a critical and appropriative narrative of such effectiveness for the absorption of Newtonian science into the eighteenth-century world-picture that it was to reign unchallenged for almost 100 years after it was published. Although there were some significant eighteenth-century critiques of Locke,[13] it was not until the advent of Romanticism nearer the end of the century that a different arrangement of existing knowledge was widely accepted as possible.[14] Ironically, this view of Newton was also to earn the hatred of another major intellectual figure whose

---

[11] Joseph Addison, 'The Pleasures of the Imagination' (1712), *Spectator*, 413.

[12] See also Henning Graf Reventlow, *The Authority of the Bible and the Rise of the Modern World*, trs John Bowden, SCM Press, 1984, p. 338.

[13] See, for instance, that of John Wesley, who, in 1774, anticipated the later 'realist' criticism, by arguing that since secondary qualities were as much a product of the senses as the primary ones, they were therefore just as *real*. For a discussion of Wesley's views on Locke, see Richard E. Brantley, *Locke, Wesley, and the Method of English Romanticism*, Gainsville: University of Florida Press, 1984, pp. 70–3.

[14] For a fuller discussion of this, and its relation to Wordsworth's theory of the Imagination, see Stephen Prickett, *Coleridge and Wordsworth: The Poetry of Growth*, Cambridge University Press, 1970, pp. 6–11.

ambition it was to challenge the whole thrust of what he understood to be Newtonian science: Johann Wolfgang von Goethe[15] – from whom, one suspects, the German-educated Henry Kissinger may indirectly have obtained his own oddly distorted notion of Newtonianism, if not Goethe's conclusions.

Once again we are dealing with different levels of narrative. We are so familiar with what Lyotard would call the 'vulgar' myth of Newton's 'discovery' of gravity – the story of the apple falling, etc. – that we somehow accept as obvious the sheer mystery of the phenomenon described. It takes works like Arthur Koestler's *The Sleepwalkers* or Richard Feynman's *The Character of Physical Law*, to defamiliarize gravity, and to make us realize afresh the sheer peculiarity of the fact that mass should attract mass, and that bodies should exert a pull on one another, not just in East Anglian apple orchards, but stretching invisible and undetectable tentacles across millions, even billions of miles in inter-stellar space. It happens without physical contact, without emissions, rays, or any other known or hypothetical links. We believe in it not because it is even remotely credible to our imaginations, but because it is mathematically calculable and predicatable to the highest degree of accuracy that our instruments permit. Small wonder that Newton himself was so cautious about his own findings, constantly using phrases such as 'it is as if . . . ' in his private letters to his friend Bentley.

As we sometimes need reminding, the foundations of modern science lie not in the Aristotelian empiricism, apparently embraced by Kissinger, but in the ironic sense of a hidden reality behind Platonic and even Hebrew mysticism.[16] The importance of these Greek and Hebrew assumptions behind the growth of Western science can scarcely be over-estimated. Comparison with what was, until recently, a much more technically advanced civilization illustrates the difference. China's failure to develop a theoretical science to match its advanced technology has long intrigued historians. Joseph Needham, the greatest Western interpreter of Chinese science finds the explanation in the comparative metaphysics of the two societies. In China

the highest spiritual being known and worshipped was not a Creator in the sense of the Hebrews and the Greeks. It was not that there was *no* order in Nature for the Chinese, but rather that it was not an order ordained by a rational personal being, and hence there was no guarantee that other rational personal beings

---

[15] See Roger Stephenson, *Goethe's Conception of Knowledge and Science*, Edinburgh University Press, 1995, p. 68.
[16] Burtt, *Metaphysical Foundations of Modern Science*.

would be able to spell out in their own earthly languages the pre-existing divine code of laws which he had previously formulated. There was no confidence that the code of Nature's laws could be unveiled and read, because there was no assurance that a divine being, even more rational than ourselves, had ever formulated such a code capable of being read.[17]

Chinese descriptions of nature were often meticulous, but the things so described were not seen as following universal principles, but as operating under particular rules followed by those entities in a harmonious cosmic order.[18] Here metaphor is absolutely central to thought. European Christianity – especially the Roman, and its offshoot Protestant traditions – thought in terms of a divine legal system embracing the whole of creation. However much this may originally have been a quite literal belief (and in the case of writers like Augustine the matter is debatable) it was in *linguistic* terms always a metaphor. We only have to look at Needham's English in the passage quoted to see how impossible it is to think of the operations of nature without using legal metaphor. Not just the word 'law' but 'code', 'read' and even 'order' and 'assurance' smack of the law-court.

In China there were both linguistic and historical reasons for a quite different way of thinking. Paradoxically, the workings of nature had been relatively *more* important in traditional Chinese thought than in European, but those processes had their own specific word. 'Law' was a concept that applied (quite logically) only to human society.[19] Moreover, for particular contingent and historical reasons, the idea of abstract codified law was unattractive. During the transition from feudalism to bureaucracy in the Ch'in dynasty (221–206 BCE) Chinese law had been rigidly quantified by the 'Legalists', working on the assumption that people are fundamentally antisocial and must be coerced into obeying laws that placed the power of the state above any personal needs or aspirations.[20] For a people who today still apparently remember with hatred the tyranny of the First Emperor ruthlessly using forced labour to build the Great Wall, the idea of nature as an extension of their own experience of the law was instinctively – and quite understandably – abhorrent. That revulsion is visible even today in the current Chinese

---

[17] Joseph Needham, *Human Law and the Laws of Nature in China and the West*, L.T. Hobhouse Memorial Trust Lecture, Cambridge University Press, 1951, pp. 41–2.

[18] See Edward O. Wilson, *Consilience*, Abacus, 1998, p. 32. See also *The Shorter Science and Civilization in China: An Abridgement of Joseph Needham's Original Text*, Vol. I, prepared by Colin A. Ronan, Cambridge University Press, 1978.

[19] Needham, *Human Law and the Laws of Nature*, p. 39.

[20] Wilson, *Consilience*, p. 32.

translation of our commonplace phrase, 'laws of nature': *tzu-jan fa*, 'spontaneous law' – a phrase which, as Needham puts it, 'uncompromisingly retains the ancient Taoist denial of a personal God, and yet is almost a contradiction in terms'.[21]

Though the European idea of natural law was, of course, formed as a metaphor from human law, because it was inevitably *seen* as the other way round, it was always possible to separate human tyranny from divine order. The argument from 'natural justice' invoked by English lawyers in a variety of contexts over the centuries draws its force from the still powerful latent notion of an even greater legal system permeating the cosmos, to which our own imperfect copy has somehow failed to properly correspond. In particular the legal right to rebellion against an unjust civil power was central to seventeenth-century English politics. Though interpretation might only be decided by civil war, the laws of man had in some way to reflect the greater laws of God. Some historians of science have been baffled by the fact that the great Sir Isaac Newton, the apparent epitome of Enlightenment rationality, should actually have spent at least half his working life in trying to interpret biblical and other ancient prophecies. Yet to make sense of Newton at all, we have to accept that these researches into biblical prophecy were not, as it were, an endearing eccentricity, the private 'hobby' of an otherwise eminent scientist and mathematician, but, for him, as much a valid part of his work in discovering the true nature of things, as the *Principia* and the *Opticks*.

Even for some of his contemporaries this was hard to take. Critics were quick to observe that not merely did Newton *not* draw the kind of clear distinction between science and occult or metaphysical forces that was second nature to many of his rationalist contemporaries, but, even worse, such occult forces were actually pivotal to his science itself. Newton's gravity was, as we have seen, an essentially mysterious force which could only be described in the language of 'innate qualities' used by the discredited mediaeval scholastic philosophers – who said, with unassailable logic, but to our ears somewhat tautologically, that things had a 'tendency to fall'. For an age dominated by 'corpuscular' physical theory, where any action had to have a demonstrable mechanical cause, the lack of such a mechanical explanation of gravity was one of the most challenging problems. Newton himself devoted much time to it, as did many of his eighteenth-century successors. The alternative, however, was

---

[21] Needham, *Human Law and the Laws of Nature*, p. 40.

to reject Newton's theory altogether for its failure to explain gravity – as, of course, many contemporaries did, for precisely that reason.[22]

REVOLUTIONS AND PARADIGMS

In fact, as Thomas Kuhn reminds us in his epoch-making study, *The Structure of Scientific Revolutions*, Newton's theory was *not* generally accepted, particularly on the Continent, for more than half a century after the *Principia* appeared.[23] But, from a practical point of view, the total package proved in the end irresistible. Unable either to practise science without the *Principia*, or to make its central theory conform to the corpuscular standards of the seventeenth century, scientists gradually accepted the view that gravity was indeed innate. 'By the middle of the eighteenth century', writes Kuhn, 'that interpretation had been almost universally accepted, and the result was a genuine reversion (which is not the same as a retrogression) to a scholastic standard. Innate attractions and repulsions joined size, shape, position, and motion as physically irre-ducible primary properties of matter.'[24] The new Newtonian paradigm had ceased to be controversial, and, according to Kuhn, passed into the realm of 'normal science', providing an unquestioned background for scientists to get on with what they do best: small scale problem-solving.

For Kuhn, such 'reversions' illustrate a fundamental point about what he calls scientific 'paradigms'. These are the larger, and largely unques-tioned frameworks of ideas within which the normal science of any given period is practised. As with the Newtonian 'revolution', a paradigm is based on 'universally recognized scientific achievements that for a time provide model problems and solutions to a community of practitioners'.[25] Within any mature field of science, Kuhn argues, the current paradigm commands such a degree of universal acceptance that most scientists are unaware of its existence. Nevertheless, it is of the nature of paradigms that they will *never* manage to explain every phenomenon in their field; there will always be anomalies that do not fit.

Historically there have been two ways of dealing with these anomalies. The first is exemplified by the behaviour of the scientific community with Newton's theory of gravity. Even though it fitted *neither* with the previous corpuscular and mechanical paradigm, *nor* even with the new paradigm of Newton's own mechanics, it was provisionally accepted and put on one side in the hope either that a satisfactory explanation for the exception

---

[22] See Thomas Kuhn, *The Structure of Scientific Revolutions*, University of Chicago Press, 1962, p. 105.
[23] Ibid. p. 150.   [24] Ibid. p. 105.   [25] Ibid. p. x.

would later be found, or that, despite current appearances, it could be shown not to be an anomaly at all. In fact, as we have seen, the scientific community was finally forced to accept what Kuhn calls a 'reversion' – a return to an older and discredited notion that there could be such a thing as 'innate properties'. And this, in turn, had unexpected consequences.

The resulting change in the standards and problem-field of physical science was once again consequential. By the 1740s, for example, electricians could again speak of the attractive 'virtue' of the electric fluid without thereby inviting the ridicule that had greeted Molière's doctor [in *Le malade imaginaire*] a century before. As they did so, electrical phenomena increasingly displayed an order different from the one they had shown when viewed as the effects of a mechanical effluvium that could only act by contact. In particular, when electrical action-at-a-distance became a subject for study in its own right, the phenomenon we now call charging by induction could be recognised as one of its effects. Previously, when seen at all, it had been attributed to the direct action of electrical 'atmospheres' or to the leakage inevitable in any electrical laboratory. The new view of inductive effects was, in turn, the key to Franklin's analysis of the Leyden jar, and thus to the emergence of a new and Newtonian paradigm for electricity.[26]

And this example also shows the second traditional reaction to an anomaly in an accepted paradigm. It is often simply not *seen* at all. So conditioned are those within a specific paradigm to expect and look for certain kinds of phenomena, that those that fall outside those expectations, or fail to conform to them, are often literally invisible. Kuhn cites experiments where subjects were given quick glimpses of playing cards that were incorrect – i.e. red spades, or black hearts. The commonest reactions were either to reclassify them correctly, and 'see' them as black spades, and red hearts, or to observe that they were 'unidentifiable'. It was only when they were alerted to the possibility that there might be anomalous cards in the pack that they were able to identify them as such.[27]

Astronomy has several dramatic historical examples of this kind of influence of contemporary paradigms. Because the old Ptolemaic helio-centric model of the universe had taken the immutability of the heav-ens for granted, Western astronomers only began to see change after Copernicus. The Chinese, whose cosmological beliefs did not rule out change, had recorded the appearance of many new stars at a much ear-lier date. Similarly, because, even after Copernicus, no one believed that there could be any more planets, Uranus, which was plainly visible even

---

[26] Ibid. p. 105.   [27] Ibid. pp. 62–3.

with seventeenth- and eighteenth-century telescopes, was simply not seen as a possible planet. Astronomers' records show that it had been seen and classified as 'a star' on at least seventeen different occasions between 1690 and 1781. The astronomer Herschel, who is eventually credited with its 'discovery', when he finally realized from its movements that it could not be a star, thought at first it was a comet. 'The very ease and rapidity with which astronomers saw new things when looking at old objects with old instruments', writes Kuhn, 'may make us wish to say that, after Copernicus, astronomers lived in a different world.'[28]

As here, the point about such paradigms, Kuhn insists, is that they involve a 'revolution' in perception itself. Science does not involve a steady progression of knowledge, but has proceeded by a series of such 'revolutions' in which the definition of what constitutes 'knowledge' itself changes radically. Moreover, unless we actually read the 'pre-revolutionary documents themselves, such revolutions are almost invisible to those who come after. This is because of the way in which both scientists and laymen alike acquire their knowledge. Unlike our knowledge of, say, the literature of the past, which we gain by reading it directly, the main sources of scientific information about either the present or the past are textbooks, popularizations, and works on the philosophy of science. All three 'record the stable *outcome* of past revolutions and thus display the bases of the current normal-scientific tradition'.[29]

Unless he has personally experienced a revolution in his own lifetime, the historical sense either of the working scientist or of the lay reader of textbook literature extends only to the outcome of the most recent revolutions in the field . . . From such references both students and professionals come to feel like participants in a long-standing historical tradition. Yet their textbook-derived tradition in which scientists come to sense their participation is one that, in fact, never existed . . . The depreciation of historical fact is deeply, and probably functionally, ingrained the ideology of the scientific profession . . . '[30]

The invisibility of each previous paradigm once the new paradigm has been firmly established gives an illusion of quite unhistorical continuity to the development of science. The paradigm created by Newton was only one of many, and, as one might expect, even he was prepared to re-write the past in order to stress not the degree of change, but the degree of continuity. Thus he attributes to Galileo the discovery that the constant force of gravity produces a motion proportional to the square of the time. 'In fact,' writes Kuhn, 'Galileo's kinematic theorem does take

[28] Ibid. p. 116.   [29] Ibid. pp. 135–6.   [30] Ibid. pp. 136–7.

that form when embedded in the matrix of Newton's own dynamical concepts.'

But Galileo said nothing of the sort. His discussion of falling bodies rarely alludes to forces, much less to uniform gravitational force that causes bodies to fall. By crediting to Galileo the answer to a question that Galileo's paradigms did not permit to be asked, Newton's account hides the effect of a small but revolutionary reformulation in the questions that scientists asked about motion as well as in the answers they felt able to accept.[31]

Though at one level this is a kind of scientific 'good manners', acknowledging the essential groundwork of his predecessors, such a move also served to bolster Newton's own position, making his own contribution seem marginally less revolutionary than it actually was. But, whether intended or unintended, the overall effect was to stress a kind of seamless 'march of the mind', despite the fact that, as we have seen with the curious case of gravity, it does not even proceed methodologically in one direction.

These characteristic shifts in the scientific community's conception of its legitimate problems and standards would have less significance . . . if one could suppose that they always occurred from some methodologically lower to some higher type. In that case their effects, too, would seem cumulative. No wonder that some historians have argued that the history of science records a continuing increase in the maturity and refinement of man's conception of the nature of science. Yet the case for cumulative development of science's problems and standards is even harder to make than the case for cumulation of theories. The attempt to explain gravity, though fruitfully abandoned by most eighteenth-century scientists, was not directed to an intrinsically illegitimate problem; the objections to innate forces were neither inherently unscientific nor metaphysical in some pejorative sense. There are no external standards to permit a judgement of that sort. What occurred was neither a decline nor a raising of standards, but simply a change demanded by the adoption of a new paradigm. Furthermore that change has since been reversed and could be again. In the twentieth century Einstein succeeded in explaining gravitational attractions, and that explanation has returned science to a set of canons and problems that are, in this particular respect, more like those of Newton's predecessors than of his successors.[32]

As here, this shift between paradigms is never simply a matter of adding new knowledge. It is, Kuhn claims, a fundamental 'flip' of perception

---

[31] Ibid. p. 138. For Newton's remark see Florian Cajori (ed.), *Sir Isaac Newton's Mathematical Principles of Natural Philosophy and his System of the World*, Berkeley, Calif.: University of California Press, 1946, p. 21. Cf. Galileo's own discussion in his *Dialogues Concerning Two New Sciences*, trs H. Crew and A. de Salvio, Evanston, Ill., 1946 pp. 154–76.

[32] Ibid. p. 106.

more akin to the way in which we change our 'way of seeing' in the well-known rabbit or duck experiment. One of the words he repeatedly uses for this process is 'conversion'. Clearly many scientists never make the transition, never experience this semi-voluntary conversion at all, and the ultimate success of the new paradigm depends on a new generation, for whom it seems obvious and natural, taking over as its opponents withdraw and die.

But there remains an important distinction between rabbit/duck pictures and scientific paradigms. The experience of seeing such puzzle pictures as first one thing, and then another, depends on the subject knowing for certain that the object itself has *not* changed. 'Unless there were an external standard with respect to which a switch of vision could be demonstrated', Kuhn points out, 'no conclusion about alternate perceptual possibilities could be drawn.'

With scientific observation, however, the situation is exactly reversed. The scientist can have no recourse above and beyond what he sees with his eyes and instruments. If there were some higher authority by recourse to which his vision might be shown to have shifted, then that authority would itself become the source of his data, and the behaviour of his vision would become a source of his problems (as that of the experimental subject is for the psychologist).[33]

In other words, contrary to the kind of popular assumptions that, as we have seen, Locke was able to draw on in his appropriation of Newton, we have in science no assurance of a stable and neutral base from which to demonstrate the uncertainty and subjectivity of our perceptions. And here the argument begins to become very interesting indeed. It is as if Kuhn has himself discovered an anomaly in the paradigm of mid-twentieth-century science in which he has come to consciousness as a working practitioner, and is unsure of quite how to develop his argument.

But is sensory experience fixed and neutral? Are theories simply man-made interpretations of given data? The epistemological viewpoint that has most often guided Western philosophy for three centuries dictates an immediate and unequivocal, Yes! In the absence of a developed alternative, I find it impossible to relinquish entirely that viewpoint. Yet it no longer functions effectively, and the attempts to make it do so through the introduction of a neutral language of observations now seem to me hopeless.[34]

Whether Kuhn intended it or not, this is language for which the rest of his book has been carefully preparing us – anomalies that no longer permit

---

[33] Ibid. p. 113.   [34] Ibid. p. 125.

the current paradigm 'to function effectively', and 'hopeless' attempts to rescue it through new adjustments already too late to be effective, are the terminology of a paradigm-shift in operation. Like C.S. Lewis, part of him, at any rate, would like to believe in a stable and monistic universe where, as in Donne's poem

> On a huge hill,
> Cragged and steep, Truth stands, and he that will
> Reach her, about must, and about must go,
> And what the hill's suddenness resists, win so;[35]

For Donne, as for Lewis, the problem with 'Truth' lies in ascending the huge hill, and somehow finding it. Truth itself is not a problem when you get there. But the whole tenor of Kuhn's argument tells a quite different story. As a scientist and as a historian he finds that it is no longer possible, even in 1962, to believe in such a world. What he has been describing instead is a universe where there is never a whole and seamless picture, and where no paradigm ever explains all the phenomena in its field. What his history of science shows is a constantly shifting mosaic pattern of pieces of differing sizes and significance, constantly switching from positive to negative, and back. Indeed,

no paradigm that provides a basis for scientific research ever completely re-solves all its problems. The few that have ever seemed to do so (e.g. geometric optics) have shortly ceased to yield research problems at all and have instead become tools for engineering. Excepting those that are exclusively instrumental, every problem that normal science sees as a puzzle can be seen, from another viewpoint, as a counterinstance and thus as a source of crisis.[36]

As he is well aware, this is more than a portrait of complexity; it is one of fundamental and irreconcilable ambiguity. One of the most disturbing features of paradigm-shifts is that the new paradigm not only serves to explain problems or anomalies that were previously inexplicable, but it also often provides new explanations for phenomena that, from the point of view of the old paradigm, *already had* perfectly satisfactory explanations. Moreover, as we have seen in the case of Newton's regression to the older discredited idea of 'innate qualities', the explanation offered by the previous paradigm may, to a still later paradigm, seem to offer a 'better' explanation. From a purely scientific point of view, this is a universe that, even as we learn progressively more and more about it, remains in the end tantalizingly unknowable. Despite our growing technical skills

---

[35] John Donne, 'Satire 3', lines 79–82.   [36] Kuhn, *Structure of Scientific Revolutions*, p. 79.

in predicting and manipulating such forces as electricity or gravity, we are in the end no wiser about what they actually *are*. Indeed, for many scientists, such a naively essentialist question is one that would only be asked by an ignorant layman.

No doubt as a result of such awkward implications, even after forty years Kuhn's work remains controversial. For obvious reasons, it proved to be much more popular with social scientists than with physical scientists, and, as we shall see, even more so with such nominalistic irrationalists as Richard Rorty. Kuhn himself, it should be clear, has been increasingly anxious to distance himself from many of those most keen to apply his ideas to the social sciences and to the humanities – areas that he considers 'pre-paradigmatic'.

Not least of the problems that have irked dedicated members of the scientific community in particular is that the 'scientific method' is made to seem no more than a branch of other human cultural activities, and to be reducible to the methods and analyses of the social sciences, which had long been a by-word for pretensions unsupported by genuine incremental growth of knowledge among those who regarded themselves as 'real' scientists. As Barry Barnes says,

> Whereas on a rationalist view routine scientific work is a matter of passive obedience to rules, on Kuhn's account it involves the active elaboration of existing custom and convention...On this account, paradigms, the core of the culture of science, are transmitted and sustained just as is culture generally: scientists accept them and become committed to them as the result of training and socialisation, and the commitment is maintained by a developed system of social control.[37]

The suggestion that science was *socially* constructed in the same way as literature, politics or religion, despite the difference in its content, was (and still is) as unwelcome to many research scientists, including Kuhn himself, as it was welcome to such social scientists as Lyotard, who, of course, himself draws heavily on unacknowledged Kuhnian assumptions to portray science as yet another area of social control.

Equally appealing to social scientists and repugnant to many physical scientists was Karl Popper's notion of 'falsifiability'. The process of logical induction by which scientific laws were supposed to be discovered was, he claimed, largely nonsense. For Popper the only scientifically respectable beliefs were those that had been subjected to a 'crucial experiment' designed to falsify them. This was the way, he maintained,

---

[37] Barry Barnes, 'Thomas Kuhn', in Skinner (ed.), *The Return of Grand Theory in the Human Sciences*. Cambridge University Press, 1985, p. 89.

that most scientific beliefs are in the end refuted. If, on the other hand, no such experiment could be devised, even in theory, we have good reason to suppose that nonsense is being talked – and that we are in the realm not of physics, but metaphysics.[38] To verify the supposed law 'all ravens are black', for instance, it would be necessary to check all known ravens. The discovery of even one miserable albino bird would bring the whole structure crashing down. But the painstaking, even clumsy mode of refutation this involves tells us something else. We move from one provisional, and falsifiable hypothesis to the next. Science cannot establish certain and definitive knowledge; there is no definitive theory, no definitive knowledge.

As these examples suggest, debates about 'how science actually works' have always appealed more to philosophers and social scientists than to scientists themselves. Physicists such as Paul Davies who have attempted to popularize developments in cosmology and to discuss possible theological implications have proved more popular with the public than with colleagues.[39] It is no accident that much of the debate over paradigms and the supposed limits of scientific method has been conducted not among scientists but philosophers.[40] Thus a 1982 volume entitled *Scientific Revolutions*, with essays by Kuhn, Popper ('The Rationality of Scientific Revolutions') and the anarchist philosopher, Paul Feyerabend ('How to Defend Society Against Science') drew a ferocious counterblast from another philosopher, D.C. Stove, who lumped Kuhn and Popper together with Feyerabend and the Hungarian Marxist refugee, Imre Lakatos, as 'four modern irrationalists', all of whom, according to Stove, simply seek to deny by literary and rhetorical tricks 'the accumulation or growth of knowledge in the last four hundred years'.[41] Such an extreme position ignores the gulfs that separates all four writers, but is indicative of the passions that such debates generate.

Among philosophers these arguments tend, very properly, to concentrate on exact nuances of interpretation. If Popper is opposed to Lakatos, and both oppose Kuhn and (later) Feyerabend, what are we to make of their all contributing to *Scientific Revolutions*? Did Kuhn ever intend his work to be applied outside the sphere of science? How far did Kuhn's later repudiation of the sociological applications of his ideas have to do with his perceived standing within the scientific community? What is

[38] Karl Popper, *The Logic of Scientific Discovery*, Hutchinson, 1959, pp. 78–92.
[39] E.g. Davies, *The Mind of God*.
[40] See, for instance, Paul Thagard, *Conceptual Revolutions*, Princeton University Press, 1992.
[41] D.C. Stove, *Popper and After: Four Modern Irrationalists*, Oxford: Pergamon Press, 1982.

rarely considered in such debates are the wider questions of how (and why) new ideas are taken from one sphere and appropriated to others. The history of ideas is also the history of mis-appropriations, misunderstandings, misreadings – many with powerful results. The history of the concept of 'revolution' itself is a case in point.[42] Einstein, famously, could never accept Bohr's 'Copenhagen' interpretation of the quantum theory – which his own work had done so much to prepare the ground for.[43] From the point of view of a historian of ideas, the applicability of Kuhn's notions of a 'paradigm' to the social sciences has in the end little to do with the question of whether Kuhn did, or did not, agree with it. The historian simply notes that the word 'paradigm' underwent a significant change of meaning, and application, in the second half of the twentieth century. A new kind of narrative, a new description of the world, had been introduced, and gained widespread acceptance.

The dangers of repudiation by the scientific community are, however, illustrated by the fate of an even bolder speculative theorist. Rupert Sheldrake, one-time academic biologist and fellow of Clare College, Cambridge, has outraged many members of the scientific establishment by arguing that there are *no* natural laws in the accepted sense at all. For him the universe is governed by what he calls 'morphic resonance'. This means that, in effect, the material world operates by 'habit'. Once a thing has happened by chance in a particular way, it will happen that way again. For instance, newly synthesized compounds can be very difficult to crystallize to begin with, but they become progressively easier the more often they are made. Though in theory these artificial compounds could have a number of possible structures, they seem always to 'choose' one particular form. Conventional explanations include fragments of previous crystals being carried around the world as dust particles in the atmosphere, or even in chemists' beards! Morphic resonance, Sheldrake argues, provides an alternative explanation. Once established, anywhere in the world, all other experiments will follow the same course.[44] A more homely example of Sheldrake's that has aroused even wider controversy was his argument that it was easier to do the *Times* crossword puzzle in the afternoon of the day it was published because so many people had already completed it in the morning. An experiment designed to test this hypothesis was carried out, with apparently positive results, but (as Kuhn might have predicted) a large body of scientific opinion was less than impressed!

---

[42] See below, pp. 80–1.   [43] See below, pp. 243–7.

[44] Rupert Sheldrake, *The Presence of the Past: Morphic Resonance and the Habits of Nature*, Collins, 1988, p. 131.

Though such rejection is what the Kuhnian paradigm theory would, of course, predict for any attempt at radical restructuring of the existing pattern of scientific thought, it may also stem from an innate suspicion of theories that explain *too much*. Sheldrake's 'morphic resonance', at least in its present stage of development, amounts in practice to a 'grand Theory of Everything'. As we have consistently seen at every level of human experience, such universal explanations fly in the face of a long tradition, both in theory and practice, of 'incompleteness'. Nevertheless, it will, I hope, be clear to readers that it is no part of the present work to assess the truth or falsity of the scientific theories discussed (or even whether terms such as 'true' or 'false' are appropriate at all for theories with an inevitably short shelf-life). My theme here, and throughout, is the way in which scientific theories have interacted with those of literature and theology to 'construct' the worlds which we have collectively assumed that we inhabit, showing not merely how such assumptions (which have very rarely been sufficiently conscious for us to apply the word 'belief') have subtly shifted and changed over the past 300 years, but also their inevitable fragmentation and incompleteness. What we are concerned with are models of reality – and such models are usually verbal and almost invariably narrative. As we shall be seeing, from our point of view, one of the most interesting things about Kuhn's notion of paradigms is the way in which they correspond to other similar patterns of representation in art, social thought, and religion. Whether Sheldrake's arguments are more than just an amusing footnote to twentieth-century science remains to be seen.

MODELS OF REALITY

Though Kuhn gives more weight to the social inertia of the scientific community than Popper, their theories are by no means incompatible, and despite their marginalization from the mainstream of scientific action, the questions raised by both have not gone away. In particular the problem of whether this growing ambiguity and elusiveness of our knowledge is simply a matter of our ignorance, and the provisional state of our understanding in general, or whether this is a fundamental limitation – as it were, part of the natural order of things – has become an increasingly controversial question. Though, as has been observed, some physical scientists – most notably cosmologists – hanker after what they call 'a grand Theory of Everything', it is interesting that this call comes from what must be the most provisional and rapidly changing science of all.[45]

This current debate, however, seems to be fundamentally different from all apparently similar debates about the limits of knowledge in the past. The history of the past 500 years has been one of continual, and futile, attempts to set limits to the nature and scope of scientific knowledge. For centuries, the Catholic Church notoriously insisted that what it saw as biblical Revelation (actually the Ptolemaic model) should take precedence over human observation. Nevertheless, as Galileo is supposed to have muttered under his breath when forced, under threat of torture, publicly to recant his claim that the earth goes round the sun, *eppur si muove* ('but it *does* move'). Similarly, the Bishop of Oxford's (equally mythical[46]) attempt to refute Darwin by ridicule in the debate at the Pitt-Rivers Museum in Oxford simply contributed another anecdote to the long narrative of successive scientific victories over superstition and obscurantism. Even predictions of the limits of science by scientists themselves have almost always been confounded. The comment by Sir Bernard Lovell, Astronomer Royal in the 1960s, that space travel would never be possible, has already been disproved, and the many voices raised in mid-century to assert that man cannot 'create life' have fallen oddly quiet in recent years.

What is different about about this claim, therefore, is not merely that it comes from scientists themselves, but that it comes, as it were, from *inside* science. Moreover this is not a matter of technology, whose boundaries at the end of the twentieth century seem almost non-existent, but of theory. The claim is being made not by those who wish, for whatever reason, to derive their boundaries from some external non-scientific criteria – whether biblical Revelation, common sense, or simply fear of the unknown – but from those who have detected what seem to them inherent contradictions emerging within science itself.

The French physicist, Bernard D'Espagnat, for instance, shares many of the reservations of the practising scientific community about Kuhn, but he does so from a disconcerting angle. For him the difficulty lies in the relation between the raw material of science, the empirical phenomena (or 'physical reality') we experience either directly through our senses or, increasingly, through our specialized instruments, and independent reality. This relationship, he argues, is deeply problematic, and is likely to remain so.

---

[45] Even the precise meaning of this term, 'theory of everything', has, however, proved to be controversial. See David Deutsch, *The Fabric of Reality*, Harmondsworth: Penguin 1997, p. 2.

[46] See Stephen Jay Gould, *Bully for Brontosaurus*, pp. 385–401.

Like most physicists, I am of the opinion that the value of such 'socio-epistemological' theories [as Kuhn's or Popper's] does not match the stir they have created. Since fallibilism had spread the idea that theories successively collapsed, it was probably inevitable that purely sociological, perhaps even irrationalist, interpretations of science should appear and enjoy the limelight for the moment. But what has been said above about the solidity of experimental facts and theoretical equations is enough to dispose, in general terms, of the thesis of successive collapse. Whether applied to theories, as the fallibilists apply it, or to paradigms, as the socio-epistemologists apply it, the thesis can – given the solidity of experimental facts and theoretical equations – only affect *interpretations*. It is therefore meaningful only within physical realism ... And as we shall see ... physical realism now faces insurmountable problems and should therefore preferably be left aside in connection with the matters in hand – which deprives 'sociologism' of its substance.[47]

If that were all there were to Kuhn, such a dismissal would perhaps be just from D'Espagnat's point of view. But, as we have seen, there is more to Kuhn's argument than a sociological analysis of paradigms. 'Physical realism', the notion that science deals directly with a real and knowable world, is not exactly the haunt of the lunatic fringe. As D'Espagnat himself admits, it is the working model most scientists use most of the time. Some, if pressed, would refine their positions to that of 'instrumentalism' – the idea that scientific knowledge refers only to experience, not to reality – thus leaving open the question of what reality might be, but in practice physicists behave, at least, like simple physical realists. For this credo to be under challenge, if only in theory, is remarkable.

Underlying that are much more disturbing questions: why, for instance, do so many paradigms nearly, but never quite, explain the same phenomena? How far can reality be pushed and pulled in different directions to suit first one schema, and then another? For D'Espagnat, the problem lies in the disconcerting gap between 'empirical reality', which is the realm of science, and what he calls 'independent reality'. For him, 'physical realism', or the view that the empirical world of scientifically measurable phenomena constitutes the ultimate reality, is no longer a tenable *scientific* position. So far from seeing science as providing an adequate description of the world, therefore, D'Espagnat insists that any account it provides can never be more than partial – or in his terms 'veiled'.

This notion, for me the central one, of veiled reality can perhaps best be grasped by means of an analogy inspired by an idea of Bertrand Russell, in which

---

[47] D'Espagnat, *Reality and the Physicist*, p. 256.

independent reality is compared to a musical concert while empirical reality – the ensemble of phenomena – is compared to a recording of the concert on, say, a disc. Obviously the pattern of the disc is not totally independent of the structure of the concert, but obviously too the recording, consisting of a spatial arrangement in the form of minute hills and hollows in grooves, cannot be identified purely and simply with the concert, which is arranged in time. It would clearly be absurd to suppose that concert and disc constitute one and the same thing. Besides, a Martian who landed on Earth and discovered the disc would never, by studying its detailed spatial structure, be able to reconstitute the concert, whatever abilities he might be endowed with . . . [48]

There are several points here that are worth considering. The first is that D'Espagnat is at some pains to write as a philosopher *and* scientist. That is to say, he sees himself working within the rules and practices (the 'paradigms') of both academic communities. When, for instance, he says that the scientific school of thought which he designates 'physical realism' now 'faces insurmountable problems' he does not intend this so much as an expression of his own opinion, as a simple statement of fact, which can be verified by anyone who has the necessary knowledge (such as a fellow-member of the scientific community) and who takes the trouble to follow his arguments.

The second is that D'Espagnat's model, despite its contemporary trappings, is in essence a very old one indeed, and owes its origins to a way of thinking that is not in the least scientific in our modern sense. It has at least a strong 'family resemblance' to Plato's cave-myth and, despite his specific denials, to Kant's distinction between 'understanding' and 'reason'. For Plato the human condition was like that of prisoners in a cave, facing away from the entrance so that all they could see of the 'real' world outside the cave were shadows cast by things as they passed the entrance. Only with the aid of the strictest philosophical training might people aspire to turn around and face the other direction, towards the light. For Kant, similarly, we live in a world of appearances, to which the 'understanding' or 'empirical reason' gives us some access, and by means of which we can practise science. True reality, however, and the nature of things-in-themselves is forever hidden from us, despite the possibility offered by 'pure reason' and (in the Third Critique) some works of art. Though no doubt D'Espagnat is correct in trying (as he does) to distance himself from the precise formulations of either, such extended metaphors are not matters of precise formulation, but images of disjunction and imprecision.

[48] Ibid. p. 208.

And this brings us to a third, and from our narrative point of view, perhaps most important point. Such metaphors of shadows in a cave, of the essential unknowability of things in themselves, or of a veiled reality revealed to us only as a disk (78, LP, CD, or DVD, it matters not!) records a live orchestra, provide a language fraught with irony, both in the original Greek sense of something 'hidden', and in the modern extended meaning of our being *aware* of a gap between what is being said, and what we are expected to understand by what is being said. This can take the very simple form of rhetorical understatement (*litotes*) – the soldier who describes a battle as being 'a spot of bother' or 'a bad show' – or the much more subtle form where the narrator implies either that there is more to the story he is telling than the narrative admits, or that we are expected to read more into it. Shakespeare's *Macbeth*, which, as we all know, is full of the more flamboyant forms of dramatic irony, has also a very fine example of this quieter more deadpan kind, when Lennox (a Lord who says practically nothing else of significance) comments:

> The gracious Duncan
> Was pitied of Macbeth; marry he was dead.
> And the right valiant Banquo walk'd too late,
> Whom you may say (if't please you) Fleance kill'd,
> For Fleance fled. Men must not walk too late.
> (III, vi, 3–7)

This is, of course, language under political repression. Lennox does not know, for certain, who killed Duncan or Banquo; nor, indeed, whether he can trust the (unnamed) person he is speaking to. Therefore he says nothing that could be construed as questioning the official version of events, or that could be interpreted as critical of the new regime. Yet the (unspoken) message is perfectly clear.

More complex still, however, is the irony of ultimate uncertainty, where the message is *not* clear at all. The only thing that is clear is that there is more going on than meets the eye. Perhaps the most famous example would be the words of the angel at the tomb of Jesus on Easter morning: 'He is not here.' Yes, indeed, they can all see that! But what is *hidden* behind this enigmatic truism?

The scientific equivalent of this is the language of ironic understatement and uncertainty. When D'Espagnat insists that the language of physics, and the notion of physical realism are analogous to a recorded disk found by that ultimate innocent observer, the man from Mars, who can even discover how to play it, but not what went into making the sounds, he is (consciously or not) tapping into level upon historic level of ironic resonance. Consider this, for instance:

In crossing a heath, suppose I pitched my foot against a *stone*, and were asked how the stone came to be there, I might possibly answer, that, for anything I knew to the contrary, it had lain there for ever; nor would it perhaps be very easy to shew the absurdidty of this answer. But suppose I had found a *watch* upon the ground, and it should be enquired how the watch happened to be in that place, I should hardly think of the answer which I had before given . . . For this reason, and for no other, viz. that when we come to inspect the watch, we perceive (what we could not discover in the stone) that its several parts are framed and put together for a purpose . . . [49]

The writer is William Paley, and the book *Natural Theology*, published in 1802. In this narrative, the high-tech artifact does not so much conceal its origins, and what lies behind it, as advertise to every reader that it tells a story. This is the classic statement of the argument for the existence of God from the design of the universe – using the analogy of a watch first used by the British scientist, Robert Boyle, popularized by the French philosopher, Leibniz, and developed with minute precision by Paley's contemporary, Pierre Laplace. Paley's 'watch', however, is not, like Leibniz', an image of the solar system. Though he does devote one chapter to astronomy, he is here much more interested in the operations of the organic world, and, in particular, of comparative anatomy and physiology. His message is that the minutely detailed description of *how* those individual parts of the man-made watch work together to produce a purposeful and efficient machine can be paralleled, even exceeded, by the seemingly miraculous properties of created life: 'every indication of contrivance, every manifestation of design, which existed in the watch, exists in the works of nature; with the difference, on the side of nature, of being greater and more, and that in a degree which exceeds all computation'.[50]

Paley's famous watch, though of course presented within a framework of naive physical realism, is a classic 'proof' of God. But, in the history of science, his Leibnizian argument does not only come down to us directly, but also through a further level of mediation. Charles Darwin

---

[49] William Paley, *Natural Theology: or Evidences of the Existence and Attributes of the Deity, Collected from the Appearances of Nature*, 3rd edn, 1803, pp. 1–2.
[50] Ibid. p. 19.

had originally been sent to Edinburgh University to read medicine, but, when it became clear that his son had no desire to practise as a doctor, his father decided that he should become a clergyman instead and sent him in 1828 to Cambridge – to Paley's old college, Christ's, where in his first year, he actually occupied Paley's old rooms.[51] Darwin afterwards recalled that the logic of Paley's *Evidences* and *Natural Theology* gave him 'as much delight' as reading Euclid[52] – and he claimed to have learned it by heart.[53] The patient step-by-step reasoning of mathematics, and the very genuine enthusiasm for the subject, are both significant in the light of Darwin's later use of this material. Paley, for instance, following what he believes to be the workings of science, finds in the mechanism of the human eye, and the fineness of the image on the retina, a perfect example of the Locke/Newton theory of vision:

In considering vision as achieved by the means of an image formed at the bottom of the eye, we can never reflect without wonder upon the smallness, yet correctness, of the picture, the subtility [sic] of the touch, the fineness of the lines. A landscape of five or six square leagues is brought into a space of half an inch diameter; yet the multitude of objects which it contains are all preserved; are all discriminated in their magnitudes, positions, figures, colours. The prospect from Hampstead Hill is compressed into the compass of a six-pence . . . If anything can abate our admiration of the smallness of the visual tablet compared with the extent of vision, it is a reflection, which the view of nature leads us, every hour, to make, viz. that, in the hands of the Creator, great and little are nothing. Sturmius held, that the examination of the eye was a cure for atheism.[54]

Every image in this sequence reinforces the initial analogy between the parts of the body and those of a purposefully designed machine: illustrating the wonder and beneficence of God's creation. 'I know of no better method of introducing a subject', writes Paley, 'than of comparing a single thing with a single thing; an eye, for example, with a telescope. As far as the examination of the instrument goes, there is precisely the same proof that the eye was made for vision, as there is that the telescope was made for assisting it.'[55]

---

[51] On G staircase. See Adrian Desmond and James Moore, *Charles Darwin*, Michael Joseph, 1991, p. 64, and *Darwin's Autobiography of Charles Darwin*, Watts & Co., 1929, pp. 19–20. Darwin's self-proclaimed academic indolence and lack of ambition are not unlike those attributed to Paley himself during the nineteenth century. See the anecdote in Samuel Smiles, *Character*, London: John Murray, 1884, p. 69.

[52] Darwin, *Autobiography*, p. 22.   [53] Desmond and Moore, *Darwin*, p. 78.
[54] Paley, *Natural Theology*, p. 34.   [55] Ibid. p. 20.

William Paley was one of a group of leading divines and natural theologians centred on Cambridge in the second half of the eighteenth century.[56] From 1766–75 he was a fellow of Christ's College, Cambridge. His friend and patron, Edmund Law, was master of Peterhouse from 1754–87 and for part of that time (1767–87) concurrently Bishop of Carlisle. In 1777 Law had produced a new edition of Locke, stressing in particular the idea of progress or development in religion – anticipating Lessing,[57] and perhaps later influencing Newman. Under his patronage Paley became first prebendary and then Archdeacon of Carlisle. Paley's books, *Evidences of Christianity* (1794), *Principles of Morals and Political Philosophy* (1785), and *Natural Theology* (1802), were best-sellers, and required reading for all Cambridge undergraduates until well into the 1850s.

By the time the last of these, *Natural Theology*, was published, the Lockean epistemology on which it tacitly rested had already been convincingly challenged by Kant and a whole subsequent tradition of German idealist philosophers, as well as by a number of English thinkers, from Coleridge to Blake, who were to various degrees in touch with developments in continental philosophy.[58] None of this impinged directly on Paley, however, whose Cambridge environment was peculiarly well-insulated from new intellectual movements from the Continent, and who was able to summarise the *a posteriori* arguments for the existence of God with a verve and meticulousness that suggest a total confidence in his methodology.

Harold Bloom, in his book *Anxiety of Influence*, has suggested how certain artists feel so threatened by particular immediate predecessors that they are driven to challenge and try to surpass them just as Freud supposed sons to wish to rival and even symbolically 'kill' their own fathers. If so, this is not a phenomenon confined to artists, but can be seen in the case of many of the most innovative scientists. Not merely did Darwin, for instance, come from the same background as Paley a couple of generations later, but, in occupying his old rooms, had already enacted physically what he was about to do in terms of his ideas. It is even a speculative possibility that Darwin's idea of biological evolution was influenced

---

[56] For a more detailed account of this group, see Stephen Prickett, *Romanticism and Religion: The Tradition of Coleridge and Wordsworth in the Victorian Church*, Cambridge University Press, 1976, pp. 77–8.

[57] See J.M. Creed, *The Divinity of Jesus Christ*, Cambridge, 1938, p. 14.

[58] Coleridge had been critical of Locke for some time, and by 1800 had read *Kant's Critique of Pure Reason* and probably knew something of Fichte as well. Though we have no evidence of Blake having read Kant, he was, of course, very familiar with the ideas of Swedenborg which formed such an important trigger to Kant's own thinking.

by Law's re-interpretation of Locke as a religiously 'evolutionary' writer. It is no surprise therefore that Darwin too, when he came to write *The Origin of Species*, made the eye central to *his* case, since it presents at first sight the most difficult problem any evolutionary theory has to account for. In doing so, he reveals most clearly the influence of his compulsory undergraduate reading – by taking and neatly inverting Paley's argument from design. He continues 'It is scarcely possible to avoid comparing the eye to a telescope. We know that this instrument has been perfected by the long-continued efforts of the highest human intellects; and we naturally infer that the eye has been formed by a somewhat analogous process.'[59]

Editors of Darwin have long noted how his need to undermine the doctrine of special creation, in order to provide his own evolutionary answer, makes *The Origin of Species* read in places like an answer to Paley.[60] But there is another reason, less logical but more deep-seated. By the time Darwin came to write *The Origin* he had clearly appropriated Paley to the point where the structure and contents of *Natural Theology* were a part of his own mental furniture. In that sense the *argument* of Paley's textbook was the least memorable, or, perhaps, the most easily altered part of the whole structure. In the endless patiently assembled detail of anatomy and biological organization his rejected teacher had in effect provided Darwin with not just the architect's model for his revisionary work, but with the scaffolding and bricks as well.

Bertrand Russell, with whom D'Espagnat's metaphor of the disk originates, undoubtedly knew his Paley as well as his Darwin. We cannot be sure that D'Espagnat had read Paley, though given his philosophical training it is more than likely. But, like Russell, he also knows Plato, Leibniz, Laplace and Kant – not to mention Darwin. The point of this little historical excursus is simply that no metaphor – and certainly no such metaphor in such a context – comes to us empty-handed. From Leibniz onwards, the image of the universe as a complicated artifact has been thrown backwards and forwards, first as an image of its design and intelligibility (Leibniz, Laplace and Paley), and now as a metaphor for its exact opposite: its ultimate unknowability. Between these poles lies Darwin, who, while he nowhere uses the watch metaphor, makes use of its parallel, the telescope, to show how natural selection, through random mechanisms, can give a quite *false* impression of order and design.

[59] Charles Darwin, *The Origin of Species*, Harmondsworth: Penguin, 1968, p. 219.
[60] J.W. Burrow, Editor's Introduction, ibid. p. 22.

Not even the most basic metaphors of this scientific debate come without a previous content. Take, for instance, Kuhn's own central metaphor of 'revolution'. The word itself changed its meaning radically – and from our point of view, very significantly, in the late eighteenth century. Its original sense was astronomical, meaning to go round in a circle, as for instance the planets were believed to circle the earth in pre-Copernican cosmology, or later to circle the sun. This is the prime meaning given, for instance, in Johnson's dictionary of 1755. From this developed a range of other 'cyclic' meanings, including the movement of the hands of a clock around the dial, and even the act of winding a clock. The figurative meaning, therefore, was of a return to the original starting-point. Thus, in politics, the so-called 'Glorious Revolution' of 1688, when James II was expelled, and William and Mary were invited by Parliament to accept the throne, was so called because it was believed to be a *return* to the original starting point. By contrast, the English Civil War, which saw Charles I's head cut off, and brought Cromwell to power, was called the 'Great Rebellion'. It was not a 'revolution' because things were not afterwards restored to the *status quo ante bellum* ('as things were before the war'). That 1688 was by no means a return to the time of Charles I, and that the 'ancient liberties' it was supposed to have restored were largely mythical is beside the point. Naming the 1688 settlement a 'revolution' was itself a piece of political rhetoric emphasizing its continuity and lack of change.[61]

The decisive alteration – the 'revolution' – in the meaning of the word comes in the 1790s with the events in France. British sympathizers had hailed the early developments in 1789, with the summoning of the Estates General, and the apparent promise of the kind of liberties enjoyed north of the Channel as a 'Revolution', with deliberate reference to 1688.[62] Burke's indignant counterblast, *Reflections on the Revolution in France*, was intended as a savage irony. For him what had happened in France could by no stretch of imagination be seen as a 'revolution', since it did not restore anything. The real irony is that his title rapidly became a straight description, and within a few years, by the mid-1790s, we find the word used in both Britain and France to mean a violent overthrow of an existing government, and the substitution of a new social order.

The phrase 'industrial revolution' is a no less political coinage. It was originally produced in France in the 1820s by revolutionary socialists

---

[61] See Stephen Prickett, *England and the French Revolution*, Macmillan, 1988, p. 2.

[62] The Welsh preacher, Richard Price, had used the term in his sermon to the 'Revolution Society' – a constitutional club devoted to commemorating 1688.

(forerunners of the Commune of 1870) who believed that changes in the means of production would bring down the government and workers to power. It was first used in English much later in the century, and only became a commonplace (with no political connotations) in the twentieth century. Whether or not he was aware of the history of the word, Kuhn's choice of 'revolution' as metaphor for a paradigm shift is highly ironic. Yet it is also peculiarly apt, since it captures *both* the sometimes dramatic changes involved in moving to a new paradigm, *and* the older meaning of restoration and continuity which the history of science has seemed to present to outside viewers.

AMBIGUITY AND IRONY

As we suggested in the last chapter, no modern science has a narrative that can be described as totally un-ironic. Any metaphor, whether of change, design, or of unknowability, has a hidden history that bears on our understanding of its present use, making us aware not merely of how it has been used in the past, but of its essentially *provisional* nature. Anyone who knows of its history, is also well aware of how many different ways it may have been used in the past – even to prove opposing points – and that it may be used yet again as part of a new idea, new theory or new paradigm.

But, someone may object, though this may well be true for the history of scientific metaphors, metaphors are anyway inexact and ambiguous things. For that reason physical scientists and astronomers do not work in linguistic metaphors, they work in the exact and precise language of mathematics, which is totally unambiguous. The difficulties only arise because, when they are trying to popularize their ideas, they are like fish out of water trying to explain the unambiguous clarity of advanced mathematical concepts in the hopelessly inexact language that a non-mathematician can understand. Language may be ambiguous and ironic; mathematics cannot be either.

Here, significantly, the evidence of mathematicians themselves becomes very ambiguous indeed. We have seen that the great mathematicians of the seventeenth century, Descartes and Newton, for instance, were unabashed Platonic mystics, seeking to discover the ways of a God who, in Pythagoras' words, 'was always doing mathematics'. In the last two centuries, however, the prevailing influence of empiricism and positivism in academic philosophy has made Platonism unfashionable and favours instead a philosophy of mathematics called formalism, according to which much, if not all, of mathematics is merely an intellectual game, without any ultimate meaning. But more detailed investigation seems to suggest that modern mathematicians are not necessarily as formalistic as their official rhetoric might indicate:

> The majority of writers on the subject seem to agree that most mathematicians, when doing mathematics, are convinced that they are dealing with an objective reality, but then if challenged to give a philosophic account of this reality find it easier to pretend that they do not believe in it after all . . . The typical mathematician is both a Platonist and a formalist – a secret Platonist with a formalist mask that he puts on when the occasion calls for it.[63]

This is a point echoed by Paul Davies, who points out that the psychology of mathematical discovery is fundamentally at odds with the prevailing cultural ethos of the twentieth century.

> It is often said that mathematicians are Platonists on weekdays and formalists at weekends. While actually working on mathematics, it is hard to resist the impression that one is actually engaged in the process of discovery, much as in an experimental science. The mathematical objects take on a life of their own, and often display totally unexpected properties. On the other hand, the idea of a transcendent realm of mathematical Ideas seems too mystical for many mathematicians to admit, and if challenged they will usually claim that when engaging in mathematical research they are only playing games with symbols and rules.[64]

Nevertheless, even in our own century a number of prominent mathematicians, like Kurt Gödel and Roger Penrose, have unequivocally 'come out' as Platonists.

Platonism, as we have seen, is an essentially ironic philosophy, moving always between appearances and a hidden reality. Though its formulations may be more precise than words, mathematics, too, has a history, a context, and a philosophy. Like the English language we are using as our present means of communication, mathematics is as ambiguous or as unambiguous, as ironic or non-ironic as its history, context, and philosophy make it. Moreover, as was demonstrated by Gödel, perhaps the greatest logician of the twentieth century, even formalism is not exhaustive of meaning, and allows once again the now-familiar ironic 'gap'. Gödel's famous 'incompleteness theorem' demonstrated that no matter which formal system is chosen, either that system is itself inconsistent (and so contains its own internal 'paradoxes') or else it is incomplete in

[63] P.J. Davis and R. Hersh, *The Mathematical Experience*, Harmondsworth: Penguin, 1983.
[64] Paul Davies, *The Mind of God*, Simon & Schuster, 1992, p. 142.

the sense that there are true mathematical statements that lie beyond its scope.[65]

Perhaps one of the most intriguing problems in the history of mathematical irony is Euler's enigmatic 'proof' of God. Leonhard Euler (1707–83), was one of the world's great mathematicians. A Swiss by birth, he was elected to both the Prussian Academy of Sciences and the St Petersburg Academy (at a time when the two countries were at war), as well as being a foreign member of the French Academy. If collected, his total published works would occupy some 60–80 volumes, many of which were published during the last twenty years of his life when he was virtually blind. He had what would nowadays be called a 'photographic' memory, and, for instance, not merely knew the whole of Virgil's *Aeneid* by heart, but could give the first and last lines of every page of the edition used.

Since he was known to be a strict and deeply religious Swiss Calvinist, while he was in St Petersburg some sceptical Russian scientists challenged him to produce a mathematical proof that God existed. To their complete bafflement, his reply was the equation: '$e\pi i = -1$'. Opinion has been divided ever since as to whether he was calling attention to the beauty of the 'transcendental numbers', e and π (so-called because they are not the solution of any algebraic equation ($i = \sqrt{-1}$)) and thus (as a good Platonist) to the entire mystery of the God who had created such an aesthetically satisfying universe – or ironically dismissing the whole game, and mocking those who supposed they could understand such a proof, even if it were placed before them.

No one was more aware of the ironies of his craft than the late Richard Feynman, the American physicist, who is widely regarded as being one of the most brilliant scientists of the twentieth century. His account of the history and development of the concept of physical laws shows the influence of both Kuhn and Popper.[66] His description of what eventually happened to Newton's mysterious 'innate attraction' of gravity is a classic piece of twentieth-century scientific irony. What happened was not that gravity was 'explained', but that parallel, and less disconcerting formulations were found to describe it: 'You may not like the idea of action at a distance. How can this object know what is going on over there? So there is another way of stating the laws, which is very strange, called the field way . . .'[67]

---

[65] See, for instance, Roger Penrose, 'Ingenious Ingénue', *Times Higher Education Supplement*, April 3, 1998, p. 20.

[66] Richard Feynman, *The Character of Physical Law*, BBC, 1965, pp. 157–8.

[67] Ibid. p. 50.

Mathematically each of the three different formulations, Newton's law, the local field method and the minimum principle, gives exactly the same consequences. What do we do then? You will read in all books that we cannot decide scientifically on one way or another. That is true. They are equivalent scientifically. It is impossible to make a decision, because there is no experimental way to distinguish between them if all the consequences are the same. But psychologically they are very different . . . [68]

Gravity can be described by not one, but by several alternative narratives, *all* of which describe the phenomenon correctly, but so differently that any one model precludes reference to the others while it is in use. Physicists choose their model not according to the mathematics, but according to what they are trying to do with the formulation. This is, in effect, another rabbit/duck puzzle – with not two but *three* possible solutions. Moreover, whichever model is chosen carries with it an awareness of the ambiguity of the phenomenon – and of other possible routes not chosen. 'One of the amazing characteristics of nature', Feynman writes, 'is the variety of interpretational schemes which are possible.'[69] But because of the way in which a theory will be embedded in a total notional scheme of things, a tiny change in theory may necessitate an enormous re-shuffle of the general scientific paradigm.

For instance, Newton's ideas about space and time agreed with the experiment very well, but in order to get the correct motion of the orbit of Mercury, which was a tiny, tiny difference, the difference in the character of the theory needed was enormous. In order to get something that would produce a slightly different result it had to be completely different. In stating a new law you cannot make imperfections on a perfect thing: you have to have another perfect thing. So the differences in philosophical ideas between Newton's and Einstein's theories of gravitation are enormous.[70]

Among Feynman's many gifts (which included playing the bongo-drums at a professional level) was a flair for the memorable parable to illustrate a particular point. One such concerns an imaginary incident in one of the few non-European societies to practise mathematical astronomy, and so present the kind of rival to the Newtonian tradition held in such esteem by Kissinger: the Mayas of Central America.

For those people who insist that the only thing that is important is that the theory agree with the experiment, I would like to imagine a discussion between a Mayan astronomer and his student. The Mayans were able to calculate with great precision predictions, for example, for eclipses and for the position of the

---

[68] Ibid. p. 53.   [69] Ibid. p. 54.   [70] Ibid. p. 169.

moon in the sky, the position of Venus, etc. It was all done by arithmetic. They counted a certain number and subtracted some numbers, and so on. There was no discussion of what the moon was. There was no discussion even of the idea that it went around. They just calculated the time when there would be an eclipse, or when the moon would rise at the full, and so on. Suppose that a young man went to the astronomer and said, 'I have an idea. Maybe those things are going around, and there are balls of something like rocks out there, and we could calculate how they move in a completely different way from just calculating what time they appear in the sky.' 'Yes', says the astronomer, 'and how accurately can you predict eclipses?' He says, 'I haven't developed the thing very far yet.' Then says the astronomer, 'Well, we can calculate eclipses more accurately than you can with your model, so you must not pay any attention to your idea because obviously the mathematical scheme is better.' There is a very strong tendency, when someone comes up with an idea and says, 'Let's suppose that the world is this way', for people to say to him, 'What would you get for the answer to such and such a problem?' and he says, 'I haven't developed it far enough.' And they say, 'Well we have already developed it much further, and we can get the answers very accurately.' So it is a problem whether or not to worry about philosophies behind ideas.[71]

Needless to say, we have no evidence at all that the Maya thought like this. Nevertheless the story gained wide currency among professional physicists, and in the process acquired modifications that illustrate very well the curious dynamic tendencies of narrative. D'Espagnat, for instance, introduces his own version of Feynman's story by saying that it is 'part of the mental furniture' of many physicists. He then proceeds to retell it, at somewhat greater length,[72] concluding with the following explanation by the Mayan astronomer:

The fact of the matter was that in the field in which they were working, all the rules of prediction were already available. Taken together, these constituted science and all there is to science. Remember, he went on, only *phenomena* are meaningful. Our rules are valid for everyone and are therefore rigorously objective. Imagining the Sun and Moon to be material as you do is pointlessly to seek *explanations* of laws; in other words, it amounts to stubbornly introducing the old anthropomorphic idea of 'cause' into a field where it only complicates description to no avail. To put matters plain and simply, it is to indulge in *metaphysics*, a quite fruitless and indeed shameful thing to do, as our most eminent philosophers will tell you.

So, in essence, runs Feynman's tale. It provides in agreeable fashion a good illustration of the sense of absurdity experienced by most physicists when faced

---

[71] Ibid. pp. 169–70.
[72] Thirty per cent more: 470 (in the English translation) as against 325.

with the systematic negation of the concept of independent reality and the refusal to take seriously anything other than mere observable regularities.[73]

Feynman's story has indeed remained more or less the same. But what has happened to the conclusion? Feynman, we recall, did not point his moral directly. His fable seems to be ambiguous. Are we to conclude that no theory, however well supported by experimental evidence, should become totally detached from physical reality? Or that the fact that we already have accurate answers to the kinds of questions we are asking shouldn't prevent us from looking at a different theory, whose answers are as yet less satisfactorily developed? The question he actually asks is related to both problems: whether a general scientific 'philosophy' (that is, a grand narrative in his terms) is a help in discovering specific natural laws, or whether all one needs is simply agreement between theory and experiment? The answer to that seems to be the not-unfamiliar paradox that a general theory is both a nuisance, and essential.

D'Espagnat's version, however, is different again. For him, it illustrates 'the sense of absurdity experienced by most physicists when faced with the systematic rejection of the concept of independent reality . . . ' While this is by no means an illegitimate inference, it is (as we might expect!) a much more accurate reflection of *his* immediate concerns than Feynman's. He is obviously retelling the story here from memory, without having re-read the original.[74] Like the famous children's 'whispering game', each repetition of the story moves further away from the original, and contains new elements introduced by the re-teller. Feynman was not concerned at all with the problems of 'independent reality', in the metaphysical sense of 'things-in-themselves', which concern D'Espagnat, but only of 'physical reality' in the much simpler sense of 'something like rocks out there' in space.

Feynman had a strong sense of the ironies of science, and this little story is no exception. The mere fact that it has a multiplicity of possible interpretations suggests how much is 'hidden' within it, and how, in Kuhn's terminology, a number of different paradigms can be brought to bear on a particular set of phenomena, without totally exhausting the potential meaning to be found in it. At the micro-level of quantum physics the question of multiple interpretations has had to be built into the theory itself. Heisenberg's famous 'uncertainty principle', that measurement

---

[73] D'Espagnat, *Reality and the Physicist*, pp. 144–5.

[74] Revealingly, his footnote reference is incomplete, giving the name of the book, but no page number.

alters what is being measured in ways that cannot be fully predicted, is like Gödel's theorem in that it seems to set absolute limits to what *can* be known. As we shall see in Chapter Seven, quantum theory is also uniquely ironic in that its implications are so bizarre as to demand further levels of essentially speculative interpretation before it can be grasped. The majority of modern interpretations, for instance, seem to favour what is called the 'many universes' hypothesis: that is, that each 'choice' between unpredictable alternatives at the quantum level involves a corresponding splitting of universes – so that, presumably, all possible universes 'exist' simultaneously.[75] For the physicist Paul Davies, however, such a theory is no more than a last-ditch attempt by traditional physical scientists to avoid the re-introduction of mind into the physical universe.[76]

A historian of science might liken such a vast and unprovable theory to the last stages of 'saving the appearances' by the defenders of the Ptolemaic earth-centred universe before Copernicus' revolutionary sim- plification of the heliocentric system. The difference, of course, lies in the modern sense of the ever-growing gap between what can be tested, and whatever we may suppose true reality to consist of. That modern sense of irony has no counterpart in the late mediaeval world. As has been suggested, too great a feeling of irony may also be a sign of strain between paradigm and phenomena. Anyone who has followed Kuhn's arguments so far may note in D'Espagnat's language of anomaly and counterinstance the signs that so often in the past have presaged a major paradigm shift. Kuhn's own sense that though he might not quite be able to put his finger on what was happening, he was perhaps himself expe- riencing, or was at any rate in the midst of, another paradigm change is no less significant. His book was epoch-making, in that it changed for ever the way in which the history of science was understood. But in his footnotes he acknowledges the influence of two other seminal works which had just appeared, and which, in their own ways, were to make almost as great an impact as his own. The first was Michael Polanyi's

[75] For a recent account of the multiple universes theory (the 'multiverse') see Deutsch, *Fabric of Reality*. His most startling piece of evidence concerns 'Shor's algorithm' discovered in 1994 which, Deutsch claims, used the computational powers of other universes on a grand scale to augment those available to him here. To sceptics Deutsch throws down the challenge: 'When Shor's algorithm has factorized a number using 10^{500} or so the computational resources that can be seen at present, where was the number factorized? There are only about 10^{80} atoms in the entire visible universe, an utterly minuscule number compared with 10^{500}. So if the visible uiverse were the extent of physical reality, physical reality would not even remotely contain the resources required to factorize such a large number. Who did factorize it then? How, and where, was the computation performed?' (p. 217).

[76] Conversation between Paul Davies and Phillip Adams, ABC Television, June 7, 1998.

Personal Knowledge, published in 1958; the second, E.H. Gombrich's *Art and Illusion*, 1960. We shall be discussing Polanyi in a later chapter; what I want to consider here for a moment are the extraordinary parallels between Gombrich's pioneering work and Kuhn's own.

Gombrich, a professional art-historian, begins with one of those deceptively simple questions that lead inexorably into some of the most complex and bewildering areas of human experience. 'Why is it that different ages and different nations have represented the world in such different ways?'[77] On the first page he shows us a modern cartoon by Alain from the *New Yorker* of an ancient Egyptian life-class, where a naked girl is actually standing side-on to the viewer in precisely the position thousands of similar figures are to be seen in Egyptian bas-reliefs. The cartoonist's joke, of course, is the idea that such an obvious stylization should be assumed to be true-to-life: that ancient Egyptians really did stand around like that. But, as in the case of D'Espagnat's retelling of Feynman, there are ironies of interpretation. Another art historian, W.J.T. Mitchell, in a recent discussion of the picture, claims that Gombrich has mis-read the joke. 'What is funny about the cartoon, I take it, is not that the ancient Egyptians are shown (as we might expect) to be exotic, alien, and different from us, but that they are shown (against all expectation) to be just like us.' Already we are into the realm of ambiguity. Mitchell concludes,

the two readings . . . stand in a dialectical relationship, by which I mean that they contradict one another, oppose one another, and yet they also require, give life to, one another. Whatever these cartoons amount to as totalities, as metapictures, is not reducible to one reading or the other but is constituted in the argument or dialogue between them.[78]

Not surprisingly, Gombrich's own question: 'Why is it that different ages and different nations have represented the world in such different ways?' now takes on a quite different spin. If even a simple cartoon – and one in which the joke seems at first sight quite obvious – can be read in such radically opposed senses, is it surprising that the real world proves so elusive?

Gombrich's solution, as proposed by *Art and Illusion*, presents astonishing parallels with Kuhn's own theory of paradigms. Different periods, argues Gombrich, really have literally 'seen' their worlds in radically

---

[77] E.H. Gombrich, *Art and Illusion: A Study in the Psychology of Pictorial Representation* (1960), revised edn, Princeton University Press, 1961, p. 3.

[78] W.J.T. Mitchell, *Picture Theory*, University of Chicago Press, 1994, p. 44.

different ways. So far as we know, ancient Egyptians did *not* actually always stand sideways to each other in long lines (we do, as Gombrich shows, actually have some amazingly lifelike portraits from that period) but they did genuinely see things very differently from, say, the ancient Chinese or the classical Greeks. And here, as Kuhn himself notes, the resemblance to his thesis is uncannily close. Though, until very recently, we have tended see the history of art in terms of a steadily developing technical realism, such a view is totally a-historical because it conceals the way in which different 'schemata' (in Gombrich's terminology[79]) have dominated ways of seeing. One later art-critic drew even more explicit parallels:

We now know that scientific progress requires more than merely 'adding to' existing knowledge and the systematic building up of achievement. We also know, since the shift into Modernism, that progress [in art] is not made, as was once thought, by the accumulation of knowledge within existing categories: it is made by leaps into new categories and systems.[80]

Not merely do all artists learn more from other artists than they do from observation of life, it seems that without previous artists to guide them, they would 'see' very little. But, equally, what does not correspond to the dominant schema is very difficult to see at all. In an almost exact visual parallel to the way in which we are driven to make stories to conceptualize and understand facts, so, it has been discovered, we do not 'see' what we cannot comprehend. Interpretation is an integral part of perception. We have all had the experience at one time or another of 'seeing' a friend at a distance, and even observing familar features of them, before discovering that we were mistaken – and then finding that the person in question has few or even none of the characteristics we had just been convinced we could actually 'see'.

One of Gombrich's most interesting examples involves comparing two pictures of Chartres Cathedral. The first, by Robert Garland, a popular nineteenth-century English engraver was made in 1836; the other is a recent photograph. What is remarkable is the way in which Garland's expectations of Chartres as the epitome of mediaeval Gothic architecture have conditioned him to see the windows of the West Front as pointed, when, as the photograph clearly shows, they are in fact Romanesque, and rounded at the top.[81] Since we know that these windows have not been

---

[79] Borrowed, in turn, from one of the pioneer works on memory research, F.C. Bartlett, *Memory*, Cambridge University Press, 1932.
[80] S. Gablik, *Progress in Art*, New York: Rizzoli, 1977, p. 159.
[81] *Art and Illusion*, pp. 72–3.

altered (not, at least, since 1836) we have precisely the case that Kuhn himself was invoking in his discussion of the 'rabbit/duck' pictogram. The photograph gives us the hard reality from which perception can be shown to deviate.

But does it? Though this particular photo of Chartres is undoubtedly enough to settle the question of whether the windows in question were round or pointed, the photographs are themselves highly stylized representations of appearances. Not merely was this particular one reproducing a world that we see in terms of colour (i.e. a certain quite narrow band of electromagnetic light waves to which the human eye is sensitive) in black, white and numerous shades of grey, but it was also reducing a three-dimensional building to a small flat piece of glossy paper. Other conscious choices by the photographer included depth of focus, speed of film, angle of the light and position of the camera. It would, no doubt, have been quite possible to take a photo of the West Front of Chartres Cathedral in which it would be almost impossible to see whether the lower windows of the towers were round *or* pointed. Because the photograph is very much a standard part of the twentieth-century Western cultural schemata that we have grown up with from our earliest infancy, it is very easy for us to forget just how strange and conventionally stylized a medium it actually is. Only on the, now rare, occasions when explorers encounter some really isolated people who have never seen a camera before, and try to demonstate what it does, do we discover that, to begin with, they can't see anything *in* the picture at all. All they can see is a small flat rectangular object with some markings on it. If, and when, they do see *into* the picture, it is not with a slow working out of what individual objects must be, but with a flash of total recognition, akin to the switch in the rabbit/duck puzzle. We do not, Gombrich reminds us, see what we cannot interpret. Interpretation is in integral part of perception. We perceive mistakenly rather than perceive nothing.

As we shall see in a later chapter, the obvious parallel here is with literacy itself. What you have before you at this moment are some dark marks on a sheet of paper. Were you illiterate, that is *all* you would see. As a reader, however, you are so conditioned by education and culture to make words from those marks, and to construct from those words an intelligible meaning, that you are very rarely conscious of the complexity of the activity – or that whatever picture you may have in your head as a result of that reading is the product not merely of advanced symbolism, but of a very high degree of abstraction. For that reason, of course, newspapers like to include pictures (usually photographs) with every report.

More immediately, this perceptual process of what Gombrich calls 'making and matching' of schemata has an obvious family resemblance to the paradigms through which Kuhn sees the work of science operating. Since Kuhn has appropriated the word 'paradigm' specifically for the way in which the scientific community inculcates and perceives its function at any point in time, and Gombrich has given the word 'schema', and its plural, 'schemata', a similarly precise meaning for visual perception, we may leave them with those metaphors – pausing only to note that they *are*, of course, metaphors – and note instead that though neither paradigms nor schemata depend on total verbalization, both constitute 'narratives' in the broad sense in which the word emerged in the last chapter.

Gombrich's schemata are not, of course, verbal at all. They are essentially visual blue-prints, mental formations by which we construct the 'pictures' that we see. As we shall see, though our understanding of the perceptual mechanisms involved comes largely from twentieth-century psychology experiments, the theory behind such a process goes back to Kant and late eighteenth-century German Romanticism. But there is no need for a narrative to be verbal. Every picture tells a story. Mediaeval art, comic strips and silent films all tell the most elaborate narratives without a word being uttered. In the twentieth century the very writers who have become worried that pictures, from television and photo journalism, have replaced words and contributed to a general dumbing-down of our culture, are prepared to pay money to go and see a picture like Picasso's *Guernica*.

In the case of paradigms, the narrative is partly verbal, but consists partly also of what Kuhn calls 'tacit knowledge' – a term he takes, with approval, from the Hungarian/British philosopher Michael Polanyi (of whom more in Chapter Five). This consists of the knowledge that is acquired through practice within a specific scientific community, and which cannot be articulated explicitly.[82] As in any relatively closed community, such tacit knowledge may in fact constitute more important knowledge than anything that is made explicit – and here we, with our wider interest in the nature of the narrative being told, may extend our view of that knowledge somewhat wider than either Kuhn or Polanyi would allow. A laboratory is not merely a scientific community, with its own tacit knowledge of how research is best done, it is also a human community,

---

[82] Kuhn, *Structure of Scientific Revolutions*, p. 44; Michael Polanyi, *Personal Knowledge*, Routledge, 1958, Chs. 5 and 6.

with a quite different repository of tacit knowledge. The most fully qualified outsider in scientific terms still has to learn about the ways things
are in a new institution. The fact that x and y are not on speaking terms;
that p and q are having an affair; or that the departmental secretary is
a much more powerful and influential figure than the director when it
comes to allocating funds or office space, are all vital pieces of knowledge
for anyone actually working there, and it may be that none of these are
matters people will speak about – certainly not to strangers. This may
not be science, but it is nevertheless necessary background knowledge
for scientific work in that context.

Locke's appropriation of the Newton legend hardly counts as a scientific paradigm in Kuhn's sense, but it played so large a part in the
apparent scientific underpinning of the English Enlightenment, that it
can hardly be dismissed as simply an aberration either. What it highlights
is the fact that the scientific paradigm is only the most formalized of a
whole series of such narratives providing parallel but often incompatible
systems of interpretation that run concurrently though every part of our
lives. Such paradigmatic narratives are, perhaps, most clearly visible in
the history of science, because science is more precisely documented than
most of our activities. It shows us the normal processes of thought writ
large. If, on the one hand, practising scientists are highly dependent on
the narrative provided by the reigning paradigm at that period for their
own work, they are no less dependent on what one might call subsidiary
or peripheral paradigms for news of what is going on elsewhere in the
discipline – or outside.

And this, of course, brings us back to the popular narrative of Newton
with which we began. Kissinger's view of the Newtonian revolution typifies a much wider misconception both of what Newton actually did, and
of his subsequent influence. Indeed, it is hard to know which is the more
mistaken, Kissinger's idea that 'knowledge consists of recording and classifying data – the more accurately the better', or his belief that in 'the
pre-Newtonian view . . . the real world is almost completely *internal* to the
observer'. What links the two, of course, is what D'Espagnat calls 'vulgar
positivism': the idea that the 'facts' about the world – which are here
presumed to be the raw material of science – are wholly external and
independent of the knower, and that 'knowledge' therefore consists of
collecting and classifying as many of those facts as possible. On the contrary, as we have seen, there can be no 'facts' independent of the knower,
and the cultural, social and scientific context from which that individual
starts. Is gravity an occult and innate force, a field, or best described as

a minimal principal, or none of these? Historically it will depend under which paradigm you happen to be working; currently, it will also depend on which mathematical theory you wish to apply. What makes us perceive things in one way, rather than another? How do we construct our pictures of the world around us? Not by passive receptivity, but by an active process of 'making and matching'; by an act of the imagination which allows us to interpret the raw material of sense-data and construct from it something that 'makes sense' to us. The irony is not merely that Kissinger's version of Newton, and of the workings of science in general, is almost the complete inverse of the truth, but that it was precisely in the eighteenth century, just at the time when Kissinger apparently believed that in the West the real world had finally been externalised and objectified, that the very process of internalisation so essential to understanding modern science and philosphy actually reached its climax. This will be the subject of our next chapter.

CHAPTER 3

Learning to say 'I': Literature and subjectivity

INTERIOR AND EXTERIOR WORLDS

Let us go back for a moment to the one part of Said's quotation from Kissinger which we have not so far discussed: the statement that pre-Newtonian cultures saw the 'real world as being almost completely *internal* to the observer'. This can be understood at two levels. At one level he is here, I take it, referring to what anthropologists would call 'primal consciousness': that supposedly undifferentiated state of being, where there is little or no personal sense of distinction from the natural environment, not to mention the family, group or tribe. Thomas Mann's great re-creation of the Old Testament world in his epic tetralogy of novels, *Joseph and his Brothers*, has one of the best descriptions of what it means to be still within this world of primal consciousness, when he describes Eliezer, Jacob's (hereditary) steward.

... the old man's ego was not quite clearly demarcated, that it opened at the back, as it were, and overflowed into spheres external to his own individuality both in space and time; embodying in his own experience events which, remembered and related in the clear light of day, ought actually to have been put into the third person ... The conception of individuality belongs after all to the same category as that of unity and entirety, the whole and the all; and in the days of which I am writing the distinction between spirit in general and individual spirit possessed not nearly so much power of the mind as in our world of today ... It is highly significant that in those days there were no words for conceptions dealing with personality and individuality, other than such external ones as confession, religion.[1]

Just as personality and individuality could only be expressed through the language of external things, so what we would now call 'nature' was not yet distinguished from the self. In the Old Testament there is no word for 'nature', and indeed little concept of it in our sense. Everything,

[1] Mann, *Joseph and his Brothers*, trs. H.T. Lowe-Porter, Penguin, 1988, p. 78.

94

from the rising of the sun in the morning to Elijah being taken up to heaven in a fiery chariot is attributed directly to God, Yahweh, who, therefore, has little difficulty in stopping the passage of the sun across the sky for Joshua at Gibeon for a whole day in order for him to finish smiting the Amorites (Joshua 10: 13–14). This is essentially similar also to the legendary 'Dream Time' of the Australian aborigines, when human consciousness was indistinguishable from that of the gods and the natural world. In such a condition the world is perceived as cyclical, repetitive and unchanging, rather than in linear terms of historical development. Kissinger is, of course, entirely right in seeing this as an essentially pre-scientific state of mind. For science to develop at all, there had to be a break between observer and observed. Individuation is a necessary condition of the experimental method.

The new sense of self and individuality experienced by the Enlightenment was not merely a matter of scientific standpoint. If Kissinger's 'real world' was from henceforth now composed of the recording and classifying of objective data, that 'objectivity' was underpinned by the corresponding new sensation of 'subjectivity' by the observer. It is no accident that the early eighteenth century, the formulative period for the principles of the so-called 'Enlightenment project', was also one that saw the rise of a new art-form, the 'novel', devoted to a new sense of the individual as an autonomous centre of consciousness. Moll Flanders, no less than Defoe's other great protagonist, Robinson Crusoe, inhabits an island of her own making, surrounded by a great sea of alien humanity. The growth of objectivity of the external world was progressively matched by a growing sense by the observer of his or her personal identity.

At another level, however, Kissinger is throwing his hat into the ring with the civilizers rather than with the culturalists. If what we mean by the 'real world' is one structured by objectively verifiable and calculable scientific laws, there is little place for regional and cultural variation. Those societies that make scientific discoveries do so merely because their culture is more 'realistic'. Though the power of the dominant group is explicitly seen as the product of historical and cultural conditions – certain countries, after all, *have* been through the process of discovering Newtonian science, while others have not – this is not seen as a reason for cultural variables to play any part. That American technical know-how could be successfully countered by a quite un-Enlightenment fanaticism binding together the sub-culture of the Viet Cong was never considered in Kissinger's philosophy.

But however dramatic was the impact of this assumption about the nature of the 'real world' on twentieth-century history, the eighteenth-century debate that lies behind it was to have an even more momentous effect on the shaping of our modern world. For the seventeenth-century clergymen–scientists of the Royal Society there seemed little reason to doubt that the advance of natural philosophy would inevitably prove and strengthen the great revealed truths of the Christian religion. By the end of the eighteenth, that anticipated growth of knowledge, though it had vastly exceeded all expectations, had not merely failed to deliver the expected religious rewards, but, so far from reinforcing faith, the new mechanical world-picture, together with the questions raised by biblical criticism, had presented a whole spectrum of fresh challenges to it.

It was in particular the challenges presented by the Scottish sceptical philosopher, David Hume, that, we are told, aroused Immanuel Kant from his 'dogmatic slumbers' in Königsberg. The publication of Kant's *Critique of Pure Reason* in 1781 was to alter the course of European thought. Though it was a diabolically difficult book even in German, let alone in the curious Latin version in which it first seems to have reached the English-speaking world,[2] it was destined eventually to transform every branch of human knowledge: science, literature and even theology. Whereas previous philosophical systems had been ultimately grounded in the idea of a stable and objective natural order, Kant's aim, in the true spirit of Enlightenment, was to make the human mind itself the ultimate ground of truth. But like those other icons of Enlightenment secularity, Newton and Descartes, he seems in fact to have been motivated by a strong, if not very orthodox, personal piety. It was not a spirit of atheism, but the realization that Hume's attacks on conventional religion were on the whole justified, that prompted Kant to find some more secure 'space' for the idea of God. Such a God could never be 'proved' in the way earlier theologians had hoped, for that would eliminate freewill; nor could his system give any form to the idea of God, for that could only reflect the individual's own culture and experience. We live in two worlds, one, that of everyday experience, in which we exercise what he calls (in the somewhat inadequate English translation) our 'practical Reason'; the other, that of 'pure Reason', is one of spiritual awareness, whose ideas of 'God, freedom, and immortality' *cannot* be derived from experience and are, he argued, innate.[3] God is not *part* of the world, and cannot

---

[2] See Dugald Stewart's comments on Kant in his *Philosophical Lectures* (1816) and René Wellek, *Immanuel Kant in England*, Princeton University Press, 1931.

[3] See Hazard Adams, *Philosophy of the Literary Symbolic*, Tallahassee: Florida State University Press, 1983, Ch. 2: 'The Kantian Symbolic'.

therefore ever be proved (or disproved) within it. Kant concluded that our perceptions, instead of being formed by external objects, can only conform to the categories imposed by our own minds – which included even such apparently objective external conditions as space and time. For him, the 'real' world of 'things-in-themselves' was both unknown and unknowable. We inhabit a universe structured and indeed limited by our own senses and mental capacities.

Kant's *Critique*, for all its radical subjectivity, did not, of course, begin the long process of internalization. An interiorized self-consciousness goes back at least as far as St Augustine's *Confessions*, written in the last days of the Roman Empire, in the fourth century CE. As Charles Taylor shows, in his monumental book on the making of the modern sense of identity, *Sources of the Self*, Augustine's most revolutionary contribution to human thought lay in the discovery – or rediscovery – of introspection. Whereas Plato had urged his followers to make a spiritual *turn*, to face away from appearances towards what he believed was the reality of ideal forms, it was still conceived in outward terms. Augustine urges us to turn inward. *Noli foras ire, in te ipsum redi; in interiore homine habitat veritas.* (Do not go outward; return within yourself. In the inward man dwells truth.)[4] Inward lies the road to God. For Augustine,

> God is not just the transcendent object or just the principle of order of the nearer objects . . . God is also and for us primarily the basic support and underlying principle of our knowing activity. God is not just what we long to see, but what powers the eye which sees. So the light of God is not just 'out there', illuminating the order of being, as it is for Plato; it is also an 'inner' light.[5]

The sixteenth and seventeenth centuries in Europe were to see an immense flowering of Augustinian spirituality, affecting both Catholic and Protestant traditions alike. We have already seen the ironic paradox of Montaigne's choice to 'look within himself' and to make introspection the source of his own self-consciousness.[6] In England Montaigne had always been popular. A generation before the Romantics, we find an increasing stress on originality as a proof of individuality. 'Thyself so reverence, as to prefer the native growth of thy own mind to the richest import from abroad', wrote Edward Young in his *Conjectures on Original Composition* (1759), 'such borrowed riches make us poor'.[7] The

---

4 *De Vera Religione*, XXXIX, 72.
5 Charles Taylor, *Sources of the Self*, Cambridge University Press, 1989, p. 129.
6 Montaigne, *Essays*, p. 596.
7 Edward Young, *Conjectures on Original Composition in a Letter to the Author of Sir Charles Grandison*, London, 1759, p. 54. See also Kevin Hart, *Samuel Johnson and the Culture of Property*, Cambridge University Press, 1999, p. 70.

Augustinian tradition, whether or not filtered through Montaigne, was to become a prime source of romantic feelings and values. Indeed, at least one modern critic has seen in St Paul and St Augustine the first real Romantics.[8] It is no accident that the first full-length version of Wordsworth's great autobiographical poem, *The Prelude*, was divided into thirteen books, the same number as Augustine's own classic autobiography, *The Confessions*. But if Kant was to have a less significant immediate impact than Augustine, it is worth remembering that he, of course, like Wordsworth, had also read Augustine. In that sense, Kant did not so much invent the subjectivity of the self as give the most powerful philosophic expression to what had previously been more of a religious and aesthetic orientation than a philosophic system.

But the new Romantic and post-Romantic internalization was in one sense very different from that of the earlier tradition. Augustine, like Plato, had never doubted that however much God was to be found within himself, the values so revealed were universal ones, centred on divine law. For the new Romantic sense of individuality, whether in its directly Kantian German form, or its more Augustinian English manifestation, the individual was *also* the prime source of values.[9] We see one of the most dramatic examples of this in John Henry Newman, the great nineteenth-century English convert to Catholicism, who, while submitting his views and total obedience to his new-found Church, made it perfectly clear that his doing so was not an act of blind obedience, but a voluntary act of conscience. Nor could this be a single, once-and-for-all submission. Every such act of obedience was also an act of conscious and fully responsible choice. The moral centre of his life lay *neither* in the teachings of his Church, *nor* even in his personal devotion to God, but inalienably *within* himself.[10]

The contrast with classical Greek literature could hardly be more stark. The Homeric, and even the Sophoclean hero, has no interior space. Character is not recognized as what it is until it is spoken or acted. Protagonists are primarily aware of themselves as they appear to others. Achilles sulks in his tent at the beginning of *The Iliad* because his concubine Briseis has been reclaimed by Agamemnon, the supreme commander of the Greeks, and Achilles' superior. He is not apparently mourning the loss of the woman he loves (the question of whether he loves her, an essentially *interior* experience, is not even raised); he is furious because he

---

[8] Simon Haines, 'Romantic Souls and Realist Lives', unpublished manuscript.
[9] Taylor, *Sources of the Self*, p. 143.   [10] See Prickett, *Romanticism and Religion*.

has lost face in public. He has no choice but to see himself through the eyes of others. This shift in sense of identity between the classical world and modern Europe was acutely observed by one of Newman's near-contemporaries, Julius Hare, who remarks that in Seneca's late-Roman play, *Medea*, the protagonist, Medea herself, describes her abandonment by Jason in the third person. At this point, at the tragic climax of the play, she says simply *Medea superest* ('Medea remains' [behind]). 'An English poet', Hare writes, 'would hardly say *Medea remains.*' Though he can find no directly comparable modern play, an Italian 'modern opera of little worth' illustrates Hare's point by making Medea reply to Jason's question *Che mi resta*; with the simple pronoun *Io*. 'An ancient poet could not have used the pronoun; a modern poet could hardly use the proper name.'[11] In other words, even as late as the end of the Roman Empire (indeed, more or less the same time as Augustine is writing his *Confessions*) Seneca can still only portray Medea as seeing her tragic predicament *from the outside* – as the abandoned lover, but not sufficiently 'interiorized' to be able to say of herself, 'I'. For us, in the twenty-first century, Hare's fascination with the shift in self-consciousness is itself another revealing step in the narrative.

For an example from contemporary early nineteenth-century fiction we need look no further than Charlotte Brontë's Jane Eyre, one of the first, and most powerfully realized, examples of the new interiority. When Jane is struggling almost to the point of breakdown with her conscience over whether to become Rochester's mistress, she puts the question to herself 'Who in the world cares for *you*?' The reply is a passionate statement of inner principle that would have been incomprehensible to Medea's contemporaries:

I care for myself. The more solitary, the more friendless, the more unsustained I am, the more I will respect myself. I will keep the law given by God; sanctioned by man. I will hold to the principles received by me when I was sane, and not mad – as I am now. Laws and principles are not for the times when there is no temptation: they are for such moments as this, when body and soul rise in mutiny against their rigour: stringent are they; inviolate they shall be. If at my individual convenience I might break them, what would be their worth? They have a worth – so I have always believed; and if I cannot believe it now, it is because I am insane – quite insane: with my veins running fire, and my heart beating faster than I can count its throbs. Preconceived opinions,

---

[11] *Guesses at Truth by Two Brothers* (Augustus and Julius Hare) London, 1827, pp. 116–17.

foregone determinations, are all I have at this hour to stand by: there I plant my foot.[12]

If we suspect that narrative precedes philosophy, it will come as no surprise to find the twentieth century still struggling to come to grips with the philosophical import of such an outburst. Here, for instance, is Stuart Hampshire, addressing the experience, if not the sex, of the protagonist:

A person . . . explains himself to himself by his history, but by the history as accompanied by unrealized possibilities . . . His individual nature, and the quality of his life . . . emerge in the possibilities that were real possibilities for him, which he considered and rejected for some reason or another. From the moral point of view, it is even a significant fact about him . . . that a certain possibility, which might have occurred to him as a possibility, never actually did occur to him. In self-examination one may press these inquiries into possibilities very far, and this pressure upon possibility belongs to the essence of moral reflection.[13]

But not merely does narrative precede philosophical reflection, it is in some sense an on-going part of it. As Rowan Williams has put it:

Every 'telling' of myself is a retelling, and the act of telling changes what can be told next time, because it is, precisely, an *act*, with consequences, like other acts, in the world and speech of others. The self lives and moves in, and only in, acts of telling – in the time taken to set out and articulate a memory, the time that is a kind of representation (always partial, always skewed) of the time my material and mental life has taken, the time that has brought me here . . .

   The process of 'making' a self by constructing a story that is always being told is a prosaic and universal one . . .[14]

The act of narration – whether aloud, or only to the self, is central. Following the philosopher Walter Davis, Williams claims that 'a self is only really definable *in* the act of self-questioning; reflecting on the self can't be a way of thinking about an "item" that will stay in focus while we look at it . . .'[15] In a passage that might almost have been written in commentary on Jane Eyre, he cites Davis that 'Inwardness develops not by escaping or resolving but by deepening *the conflicts that define it.*'[16] As we shall see, this is not merely a psychological, but a historical phenomenon.

---

[12] Charlotte Brontë, *Jane Eyre* (1847), introduction by Margaret Smith, Oxford: Clarendon Press, 1975; re-issued as World's Classics paperback, 1991, Vol. 3, Ch. 1, pp. 321–2.

[13] Stuart Hampshire, *Innocence and Experience*. Cited by Kekes, *Morality of Pluralism*, p. 99.

[14] Rowan Williams, *Lost Icons: Reflections on Cultural Bereavement*, Edinburgh: T. & T. Clark, 2000, p. 144.

[15] Walter Davis, *Inwardness and Existence: Subjectivity in / and Hegel, Heidegger, Marx and Freud*, Madison, Wis., 1989, p. 105. Cited in Williams, *Lost Icons*, p. 146; Rowan Williams' italics.

[16] Davis, *Inwardness and Existence*.

It is no accident that Hare's two examples of self-consciousness are taken from one of the most agonizing classical stories about identity: that of Medea, who seeks to punish Jason's infidelity by killing her (and his) children. Seneca's play, like the nineteenth-century one, both stand in the shadow of Euripides', one of the most soul-searching and cathartic works ever to emerge from the ancient world.

Moreover, Hare points out, ever since the Renaissance, conscious-ness had been experienced more and more as an internal and private phenomenon, while nature (and therefore its scientific investigation) was increasingly felt not as a part of the self, but as an external force act-ing upon us from the outside. One of the most acute twentieth-century observers of this process of internalization, Owen Barfield, has noticed that this dual action between an increasingly objective universe and an increasingly subjective observer, was accompanied by a corresponding shift in our language itself. He highlights in particular what he describes as 'a sharp divergence in the behaviour of two broad classes of words':

Of those which refer to nature, or what we now call nature we observe that *the further back we go*, the more they appear to connote sentience or inwardness. Of those on the other hand which refer to human consciousness, the opposite is the case, and their meaning, if I may put it so, becomes more and more outward. Nature as expressed in words, has moved in the course of time from inwardness to outwardness; consciousness, as expressed in words, has moved from outwardness to inwardness.[17]

Though Barfield does not himself use the example, we can see this pro-cess at work even in the history of the word 'nature' itself. The Latin root, *natura*, referred to the qualities given to somebody (or, by exten-sion, something) at birth. The native Anglo-Saxon equivalent which, as so often in English, has survived alongside the Latin, is 'kind'. Thus, though, as we have said, there is no word in Old Testament Hebrew for 'nature', we find in the English King James Bible of 1611, that at the Creation God says 'Let the earth bring forth grass, the herb yielding seed, and the fruit tree yielding fruit after his kind' (Genesis 1: 11). By the late seventeenth century this idea of nature as a sort of inward quality of birth had largely given way to the Newtonian concept of natural law – something which could be mathematically measured and verified. Con-trariwise, as Barfield observes, the words we use to describe mental states are, without exception, derived metaphorically from words that origi-nally had only an outward meaning.[18] We recall how the word 'feelings'

---

[17] Owen Barfield, 'The Nature of Meaning', *Seven*, Vol. II, 1981, p. 38.   [18] Ibid.

is nowadays more commonly used for our emotions than for fingertip sense-impressions. Barfield himself cites, among other examples, how the word 'scruple', from the Latin *scrupulus*, a small sharp stone that could get in your sandal and inhibit walking with a firm tread, has ceased to have any connection with shoeleather and now refers exclusively to moral impediments.

In an earlier, and now classic work, *Saving the Appearances*, Barfield suggests that this historical linguistic movement reflects a corresponding shift in consciousness spanning the eighteenth century and argues that this implies, in effect, an 'awakening' from what we might call the European Dream-Time into historical time.[19] In other words, the *idea* of primal or original participation is only possible for those who no longer possess it. It was only by separating ourselves from the natural world that our idea of 'nature': whether in the form of eighteenth-century Natural Law, Wordsworthian greenery, or Stephen Hawking's Black Holes, becomes possible.

As if on cue, enter Jung. On a visit to East Africa in 1925, thirty years before Barfield was writing, Carl Gustav Jung recorded his impressions from a hill looking down on the savannah stretching to the far horizon, watching gigantic herds of gazelle, antelope, gnu, zebra and warthog grazing and moving forward like slow rivers. As he watched, he was overwhelmed by a feeling of 'the cosmic meaning of consciousness'. Without human consciousness the scene before him would remain in a state of non-being. Consciousness, it now seemed to Jung, had given the world objective existence.

Now I knew what it was, and knew even more: that man is indispensable for the completion of creation: that, in fact, he himself is the second creator of the world, who alone has given to the world its objective existence – without which, unheard, unseen, silently eating, giving birth, dying, heads nodding through hundreds of millions of years, it would have gone on in the profoundest night of non-being down to its unknown end. Human consciousness created objective

[19] 'The elimination of original participation involves a contraction of human consciousness from periphery to centre – a contraction from the cosmos of wisdom to something like a purely brain activity – but by the same token it involves an *awakening*. For we wake, out of universal into self-consciousness. Now a process of awakening can be retrospectively surveyed by the sleeper only after his awakening is complete; for only then is he free enough of his dreams to look back on and interpret them. Thus, the possibility to look back at the history of the world and achieve a full waking picture of his own gradual emergence from original participation, really only arose for man ... in the nineteenth century.' (Owen Barfield, *Saving the Appearances*, N.Y.: Harcourt Brace, 1957, pp. 182–3.)

existence and meaning, and man found his indispensable place in the great process of being.[20]

Two very important corollaries follow from this line of thought. The first is that our distinctively modern idea of objectivity is the direct product of subjectivity: logically and historically, subjectivity *precedes* objectivity. The objective existence of things is, as it were, no more than a freebie, a by-product of the long process of learning to say 'I'. The second point is one that we shall return to in Chapter Seven, and that is the idea, pioneered by the physicist Eugene P. Wigner, that the human mind (and therefore human perception) is part of the given structure of the physical world with which science must deal. In this context, Kissinger's assumption that 'knowledge consists of recording and classifying data' makes perhaps some sense. The problem, of course, is that it makes an extremely poor description of 'knowledge'.

But, as we have seen, even our definition of what might constitute 'knowledge' is influenced by the master-narrative of which it is a part. The account I have just given, beginning with Mann's description of an undifferentiated consciousness, and culminating in Jung's vision of how human consciousness gives meaning and objectivity to the universe, is itself part of a particular modern narrative of 'progress'. This story of the slow growth of human self-consciousness, and our emergence from primal participation into a modern sense of individuality, has become one of the dominant narratives of the nineteenth and twentieth centuries – complementing the story of Newtonian science and Enlightenment rationality we looked at in Chapter Two. Its roots tap into eighteenth-century theories of development, from Lessing's *The Education of the Human Race* (1780), Schiller's *The Aesthetic Education of Man* (1795), to Hegel's *Phenomenology of Mind* (1807) and Feuerbach's *Essence of Christianity* (1841) – both of which were given a new materialist twist by Marx (1867). In different forms it underlies the new disciplines of philology, anthropology, sociology and psychology, and has been used to provide a context and retrospective explanations for the scientific revolution of the seventeenth century, the rise of the novel and the associated eighteenth-century print culture, the phenomenon of Romanticism, the emergence of the modern secular idea of 'history', and the higher criticism of the Bible. The fact that this is one of the foundational 'grand' narratives of our time

---

[20] C.G. Jung, *Memories, Dreams, Reflections*, ed. Aniela Jaffé, trs Richard and Clara Winston, Collins, 1963, pp. 240–2.

(and therefore one that we are often scarcely aware of) does not make it any less of a narrative in the sense we have been exploring. Indeed, it is as much as anything from the attacks that have been made on it in recent years that we have become conscious of its status as a dominant narrative – and of the possibility that we may have accepted it for reasons more to do with our cultural self-image than the compelling logic of the evidence. But, as we are reminded by critics of this narrative, neither our logic nor sense of evidence themselves come to us free from cultural baggage.

At its simplest, such baggage is assumed in the claim that consciousness is itself culturally constructed. Though Richard Rorty, the American philosopher, cites Kuhn to support his claim that science, like all knowledge, is no more than a convenient way of talking about the world, his argument is much more extreme than Kuhn's.[21] Rorty confesses himself uneasy with the word 'consciousness' in any sense, and prefers Foucault's term, 'discourse', the linguistic apparatus through which the articulation of knowledge becomes an expression of power – because that is what he believes the narrative outlined above is really about.[22] Lyotard, as we have already seen, finds Western science indivisible from European imperialist ethics and politics. Similarly, Edward Said sees philology, like anthropology, as nothing less than a covert instrument of Western imperialism, used by the European nations to study, classify, and so create an objective 'other' out of subject peoples in other parts of the world. According to this view, the study of Asian or Arab cultures, by, for instance, Sir William Jones in India, or by the savants accompanying Napoleon in his Egyptian expedition of 1798, must be viewed not so much as scholarship, as an act of imperialist appropriation. At the heart of this endeavour is, once again, the recording and classifying of data. Thus Said sees the scientific results of Napoleon's (primarily military) expedition, finally published between 1820–30 in the monumental *Description of Egypt*, as an organized displacement of Egyptian or Oriental history as a history possessing its own coherence, identity and sense. This French version of Egyptian history, he claims, was designed to undermine local and indigenous versions by identifying itself directly and immediately with world history, 'a euphemism for European history'.[23]

[21] See Paul A. Boghossian, 'What is Social Construction?', *Times Literary Supplement*, February 23, 2001, pp. 6–8; also Chapter 6, below.

[22] Rorty, 'Universality and Truth', *Rorty and his Critics*, ed. Robert B. Brandom, Oxford: Blackwell, 2000, p. 9.

[23] Said, *Orientalism*, p. 86.

Similarly anthropology has been accused of being, at best a faithful servant of imperialism, and, at worst a patronizing and insulting attempt to construct 'the primitive' from other cultures, no less rich and complex than the anthropologist's own. The whole idea of 'primal participation' is nothing more or less than a way of differentiating the imperialist from the colonized peoples. For Said, philology, and indeed the whole concept of the scientific study of languages, is more like a conspiracy than an academic discipline. But here he recognizes the agenda concerns much more than the construction of a primitive and immature 'orient', and is inextricably linked with a particular 'scientific' view of reality itself.

Philology problematizes – itself, its practitioner, the present. It embodies a particular condition of being modern and European, since neither of those two categories has true meaning without being related to an earlier culture and time...The job of philology in modern culture (a culture Renan calls philological) is to continue to see Reality and nature clearly, thus driving out supernaturalism, and to continue to keep pace with discoveries in the physical sciences. But more than all this, philology enables a general view of human life and of the system of things...[24]

Objections to Said's view have been well summarized by John Mackenzie, who points out how in the past decade the word 'orientalism' has been transformed by Said and his followers from being a word with wholly sympathetic connotations (orientalists saw themselves as studying 'the languages, literature, religions, thought, arts and social life of the East to make them available to the West, even in order to protect them from occidental cultural arrogance in the age of imperialism') to 'an expression of intellectual and technical dominance and a means to the extension of political, military, and economic supremacy'.[25] But despite the severe historical weaknesses of Said's principal thesis, what is interesting about his argument from our point of view is how firmly it is rooted in the very nexus of nineteenth-century disciplines that he wishes to attack. The idea that the whole edifice of Western knowledge, the recording and classifying of data, should be seen as an instrument of imperialism is an externalized and racialized adaptation of Foucault's idea of 'discourse' as the language of power, while the parallel notion of cultural hegemony, through which power of an elite is maintained over the masses, is adapted from the Italian Marxist sociologist, Antonio Gramsci, whose analysis, of

[24] Ibid. p. 132.
[25] John M. Mackenzie, *Orientalism: History, Theory and the Arts*, Manchester University Press, 1995, p. xii.

course, was intended to describe not race but class relations.[26] Gramsci, like Foucault, coming from the context of the twentieth-century clash of Fascism and Communism in continental Europe, had an exaggerated belief in the coherence and efficacy of human organization. Nonetheless his whole concept of consciousness and the social context of ideas, however different from that of, say, Barfield or Jung, is ultimately derived from the same dominant developmental narrative.

But behind this charge of a sinister hidden agenda of power and dominance, there lurks an even more serious contention from those who would deny that there is any such thing as a stable and coherent individual personality at all. For them, the 'self' is nothing more than yet another fiction we compose about ourselves to explain who we are – to impress others or (as often) to reassure ourselves. Though this is a common postmodernist manoeuvre, its origins lie at least as far back in the nineteenth century as Dostoyevski's *Notes from Underground*. It occurs again, in works as different as Joseph Conrad's *Nostromo*, James Joyce's *Ulysses*, and Virginia Woolf's *Mrs Dalloway*. Though we cover these authors with the blanket term 'modernist', they have little else in common, and were certainly never a 'movement' of a literary or any other kind. 'Characters', wrote Woolf, concerning her own technique, 'are to be merely views; personality must be avoided at all costs.' In one of his very earliest essays, 'The Nothingness of Personality', the twenty-three-year-old Argentinian writer Jorge Luis Borges wrote in 1922:

I want to tear down the exceptional pre-eminence now generally awarded to the self... I propose to prove that personality is a mirage maintained by conceit and custom, without metaphysical foundation or visceral reality. I want to apply to literature the consequences that issue from these premises, and erect upon them an aesthetic hostile to the psychologism inherited from the last century...[27]

Well, maybe... but whence this 'I' who wishes to do these things? He is certainly not the product of the old undifferentiated consciousness of Mann's Elieazor. Borges was always an ironist, and that insistent pronoun beginning every sentence signals a self-mockery quite as complex as anything in Montaigne. How different, too, is this from Rowan Williams' assertion that 'the self lives and moves in, and only in, acts of telling...'?

[26] 'But whereas Foucault was often more interested in the internal topography of his apparatus, Said was concerned to apply it to a large body of heterogeneous texts. And where Gramsci dealt with class in a European context, Said transferred his hegemonic principles to racial representation and control in an imperial frame.' Ibid. pp. 3–4.

[27] Jorge Luis Borges, *Selected Non-Fictions*, trs Esther Allen, Suzanne Jill Levine and Eliot Weinberger, ed. Eliot Weinberger, N.Y.: Viking, 1999, p. 3.

THE IDEA OF LITERATURE

This narrative of the internalization of identity and externalization of nature was paralleled aesthetically by the growth in popularity of the novel. In the eighteenth century such interiorization had already been anticipated by Laurence Sterne. Among the elements of genius in his great rambling novel, *Tristram Shandy*, is the way that Sterne sees how Locke's account of the interaction of external and internal worlds was far more satisfyingly bizarre and ironic than any satire.[28] Not surprisingly, Sterne was also a major influence on the German Romantics, providing an example of the kind of 'inner space' implicitly demanded by Kantian aesthetics.

The three Critiques which constituted Kant's own intellectual 'Copernican revolution', coincided so closely in time with the political upheavals in France that it seemed to many of those (mostly German) observers who were aware of his work at the time that it partook of the same irresistible metaphysical force. For critics and writers it was clear from the start that the subjectivity of Kant's philosophy posed a special problem, as well as a special opportunity, to theories of literature and art. Almost from the appearance of the First Critique, philosophers have been deeply divided whether it necessarily implied an unbridgeable gap between mind and the real world.[29] But certainly most Kantians, then and now, have seen the purpose of Kant's Third Critique, *The Critique of Judgement* (1790), as being to discover a bridge between the realms of the two earlier Critiques – the 'Understanding' and the 'Reason'. For Kant, it is what he calls reflective 'judgement' that enables us to discover and distinguish between aesthetic qualities, and in particular those poles of eighteenth-century taste, the sublime and the beautiful.

In the Third Critique Kant sees sublimity and beauty reflected in both nature and art, but subsequent philosophers, following the ideas of the poet Schiller in *The Aesthetic Education of Man*, tended to see art rather than nature as central in the construction of the human world. Taken to its logical conclusion, this could be interpreted as meaning that visual, poetic or literary descriptions, simply because they were *not* sense perceptions but aesthetic constructs of the mind, were actually *more* real than direct sense-data, which, in the last resort, have no access at all to things-in-themselves. Art and literature could thus be seen as in some sense *the*

---

[28] See Nuttall, *Common Sky*.

[29] See, for instance, Henry E. Allison, *Kant's Transcendental Idealism*, New Haven: Yale University Press, 1983.

mediators of reality. Hegel, for instance, explicitly reverses the Kantian priorities: for him beauty in art possessed higher status than natural beauty.[30]

Oddly enough, this historic revaluation of aesthetics was not confined to the arts. In the last two centuries an increasing number of mathematicians have openly made beauty a guide to truth, and many more privately admit to being guided as much by aesthetics as logic. The Nobel Prizewinner Paul Dirac, constructed his equation for the electron, which was to lead to the prediction of antimatter, on aesthetic criteria, claiming that 'it is more important to have beauty in one's equations than to have them fit the experiment'.[31] How far the aesthetic of mathematics can be compared with that of the visual or literary arts is an interesting question, but there is presumably no *prima facie* reason why, for a Kantian, the beauty of mathematics should not give as great an access to reality as any beauty in the arts. Indeed, the abstraction of theoretical mathematics provides one area which is arguably more real than the behaviour of the matter which seems to be governed by its rules.

There is a certain historic irony in the fact that the origins of this debate over the nature of literature and art, with its seemingly paradoxical implications, should have begun in Germany at all. German literature was still remarkably undeveloped in comparison with that of either France or Britain. Despite Germany having one of the highest literacy rates in Europe, supporting the publication of more books and perodicals than anywhere else,[32] the German novel, compared with the English and French, was a low-status art-form, and scarcely existed at the end of the eighteenth century.[33] When Goethe, for instance, in *Wilhelm Meister* (1796), which is often seen as being the first great German novel, wants to refer to other works his examples are almost invariably from English.[34] Even as late as the end of the nineteenth century, when Germany's greatest novelist, Thomas Mann, was beginning his career, literature was still widely considered to be the domain of the lyric poet (*Dichter*) while novelists were classed with journalists under the general tag of 'writer' (*Schriftsteller*).[35]

---

[30] Andrew Bowie, *From Romanticism to Critical Theory*, Routledge, 1997, p. 133.
[31] Paul Davies, *The Mind of God*, pp. 175–6.
[32] R.R. Palmer, *The World of the French Revolution*, Allen & Unwin, 1971, p. 233.
[33] The possible exception would be Wieland.
[34] 'Grandison, Clarissa, Pamela, the Vicar of Wakefield, Tom Jones . . .', *Wilhelm Meister's Apprenticeship and Travels*, trs Thomas Carlyle, 2 vols., Centenary Edn, Carlyle: *Works*, Chapman and Hall, 1896–1903, Vols. XXIII and XXIV, Vol. I, p. 345.
[35] Anthony Heilbut, *Thomas Mann: Eros and Literature*, N.Y.: Knopf, 1995, p. 32.

What Germany lacked in creative writers, however, it made up by some of the most intelligent, ingenious and innovative critics. The group of young self-consciously styled 'Romantics' that had formed in Jena in 1798 around the Schlegel brothers, August and Friedrich, included the philosophers Fichte and Schelling, Caroline Michaelis, August's mistress (later to marry Schelling) and Dorothea Mendelssohn, who was later to marry Friedrich. Closely associated with this core were poets such as Novalis (the pen-name of the aristocratic Friedrich von Hardenberg) and Tieck; a reformed (Calvinistic) clergyman, Friedrich Schleiermacher; and, somewhat more distantly and intermittently, other literary and philosophic figures such as Brentano, Hölderlin, Hegel and Steffens. They had initially been drawn to the university at Jena by its closeness to Herder and Goethe at Weimar; with the publication of their journal, the *Athenaeum* in 1798, they rapidly, if briefly, acquired a powerful intellectual and critical momentum of their own. Produced primarily by the Schlegel brothers and Schleiermacher, the *Athenaeum* gives the first signs of the new literary theories that were to change the course of German, and ultimately European, thought.

Perhaps because of the weakness of German fiction, from the first their theories of literature were more to do with language and the representation of reality in general. Just as we have seen that new scientific paradigms frequently explain in quite different terms, or give a new significance to, phenomena for which the old paradigm had already provided what had hitherto seemed to be a perfectly 'satisfactory' explanation, so Kant's philosophic subjectivity was to transform the significance of literature and the creative arts in general. If telling stories about it was the closest we might ever get to the real world, then the art-form that had always specialized in telling stories suddenly assumed a new and quite undreamed-of significance. In particular, this new concept of an art-form did not see its function as merely to describe the world as it was conventionally perceived. For the German Romantics art invents new ways of seeing, new ways of describing things. It is essentially creative. 'Art is not a descriptive statement about the way the world is, it is a recommendation that the world ought to be looked at in a given way.'[36]

It is no accident, therefore, that the modern conception of 'literature', as a form of writing of inherent value over and above its ostensible subject should date from precisely this period at the end of the eighteenth

[36] S. Gablik, *Progress in Art*, p. 159.

century.[37] For the ancient Greeks art had been an essentially imitative activity, and artists were classed primarily as craftsmen. Though post-Renaissance European civilization had raised the status of the artist, the belief that art was essentially a matter of imitation had remained. As we have seen, the quality of art was judged primarily on its ability to appear 'lifelike'. Similarly, though the Enlightenment had valued and admired its literature, producing some great writers, no one had suggested that the status of fiction could ever be more than a decorative (or 'polite') adjunct to civilized thought. In Alexander Pope's words, 'true wit' was 'what oft was thought, but ne'er so well expressed'. Literature, especially as satire, could also convey moral values, correcting and instructing the reader by pleasing. But for that reason, if for no other, its status was always secondary and dependent on intellectual developments that took place elsewhere – in science, history or philosophy. In the end there was always the possibility that it would be dispensable. As Shelley's friend, Thomas Love Peacock, ironically wrote of poetry (still then the dominant narrative and literary form):

> As the sciences of morals and of mind advance towards perfection, as they become more and more enlarged and comprehensive in their views, as reason gains the ascendency in them over imagination and feeling, poetry can no longer accompany them in their progress, but drops into the background, and leaves them to advance alone.
>
> Thus the empire of thought is withdrawn from poetry, as the empire of facts had been before.[38]

As one might guess from the style of this prophecy, Peacock's argument is not un-ironic, but it also represents a very real fear on his part that what he describes might actually be already happening. Moreover, if we recall that, even as he wrote in the early nineteenth century, prose was inexorably replacing verse as the main literary form of expression, this was a very acute observation. As Peacock had hoped, however, his tongue-in-cheek prophecy of poetic obsolescence was to provoke Shelley into writing his *Defence of Poetry*, one of the most powerful restatements of the role of literature ever produced.[39] In it Shelley draws on the quite new kind of aesthetic arguments that had first made their appearance

---

[37] See Philippe Lacoue-Labarthe and Jean-Luc Nancy, *The Literary Absolute: The Theory of Literature in German Romanticism* (1978), trs Philip Barnard and Cheryl Lester, Albany: State University of New York Press, 1988, p. xiv.

[38] *The Four Ages of Poetry*, ed. H.F.B. Brett-Smith, Percy Reprints, No. 3, Oxford: Blackwell, 1953, p. 9.

[39] See Stephen Prickett, 'Peacock's Four Ages Recycled', *British Journal of Aesthetics*, Spring, 1982.

in the pages of the *Athenaeum* only a few years earlier. For Shelley, as for the Schlegels and their circle, our construction of the world in narrative terms is much more than just a 'primitive' story-telling capacity. It was not *a* way of organizing our perceptions, it was *the only* way. Poets were 'the unacknowledged legislators of the world'. In this sense our worlds are inescapably 'poetic'. Narrative lies at the core of all other activities.

Strong as this statement might seem to an English-speaking reader whose assumptions of art have been gleaned from within the empiricist tradition, poetry was to be given even higher status within twentieth-century German thought. This is Martin Heidegger, by common consent the greatest German philosopher of the century, and for many outside Germany, despite his Nazi past, the greatest twentieth-century philosopher in the world.

Poetry is not merely an ornament accompanying existence, not merely a temporary enthusiasm or nothing but an interest or amusement. Poetry is the foundation which supports history, and is therefore not mere appearance of culture . . . it is poetry which first makes language possible. Poetry is the primitive language of a historical people. Therefore, in just the reverse manner, the essence of language must be understood through the essence of poetry.[40]

That, at least, was the new idea of 'literature' that was about to emerge from Germany at the end of the eighteenth century. Owing in part to the underdeveloped nature of German prose fiction, and in part to the meaning of the German word, *Poesie*, which like the older English word 'poesie', refers to all imaginative literature, rather than just verse, Kant took poetry, in this sense, as his representative aesthetic form:

Of all the arts poetry (which owes its origins almost entirely to genius and will least be guided by precept or example) maintains the first rank. It expands the mind by setting the imagination at liberty and by offering, within the limits of a given concept, amid the unbounded variety of possible forms accordant therewith, that which unites the presentment of this concept with a wealth of thought to which no verbal expression is completely adequate, and so rising aesthetically to ideas.[41]

Even if such turgid philosophical prose confirms that Kant was not over-sensitive to literary values himself, there were plenty who were. In such a context there is nothing very surprising in the tone of the aphoristic 'fragments' which adorned issues of the *Athenaeum*, the journal

---

[40] Martin Heidegger, 'Hölderlin and the Essence of Poetry', trs Douglas Scott, *Existence and Being*, Vision Press, 1949, pp. 306–7.
[41] Kant, *Critique of Judgement*, trs J.H. Bernard, N.Y.: Hafner, 1951, pp. 170–1.

begun by the Schlegel brothers and their friends from Jena. Here, for instance, Friedrich Schlegel gives his definition of what he expects the new Romantic literature to be like:

Romantic poetry is progressive, universal poetry. Its aim isn't merely to unite all the separate species of poetry and put poetry in touch with philosophy and rhetoric. It tries to and should mix and fuse poetry and prose, inspiration and criticism, the poetry of art and the poetry of nature; and make poetry lively and sociable, and life and society poetical; . . . It embraces everything that is purely poetic, from the greatest systems of art, containing within themselves still further systems, to the sigh, the kiss that the poeticising child breathes forth in artless song . . . It alone can become, like the epic, a mirror of the whole circumambient age . . . It is capable of the highest and most variegated refinement, not only from within outwards, but also from without inwards; capable in that it organises – for everything that seeks a wholeness in its effects – the parts along similar lines, so that it opens up a perspective upon an infinitely increasing classicism . . . Other kinds of poetry are finished and are now capable of being fully analysed. The romantic kind of poetry is still in the state of becoming; that, in fact, is its real essence: that it should forever be becoming and never be perfected. It can be exhausted by no theory and only a divinatory criticism would dare to try and characterise its ideal. It alone is infinite, just as it alone is free; and it recognises as its first commandment that the will of the poet can tolerate no law above itself. The romantic kind of poetry is the only one that is more than a kind, that is, as it were, poetry itself: for in a certain sense all poetry is or should be romantic. (*Athenaeum* Fragment 116)[42]

The boundaries between description and prescription have here been completely blurred. Is Schlegel describing something that already existed, or recommending a new kind of art that was yet to be written? The evasion is deliberate. What did exist was English and French literature (which Schlegel read, borrowed wholesale from, and loudly professed to despise), the poetry of Schiller, and Goethe's prose novel *Wilhelm Meister*, which Friedrich Schlegel had hailed in a review as 'all poetry – high pure poetry'. The only problem was that Goethe insisted that he was a classicist, and would have no truck with the word 'Romantic', which was an invention of the Jena group. The safest policy was to appropriate: to proclaim Romanticism not a thing, but as an Aristotelian *entelechy*, a process of becoming – as much a reinterpretation of the past as a programme for the future.

---

[42] Fragments reproduced in Friedrich von Schlegel, *Friedrich Schlegel's Lucinde and the Fragments*, trs and introduction Peter Firchow, Minneapolis: University of Minnesota Press and Oxford University Press, 1971.

Athenaeum Fragment 153, also by Friedrich Schlegel, continues this theme:

The more popular an ancient author, the more romantic. This is the governing principle of the new anthology that the moderns have in effect made from the old anthology of the classics, or, rather, that they are still in the process of making.

Schlegel is not referring to any particular anthology here, what concerns him is the way we perceive the past. To appropriate it we construct – or rather, are *constantly* constructing: the unfinished nature of the process is important – our own 'anthology' of what is significant to us from the literature of antiquity. Romanticism, is thus, in effect, a re-reading of everything that has gone before it; a particular selection, or anthology, of classical works.

This was, of course, true in the literal sense that the Romanticism represented by the *Athenaeum* and its circle had begun as an attempt to break away from modern literature and recapture the spirit of the classical world. The Schlegels started out not with a revolutionary programme for the future, but a new vision of the poetry of antiquity inspired by Winckelmann – and, in the footsteps of Goethe, a search for ways of recreating the classical moment in modernity. Ironically, it was Friedrich Schlegel's own distinction between the classic and the romantic that had led him towards classicism. For him modern literature emphasized the miraculous, fictitious, purely imaginative and unrealistic to an extent that was incompatible with the kind of true classical objectivity that he so much admired in, for instance, Goethe's *Wilhelm Meister*.[43]

This indicates something of the paradox that lies at the heart of Jena Romanticism. Any modern reader of *Wilhelm Meister* – especially in Carlyle's influential English translation of 1824 – can be forgiven for thinking that it represents the epitome of the Romantic novel.[44] Though, on the one hand, Schlegel's definition of the 'Romantic' includes all post-Renaissance literature, and therefore embraces the entire modern period, there is a second implicit definition contained, as it were, within the main one that defines Romanticism more by the way it seeks to appropriate the past than by the way it describes the present. Indeed we might say that German Romanticism uses the idea of revolution, and therefore its sense of the historical difference between past and present,

---

[43] Hans Eichner, *Friedrich Schlegel*, New York: Twaine, 1970, pp. 22; 65.
[44] See Stephen Prickett, 'Fictions and Metafictions: *Phantastes, Wilhelm Meister* and the idea of the *Bildungsroman*', in *The Gold Thread: Essays on George MacDonald*, ed. William Raeper, Edinburgh University Press, 1991, pp. 109–25.

as a way of assimilating and coming to terms with the works of the past. As has been suggested, Kuhn's idea of a scientific paradigm itself stands in this Romantic tradition of reinterpreting the past.

In one of the most interesting recent discussions of German Romanticism, Andrew Bowie writes:

It is in this dimension of understanding, which is not a registering of pre-existing truth-determinate objects 'out there' in the world independent of what we say about them, that the potential aesthetic aspect of our relationship to language becomes apparent . . . What something is 'seen as' is historically variable, in ways which cannot be circumscribed by a definitive scientific description of what the thing 'really is'. This approach begins to suggest good theoretical reasons why 'literature' might continue to be a major source of the ways in which we make sense of the world, a fact that has, for example, become increasingly important in recent work in the history of science.[45]

There follows from this an even more important conclusion – one which, as we have already seen, underlies modern science from Gödel's incompleteness theorem to Kuhn's model of paradigms: however full and detailed our seeing or describing the world may be, it is never complete, never exhaustive, and above all, never entirely predictable. There will always be something to be added, more to be said, a different way of interpreting it by those who come after. Moreover, such endless possibility was as rich a source of irony as any hidden meaning. Indeed, it meant that meaning itself had become an infinite term.

But what is true of our senses is no less true of our descriptions. If there is no such thing as a complete description of anything, then all we can ever hope for are partial insights and fragments of an unachievable whole. 'Irony', writes Friedrich Schlegel in one of his fragments, 'is clear consciousness of eternal agility, of an infinitely teeming chaos.'[46] For him, it was the inseparable twin of the fragment – the natural mode of a pluralistic society. For the Romantics this was not so much a problem, as an opportunity.

THE IDEAL OF THE FRAGMENT

If irony was to become the mode of pluralism, the fragment was to become its most typical expression. The fragment (or ruin), which had grown steadily in popularity and significance throughout the eighteenth

---

[45] Bowie, *From Romanticism to Critical Theory*, p. 18.   [46] *Ideen*, 1800.

century, was the endemic form of Romanticism.[47] Rather than neglecting or pulling them down, English country landowners admired any ruins littering their estates as an aesthetic addition to the landscape. Indeed, where their ancestors had been careless enough not to leave any, they built new ones for themselves.[48] Longer literary works, from Coleridge's 'Christabel' and Keats' 'Hyperion' to Byron's 'Don Juan' were published uncompleted. Others, from Henry Mackenzie's *Man of Feeling*, to Coleridge's 'Kubla Khan', were presented to the reader as being 'fragments', even when they were not. Horace Walpole's best-selling *Castle of Otranto*, widely regarded as the first Gothic novel, not merely presents itself as a fragment from a lost manuscript, but is all about giant ghostly fragments that only in the final apocalypse assume a unified body. Above all, the aphorism becomes an art-form in itself.

Though collections of proverbs, or maxims, had always been around, from the Old Testament Book of Proverbs, to La Rochefoucauld, the *Pensées* of Pascal, or La Bruyère's *Caractères*, the Romantic aphorism differs from its predecessors in that it relies upon its own incompleteness. Whereas the traditional aphorism aimed to impart rules of behaviour or practical wisdom, the Romantic aphorism typically consisted of a brief, witty, ironic and often puzzling statement, designed to provoke thought rather than complete it. William Blake's 'Proverbs of Hell' from *The Marriage of Heaven and Hell* have notoriously aroused controversy over their meaning ever since. Is 'sooner murder an infant in its cradle than nurse unacted desires' an incitement to every kind of crime? a proto-Freudian observation on the complexity of the human mind? or advice against 'nursing' unrealistic fantasies? As we have seen, many of the Schlegel brothers' fragments in the pages of the *Athenaeum* are scarcely less gnomic.

Much of this new delight in cryptic aphorisms, especially in England, of course, owed nothing directly to the problems raised by Kant.[49] But, as

---

[47] Thomas McFarland, *Romanticism and the Forms of Ruin*, Princeton University Press, 1981.

[48] Among the best examples of such constructed landscapes of fragments are the great gardens at Stowe and Stourhead. See Monique Mosser and Georges Teyssot (eds.), *The History of Garden Design: The Western Tradition from the Renaissance to the Present Day*, Thames and Hudson, 1991; John Dixon Hunt and Peter Willis (eds.), *The Genius of the Place: The English Landscape Garden 1620–1820*, 2nd edn, Cambridge, Mass.: MIT Press, 1988; Kenneth Woodbridge, 'The Sacred Landscape: Painters and the Lake Garden at Stourhead', *Apollo*, 88, 1968, pp. 210–14; Edward Malins, *English Landscape and Literature 1660–1840*, London, 1966; Christopher Hussey, *English Gardens and Landscapes 1700–1750*, London, 1967; Ronald Paulson, *Emblem and Expression: Meaning in English Art of the Eighteenth Century*, Cambridge, Mass.: Harvard University Press, 1975, Ch. 2; Malcolm Kelsall, 'The Iconography of Stourhead', *Journal of the Warburg and Courtauld Institutes*, Vol. 46, 1983, pp. 133–43; and Stephen Prickett, *Origins of Narrative*, Ch. 3.

[49] Rodolphe Gasché, 'Foreword' to *Philosophical Fragments*, pp. x–xi.

so often, the Schlegels' use of aphoristic fragments in the *Athenaeum* gives a new form and theoretical structure to an existing trend. If no description can ever be complete, no account fully adequate, all we can ever produce is a fragment of the truth. For Kant, no description can ever be complete; aesthetic ideas always invoke 'more thought than can be expressed by words'. But simply because aesthetic ideas cannot be fully expressed or presented, they can only be perceived by us in terms of fragments. Such fragments, however, are not to be seen as broken, leftover, or otherwise detached pieces, but represent the only way in which the supersensible can actually become present.[50] They represent an incompleteness that is universal, essential, and which has nothing to do with the accidental incompleteness traditionally associated with fragments.[51]

In the case of Friedrich Schlegel, Kant's arguments certainly fell on immediately fertile ground: fragmentary aphorisms became for him such a compulsive medium that by the time of his death he had filled some 180 notebooks with jottings, aphorisms and fragments, revealing a veritable torrent of ideas as they were 'written on the spur of the moment'. Even the hundreds with which he filled the *Athenaeum* – often against the advice of his friends – represent only a tiny fraction of the whole. Though the *Athenaeum Fragments* make up the main bulk of the fragments published in the *Athenaeum* between 1798 and 1800, there are two other significant sequences: the *Critical Fragments* (also sometimes known as the *Lyceum Fragments*) and another group simply known as *Ideas*. In addition to creating them, Friedrich – as ever – theorized about them. *Athenaeum* Fragment 24 comments enigmatically, 'Many of the works of the ancients have become fragments. Many modern works are fragments as soon as they are written'; Fragment 206 adds: 'A fragment, like a miniature work of art, has to be entirely isolated from the surrounding world and to be complete in itself like a porcupine.' Slightly less gnomically, Fragment 77 declares that:

A dialogue is a chain or garland of fragments. An exchange of letters is a dialogue on a larger scale, and memoirs constitute a system of fragments. But as yet no genre exists that is fragmentary both in form and content, simultaneously completely subjective and individual, and completely objective and like a necessary part in a system of all the sciences.

The original meaning of 'anthology', we recall, is a collection (or garland) of flowers.

---

[50] Ibid. pp. xxv–xxvii.   [51] Ibid. p. xxx.

The quest for a new genre that would be adequate to all the theoretical requirements being heaped upon it by the fertile aphoristic genius of Schlegel and his friends becomes a familiar one in the pages of the *Athenaeum*. Sliding between the present and conditional tenses, the famous 'definition' of 'romantic poetry' in Fragment 116[52] is not so much a description as a call to action – a theoretical programme. Given the declared impossibility of achieving such multitudinous goals with any degree of completeness, the fragment makes not merely philosophic but practical sense as well. Indeed, there is a sense in which the fragment could be held to symbolize the condition of human perception and knowledge. The very incompleteness of any statement, any view of the world, demands our own imaginative participation to complete it. In this, it operates in exactly the same way as sense-perception itself.

> ...many a work of art whose coherence is never questioned is, as the artist knows quite well himself, not a complete work but a fragment, or one or more fragments, a mass, a plan. But so powerful is the instinct for unity in mankind that the author will himself bring something to a kind of completion at least directly with the form which simply can't be made a whole or a unit; often quite imaginatively and yet completely unnaturally. (Critical Fragment 103)

Because of the extensive theorizing that accompanied these fragments, we have so far drawn the bulk of our examples from the *Athenaeum*. But, as has been suggested, German Romanticism was not alone in its stress on the importance of the fragment as an instrument of thought. Blake's 'Proverbs of Hell', for instance, predates the Jena Romantics by a decade. Also it would be a mistake to assume that, because Kant was still totally unknown in England at this period, Blake's interest in the fragment springs from a totally different source. Though he had not read Kant, Blake was well read in the works of the Swedish scientist and religious mystic Emanuel Swedenborg, who had been a major influence on Kant, and whose largely intuitional and visionary statements uncannily anticipate many of the main planks of Kant's philosophical system. In particular, Swedenborg also makes extensive use of gnomic fragments.

Though England, handicapped as ever by the poor quality of language-teaching in its schools, knew little of German thought, educated Germans were often widely read in both English literature and philosophy. Scotland, with its strong traditional stress on education, was somewhat better off. In the early nineteenth century probably the best place in Britain to encounter new German ideas was Edinburgh. We

---

[52] See p. 112.

recall that it had been the challenge posed by a Scot, David Hume, which had fired Kant into creating his philosophical revolution in the first place. But the fact that a few literary figures, such as the Edinburgh-educated Thomas Carlyle, Samuel Taylor Coleridge and Thomas De Quincey, were enthusiasts for the new ideas, could hardly outweigh the patronizing ignorance of most English thinkers. The story of James Mill, the English Utilitarian philosopher, flipping through a volume of Kant's *Critique of Pure Reason* and remarking, 'Ah, yes. I see what poor Kant would be at' is probably, alas, apocryphal, but it captures very well the prevailing mood in England. It certainly is true that when, in 1821, Edward Bouverie Pusey, later to become Regius Professor of Divinity at the University of Oxford, wanted to find out about recent developments in German theology (including, as we shall see, the work of Schleiermacher) he could find only two men in the whole University of Oxford who knew any German at all.[53] Cambridge was only marginally better off. Herbert Marsh, the translator of Michaelis' *Introduction to the New Testament* (1793–1801) had become Lady Margaret Professor of Divinity there in 1807, and had introduced some knowledge of German scholarship. More influential in the long run, however, was Julius Hare, a Fellow of Trinity College and later rector of Hurstmonceux, in Sussex, who was to become one of the finest German scholars in England. His Rectory at Hurstmonceux was said to contain more than 2,000 books in German alone.[54] He had been partly brought up in Germany, and in the 1820s produced a series of translations of German works, including both fiction and history. It was he, if anyone, who finally anglicized the Schlegelian fragment, and brought together the German and English Romantic aesthetic traditions.

Neither Blake's works, whose sales were virtually non-existent, nor the *Athenaeum*, which was almost unknown outside a tiny circle in Germany, were to have anything like the immediately popular success of Hare's *Guesses at Truth*, a collection of literary, philosophic and religious

---

[53] David Newsome, *The Parting of Friends*, John Murray, 1966, p. 78.

[54] 'You entered and found the whole house one huge library, – books overflowing in all corners, in hall, on landing-places, in bedrooms, and in dressing-rooms. Their number was roughly estimated at 14,000 volumes, and, though it would be too much to say that their owner had read them all, yet he had at least bought them all with a special purpose, knew where they were, and what to find in them, and often, in the midst of discussion, he would dart off to some remote corner, and return in a few minutes with the passage which was wanted as an authority or illustration. Each group of books (and a traceable classification prevailed throughout the house) represented some stage in the formation of his mind, – the earlier scholarship, the subsequent studies in European literature and philosophy, the later in patristic and foreign theology.' 'Memoir of Julius Hare', *Guesses at Truth*, Macmillan, 1871, p. xlv.

fragments, jointly composed with his brother, Augustus, and first published anonymously in 1827. In spite of its distinctly down-beat title, it was to maintain an astonishing popularity throughout much of the century, going through a second, much enlarged, edition in 1838, a third in 1847, and being reprinted thereafter in 1867, 1871, and 1884. We have records of Charlotte Brontë buying herself a copy in 1849. Though most English contemporaries were reminded of the more familiar maxims of Pascal or La Bruyère, to anyone familiar with the *Athenaeum* the much greater debt to the Schlegels and the Jena circle is obvious. In fact there is circumstantial evidence of his knowledge of the *Athenaeum* as early as 1816. Responding to the comment of one of his colleagues, William Whewell, that he was too ready to adopt the philosophy of 'certain writers' (from the context, one suspects Wordsworth and Coleridge) because he admired their poetry, Hare is reported to have replied with an argument apparently as startling to his Cambridge audience as it would have been familiar to readers of the *Athenaeum*: 'But poetry is philosophy, and philosophy is poetry.'[55]

Though it seems clear that Julius and Augustus Hare (together with a third brother, Marcus) saw themselves as in some way the English counterpart of the Schlegel brothers, theirs was no slavish imitation of the Jena model. Indeed, it would be much better to describe the various editions of *Guesses at Truth* as an extended critical dialogue with the fragments of the *Athenaeum*, and with Friedrich Schlegel in particular. From contemporary accounts of his inordinately lengthy sermons, both at Hurstmonceux and Cambridge, it may be that fragments were best suited to Hare's particular gifts. Interspersed with one-liners on religious and aesthetic topics are much longer essays on specific points of history, philology and literary criticism. These essays are augmented and increase in number in later editions, constituting perhaps the best source of second-generation Romantic critical theory in the English language, and developing ideas that are only latent or embryonic in the more famous *Four Ages of Poetry* by Peacock or Shelley's *Defence of Poetry*. Though Hare shows himself better aware of current German theory than any of his contemporaries, with explicit references to and quotations from Goethe, Novalis, Schiller, the Schlegels, Schleiermacher and Tieck, the theoretical emphasis is subtly different.

For instance, as one might expect from the relative strengths and histories of English and German literature at this period, the Hares show

---

[55] *Guesses at Truth* (1871), p. xxii.

a much more powerful sense of an existing and socially engaged literary tradition. Hare is as concerned as the Schlegels with a philosophy of literature, but it is a historical rather than an idealist aesthetic. Whereas Friedrich Schlegel's views on the novel are derived from only a handful of examples, Hare has a sense not merely of the enormous range and diversity of his own literary heritage, but also of how far it had developed and changed over the years:

> ... Goethe in 1800 does not write just as Shakespeare wrote in 1600: but neither would Shakespeare in 1800 have written just as he wrote in 1600. For the frame and aspect of society are different; the world which would act on him, and on which he would have to act, is another world. True poetical genius lives in communion with the world, in a perpetual reciprocation of influences... Genius is not an independent and insulated, but a social and continental, or at all events a peninsular power...[56]

The similarities and differences between the Hares' and Schlegels' aesthetics is nowhere better illustrated than in their aphoristic theories themselves. The first edition of *Guesses at Truth* carries a prefatory motto from Bacon's *Advancement of Learning*:

> As young men, when they knit and shape perfectly, do seldom grow to a further stature; so knowledge, while it is in aphorisms and observations, it is in growth; but when once it is comprehended in exact methods, it may perchance be further polished and illustrated, and accommodated for use and practice; but it increaseth no more in bulk and substance.

The key to the Hares' theory is biological: for them the best metaphor for human consciousness was that of an organism.[57] 'Some thoughts are acorns', writes Julius, 'Would that any in this book were.'[58] The idea of thoughts as seeds is part of a theory of aesthetics in which the book has become a symbol for life itself:

> Life may be defined to be the power of self-augmentation, or of assimilation, not of self-nurture; for then a steam-engine over a coalpit might be made to live.[59]

There is a powerful debt here to Goethe's biological theories. For him a plant was both inner-determined in its own growth, but simultaneously in a dialectical relationship to its environment. This idea was to become

---

[56] Ibid. Vol. II, pp. 136–40.
[57] For a fuller account of organic theories of mental growth, see Prickett, *Coleridge and Wordsworth*.
[58] *Guesses at Truth* (1827), Vol. II, p. 79.   [59] Ibid. p. 16.

part of both the Schlegel brothers' aesthetics in the *Athenaeum*. The series of aphorisms published by Novalis in the 1798 issue is entitled *Blütenstaub* ('Pollen') and is prefaced by a reference to Christ's parable of the sower: 'Friends, the soil is poor, we must sow a lot of seed properly in order to achieve a reasonable harvest.'[60] Four of the 'grains' that follow are by Friedrich Schlegel himself. Nevertheless, the Schlegelian theory of the fragment is as much philosophical as organic: an acknowledgement of the essential incompleteness both of human knowledge and of the hopelessness of trying to put that knowledge fully into words. In contrast, the word 'fragment', though familiar even from the German title *Athenaeum Fragmente*, is not one that the Hares ever use. For them the contrast between the organic 'seed' and the random broken quality of the inorganic 'fragment' is absolute:

Second thoughts . . . are only fragments of thoughts; that is, they are thought by a mere fragment of the mind, by a single faculty, the prudential understanding . . . Now man . . . should studiously preserve the unity of his being . . .'[61]

A thing may be complete and yet unfinished; finished and yet incomplete. This distinction serves as the basis for a further distinction, that between the classic and Gothic spirit:

Is not every Grecian temple complete even though it be in ruins? just as the very fragments of their poems are like the scattered leaves of some unfading flower. Is not every Gothic minster unfinished? and for the best of reasons, because it is infinite . . .[62]

TWO KINDS OF TRUTH?

Though the bulk of the fragments in the *Athenaeum* were composed by the two Schlegel brothers, there were other contributors as well. By far the most significant was their young clergyman friend Friedrich Schleiermacher. Fragment 350, for instance, while closely in agreement with the Schlegels' general aesthetics, also shows concerns that were to be distinctive to Schleiermacher's later work.

No poetry, no reality. Just as there is, despite all the senses, no external world without imagination, so too there is no spiritual world without feeling, no matter how much sense there is. Whoever only has sense can perceive no human being, but only what is human: all things disclose themselves to the magic wand of

---

[60] My translation. *Athenaeum 1798–1800*, Stuttgart: J.G. Cotta'sche Buchhandlung Nachf, p. 70.
[61] *Guesses at Truth* (1827), Vol. II, p. 96.   [62] Ibid. p. 250.

feeling alone. It fixes people and seizes them; like the eye, it looks on without being conscious of its own mathematical operation.[63]

It is art, not our perceptions of the world around us, that gives access to a reality that is in part our own creation. This post-Kantian orthodoxy was expanded by Julius Hare, an avowed admirer of Schleiermacher, to include the way in which poetry (or poesie in its broader archaic English sense) affects our construction of nature:

> The commentator guides and lights us to the altar erected by the author, although it is at the flame upon that altar that he must have kindled his torch. And what are Art and Science, if not a running commentary on Nature? What are poets and philosophers but torch-bearers leading us toward the innermost chambers of God's holy temples, the sensuous and the spiritual world? Books, as Dryden has aptly termed them, are spectacles to read nature. Homer and Aristotle, Shakespeare and Bacon, are the priests who preach and expound the mysteries of the universe: they teach us to decypher and syllable the characters wherewith it is inscribed. Do you not, since you have read Wordsworth, feel a fresh and more thoughtful delight whenever you hear a cuckoo, whenever you see a daisy, whenever you play with a child? Have not Thucydides and Dante assisted you in discovering the tides of feeling and the currents of passion by which events are borne along in the ocean of Time? Can you not discern something more in man, now that you look on him with eyes purged and unsealed by gazing upon Shakespeare and Goethe? From these terrestrial and celestial globes we learn the configuration of the earth and the heavens.[64]

From this assertion of the power of literature to transform our perception of the world, it is only a short step to the even more radical assertion that there are two kinds of 'truth'. In addition to the traditional definition, which relates to events or concepts in the world of our perceptions (whatever may be the relationship of such 'truth' to the more intangible world of things-in-themselves), there now comes into being a second definition linking truth to art. If, as we have seen, art has the capacity to reveal reality in ways denied even to our senses, it is, in effect, creating new ways of seeing the world that constitute valid truths in themselves.[65] We recall Bloom's quotation from Nuttall to the effect that Shakespeare shows us aspects of reality that we could not see without him. The interesting question, of course, is whether, and, if so, in what sense, those aspects of reality existed before Shakespeare put them into words?

---

[63] *Philosophical Fragments*, in Schlegel, *Fragments*, p. 71.
[64] *Guesses at Truth*, 1st edn, 1827, p. 80.
[65] See Bowie, *From Romanticism to Critical Theory*, p. 17.

Such a question is rather like the question of the formation of new words from existing roots. We have already seen something of the confused history of 'postmodernism'. For the first three-quarters of the twentieth century, someone who supported the political, social and economic ideas of Karl Marx was called a 'Marxist'. In the last twenty years or so – especially with the ideological collapse of world Communism – a new word, 'Marxian', has appeared, which is used to mean those who were heavily influenced by some non-political aspect of Marx's thought, usually his economic or social analysis, but not his political thought, and wish to distance themselves from any form of Communist dogma. Are such words 'new' inventions, denoting genuinely new concepts, or do they just clarify meanings that were latent, but always there, lurking within the cloudy imprecision of their parent word? Were there no consciously selective or half-hearted Marxists before the last part of the twentieth century?

What, too, for instance, of the word 'sentimental'? which, if it was not invented by Sterne in his novel, *A Sentimental Journey*, was certainly given common currency by it.[66] In this original sense it described a refined and elevated quality of feeling (only later did it acquire its modern derogatory meaning of being swayed by an inapproprate excess of emotion).[67] Did the emotional quality so described only come into existence when there was a word for it? Or should we rather say that, once they had a word for it, our eighteenth-century ancestors not merely recognized an already familiar cast of mind, but, seeing it become fashionable, thereafter consciously tried to practise it as proof of their own cultivated feelings? Yes, indeed – but there is a further point here not to be missed. Sterne was one of the great ironists of all time. His adoption and ironic undercutting of the word are almost simultaneous. It is very hard to say whether the word 'sentimental' *ever* had quite the refined and elevated quality ascribed to it by most dictionaries. The hero of the *Sentimental Journey*, Sterne's fictional alter-ego, parson Yorrick, constantly sees himself as expressing such sentiments while chasing various women, from ladies to their maids, through a variety of faintly ridiculous and hypocritical adventures. The ambivalence of Sterne's use of the word is beautifully captured in a brief episode when he pities a caged starling. Our hero

---

[66] The *OED* gives 1749 as the date of its first use.

[67] As so often, it is as impossible to give precise meanings to such vogue-words as 'sensibility' and 'sentimental' at this period as it is to give exact dates to shifts of tone and meaning. See Markman Ellis, *The Politics of Sensibility: Race, Gender and Commerce in the Sentimental Novel*, Cambridge University Press, 1998, p. 5.

meditates on its captivity, attributing to it the pathos of captivity and slavery everywhere, sheds tears of sympathy for it – but makes no effort at all to open its cage and set it free.

Such new words and concepts are precisely what the German Romantics meant by the creation of 'new' truth – in the case of 'sentimental' perhaps the more so for its acceptance that the word captures both the nobility of aspiration and the faint ridiculousness of human emotions. Once we accept the idea that truth may not necessarily be a Platonic absolute, but can be the creation of particular circumstances, at a particular moment in time and space, and express not simple qualities of the human mind, but simultaneously its ironies and contraditions, we may also begin to wonder how different such truths are from the kinds of objective mathematical and scientific laws that have traditionally been associated with the word 'truth'.

At first sight, this distinction between objective and eternal truth, and subjective and creative truth, may look like a re-run of Lyotard's distinction betwen 'scientific knowledge' (which is objective) and 'narrative knowledge' (which is subjective). Yet, as in the case of that distinction, such neat polarities have a disconcerting way of collapsing into each other. If we were Platonists, for example, we would be likely to claim that the eternal truths of mathematics, or the laws of nature, had 'existed' long before they were ever articulated. Many modern theoretical physicists, such as Paul Davies, who would deny being Platonists, would nevertheless agree. But even such apparently immutable laws as those of nature are open to question.

To begin with, in talking of 'laws' we are talking not of an abstract form, but (as we have seen in the case of Chinese science) of a human metaphor with as clear a history of meaning and application as the word 'sentimental'. As Rupert Sheldrake points out:

The concept of laws of nature is metaphorical. It is based on an analogy with human laws, which are binding rules of conduct prescribed by authority and extending throughout the realm of sovereign power. In the seventeenth century, the metaphor was quite explicit: the laws of nature were framed by God, the Lord of all Creation. His laws were immutable; his writ ran everywhere and always.[68]

But, of course, many people today do not believe in such a God, even while they may accept the idea of universal and immutable laws whose existence was historically dependent on Him. In that sense, the idea of

---

[68] Sheldrake, *The Presence of the Past*, p. 11.

'laws of nature' is the last great surviving legacy of the old cosmology, and, even if it was once used in a totally non-ironic sense, can no longer be so. Real laws, framed by real people for actual human societies, do, of course, evolve and develop all the time. Indeed, the concept of English common law *depends* not on immutability, but on just such a process of continual modification and adaptation. So do post-eighteenth century concepts of science. Darwinian evolution, though almost as far-reaching in terrestrial science as any of the Newtonian laws of mechanics, is rarely actually called a 'law' – presumably for that reason.

Whatever may be the niceties of such debates, what is grammatically certain is that even to use such metaphors as 'law' in this context is once again to invite irony. Between image and reality (whether knowable or unknowable) lies a gap. Whereas it was possible for a seventeenth-century clergyman–scientist to talk of the laws of the universe as facts that were neither changeable nor debatable, for a twentieth-century physicist, such as Feynman, even to use a title like *The Character of Physical Law*, is, as he recognizes, inescapably to enter a realm of ambiguity and irony. But it is important to recognize that, as we saw in the case of Darwinism, such ambiguities are not *entirely* a linguistic problem.

Consider, for instance, the following argument:

Water boils in the same way in Scotland, Thailand, and New Guinea, and everywhere else too. Under given conditions it boils at predictable temperatures – for example at 100 °C at standard atmospheric pressure. Sugar crystals form in much the same way under similar conditions all over the world . . . We usually assume that all these things happen because the appropriate materials, under the appropriate physical and chemical conditions, are under the influence of natural laws – laws that are invisible and intangible, but are nevertheless present everywhere and always. There is order in nature; and the order depends on law.

These hypothetical laws of nature are somehow independent of the things they govern. For example, the laws governing the formation of sugar crystals do not just operate only inside and around the growing crystals, but exist outside them. . . . The sugar crystals that are forming today in sugar factories in Cuba are not following local Cuban laws, but rather laws of nature which apply everywhere on earth, and indeed everywhere in the universe. These laws of nature cannot be altered by any laws the government of Cuba may pass, and they are not affected by what people think – not even by what scientists think. Sugar crystals formed perfectly well (as far as we know) before the structure of sugar molecules was worked out by organic chemists and before the structure of their crystals was worked out by crystallographers; indeed, these crystals were forming perfectly well before there were any scientists at all. Scientists may have discovered and more or less precisely described the laws governing the formation of these crystals, but the laws have an objective existence quite independent of human beings, and even independent of the actual crystals themselves. They are eternal. They existed before the first sugar molecules arose anywhere in the universe. Indeed they existed before there was a universe at all – they are eternal realities which transcend time and space altogether.[69]

But at this point, as Sheldrake, the author of this passage, points out, something very odd has happened to the argument. How, for instance, could we possibly know that the laws of nature existed before the universe came into being? What we are confronting, not for the first time in this book, is that process by which legitimate science is imperceptibly transformed into metaphysics. We start with a more or less simple and obvious proposition, and move, by a series of steps, each of which appears in itself to be totally safe and logical, to a position that has become a totally unprovable (and unfalsifiable) hypothetical construct. Whether the truths that form these laws are, in fact, eternal, or whether they are themselves in a process of evolution is simply beyond our competence to judge at the present time – and maybe for ever. (What kind of practical experiment could we conduct on the processes of inter-stellar physics?)

As in other cases we looked at in the last chapter, the apparently objective absolutes of science, on inspection, turn out to be not so much timeless truths, as narratives we tell ourselves about the timeless nature of our world. Indeed, the idea of 'truth' itself seems increasingly inaccessible – so much so that Richard Rorty has argued that, in the parallel case of philosophy, the only way to break its failed Platonic obsession with the idea of the truth in some absolute sense is for it to think of itself instead as a kind of literature, yet another of the stories we tell ourselves about the universe. We seem to have come full circle to the *Athenaeum* fragments, and the insistent blurring of philosophy and literature. Friedrich Schlegel again:

Philosophy . . . is the result of two conflicting forces – of poetry and practice. Where these interpenetrate completely and fuse into one, there philosophy comes into being; and when philosophy disintegrates, it becomes mythology or else returns to life. The most sublime philosophy, some few surmise, may once again turn to poetry . . . (*Athenaeum* Fragment 304)

As Schleiermacher observed in the quotation on poetry and reality, the two worlds of interior and exterior, subjective and objective, become more and more difficult to separate. Just as there is 'no external world without imagination, so too there is no spiritual world without feeling'.

[69] Ibid. pp. 10–11.

If the first part of the sentence was orthodox Kantianism, the second part was pure Schleiermacher. In it were the seeds of an entire new theory of interpretation, which was to become known to the world as 'hermeneutics'. In the next chapter, therefore, we will follow through one example of the way in which this new nexus of ideas was to influence even that most conservative of human activities, religion.

CHAPTER 4

Reconstructing religion: Fragmentation, typology and symbolism

FROM RELIGION TO RELIGIONS

Christianity was the original grand narrative. Unlike either Judaism, or the various pagan cults it had supplanted in the late Roman world, for more than 1,000 years it seemed to many of its adherents to offer the final and coherent Theory of Everything. This fundamental consilience (to use E.O. Wilson's re-coined word[1]) included not merely the dramatic sweep of the Bible narrative itself, beginning with the Creation and ending with the Apocalypse, but cosmology, botany, zoology and even secular literature, integrated into a single vast all-encompassing system. In its most developed form not merely human society, but animals, plants, minerals, and even angels themselves, were arranged in a divinely ordered Great Chain of Being whose golden links reached from the throne of God to the lowliest inanimate parts of Creation.[2] The earth-centred Ptolemaic universe, the providential powers of medicinal herbs, and the hierarchies of mediaeval bestiaries, all bore witness to the divine scheme of the universe. The very completeness of the narrative by the late middle ages made the idea of an alternative story almost unthinkable.

Even the one apparent cultural exception to this order, the literature of classical antiquity, was ingeniously incorporated into this great universal narrative. As early as the first century, Philo, a Hellenized Jew, claimed that the Greek philosophers such as Plato were not merely compatible with the Hebrew scriptures, but had actually been influenced by them.[3] Other commentators applied to classical literature the same allegorizing

---

[1] *Consilience: The Unity of Knowledge*, Little, Brown & Co., 1998.

[2] The best account of this is A.O. Lovejoy, *The Great Chain of Being*, Harvard University Press, 1936.

[3] See E.R. Goodenough, *Introduction to Philo Judaeus*, 2nd edn, Oxford: Basil Blackwell, 1962 (1st edn, New Haven, Conn.: Yale University Press, 1940); and Henry Chadwick, 'Philo', in A.H. Armstrong (ed.), *Cambridge History of Later Greek and Early Mediaeval Philosophy*, Cambridge University Press, 1967, pp. 137–57.

techniques that had first been used in the Christian appropriation of the Old Testament. Virgil's fourth *Eclogue*, with its prophecy of a coming ruler, was understood as a foretelling of Christ and a parallel to Isaiah. His *Aeneid* was even read as a parable of the Christian soul's journey through life. By the sixth century Cassiodorus was able to accommodate the whole of classical learning to an organized programme of Christian education.[4] Thus sanctified, the classics were embraced by the Renaissance writers as religious authorities almost on a par with the biblical writers. Dante makes the pagan Virgil his guide through a Christian Hell and Purgatory that contains both biblical and classical figures. Milton, in *Samson Agonistes*, creates a classical tragedy out of a biblical story – reminding us in his prologue that 'The Apostle Paul thought it not unworthy to insert a verse of Euripides into the text of Holy Scripture, I Cor. xv. 33.' 'Of the style and uniformity and that commonly called the plot . . . they only will be best judge who are not unacquainted with Aeschylus, Sophocles, and Euripides, the three tragic poets unequalled yet by any, and the best rule to all who endeavour to write tragedy.'[5] All human learning: literature, art, science and religion could be seen as being in perfect harmony.

Like all such generalizations, this is of course a vast over-simplification. No synthesis of this magnitude and complexity is univocal, or tells only one story. Even that musical image of 'harmony' implies at least different voices or instruments playing related parts within a single tune. Another analogy might be that of a thick rope composed of many individual narrative strands. Perhaps the best metaphor of all would be that of a Kuhnian paradigm. Within a common overall way of thinking there could be wide areas of disagreement. Aquinas' great *Summa Theologica*, now often seen as the supreme statement of the mediaeval synthesis, was sharply attacked, and even seen as heretical in its own time. What finally broke the paradigm, however, was not any single point of debate, but rather the collapse of the idea that a total common synthesis was possible at all.

Among the ideas that had been incorporated into Christianity from Greek thought was the Platonic one of the 'ontic logos', where scientific knowledge and moral vison were inextricably linked. The loss of this strand of the great synthesis, and the consequent realization that science and morals might operate in totally different realms that could not be

---

[4] See Stephen Prickett (ed.), *Reading the Text: Biblical Criticism and Literary Theory*, Oxford: Blackwell, 1991, pp. 5–7.
[5] *The Poems of John Milton*, ed. John Carey and Alastair Fowler, Longman, 1968, pp. 365, 367.

related, dealt a cruel blow to the mediaeval sense of unity. As Charles Taylor puts it:

The reading of the goodness of things in terms of Plato's order of Ideas, which we owe to the Greek fathers as well as to Augustine was one of the most influential and important syntheses which helped to form Western civilization . . . It was facilitated by Plato's creation story in the *Timaeus*, and it issues in the powerful and widely recurring idea of creatures as the signs of God, embodiments of his Ideas. Through it the notion of an ontic logos was welded for centuries into the very centre of Christian theology, so that for many people in modern times the challenge to this notion has seemed indistinguishable from atheism.

But naturally this synthesis has also been the locus of tensions, disputes, and ultimately painful ruptures in Christian civilization. Nominalists and later Reformers protested against this notion of a cosmic order, as did great numbers of others, concerned to defend above all God's sovereignty as creator and preserver. A basically Stoic theodicy, explaining away suffering and loss as a necessary and integral part of a good order, is always creeping back, with Leibniz, for example, and is always being vigorously combated, as by Kant and even more sharply by Kierkegaard.[6]

In the wake of the Reformation and the disappearance of the old Ptolemaic idea of the earth at the centre of all things, the tensions underlying the always fragile mediaeval synthesis became increasingly visible. One reason for the astonishing durability of the best Elizabethan drama is that it is shot through with this almost unendurable metaphysical tension. As A.D. Nuttall has pointed out in a recent study of Marlowe, the notion that the damnation motif in *Dr Faustus* is 'a decaying left-over from the Middle Ages' is totally a-historical. 'On the contrary', he writes, 'the Calvinistic view of man as having zero capacity, totally depraved and naturally damned, was coming, hot and strong, from the Reformers at the same time as the opposite view, enforced by Platonists, Hermeticists, and magician-scientists, that through extended knowledge man could ascend into the firmament, could become quasi-divine.'[7]

As in other examples of intellectual paradigms, there had been a kind of tacit symbiosis between the various parts. The self-evident truth of one piece of the argument seemed to reinforce other, logically unrelated, areas. Similarly, when one piece collapsed, apparently unconnected parts of the synthesis suddenly seemed less obviously right. The notion of the inherent connection between knowledge and morality was never a central Christian doctrine *per se*, but its loss nevertheless weakened the idea that there had to be a single, discernable, pattern to the universe.

[6] Taylor, *Sources of the Self*, p. 220.
[7] A.D. Nuttall, *The Alternative Trinity: Gnostic Heresy in Marlowe, Milton, and Blake*, Oxford: Clarendon Press, 1998, p. 84.

Once the idea of a unified grand narrative in this sense was questioned, it fell to pieces almost under its own entropic momentum.

This was not simply a matter of ideas. A prevailing paradigm may represent itself to its adherents primarily as a unified intellectual construct, but, as those who dare to challenge it quickly discover, it is also a locus of deeply entrenched emotions. Both the Reformation, and the Catholic Counter-Reformation had liberated huge new reserves of spiritual energy and devotion in Europe, and in both Calvinism and the new Catholic baroque sensibility what looked like new and satisfying versions of the traditional all-embracing grand narrative were painfully re-constructed. Yet the greater the vigour of the polemic against supposedly 'Christian' opponents, the more both sides were reminded that there was another possible version of events. The universal paradigm had gone. In place of a single Church were warring sects; in place of the traditional synthesis was nascent pluralism. Not unrelatedly, perhaps, by the eighteenth century religious observance in England, France and Germany had sunk to lows that have never been equalled either before, or, perhaps more surprisingly, since.[8]

Such changes in collective sensibility, however, rarely have single or simple causes. The collapse of the traditional Christian paradigm itself attracted a variety of new narratives: words like 'Reformation' or 'heresy' are themselves titles of implied narratives of heroic revolt, or triumphant fidelity. Other interpretations of European history tell other stories. One strand of conventional wisdom, for instance, has it that the old providential grand narrative was finally demolished by three great historical blows. The first, the belief that the earth we lived on was the centre of a limited cosmos, was destroyed by Copernicus, Galileo and Newton in the sixteenth and seventeenth centuries. The second, the biblical tradition that humanity was uniquely formed in God's image, was exploded by Darwin in the nineteenth century, and, finally, any assumptions of intellectual rationality bolstered by the first two were rudely shattered by Freud at the turn of this century.

One problem with this account, however, is its dating. No intellectual revolution happens all at once, but the traditional belief in the uniqueness of humanity was already being treated with great scepticism by the middle of the eighteenth century, 100 years before Darwin, who did no more than administer the *coup de grâce*. An even more important problem is its source. It was put about by Freud himself, who was, not very

---

[8] Robert Currie, Alan Gilbert, and Lee Horsley (eds.), *Churches and Churchgoers: Patterns of Church Growth in the British Isles since 1700*, Oxford: Clarendon Press, 1977.

subtly, attempting to piggy-back what he saw as his own 'revolution' on the prestige of the other two, and claim the same status in the history of thought as Copernicus and Darwin.[9] A third is that, as has been argued, the fact of the breakdown of the entire system itself was probably more significant than the questioning of any particular part.

Even by the seventeenth century we are already looking not at a single narrative, but a profusion of incompatible and competing ones. Moreover, it is significant how so many other makers and shakers of human ideas do not seem to have reacted to these blows with the horror and dismay that Freud evidently felt they should. If, in the early seventeenth century, John Donne genuinely felt that 'the new philosophy puts all in doubt' (questions of irony prevent an unambiguous reading), certainly a full century after Copernicus' death Milton, who not merely knew perfectly well that the earth went round the sun, but also believed the material of his great saga of the Fall of Man, *Paradise Lost*, to be divinely revealed in the Book of Genesis, calmly uses the obsolete Ptolemaic earth-centred cosmos as the setting for his poem. Similarly, though science may well have contributed to the growth of eighteenth-century Deism, we exaggerate its importance at that period if we attribute the scepticism of the Enlightenment solely or even principally to the scientific revolution. There were many other philosophical, religious and social roots to the Enlightenment, and, as has been mentioned, Newton's theory of gravity, for instance, was not even accepted in France until the mid-years of the century. The publication of Darwin's *Origin of Species* in 1859 certainly shook the faith of some, including, for instance, the journalist and editor John Morely, who later admitted that he had changed his mind about ordination as a result of Darwin. But the frisson that is supposed to have shaken the entire religious world loses some of its chill when we read actual eye-witness accounts of the clearly very confused debate between Huxley and Bishop Wilberforce at the Pitt-Rivers Museum, or notice that neither F. D. Maurice nor John Henry Newman, two of the most influential English theologians of the day, and far more significant figures than the meretricious 'soapy' Sam Wilberforce, seem to have been disturbed, either publicly or privately, by the new biological theory.

The changes brought about just by the breakdown of the idea of a single system of explanation – a single grand narrative – also resulted in corresponding linguistic shifts, first in English but within a century

---

[9] Sigmund Freud, *Introductory Lectures on Psychoanalysis*, Lecture 18, 'Fixation to Traumas – The Unconscious', Harmondsworth: Penguin, Vol. I, p. 326.

right across Europe. As the historian Peter Harrison has recently shown, the word 'religion' only acquired its modern meaning of a particular systemized code of belief and practice in England in the seventeenth century, as the breakdown of the mediaeval synthesis, and the religious upheavals of the sixteenth-century Reformation, allowed people, for almost the first time, to see that *more* than one such system could exist. Only then could 'a religion' be perceived as one system among several, that could be studied as it were objectively, from the outside. Only then did the word acquire its plural form.[10] In that sense, our concept of religion is itself only about 300 years old.

The concept was, moreover, born in irony. As the philosopher John Locke had put it in one of his more deadpan moments, the kings and queens of post-Reformation England had been 'of such different minds in point of religion, and enjoined thereupon such different things', that no 'sincere and upright worshipper of God could, with a safe conscience, obey their several decrees'.[11] The Vicar of Bray was a real person, responding with logic, if not with integrity, to a real dilemma. As anyone who has experienced twentieth-century totalitarianism, whether Fascist or Communist, would recognize, irony is the standard reaction to the clash of different totalizing systems.

Certainly to many contemporaries the notion of different religious systems could only come as a relief. There is ample evidence that by the late seventeenth century, after more than a century of turmoil, beginning with the Reformation and ending in the horrors of Civil War, many people were heartily tired of debates about exclusive truth. As early as the middle of the sixteenth century a Dutch commentator had observed that 'The scripture is like a nose of wax that easily suffereth itself to be drawn backward and forward, and to be moulded and fashioned this way and that, and howsoever ye list.'[12] What had begun as a polemical insult (the Papists 'make the scriptures a nose of wax, and a tennis ball'[13]) had been turned into a cynical comment on the nature of the medium

---

[10] Peter Harrison, *'Religion' and the Religions in the English Enlightenment*, Cambridge University Press, 1990.

[11] Locke: *A Letter Concerning Toleration*, in *Treatise of Civil Government and A Letter Concerning Toleration*, ed. Charles L. Sherman, NY: Appleton-Century-Crofts, 1965, p. 191.

[12] Albertus Pighuis, *Hierarchiae Ecclesiasticae Assertio*, Cologne, 1538, fo. lxxxx, sect. B, trs Jewel, *Works*, Parker Society, Cambridge 1841–53, Vol. IV, p. 759. Cited by H.C. Porter, 'The Nose of Wax: Scripture and the Spirit from Erasmus to Milton', *Transactions of the Royal Historical Society*, 5th Series, Vol. 14, 1964, p. 155.

[13] The image goes back at least to Alain of Lille (1120–1202), see Porter, 'Nose of Wax'.

itself. As Dryden put it in his poem on the Catholic–Protestant debates, 'The Hind and the Panther':

> After long labour lost, and time's expense,
> Both grant the words, and quarrel for the sense.
> Thus all disputes for ever must depend;
> For no dumb rule can controversies end.
>
> (200–3)

But pluralism was not merely a welcome pragmatic solution to an intractable problem; it was a re-writing of the entire rules of the game. What was not resolved by the new idea of 'religions' was the question of whether, and in what form, a Christianity deprived of its universal grand narrative could survive at all.

What was obvious was that the nature of all such narratives had irrevocably been altered. Though, as always, individuals might be sceptical about details, the grand narrative itself (for all its Platonic foundations) had been essentially unironic. The truth had been divinely revealed through the Incarnation of Christ, the inspired words of scripture in the form of Jerome's Latin Vulgate, and the teachings of the Church. Much might still be hidden from us, but that was no reason to suspect the permanence and validity of what was known through revelation and human reason. What had been destroyed in two centuries of acrimonious theological debate and wars of religion was a belief in the certainty of knowledge itself – that kind of 'knowledge', at least. Whatever narratives of God might replace the mediaeval synthesis were henceforth to be *either* blindly fundamentalist, abrogating human reason to absolute divine revelation (or, later, to such totalising secular creeds as scientism, Marxism and Freudianism) *or* fundamentally ironic.

The new religious pluralism, first experienced in England in the seventeenth century, meant that not even the most traditional and orthodox could any longer claim a total and complete reading of everything. The late sixteenth- and early seventeenth-century flowering of English drama, with the plays of Jonson, Shakespeare, Middleton, Webster and Tourneur, is an art-form of uncertainty, debate, and conflict. Though at one end of the spectrum such a confusion of values could be a source of comedy, it was also the basis of some of the bleakest and most powerful tragedies ever written. Any attempt at re-statement of traditional hierarchies and beliefs was instantly threatened by the possibility of ironic counter-readings. In Shakespeare's *Troilus and Cressida*, for example, Ulysses 'degree' speech (Act I, Sc. 3) is a classic re-statement of the grand narrative of a conservative and hierarchical (Christian) society. It was even quoted as such as recently as the 1980s by a member of the British Conservative government, Kenneth Baker. Yet, as its Elizabethan audience would know well, many of its assumptions (including that of the Ptolemaic universe) were already effectively demolished, and in its dramatic context of the siege of Troy and the petty squabbling of the Greek leaders, the message can be read in very different and ironic terms, as the empty rhetoric of a political cynic. It is no accident that one of the first casualties of the Civil War was the London theatres, closed down by the Puritans in 1640.

But it is significant that, however univocal and unironic the truth reflected in seventeenth-century puritan art, in practice it displayed precisely the same sense of unresolvable, ironic, and even tragic conflicts that had dominated the London theatre a generation earlier. However strong were Marvell and Milton's own religious convictions, they were writing against a pluralistic background not merely of Catholic/ Protestant divisions, but of those no less deep between Anglican and Presbyterian, Presbyterian and Anabaptist. Milton makes clear that he thinks of *Samson Agonistes* essentially in terms of a classical Greek tragedy of the fall of a great person, not one that involved the kind of moral questioning of Shakespearean drama. Yet for all the classical gestures of the poem, Samson's destruction is due not to *hamartia*, the non-moral but tragic 'mistake' of Greek drama, but to moral failure in the Jacobean tragic sense. Even more significant is the fact that *Paradise Lost*, not of course 'intended' (we must presume) as a tragedy at all, has in Satan one of the most powerful tragic protagonists ever. As generations of readers have noted, the blind poet who had given his talents to supporting Parliament against the claims of an absolute monarchy found it impossible to support the claims of an absolute Deity against a parliament of rebel angels without some feelings, however unconscious, of divided loyalty. Nor was Milton alone in his sense of the ironic complexities of the narratives he was handling. Precisely the same reserve and balance is visible in Andrew Marvell's vision of Charles as both actor and martyr upon the scaffold in his *Horatian Ode on the Return of Cromwell from Ireland*.

RELIGIONS OF NATURE AND OF THE HEART

Not surprisingly one of the most powerful impulses of the new religious context involved moving away from the dangers and fanaticisms of revealed religion towards a grand narrative based not on interpreting the Bible, but rather God's 'other book' – that of Nature. If we trace the changing meanings of that word, 'nature', over the course of the eighteenth century, we can trace with it the unfolding of a quite new religious and aesthetic sensibility.[14] Indeed, it is interesting to note that the word 'sensibility' itself, though it had been current in the English language since the fourteenth century, only acquired its modern meaning and popularity in the eighteenth century to describe a quality of feeling and apprehension associated with the increasing 'inwardness' of experience described in the last chapter.

Despite the assumptions sometimes made by historians of ideas, we have ample evidence that even the most wide-reaching intellectual changes are never more than one of a number of factors behind the religious sensibility of a particular period. What one might call the 'climate of feeling' in any period, like all climates, is made up of many conflicting forces. Current Chaos Theory, we are told, suggests that a butterfly's wings in the Amazon can eventually create hurricanes in the Atlantic; similar minor metaphorical eddies in feeling can unleash storms of emotion elsewhere. Horace Walpole's dream in his bed at Strawberry Hill of a huge mailed arm above the gothick staircase of his little house was a trivial enough incident, but the novel it inspired, *The Castle of Otranto*, was eventually to lead to the development of the historical novel.[15] A decade earlier, the 'strange warming' of John Wesley's heart in a little chapel in Aldersgate Street, in London, was to affect the religious lives of millions over the next two and a half centuries.

At the beginning of the century, however, the narrative presented by nature seemed not to be one of inwardness so much as of indifferent cosmic law. If Newton's cosmology seemed to present an escape from the controversy and ambiguity of biblical interpretation, it was into one of mathematical order and regularity, devoid of the intervention of a personal God. Small wonder that, as we have seen, Locke was able to incorporate Newton into his vision of an essentially mechanistic universe. The religious equivalent, whether unspoken or outspoken, was Deism, the belief in an impersonal God whose principal role had been to supply the philosophical necessity of a 'First Cause' to all things.[16]

---

[14] The classic treatment of this theme is, of course, Basil Willey's prosaically entitled, but highly original book, *The Eighteenth-Century Background: Studies in the Idea of Nature in the Thought of the Period*, first published in 1940 by Chatto & Windus, but which has deservedly been repeatedly reprinted since.

[15] See Stephen Prickett, *Victorian Fantasy*, Brighton: Harvester Press/Indiana University Press, 1979, Ch. 1.

[16] One of the best accounts of Deism is in Henning Graf Reventlow's monumental study, *The Authority of the Bible and the Rise of the Modern World*, trs John Bowden, SCM Press, 1984.

Such an idea was best expressed not by a grand narrative but by a simple mechanical model. The image of the universe as a gigantic watch had been first advanced by the Anglo-Irish scientist Robert Boyle, and, as we have seen, was taken up and elaborated by Leibniz, Laplace and finally by Paley. A number of highly elaborate clockwork models of the solar system were built, with each of the seven planets rotating around the sun, while the known moons of Jupiter and the Earth, together with the rings of Saturn, rotated in turn around their respective planets. They were called 'Orrerys' after Charles Boyle, a distant relative of Robert and the Earl of Orrery, in Ireland, who in 1713 first ordered one to be made.

More satisfying, but no less impersonal, was the Pantheism of Spinoza, a philosopher of Jewish descent from Amsterdam, whose immanent 'God' was everywhere present in all things, but nowhere to be found in a personal encounter. The pantheist could feel a part of the divine substance of the universe, but he was part of a God that neither felt for nor responded to His Creation. It was a system whose multiple ironies pervaded the Romantic sensibility. Thomas McFarland has traced what he expressively calls 'the spinozistic crescendo' of the eighteenth century.[17] He retells Thomas De Quincey's anecdote of Coleridge entering his room and, on seeing a copy of Spinoza's *Ethics* lying on the table, raising it to his lips, exclaiming 'This book has ever been Gospel to me.' He then put it down again, adding 'Nevertheless, it is false.' True or not, the story dramatically encapsulates what one might call the gravitational pull felt by so many of the leading intellectual figures of the period towards Spinoza's ideas – even if they did not necessarily become permanently captured by them.

It is easy for the modern reader to feel that such debates have little relevance to the modern world, but in fact they have played a vital and central part in twentieth-century history. Traditional trinitarian Christanity had always insisted that though the world was God's creation, it was in a fallen and imperfect state. There was always a gap between the immutable perfection of God and the mutability and change of nature. Similarly, there was always a gap between human ideals and aspirations, and the morally chaotic and fallen world in which we actually found ourselves. Spinoza's was the most convincing of a number of systems that purported to close that gap. For eighteenth-century Spinozists there was, in theory, no reason why humanity was not perfectible in this world. The allure of this idea of the perfectibility of man was alternately to dazzle

[17] Thomas McFarland, *Coleridge and the Pantheist Tradition*, Oxford: Clarendon Press, 1969.

and haunt the next three centuries. In a secularized form it pervades the work of Rousseau. It was central to the ideals of the French Revolution. It was present again in many of the liberal and idealistic movements of 1848. Through Hegel and Feuerbach it was taken up by Marx as the final state of the new emergent humanity under Communism. Yet, as Ernest Gellner acutely observed, the idea was ultimately fatal to every ideology it infected. 'Given its disastrous commitment to the perfectibility of man', he once said, 'it is a perpetual astonishment to me that Soviet Communism managed to survive in power for as long as seventy years.'[18]

What Deism most obviously, and Pantheism more subtly, failed to supply, however, was a religion that satisfied the new inwardness of eighteenth-century sensibility. The success of Methodism and the associated Evangelical revival demonstrated emotional need, but did not supply any corresponding grand narrative. Evangelicalism then, as now, was primarily a religion of the heart.[19] Indeed, the inherent conflict between Wesley's Arminian belief in the possibility of salvation for all, and Whitfield's Calvinistic insistence that such salvation was only for God's 'elect', those who were already predestined for conversion, would seem to illustrate how divided in theology the movement was right from the days of the Oxford 'Holy Club' where they first met.[20] Yet, as always, labels can be misleading. Wesley records a conversation with the young Charles Simeon, a Calvinist, and later to be a leading figure in Evangelical Revival and the Clapham Sect.

'Sir', said Simeon, 'I understand that you are called an Arminian; and I have sometimes been called a Calvinist; and therefore I suppose we are to draw daggers. But before I consent to begin the combat, with your permission, I will ask a few questions, not from impertinent curiosity, but for real instruction.' Permission being very readily granted, the young minister proceeded to say, – 'Pray, Sir, do you feel yourself a depraved creature, so depraved that you would never have thought of turning to God, if God had not first put it into your heart?' 'Yes', says the veteran [i.e. Wesley], 'I do indeed.' 'And do you utterly despair of recommending yourself to God by anything that you can do; and do you look for salvation solely through the blood and righteousness of Jesus Christ.' 'Yes, solely through Christ.'

---

[18] Lecture to Higher Education Foundation Conference, St John's College, Oxford, 1991.

[19] The phrase deliberately echoes Elisabeth Jay's excellent study of Evangelical writing, *The Religion of the Heart*, Oxford: Clarendon Press, 1979.

[20] The terms 'methodist' and 'evangelical' were often used so loosely in the eighteenth century as to be interchangeable. Where possible, I have tried to use the former to describe only the followers of Wesley, and the latter term to cover other associated religious movements of the period, whether Arminian or Calvinistic.

'But, Sir, supposing you were at first saved by Christ, are you not somehow or other to save yourself afterwards by your own works?'

'No; I must be saved from first to last by Christ.'

'Allowing then that you were first turned by the grace of God, are you not in some way or other to keep yourself by your own power?'

'No.'

'What then, are you to be upheld every hour and every moment by God, as much as an infant in its mother's arms?'

'Yes, altogether.'

'And is all your hope in the grace and mercy of God to preserve you unto his heavenly kingdom?'

'Yes, I have no hope but him.'

'Then, Sir, with your leave I will put up my dagger again; for this is all my Calvinism; this is all my election, my justification by faith, my final perseverance: it is in substance all that I hold, and as I hold it: and therefore, if you please, instead of searching out terms and phrases to be a ground of contention between us, we will cordially unite in those things where we agree.'[21]

If such passages illustrate how the prevailing emotional *temper* of eighteenth-century evangelicalism was always more important than theological niceties, they also illustrate the ironic consciousness of the limitations of doctrinal labels amongst its leading figures, if not among the rank-and-file. Though charges of anti-intellectualism cannot be brought against Wesley himself, who had been a Fellow of Lincoln College, Oxford, and never lost his academic rigour, from other contemporary accounts, it certainly applied to many evanglicals. As Newman, who had himself been an evangelical when he arrived in Oxford, was later to remark, their favourite text might have been 'Not many wise, not many learned.'[22] The movement was to fare better aesthetically. In John Wesley's brother, Charles, the movement acquired one of the best poets of the century, and arguably one of the greatest in the English language.

Whether or not associated with the growing pluralism of eighteenth-century England, the massive institutional decay of the Established Church itself in the period was a matter of open comment. In the words of the *Edinburgh Review*:

The thermometer of the Church of England sank to its lowest point in the first thirty years of George III. Unbelieving bishops and a slothful clergy, had

[21] Quoted from John Wesley's *Journal* by John Williamson, *A Brief Memoir of the Rev. Charles Simeon, M.A.*, London, 1848, pp. 38–41. I am grateful to Marianne Thormählen for calling my attention to this passage.

[22] John Henry Newman, 'Learning in the Church of England' (1863), *Essays*, ed. Henry Nettleship, Oxford, 1889, Vol. II, p. 268. See also Prickett, *Romanticism and Religion*, p. 253.

succeeded in driving from the Church the faith and zeal of Methodism which Wesley had organized within her pale. The spirit was expelled and the dregs remained. That was the age when jobbery and corruption, long supreme in the State, had triumphed over the virtue of the Church; when the money-changers not only entered the temple, but drove out the worshippers; when ecclesiastical revenues were monopolized by wealthy pluralists; when the name of curate lost its legal meaning, and, instead of denoting the incumbent of a living, came to signify the deputy of an absentee.[23]

Granted that, as a Scottish Whig journal, the *Edinburgh Review* was un-likely to favour a Church sometimes described as 'the Tory party at prayer', but other, more pro-Anglican sources give a similar account. The poet George Crabbe, himself a country parson in Suffolk, gives a scathing portrait of his fellow-clergy:

> A jovial youth, who thinks his Sunday's task,
> As much as GOD or Man can fairly ask;
> The rest he gives to Loves and Labours light,
> To Fields the morning and to Feasts the night;
> None better skill'd the noisy Pack to guide,
> To urge their chace, to cheer them or to chide;
> A Sportsman keen, he shoots through half the day,
> And skill'd at Whist, devotes the nights to play;
> Then, while such honours bloom around his head,
> Shall he sit sadly by the Sick Man's bed,
> To raise the hope he feels not, or with zeal
> To combat fears that ev'n the pious feel?
>
> (*The Village* (1783) lines 306–17)

Spiritual decline was not confined to rural areas. On Easter Day 1800, the most important occasion in the Anglican year, in St Paul's Cathedral in London, the principal church of what was then the largest Christian city in the world, there were a mere six communicants. Another clergyman, Thomas Mozley, describes the early years of the nineteenth century as a time when 'thousands of livings were without parsonages, and with incomes so small as not to admit of building or even renting'. As a result, 'non-residence was almost the rule in some districts, and . . . even the pastoral duties of which all clergymen are capable and which are always welcome, were discharged intermittingly and cursorily'. 'Church fabrics fell into disorder and even decay . . . bishops and dignitaries made fortunes, and used their patronage for private purposes.'[24]

---

[23] Anon. Cited by Lady Holland, *Memoir of the Rev. Sydney Smith*, 1855, Vol. I, pp. 61–2.
[24] Thomas Mozley, *Reminiscences: Chiefly of Oriel College and the Oxford Movement*, London, 1882, Vol. I, p. 184.

Even a cursory glance around the English countryside confirms these accounts of non-residence. Over and over again a mediaeval church has beside it a nineteenth-century vicarage. The chances are that this will be the *original* one.[25] In other words, before the nineteenth century there would have been no resident parson at all – though someone living miles away might be drawing a substantial income for the post. In 1807 (the first year for which we have any figures) out of some 10,000 odd benefices, no fewer than 6,145 clergy (61 per cent, or nearly two-thirds) were non-resident. Appointments depended on who you knew rather than what you knew, and were often more political than spiritual. When Sydney Smith was finally given his first living at Foston-le-Clay in Yorkshire in 1806, he went to thank his patron, who happened to be the Lord Chancellor. 'Oh, don't thank *me*, Mr. Smith', said Erskine, 'I gave you the living because Lady Holland insisted on my doing so; and if she had desired me to give it to the devil, *he* must have had it.'[26] Smith's joy was in any case premature. Arriving at Foston he found there was nowhere at all for him to live. Under the terms of the Residence Bill of 1808, he was forced to build a parsonage entirely at his own expense: a crippling imposition for a young clergyman who had no private income.

Such problems were not peculiar to England in the eighteenth century. Similar ecclesiastical laxity was widespread throughout Europe. In Catholic France many of the same forces had been at work, though a greater institutional rigidity meant that the loss of credibility was often less immediately apparent. As in England, the narrative told by the Church bore less and less relation to the narratives of people's individual lives. The open anti-clericalism of the *philosophes* and the *encyclopédistes* was mirrored by popular apathy. With the Revolution of 1789, Church lands and privileges were confiscated and monasteries dissolved with only minor popular protest. In Germany, where, as in England, local and evangelical pietistic movements, such as the Moravians, had sprung up, institutional Lutheranism was in little better condition.

MILLENARIAN FRAGMENTS AND ORGANIC WHOLES

Perhaps the only thing the new forms of religious expression within the altered and interiorized sensibility of the late eighteenth century had in common was their fragmentary and piecemeal nature. Tory Anglican

[25] At least post-Reformation. Where there had been accommodation for the pre-Reformation priest, even if it had survived, it was likely to be totally unsuitable for married clergy with families.

[26] Hesketh Pearson, *The Smith of Smiths*, Harmondsworth: Penguin, 1948, p. 154.

clergymen might preach a unified and coherent system of Church and State based on divine right left over from the seventeenth century, and modern historians like J.C.D. Clark argue that English society remained more conservative, religious, and deferential for longer than previously assumed,[27] but the fact remains that it was a dying system. Recent controversy over the supposed 'Jacobite' sympathies behind Samuel Johnson's tour of the Hebrides have only highlighted the degree to which such a synthesis could only survive as a private fantasy rather than a credible public narrative.[28]

Indeed, credible public narratives were altogether in short supply. The eighteenth century saw a steady increase in wilder antinomian and millenarian groups. Many had been around in small numbers ever since Cromwellian times. At the end of the century we find such colourful groupings as the Ranters, the Shakers and Muggletonians. Pushing the Calvinist doctrine of Election to its logical conclusion, antinomians held that since they were totally justified by God, they could do no wrong. The moral law was altogether superseded by faith, and the elect could live in perfect liberty and love. In March 1746 John Wesley had recorded in his Journal a debate with an antinomian.

'Do you believe you have nothing to do with the law of God?'
'I have not; I am not under the law; I live by faith.'
'Have you, as living by faith, a right to everything in the world?'
'I have. All is mine since Christ is mine.'
'May you then take any thing you will, any where, (suppose out of a shop), without the consent or knowledge of the owner?'
'I may, if I want it; for it is mine; only I will not give offence.'
'Have you also a right to all the women in the world?'
'Yes, if they consent.'
'And is that not a sin?'
'Yes, to him that thinks it is a sin; but not to those whose hearts are free.'[29]

Though no antinomian group could be described as 'typical', the Muggletonians are at least among the better documented. They had been founded in Commonwealth times by William Muggleton, a tailor, and William Reeves, a cobbler, who claimed to be the two Witnesses of Revelation. They continued a millenarian tradition (going back to Joachim of Fiore[30]) that there had been three world ages. In place

---

[27] J.C.D. Clark, *English Society 1688–1832*, Cambridge University Press, 1985.
[28] For the most recent discussion of this topic see Kevin Hart, *Samuel Johnson and the Culture of Property*, Cambridge University Press, 1999.
[29] Cited by Jack Lindsay, *William Blake*, Constable, 1978, p. 278.
[30] See Warwick Gould and Marjorie Reeves, *Joachim of Fiore and the Myth of the Eternal Evangel in the Nineteenth Century*, Oxford: Clarendon Press, 1987.

of Joachim's Ages of the Father, the Son and the Holy Spirit, however, were those of Moses, Jesus and Muggleton – representing water, blood and spirit, respectively. William Hurd, in his magnificently named *New Universal History of the Religions, Rites, Ceremonies, and Customs of the Whole World* (1811), tells us that:

> Their followers of the present age, still retain that notion [that the Witnesses will return]; and they believe that these two apostles, or witnesses, will meet them when they are assembled together. They meet in the evenings of Sundays, at obscure public houses in London, and converse about those of their sect who have gone before them. They have very little serious discourse, but are extremely free, sometimes going home drunk . . . There must be still a considerable number of these people in different parts of England; for only a few years ago a new edition in three volumes quarto was printed, of the rhapsodies of Muggleton Reeves, and had there not been people to purchase them they would not have been printed.[31]

As might be expected, the French Revolution gave a new impetus to such movements, and the late eighteenth and early nineteenth centuries saw a rash of new millenarian sects. By far the two largest were those of Richard Brothers (1757–1824) and Joanna Southcott (1750–1830). Brothers was a half-pay naval officer – i.e. without a ship. In 1792 he began to prophesy against the impending war with France, claiming that it was the one 'alluded to by St John, in the nineteenth chapter of Revelation, which God called a war against himself'. He proceeded to petition King George, William Pitt, the prime minister, and other members of the government. In 1794 he published *A Revealed Knowledge of the Prophecies and Times*, in which he predicted the conquest of Britain and the loss of the Empire. This, from an officer of the Crown, was going too far for a government already alarmed by fears of revolutionary movements at home, and in March 1795 he was arrested. Under the circumstances he was treated with remarkable leniency. He was declared insane and incarcerated in a lunatic asylum in Islington for the next eleven years. He was, however, still permitted to receive visits both from his followers and from revolutionary sympathizers, and was allowed to continue with his publications, which included a very detailed *Description of* [the New] *Jerusalem* (1801).

Joanna Southcott was a Devonshire farmer's daughter who had once been a Methodist. In 1792, however, she announced to the world that she had supernatural gifts, and began writing and dictating verse prophecies. A delegation of Brothers' followers came to see her in Exeter,

---

[31] Quoted in Lindsay, *Blake*, pp. 48–9.

and were won over. She was, she claimed, the woman referred to in Revelation 12:1 'clothed with the sun, with the moon under her feet, and on her head a crown of twelve stars' who, in one of the most apocalyptic passages of the Bible, was destined to bring forth a man-child who would 'rule all the nations with a rod of iron' (Revelation 12:5). In the early 1800s she came to London and began to 'seal' those who wished to secure a place among the 144,000 elect. Whether or not she had the 100,000 followers claimed for her, they were certainly spread over a wide range of society, including half-a-dozen Anglican clergy, several army officers, and an engraver, William Sharp, who was an acquaintance of William Blake.

In 1814, when she was over sixty, Southcott announced that she would be delivered of Shiloh – the miraculous son somewhat obscurely predicted by the dying Jacob in Genesis 49:10, and linked by her to the man-child of Revelation. She was examined by various doctors, some of whom declared she was indeed pregnant. When, in November 1814, Shiloh failed to appear, it was given out that she was in a trance, but in fact she was already seriously ill. She died on December 27. During her life she published sixty-five works, mostly in doggerel. Her most famous bequest, however, was her 'box'. This enormous and mysterious object apparently contained her writings and other things, and was said to weigh 165 lb. It was kept locked and preserved by her followers, who were under instructions that it was to be opened at a time of national crisis in the assembled presence of all the bishops of the realm.

These sects were only the most visible tip of a widespread but submerged popular millenarian culture in late eighteenth-century England.[32] If the actual beliefs of such movements placed them light-years away from main-stream Anglicanism, in structural terms they had one important factor in common. All represented attempts to reconstruct from a fragment a totalizing grand narrative of some kind. The Book of Revelation provided a favourite source.[33] Such apocalyptic narratives permitted neither differences of interpretation, nor ironies of understanding. Paradoxically, all were in fact 'religions', in the new sense of the word, self-confessed sects, in that they defined their constituency in terms of exclusion. Some group or other, whether Catholics, nonconformists, the un-righteous or un-elect, were by definition ineligible for membership. All, including even those who claimed to represent the historic

---

[32] See J.F.C. Harrison, *The Second Coming: Popular Millenarianism 1780–1850*, Routledge, 1979.
[33] See Christopher Burdon, *The Apocalypse in England: Revelation Unravelling, 1700–1834*, Macmillan, 1997.

and pre-Reformation Anglican tradition, now defined themselves not so much as custodians of an all-embracing truth but in relation to other religious movements, other systems, with whom they were in conflict.

Oddly enough, almost the sole exception to this was a body whose origins seemed to most people to be identical with other seventeenth-century millenarian sects: the 'Society of Friends'. Even the name by which they were normally know, the 'Quakers', seemed to place them with the Ranters and the Shakers, and there was little in the verbal violence of George Fox's and John Woolman's orations to suggest otherwise. Yet by the late eighteenth century their continuing membership had achieved a level of education and prosperity that marked them out as being superior to most other nonconformists and many Anglicans. Great Quaker families, the Frys, the Rowntrees and the Cadburys dominated the relatively new chocolate trade; the Barclays were big in banking and brewing. With such striking innovations as equal education for their women (Ackworth, in Yorkshire, was the first co-educational boarding school in the world) and new forms of treatment for the mentally ill (The Retreat, in York), the Quakers by the end of the eighteenth century were pioneering a new total vision of society. Only the Unitarians came close to them in educating women.

What was theologically interesting about the Quakers, however, was their total *absence* of theology in the normal sense. Their one and only 'doctrine', if it may be so called, was that of the 'inner light': that we have within us our own source of spiritual guidance and enlightenment which must take primacy over any externally imposed system of belief or morality. While outsiders have been quick to see in this obvious dangers of self-deceit and corruption, something in the Quaker way has enabled the sect to continue and even thrive over the succeeding years in a way few other mystically inclined groups have done, while adapting without undue pain to later intellectual developments. At the same time, they have never been numerous or had any significant appeal outside middle-class intellectual circles: present estimates of British membership are around the twenty thousand figure. Nevertheless, in the eighteenth century their stress on the inwardness of religious experience, combined with their refusal to attempt to construct any kind of external grand narrative at all, placed them in a unique position in the spectrum of religious belief.

While avoiding the obvious dangers of adherence to a fixed world-picture in a society of rapid change, the Quakers in effect gave instead complete centrality to the internal narrative. They were not, of course, the first to see their lives in such a way, but by completely discarding the conventional contemporary structure of external defining narratives, they gave a new kind of stress to their internal life. Because such a narrative by definition embraced their whole lives, describing every part of their existence, Christianity could be thus re-constituted *within them* as the ultimate grand narrative. Even if it could not explain every external thing in the way that the mediaeval world-picture had done, it could *contain* and acknowledge ironies and uncertainties, even the kind of unconscious drives and contradictions later claimed by Freud or Jung. Nor could it be fazed by new discoveries in science or biblical criticism. In that sense, at least, it was consonant with the new philosophy being developed by Kant and his idealist successors in Germany, as well as with the new ideals of sentiment and subjectivity growing in England and France. Above all, it was essentially pluralistic.

Significantly the greatest nineteenth-century attempt at reconstructing a universal Christian narrative, Frederick Denison Maurice's *The Kingdom of Christ* (1838), was sub-titled 'Hints to a Quaker Respecting the Principles, Constitution, and Ordinances of the Catholic Church', and (in its first edition) was arranged as a series of letters to a Quaker. It was a remarkable book by any standards – threatening an apotheosis of the Church of England so radical that (to invert Arnold's aphorism) Anglicans have ever since neither been able to live with it, nor live without it.[34] Yet Maurice was not even brought up in the Church of England. He had been born and raised a Unitarian. For a time in adolescence he had been strongly influenced by his mother's growing Calvinism.[35] Though both Unitarianism and Calvinism were passing phases, later transcended, there is a sense in which the two positions remained as lifelong poles in his thought. The former, with its denial of the divinity of Jesus, and a strong scientific tradition among its members, was closer to Deism in its general tenor than traditional Anglicanism. The Book of Nature was as important as biblical Revelation. Calvinism, on the other hand, was fiercely anti-naturalistic, sceptical as to both human judgement and knowledge, and stressing the inscrutability of God's ways. Thus *The Kingdom of Christ* combines an extreme theological liberalism and openness (following Coleridge's principle that people are more usually right in what they affirm than in what they deny) with an exalted view of the Church as the means of personal salvation.

For Maurice the Church is a 'universal spiritual society'. The two qualities are co-dependent. Ironically, it can *only* be universal if it is spiritual. No other kind of society could embrace everyone. But it could

---

[34] For a fuller account see Prickett, *Romanticism and Religion*, Ch. 5.
[35] *The Life of F.D. Maurice*, ed. Frederick Maurice, 4th edn, Macmillan, 1885, Vol. I, pp. 28–31.

only be spiritual if it were universal. For him openness is at the heart of the New Testament; exclusiveness is incompatible with spirituality. If at present these conditions were potential rather than actual, that is because his universal spiritual society was in a state of slow evolution. Its 'truth' has been 'working itself out into clearness for many centuries' through a 'strange and painful process'.[36] Indeed, Christianity is not a system possessing a set of clear-cut ideas at all. It would be 'hard to establish in a court of law the identity of the dogmas of the New Testament with those which prevailed in Scotland and Germany during the eighteenth century'.[37] It follows that a 'gathered church' of like-minded believers is a contradiction in terms. The model for the Church is not a group who agree, but a family – whose members are bound by deeper ties than verbal formulae. The Patriarchs of Genesis were first and foremost *relatives*. The story of Jacob, argued Maurice, bears witness to the fact that God's people were selected by family relationship and not choice.[38] The vigour of this unique society actually depends on the necessary tensions within it. Just as at a linguistic level the Bible is charged with a metaphorical tension by which the concepts of family and fatherhood acquire a new meaning from the use to which they are put, so the perpetual tension between the Church as an outward physical organization and an inner spiritual society re-shapes our ideas both of what it means to be an organization and also a spiritual society. Maurice's chosen title illustrates this tension. The 'kingship' and 'fatherhood' of God are inescapable poles of Christian experience. The 'kingdom' of Christ *is* a 'family'. 'The deepest writings of the New Testament, instead of being digests of doctrine, are epistles, explaining to those who had been admitted into the Church of Christ their own position.[39]

Though in retrospect it might seem that Maurice's vision of the Church represents the only viable attempt to create anything approaching a Christian grand narrative for the post-Kantian era, he would have been horrified by the notion. For him an all-embracing narrative – in his terms, a 'system' – was fatal to the pursuit of truth.

When once a man begins to build a system, the very gifts and qualities which might serve in the investigation of truth, become the greatest hindrances to it. He must make the different parts of the scheme fit into each other; his dexterity is shown not in detecting facts but in cutting them square.[40]

---

[36] F.D. Maurice, *The Kingdom of Christ*, 4th edn, Macmillan, 1891, Vol. II, p. 75.

[37] Ibid. Vol. I, p. 159.   [38] Ibid. Vol. I, p. 275.   [39] Ibid. Vol. I, p. 296.

[40] F.D. Maurice, *Lectures in Ecclesiastical History of the First and Second Centuries*, Macmillan, 1854, p. 222. Cited by Alec Vidler, *F.D. Maurice and Company*, SCM Press, 1966, p. 22.

A 'system', together with its outward political and ecclesiastical expression, a 'party', was for him a mental and spiritual straitjacket, permitting only pre-determined gestures towards pre-defined goals. It is the vehicle of the second-hand, holding at bay possibilities of change. It is the enemy of creativity. In contrast, following Coleridge, what he called 'method' was the pre-condition of all first-hand experience. Without it, impressions and intuitions were alike random and disorganized. 'To me', he wrote, 'these words seem not only not synonymous, but the greatest contraries imaginable: the one indicating that which is most opposed to life, freedom, variety; and the other that without which they cannot exist.'[41] The Bible afforded the perfect example of the contrast. The systematizer 'is tormented every page he reads with a sense of the refractory and hopeless materials he has to deal with', whereas the disinterested reader who does not approach it with pre-conceptions finds a unity and meaning in the very diversity of its contents. It is 'organic', providing a 'principle of progression' by which we move from the known to the unknown, and without which the infinite possibilities of the new remain unexplored because they are inaccessible.

Maurice's narrative of family development draws on many sources – Augustine, Quakerism, Coleridge and Hare (and through them the ideas of Kant and German idealism), as well as many older traditional biblical and Christian ideas. It combined the new inwardness of Quakerism with a radical re-interpretation of the traditional idea of the Church. Yet the synthesis was all his own. Though his ideas were sufficiently unorthodox to earn him genuine persecution – in 1853 he was expelled from his Chair at Queen's College, London, for his views on eternal punishment – his notion of Christianity as an organic evolving narrative, capable of living with ironies and absorbing new truths from any quarter, had sufficiently permeated the climate of thought by mid-century for many liberal Anglicans to be quite undisturbed by Darwin's *Origin of Species* when it was published in 1859.

THE AESTHETICS OF IRONY: KEBLE AND ROSSETTI

Between 1830 and 1850 a huge sea-change in aesthetic and religious sensibility swept right across Northern Europe. Some six years after Maurice's *The Kingdom of Christ*, at almost the same time as Kierkegaard was defending his thesis on irony in Copenhagen, the best-selling English poet of the century was at work on a theoretical aesthetic no less personal

---

[41] *Kingdom of Christ*, Vol. I, pp. 272–3.

and no less dependent on irony than the Dane's. John Keble was elected to the Oxford Professorship of Poetry in 1832, a post which he held until 1841. Though he had previously been a fellow of Oriel College, he was by this time a rural clergyman at Hursley, near Winchester. What had established his poetic reputation, however, was a volume of poems, *The Christian Year*, published in 1827. It had been an instant success, and over the next fifty years was to sell an average of 10,000 volumes a year – a figure only distantly challenged by that of Tennyson's *In Memoriam* (1850) and far greater than that ever achieved by the then Poet Laureate, William Wordsworth.

The Oxford Professorship is unusual in that it is not a regular academic post, and during its long history it has normally (but not always) been held by a practising poet – Robert Lowth had been one of the first holders in the 1740s. The main requirement on the incumbent is to give a series of lectures. These were traditionally given in Latin. Matthew Arnold, Professor from 1857–67, was the first to give them in English, and so gain access to a more popular audience. Keble's lectures, which were published in 1844, under the title *De Poeticae vi Medica*, were to remain virtually unknown outside Oxford until they were belatedly translated into English in 1912.

As might be expected, Keble's aesthetics start from a Romantic sense of the wholeness of the self, and constitute the most complete exposition ever devised of Wordsworth's idea of poetry as the spontaneous overflow of powerful feelings. But whereas for Wordsworth that image seems to be one of a spring of water gushing uncontrollably from the ground, for Keble, writing in the first years of the railway boom, when boiler explosions were not uncommon, the phrase seems to have suggested irresistibly something closer to the safety-valve of a steam engine – much in the way that Freud's notion of 'repression' was to do a generation later. 'My notion', Keble wrote to his friend J.T. Coleridge in 1832, 'is to consider poetry as a vent for overcharged feelings, or a full imagination, and so account for the various classes into which poets naturally fall, by reference to the various objects which are apt to fill and overpower the mind, so as to require a sort of relief.'[42]

Poetry, for Keble, was the product of tension or repression, issuing in disguised or ironic utterance. Someone who, under emotional stress, can find easy expression for their feelings is, by definition, no poet.[43] As early as 1828 he argued in a review of Lockhart's *Life of Scott*, that 'Poetry is

---

[42] J.T. Coleridge, *Memoir of the Rev. John Keble* (1869), p. 199.
[43] Keble's *Lectures on Poetry*, trs E. K. Francis, Oxford University Press, 1912, Vol. I, p. 36.

the indirect expression in words, most appropriately in metrical words, of some overpowering emotion, or ruling taste, or feeling, the direct indulgence whereof is somehow repressed.'[44] Repression or reserve – tension between what is felt and what finally finds expression – is at the creative heart of 'the poetic' – a quality, incidentally, not peculiar to poetry. All art forms, including not merely literature, but music, sculpture, painting and even architecture had, according to Keble, a 'poetical' (and therefore ironic) element in them. 'What is called the poetry of painting', he says, 'simply consists in the apt expression of the artist's own feeling' – feeling, of course, expressed under tension.[45] Such a radical re-shaping of genres would make meaningless the traditional categories that had dominated criticism ever since Aristotle. In this new 'expressionistic' framework 'there will be as many kinds of poems as there are emotions of the human mind'.[46]

For Keble there were two main classes of poets: Primary and Secondary. The Primary are 'those who, spontaneously moved by impulse, resort to composition for relief and solace of a burdened or over-wrought mind'; the Secondary, 'those who, for one reason or another, imitate the ideas, the expression, and the measures of the former'.[47] His list of Primary poets was strictly classical, ending properly with Virgil – though Dante seems to have been added as an afterthought.[48] Keble seems to have had problems with his favourite moderns. Wordsworth, despite having had the published lectures specifically dedicated to him, remains tactfully unlisted by category. As a poet, he obviously belonged to the Primary, but, as a man, he suffered from the grave disadvantage of being neither an ancient Greek, nor a Roman. Though Keble toyed with the idea of substituting 'modern examples for the Greek and Latin', mentioning Byron and Shelley as those 'mentally affected' by the intolerable tensions of their art, he never included them in the text of the *Lectures*.[49]

Keble's theory takes to its logical conclusion Wordsworth's sleight-of-hand in the Preface to the *Lyrical Ballads*, whereby the definition of a poem is framed in terms of its author's characteristics ('what is a poem? . . . a poet is . . .'). Keble now classified poetry by the emotions of the writer, who sought his own relief and health by disguised utterance. In other words, irony, the language of disguise, is also necessarily the key to mental health and stability. Poetry is, *par excellence*, the healing art. For

---

[44] Review of *Life of Scott* (1838) in *Occasional Papers and Reviews*, Oxford University Press, 1877, p. 6.
[45] Keble, *Lectures*, Vol. I, p. 38.   [46] Ibid. I, p. 88.   [47] Ibid. I, pp. 53–4.
[48] Ibid. II, p. 471.
[49] Letter to J.T. Coleridge, July 5, 1844. Coleridge, *Memoir*, p. 205.

the American critic, M.H. Abrams, writing on Keble in the mid-years of the twentieth century, this constituted nothing less than a 'radical, proto-Freudian theory, which conceives literature as disguised wish-fulfilment, serving the artist as a way back from incipient neurosis'.[50] How radical we can see from Keble's definition of poetry itself. 'Each several one of the so-called liberal arts,' he declares, 'contains a certain poetic quality of its own, and . . . this lies in its power to heal and relieve the human mind when agitated by care, passion, or ambition.'[51] This is such a bold and unexpected inversion of standard Romantic aesthetics that it is easy to miss what Keble is actually saying here. He does *not* believe that one of the powers of 'the poetic' is that it can heal or give relief to the person under strain, he believes that we must *define* 'the poetic' by this healing power. *Ibi ars medica, ubi poesis.* (Where there is healing, there is the poetic.)

As with Kierkegaard and the German Romantics, the roots of this idea go back to Greek literature – though in this case not to Greek philosophy, but to drama. Keble's idea of irony clearly owes more to the Aristotelian notion of *catharsis*, whereby tension is first built up and then released in tragedy through the emotions of pity and terror, than it does to the Socratic irony of Plato. Thus 'the poetic' involves an inherently unresolved tension between private emotion and the restraints of public expression which finally finds utterance in some veiled ironic form whose release brings with it a healing and soothing effect on both poet and reader. For Keble, unlike the German Romantic tradition, such poetic irony is entirely positive. Indeed, the word he uses for it is 'soothing'. In his 1827 Advertisement to *The Christian Year* he draws attention to the poems on the Occasional Services of the Prayer Book, which, he tells us, 'constitute, from their personal and domestic nature, the most perfect instance of that *soothing* tendency in the Prayer Book, which it is the chief purpose of these pages to exhibit'. The title of the poem for the Fourth Sunday after Epiphany gives us the full strength of this word for Keble – and presumably also for his readers. It is entitled, *The World is for Excitement, the Gospel for Soothing*. Though Keble was not immune to the search for an infantile dream-world that attracted so many Victorian writers in different guises, it is clear that the word for him also carries still much of its older meanings: 'to prove or show to be true; to assert or uphold a truth'; or 'to give support', 'encourage', or 'confirm' – by which it reaches its weaker modern sense of 'to calm' or even 'tranquillize'. The

---

[50] M.H. Abrams, *The Mirror and the Lamp*, N.Y.: Oxford University Press, 1953; reprinted N.Y.: Norton, 1958, p. 145.
[51] *Lectures*, Vol. I, p. 53.

reader's mind is finally healed and set at rest not in any mere anodyne sense: the hidden symbolic forms of poetry are 'asserting and upholding the truth'. The Prayer Book and the Gospels are essentially 'poetic' because they compellingly assert the truth. Once again, Keble's thought is grandly holistic. 'Health' is not merely a matter of a sound body, but of a well-adjusted psyche, and, finally, of right beliefs.

For Keble, the ultimate example of 'poetry' in this new 'medical' sense of his, is the Church itself. The Christian's experience of God reveals to him the poetic nature of the whole universe, in which he lives, and moves, and has his being. Poetry (such as that of the *Christian Year*) makes us all aware of the potentially sacramental nature of human experience. The Primary poets, therefore, were analogous to the founders of the Church, the prophets, apostles and early Fathers who had shaped our religious sensibilities through the Christian tradition. Like the fathers, they bring soothing and catharsis out of the intolerable tensions of our lives. The Secondary poets are, as it were, the army of saints and ecclesiastics who have kept pure the tradition of the Church, cleansing and reforming it afresh to every age and society. If, in one sense, such a structure seems no more than a dim, and even forced, analogy, Keble seems constantly to be suggesting that, like his system of natural correspondences, it is *more* than an analogy: the apostles, Fathers and saints are the true platonic types of the poets, making the unseen world visible to the faithful.

There are two aspects of Keble's argument that strike one as immediately puzzling here. The first, of course, is how this view of the Church as 'poetic' can be squared with the idea that poetry depends on inference, tension and ironic utterance. Are the prophets, apostles and saints *all* ironists then, whose words must be construed as veiled and indirect? The quick answer surely seems to be yes. That is precisely what he *does* mean. Keble has seen, as very few of his more literal-minded Victorian contemporaries did, how much of the Old and New Testaments are openly ironic – one thinks of famous passages in Hosea or Isaiah, with Israel as the whore, or dry bones in the desert. Many – perhaps the majority – of Jesus' parables and sayings recorded in the Gospels are ironic in the most obvious sense, and the disciples are recorded as being frequently baffled by them. Though it seems unlikely that he knew much of the German Romantics directly,[52] Keble could hardly *not* have known *Guesses at Truth*

---

[52] There is no evidence that Keble knew German, and (unlike Cambridge at the same period) German was scarcely known in Oxford when he was there. We recall David Newsome's anecdote (p. 118 above) concerning Keble's friend, E.B. Pusey, who, when he wanted to find out about

by Augustus and Julius Hare (published in 1827, and greatly enlarged in its second edition of 1838) from which we quoted earlier, and which sets out many of the central ideas of German Romanticism. One of the leading themes of that book is the long historical process of individuation and the corresponding growth of self-consciousness, which Julius Hare believed to be a specifically Christian achievement.[53]

No less puzzling, however, is how little this idea that Christianity is poetic, reserved, tensional and ironic spills over into Keble's own poetry, which is, for the most part, content to be completely explicit, even when expounding apparently esoteric doctrines. One of the better-known poems of the *Christian Year* (frequently used as a hymn), 'Septuagesima Sunday', certainly claims a hidden significance for the natural and visible world, but whether or not the reader is familiar with its Wordsworthian reference,[54] it could hardly be claimed as the 'indirect expression in . . . metrical words, of some overpowering emotion, or ruling taste, or feeling, the direct indulgence whereof is somehow repressed'.

> There is a book, who runs may read,
>   Which heavenly truth imparts,
> And all the lore its scholars need,
>   Pure eyes and Christian hearts.
>
> The works of God above, below,
>   Within us and around,
> Are pages in that book, to show
>   How God Himself is found.
>
> The glorious sky embracing all
>   Is like the Maker's love,
> Wherewith encompass'd, great and small
>   In peace and order move.

What he means by this was spelled out in *Tract Eighty Nine,* where he goes into great detail over the mystical significance of the visible universe. The

---

new developments in German theology, discovered only two people in the whole university who could read any German (Newsome, *Parting of Friends*, p. 78).

53 See Prickett, *Origins of Narrative*, pp. 104–14.

54 The obvious reference is to the pair of poems in the *Lyrical Ballads*, 'Expostulation & Reply' and 'The Tables Turned', especially the sixth stanza of the latter:

> One Impulse from a vernal wood
> May teach you more of man;
> Of moral evil and of good,
> Than all the sages can.

This, in turn, of course has echoes of Pope's *Essay on Man*, I, vii, 207–16.

sky, he tells us, represents 'a canopy spread over the tents and dwellings of the saints'; birds are tokens of 'Powers in heaven above who watch our proceedings in this lower world'; and waters flowing into the sea are 'people gathered into the Church of Christ'. The smell of flowers is the 'odour of sanctity'; trees and weeds are 'false principles'; the tamarisk, 'the double mind'; the palm, 'eternal purity'. 'The Sun, the greater light, is our Lord; the Moon, the lesser light, the Church.' 'He appointed the moon for certain seasons, and the Sun knoweth his going down' – or, as he puts it in 'Septuagesima Sunday':

> The Moon above, the Church below,
>   A wonderous race they run,
> But all their radiance, all their glow,
>   Each borrows of its Sun.
>
>   . . .
>
> Two worlds are ours: 'tis only Sin
>   Forbids us to descry
> The mystic heaven and earth within,
>   Plain as the sea and sky.

Despite the emphasis on the 'mystic' nature of this world 'within', the modern reader is left not with a sense of ironic reserve, but with an almost mechanical explicitness.

But if it is true that Keble's poetry fails to live up to his own (very Kierkegaardian) theory of irony, he would not be the first poet whose work fails to reflect his own poetic theory. What Keble's poetry *does* have is a strong sense of the inexhaustible significance of human perception. For him this takes the form of a multi-level universe. Everything in the visible world seems to stand for some other, unseen, quality. Normally we would classify this as allegory rather than irony, but the two categories may not be as clearly separable as we might think. Take for example a poem by another nineteenth-century poet heavily influenced by Tractarian doctrine, Christina Rossetti:

> Does the road wind uphill all the way?
>   Yes, to the very end.
> Will the day's journey take the whole long day?
> From morn to night, my friend.
>
> But is there for the night a resting place?
>   A roof for when the slow dark hours begin.

> May not the darkness hide it from my face?
>> You cannot miss that inn.
>
> Shall I meet other wayfarers at night?
>> Those who have gone before.
> Then must I knock, or call when just in sight?
>> They will not keep you standing at that door.
>
> Shall I find comfort, travel-sore and weak?
>> Of labour you shall find the sum.
> Will there be beds for me and all who seek?
>> Yea, beds for all who come.

'Uphill' is technically one of the most extraordinary poems in the English language, in that it supplies a single, totally coherent dialogue, without the usual shifts of metaphor to suggest an allegory or hidden meaning. Yet almost every reader immediately recognizes a second level of meaning. But simply to categorize the poem as an allegory does it an injustice. 'Is it fair', asks Owen Barfield, 'to say that Christina Rossetti says B but that she *really means* A? I do not think that this is a question which can be answered with a simple "yes" or "no". In fact the difficult and elusive relation between A and B is the heart of the matter.'[55] The metonymy of life as a journey and death as an inn is surely not a simple case of replacing one (explicit) term by another that is implied, but never articulated. 'Life' and 'death', however concrete in individual experience, are abstractions. We cannot envision either without recourse to *some* kind of metonymy, *some* kind of symbol. The test is simply to invite the reader to paraphrase the poem replacing B by A at every point, putting the corresponding literal statement in place of each symbol.

In a curious way, it is the very absence of explanation of A in the text of B that is so effective. G.K. Chesterton's reference to 'the decent inn of death' is clearly a conscious echo of Rossetti's 'You cannot miss that inn', but not merely does it seem somehow arch and contrived by comparison, it actually misses the point of the Rossetti line. To spell it out, even as metaphorical vehicle and tenor, diminishes its force. Barfield again:

We feel that B, which is actually said, ought to be necessary, even inevitable in some way. It ought to be in some sense the best, if not the only way of expressing A satisfactorily. The mind should dwell on it as well as on A and thus the two should be somehow inevitably fused together into one simple meaning. But if

---

55 Owen Barfield, 'Poetic Diction and Legal Fiction', in Max Black (ed.), *The Importance of Language*, Eaglewood Cliffs, N.J.: Prentice-Hall, 1962, p. 53.

A is too obvious and could be equally or almost as well expressed by other and more direct means, then the mind jumps straight to A, remains focused on it, and loses interest in B, which shrinks to a kind of dry and hollow husk.[56]

Where I differ from Barfield is in my feeling that in Rossetti's poem the two layers *do* fuse; that the surface narrative is both transparent enough to allow the reader to see the underlying meaning, while being at the same time opaque enough to make us see that underlying meaning differently. If the idea of life as a journey reaches back (at least) to the Old Testament, the image of death as an inn represents a neat inversion of the New. The birth of Christ, born in a stable because there was no room in the inn, now means that there is room for all in *this* inn.

This may, in the most formal sense, be allegory, but *rhetorically* it is surely irony. The force of the poem depends almost exclusively on what is *not* said. Not merely does the reader recognize that the poem is about the journey of life, and its conclusion in death, but he or she rapidly finds that any attempt to re-phrase it, to remove the allegory and make it a literal statement does not work. The association of room at the inn with Christ's Nativity similarly demands unspoken recognition. This is Kierkegaard's 'paper money', backed not so much by a gold-standard as by (the ultimate) self-supporting fiduciary system.

If all this seems somehow familiar, it should be. The visible and mundane are charged with an underlying meaning, at once invisible to the eye, but plain for all to see. It is, in effect, what the 'doctrine of reserve' is all about. Promulgated by Richard Hurrell Froude as a principle of religious devotion, elevated by Keble into an aesthetic theory, it is turned into living art by the studied understatement of Christina Rossetti, who allows neither the disappointments and tensions of her personal life, nor any sense of authorial detachment and superiority, to intrude.

In the process, however, something very like a new theory of language has begun to take shape. It is not so much that expression has significantly changed – as we have seen in the case of Keble's own verse, it is hard to see much change at all. It is rather that people have begun to read the grand narrative of Christianity – and, by extension, other grand narratives, including that of science – in a new kind of way. It is this 'aesthetic turn' that will be the subject of our next chapter.

[56] Ibid. p. 54.

CHAPTER 5

The ache in the missing limb: Language, truth and presence

COLERIDGE: THE LANGUAGE OF THE BIBLE

If, as previous chapters may suggest, it is possible to use the Kuhnian notion of paradigms as operating not merely in scientific discourse, but in areas like religion as well, we may suspect that such paradigms are also closely associated with theories of language. Richard Rorty has ingeniously suggested that the history of philosophy may best be understood as a series of 'turns' in which 'a new set of problems emerges and the old ones begin to fade away'. The latest of these, he argues, is the 'linguistic turn':

The picture of ancient and mediaeval philosophy as concerned with *things*, the philosophy of the seventeenth through the nineteenth century as concerned with *ideas*, and the enlightened contemporary philosophical scene with *words* has considerable plausibility.[1]

In view of what we have seen in previous chapters, the idea that we live in a period where we tend to see both things and ideas primarily in terms of words is obviously persuasive – though, as we shall see in the next chapter, not necessarily persuasive in the way that Rorty believes it to be. Indeed, it is difficult to see how any theory of narrative structure can stand independently from how we think language arose and how it functions in our present understanding of the world.

The prime example of this can be seen if we try asking the question why this interest in words only really arises in the eighteenth century. The answer seems to lie in the fact that until the breakdown of biblical literalism, the origins and nature of language had seemed to be fully explained by divine revelation. As the German philosopher Hans Georg Gadamer has observed, 'it was precisely the religious tradition of the Christian West that hindered serious thought about language, so that

---

[1] Richard Rorty, *Philosophy and the Mirror of Nature*, Princeton University Press, 1979, p. 263.

the question of the origin of language could be posed in a new way only at the time of the Enlightenment'.[2] We have already seen how Boehme in the seventeenth century, and even Herder, as late as the second half of the eighteenth, could take the biblical story of Adam naming the beasts as a satisfactory historical account of the origin of language.[3] That this might also prevent any discussion of the human and historical origins of language was clearly not something that could easily be perceived until a much larger body of secular writings, from both the modern and ancient worlds, had become easily available through printing. As is clear from the first serious modern attempts by Vico, Herder, von Humboldt and others,[4] even eighteenth-century attempts to think about the origins of language were still swayed by the massive pull of these traditional religious assumptions.

At the same time, as we have seen, secular and biblical narratives were being read in much the same way. It is often difficult for the early twenty-first-century reader, thoroughly secularized and acclimatized to the modern academic division between literary and biblical studies, to recapture the mental set in which they could not yet be experienced as requiring separate ways of thinking.[5] In England for instance, Coleridge sits uneasily at a key point in the historical separation of what we now think of as two separate academic disciplines, and is remembered as both a literary critic *and* a theologian. Yet such a dual classification, often involving a division of his works into 'literary' and 'theological', has the effect of distorting both. Take, for instance, this fragment from his *Table Talk* for June 24, 1827:

Our version of the Bible is to be loved and prized for this, as for a thousand other things, – that it has preserved a purity of meaning to many terms of natural objects. Without this holdfast, our vitiated imaginations would refine away language to mere abstractions. Hence the French have lost their poetical language; and Mr Blanco White says the same thing has happened to the Spanish.[6]

---

[2] Hans Georg Gadamer, 'Man and Language' (1966), *Philosophical Hermeneutics*, trs and ed. by David E. Linge, University of California Press, 1976, p. 60.

[3] See above, Ch. 1, pp. 46–50.

[4] See Giambattista Vico, *The New Science* (1744); Johann Gottfried Herder, 'Essay on the Origin of Language' (1772); Wilhelm von Humboldt, *On Language* (1836); and Hans Aarsleff, *From Locke to Saussure*.

[5] I am leaving out of account here that other version of postmodern theology, 'radical orthodoxy', associated with the names of Catherine Pickstock and John Milbank, for whom postmodernism is a return to the premodern. See John Milbank, *The Word Made Strange: Theology, Language, Culture*, Oxford: Blackwell, 1997; and John Milbank, Catherine Pickstock, and Graham Ward, *Radical Orthodoxy: A New Theology*, Routledge, 1999.

[6] *Table Talk*, ed. H.N. Coleridge, 1852, p. 43. The publication of Carl Woodring's admirable edition of *Table Talk* in the Bollingen Series in 1990 reveals that this has been written up from briefer notes,

It would be easy to assume at first sight that this mysterious and apparently isolated generalization was yet another expression of the common anti-Gallic prejudice that, in the wake of the French Revolution and the Napoleonic Wars, was characteristic of much popular English middle-class sentiment. In many eyes, including often his own, Coleridge's early political radicalism had been synonymous with enthusiasm for the French Revolutionary cause, and, after this had been abandoned in the mid-1790s, ritual denunciation of all things French also served as a convenient tactical shorthand for re-affirming his political correctness in other areas. Nevertheless, the comment is a genuinely elliptical and even puzzling one. In three comparatively short sentences it brings together three of Coleridge's principal lifelong intellectual concerns: the Bible – and the implications of its various translations; the relationship of words to things; and that between language and poetry.

To begin with the first of those concerns: from his unpublished notebooks we are now in a position to know what few of his acquaintances were then aware of, that the year 1827 had seen an intensification of his interest in the Bible, and particularly in the implications of current German biblical criticism. Coleridge was an almost exact contemporary of Schleiermacher. Though we cannot be certain when he first encountered Schleiermacher's work, we do know from his notebooks and letters that he had been making an intensive study of the *Speeches on Religion* in the early months of 1826.[7] Moreover, it seems very likely that his notebooks dating from 1828–30 (Nos. 37–41) were actually intended as notes towards a projected volume of biblical criticism.[8] Questions of biblical translation are a recurring preoccupation in these jottings. On March 29, 1828, for instance, he speculates on the need for a new English translation of the Bible, but, if we are to believe an undated memorandum from sometime earlier that month, this would be very far from a matter of modernizing the archaisms of the Authorized Version:

In a new translation of the Old Testament not only no word to be used of later date than Elizabeth's Reign; but from the character and genius of the Hebrew it would be most expedient to revive a number of pure Saxon words, make this proviso that they are such as explain themselves. (*Notebook* 37, f. 47)

but with substantially the same sentiments (I, 75). The coda about Blanco White and Spanish is missing. For the purposes of this discussion, I shall assume that it is nonetheless authentic, but spoken at another time and added into the text by the process of conflation and consolidation described in the Editor's Introduction (pp. lxxxiv–xci).

7 *Notebooks*, ed. Kathleen Coburn and Merton Christensen, Routledge, 1990, 5319.

8 The published Notebooks, under the general editorship of Kathleen Coburn, have now reached 1826. For a detailed discussion of the implications of the later notebooks, see Prickett, *Romanticism and Religion*, Ch. 2.

Such a principle of translation, startling as it may seem to modern eyes, would certainly be consistent with the view quoted above from the *Table Talk* of the previous year – and may even go some way to explain it. There is, in fact, nothing very new about the implied parallel between Elizabethan English and the language of the Bible. Tyndale himself had been in no doubt that the English of his own time was a much more suitable medium to convey the directness of Hebrew or the *koinē* Greek of the New Testament than the Latin of the Vulgate.

They will say that it [the Bible] cannot be translated into our tongue, it is so rude. It is not so rude as they are false liars. For the Greek tongue agreeth more with the English than with the Latin. And the properties of the Hebrew tongue agreeth a thousand times more with the English than with the Latin. The manner of speaking is both one, so that in a thousand places thou needest not but to translate it in to the English word for word when thou must seek a compass in the Latin & yet shall have much work to translate it well-favouredly, so that it have the same grace and sweetness, sense and pure understanding with it in the Latin as it hath in the Hebrew. A thousand parts better may it be translated into the English than into the Latin.[9]

Because English, like Hebrew, has a flexible word order, much of its rhetoric depends on particular choices and arrangements of words. In contrast, Latin, which is both inflected and rigid in its word-order, has of necessity a totally different rhetoric. While all three languages might be said to have their own distinctive linguistic 'character and genius', Coleridge follows Tyndale in insisting on a closer affinity between sixteenth-century English and the biblical languages.[10] We have, moreover, some clue to what he perceived as 'the character and genius of the Hebrew' in a later notebook entry on the subject of biblical imagery:

Even the Dreams of the Old Testament are for the greater part evidently *poetic*, the becoming drapery of Wisdom... Only we need not suppose, that the Hebrew Nation set to work a cold-blooded carpentry of Turners [?[11]] like the Bard or the Vision of Judgement. In those times and in that country men reasoned with the organ of Imagination, and vivid images supplied the place of

---

[9] Cited by David Daniell, *Tyndale's New Testament*, New Haven, 1989, p. xxii.

[10] Such claims were common currency among translators, and can be produced for almost every European language: e.g. See examples from David Norton, *History of the Bible as Literature*, Cambridge University Press, 1993, Vol. I, pp. 278–9: e.g. Augustinus Steuchus' claim that Hebrew poetry 'is similar to the Italian rather than to the Latin'; and Le Clerc that the 'genius' of Hebrew in its poetic form is 'conformable to that of the French tongue'. See also James L. Kugel, *The Idea of Biblical Poetry: Parallelism and its History*, Yale University Press, 1981, p. 301.

[11] The pencilled word here is very difficult to read: 'Turners' would certainly continue the carpentry image; on the other hand 'Terrors' might fit the general context better.

words, and came more readily than words in language so limited and scanty as the Hebrew. (*Notebook* 39, f. 34)

That the language here strikes us as having an almost Blakean ring is probably less due to the fact that Coleridge might have been reading Blake (though we know he had read the *Songs of Innocence and Experience* by this date) than a reminder of how much the two poets shared a vocabulary that was common to the age. Stripped of this vocabulary, much of the substance of this way of thinking is to be found in Robert Lowth's more sober assessment of the sublimity of the homely metaphors of Hebrew poetry in his epoch-making *Lectures on the Sacred Poetry of the Hebrews*, which had transformed eighteenth-century biblical studies.[12] In particular Coleridge seems to have been impressed by Lowth's argument that, contrary to the rules of neo-classical composition, the poetic nature of Old Testament language is in no small part due to Hebrew's frequent use of 'imagery borrowed from common life', employing 'more freely and more daringly that image in particular, which is borrowed from the most obvious and familiar objects'.[13] In relation to Psalm 139, verse 15, which Lowth translates himself as '. . . when I was wrought with a needle in the depths of the earth' he continues: the reader 'will miss much of its force and sublimity, unless he be apprized that the art of designing in needlework was wholly dedicated to the use of the sanctuary'.[14]

Coleridge certainly knew Lowth's works directly,[15] but a more important source may well have been Blair's version of Lowth which forms part of the argument of his *Lectures on Rhetoric and Belles Lettres* (1783) – from which Wordsworth, for instance, had also derived many of the ideas which had appeared in the Preface to the *Lyrical Ballads* thirty years before Coleridge's notebook entries. Hugh Blair, Professor of Rhetoric at Edinburgh, was not merely one of Lowth's greatest admirers in his own century, but, at a time when the *Praelectiones* were only available still in the original Latin, one of his main popularisers.[16] Blair, however, was much more than just a populariser; his concern with the history of European rhetoric had made him acutely aware of the implications of Lowth's theory of parallelism for translation theory. Above all, it offered

---

[12] For an account of Lowth's poetic principles see Prickett, *Words and the Word*, pp. 105–13.

[13] Robert Lowth, *Lectures on the Sacred Poetry of the Hebrews* (1753), trs G. Gregory, 2 vols., London, 1787; facsimile edition N.Y.: Garland, 1971, Vol. I p. 124.

[14] Ibid. p. 176.·

[15] See George Whalley, 'The Bristol Library Borrowings of Southey and Coleridge, 1793–8', *The Library*, 5th Series, 4 (1949), 11–32, p. 123.

[16] Though a translation had appeared in the *Christian's Magazine* as early as 1767, Gregory's full translation was not published until 1787.

him a scholarly basis to support Tyndale's bluff nationalistic assertion of the linguistic affinities of English with the biblical languages. Lowth had stressed that the basic structure of Hebrew poetry, with its freedom from rhyme and scansion, makes its translation into English a comparatively easy matter, so that

... a poem translated literally from the Hebrew into the prose of any other language, whilst the same form of the sentences remain, will still retain ... much of its native dignity, and a fair appearance of versification. But translated into [classical] Greek or Latin verse, and having the conformation of the sentences accommodated to the idiom of a foreign language [it] will appear confused and mutilated; will scarcely retain a trace of its genuine elegance, and peculiar beauty.[17]

The corollary, as Blair immediately saw, was that the very literalness of the Authorized Version's translation helps to convey this poetic quality of the original.

It is owing, in a great measure, to this form of composition, that our version, though in prose, retains so much of a poetical cast. For the version being strictly word for word after the original, the form and order of the original sentence are preserved; which by this artificial structure, this regular alternation and correspondence of parts, makes the ear sensible of a departure from the common style and tone of prose.[18]

Similarly, the idea that there is a distinctive character and genius to the Hebrew, as to all languages, is a common Romantic touchstone. It is central, for instance, to Herder's thesis in *The Spirit of Hebrew Poetry* (1782–3) where, following Lowth – to whom he, like Blair, also pays fulsome tribute[19] – he specifically identifies that genius with the language's 'poetic' qualities:

The genius of the [Hebrew] language we can nowhere study better, that is, with more truth, depth, comprehensiveness, and satisfaction, than in its poetry, and indeed, so far as is possible, in its most ancient poetry ... Let the scholar then study the Old Testament, even if it be only as a human book full of ancient poetry, with kindred feeling and affection.[20]

In this context, Coleridge's cryptic and apparently eccentric utterances in *Table Talk* begin to take on a much more mainstream feel. Since, so

---

[17] Lowth, *Sacred Poetry*, Vol. I, 72–3.
[18] Hugh Blair, *Lectures on Rhetoric and Belles Lettres* (1783), 2 vols., Edinburgh, 1820, Vol. II, pp. 270–1.
[19] *The Spirit of Hebrew Poetry*, (1782–3) trs James Marsh, Burlington, Vt., 1833, p. 4.
[20] Ibid. pp. 22–3.

the argument seems to run, the special and particular quality of Hebrew is best seen in the homely and everyday nature of its poetic imagery, it is a peculiar providence that the sixteenth-century English of the Authorized Version has so successfully appropriated this quality as to keep the language anchored in real things rather than the abstractions that had come to dominate French and, seemingly, Spanish as well.

This charge that French and Spanish had entirely lost their 'poetical language' through over-refinement is at first glance a puzzling one, but it also has respectable antecedents. The Reverend Joseph Blanco White was no outside commentator on contemporary Spanish culture. He had been born, raised and worked as a priest there, before escaping to England.[21] The work Coleridge is referring to is White's *Evidences Against Catholicism*, which appeared in 1825 and which, to judge again from notebook entries (*CN*, IV, 5240), he seems to have read almost at once. He obviously approved of it – not least since it confirmed many of his own observations on contemporary Mediterranean Catholicism made during his residence in Malta and visits to Italy in 1805–7. White seems to have been much in Coleridge's mind during the period 1827–9. Even the sonnet, 'Mysterious Night!', which was published in *The Bijou* in 1828 was hailed by Coleridge, rather startlingly, as 'the finest and most grandly conceived sonnet in our language'. Coleridge refers again to Blanco White's criticisms of Catholicism in his notebook for September, 1829 (*NB* 40, f. 111).

Similarly, his remarks on the unpoetic nature of French, so far from being yet another general jibe at Gallic culture, seem in fact to be derived from one of France's most eminent men of letters: Diderot. In his *Letter on the Deaf-Mutes* (1751) Diderot had himself argued that, unlike Latin and Greek in the classical world, or contemporary English and Italian, French had become increasingly abstract and analytical to the

---

[21] He had been born in Seville in 1775 of an Irish immigrant family. Apprenticed to his father's business at the age of eight, he took what seemed the only way out by discovering a vocation for the priesthood – to which he was finally ordained, after years of training, at the age of twenty-five. Within four years he had lost his faith – but was unable to resign his orders without incurring the charge of heresy, in Spain still then punishable by death. He was eventually able to escape to London during the general confusion after Napoleon's occupation of Madrid, and while in England slowly recovered his faith in Christianity, though not in Catholicism. In 1814 he became a priest of the Church of England and settled to study Greek and Divinity at Oxford – and in 1826 he became an honorary member of the Oriel common room (where Coleridge's son, Hartley, had briefly been a Fellow in 1820). At this period he was on intimate terms with Newman, Pusey and Whately. In 1831 he was to follow Whately, as tutor to his son, when he moved to Dublin. Here, however, he changed his religion once again, becoming a Unitarian; he died in Liverpool in 1841. For an account of Blanco White's Oxford career see Geoffrey Faber, *Oxford Apostles*, Faber, 1933, esp. pp. 112–14.

point where it had lost its 'warmth, eloquence, and energy' and become a language of prose best fitted for science and philosophy.[22] The exact languages he chooses for his examples are less important, however, than his conviction that poetry and prose stand at opposite ends of a continuum. The more sophisticated a language becomes, so the thesis runs, the more it moves towards the prose end of the spectrum and the less able it is to be an adequate vehicle for poetry. With variations, this is a view that was echoed by many later French literary figures: Madame de Staël, Proudhon, de Vigny, Renan and even Taine.[23] It was also adopted by a number of late eighteenth-and early nineteenth-century theorists of language: Wilhelm von Humboldt in Germany, Adam Ferguson in Scotland, and, by Thomas Love Peacock in England, whose use of the idea as an ironic polemical device was to goad his friend Shelley into writing the *Defence of Poetry*.[24] None of these, however, attempted to couple this idea that poetry is a more concrete and therefore more primitive linguistic mode with questions of biblical translation. In making this link Coleridge has not merely gone beyond his sources; he has, typically, reversed the whole thrust of their arguments.

To see how this is so, we need to look more closely at Diderot's description of the way in which poetry operates through language.

There is in the discourse of the poet a spirit that gives motion and life to every syllable. What is this spirit? I have sometimes felt its presence; but all I know about it is, that it is it that causes things to be said all at once; that in the very moment they are grasped by the understanding, the soul is moved by them, the imagination sees them, and the ear hears them; and that the discourse is not merely an enchainment of energetic terms that reveal the thought with force and elevation, but is even more a web of hieroglyphs accumulated one after the other and painting the thought.[25]

Diderot was, of course, writing before the discovery of the Rosetta Stone in 1799 – the key to the eventual decipherment of Egyptian hieroglyphics by the French scholar Jean-François Champollion in the years after 1820. For the eighteenth-century 'hieroglyph' was a word for a picture whose meaning was non-verbal – and essentially cryptic. For him, the

[22] Cited by Hans Aarsleff, 'Introduction to Wilhelm von Humboldt', in Humboldt, *On Language*, p. lvii.
[23] See Frederic E. Faverty, *Matthew Arnold the Ethnologist*, Evanston: Northwestern University Press, 1951, p. 84.
[24] See Aarsleff, 'Introduction' in Humboldt, *On Language*; Marilyn Butler, *Peacock Displayed*, Routledge & Kegan Paul, 1979, pp. 142 ff.; and Thomas Love Peacock, *The Four Ages of Poetry*, ed. H.F.B. Brett-Smith, Oxford, Blackwell, 1953.
[25] Aarsleff, 'Introduction', in Humboldt, *On Language*, pp. lvi–lvii.

'hieroglyphs' of poetry were a common feature of primitive languages, or those in their earliest years of development. In later generations it is only the outstanding geniuses who can continue to produce them. Because of this essentially hieroglyphic structure the images of such figures as Homer are highly resistant to appropriation by later European cultures: 'the more a poet is charged with hieroglyphs, the more difficult he is to render in translation'. This idea of poetry as a series of verbal hieroglyphs was to exert a powerful hold on a later generation of Romantic thinkers in two ways. Firstly, because Diderot also sees 'primitive' and poetic languages as being those of 'fiction and untruth' (*de la fable et du mensonge*), he gives a new twist to the Platonic idea that there was a very close link between poetry and lying. Creativity is invention. Secondly, it served to reinforce the already strong strand of primitivism that was latent in almost all Romantic aesthetics, but was to take a peculiarly potent form with German Hellenism. In the wave of enthusiasm for all things Greek that had affected Herder, Schiller, von Humboldt and Goethe, reaching its apogee with such figures as Winckelmann, the literature of the classical Greeks was seen as ideal, immediate and fresh, and free from the enervating hand of tradition or convention.

What makes Coleridge so interesting in this context is the way in which his thinking is at once highly derivative and yet peculiarly original. Whereas Lessing, for instance, shared with Winckelmann and their nineteenth-century successors much of this reverence for the pristine purity of the hellenistic world, this same admiration is not extended in his biblical criticism to the ancient Hebrews. Herder, on the other hand, who does have a similar enthusiasm for the culture of the Old Testament, as we have seen, remains relatively untouched by the new Higher Criticism.[26] By the late 1820s Coleridge, in contrast, shows no trace of the widespread anti-semitism, sharing all Herder's admiration and enthusiasm for the ancient Hebrew world, while being as well aware of the textual and critical problems inherent in the texts under discussion as Lessing – whom he had studied so closely that, when his *Confessions of an Inquiring Spirit* were posthumously published in 1840, his editor, J. H. Green, was obliged to add a preface to the second edition (1849) specifically to disclaim plagiarism from the German critic.

Coleridge claimed to have known some Hebrew before he went up to Cambridge, and the existence of a fragmentary verse translation of the Song of Deborah (Judges 5) in his own handwriting, apparently dating

[26] On this co-existence in Herder of a historical approach with an acceptance of miracle see Albert Schweitzer, *The Quest of the Historical Jesus*, 3rd edn, A. and C. Black, 1954, p. 36.

from about 1799, attests his early competence in the language.[27] His interest in and command of Hebrew was greatly strengthened after 1817, however, by his friendship with Hyman Hurwitz, a Highgate neighbour and Professor of Hebrew at University College, London. Hurwitz presented Coleridge with a pre-publication copy of his *Vindiciae Hebraicae* (1820), where he cites and praises *The Statesman's Manual*, and he continued to advise Coleridge on matters of Hebrew language and tradition right up to the time of the latter's death.[28] For Coleridge, this purity and freshness of language which the German Hellenists had found in ancient Greece was no less a quality of the Old Testament. Again, this was a view supported by the traditional pre-critical biblical scholarship which held that Hebrew was the most ancient of all known languages, and the nearest to the ante-diluvian language of Adam where words corresponded directly to things.

But whereas for Lowth the primitive vitality of biblical language lay in its use of natural imagery, Herder (here no doubt more influenced by Diderot than Lowth) adopts the typically Romantic stress on the creative rather than the imitative force of poetry. Coleridge's point, however, is not about the origins of poetry but about the effect of the Bible – and, in particular, of the Authorized Version – on the subsequent history of the English language. Again, there are antecedents for this approach in Lowth. In the Preliminary Dissertation to his 1778 *Isaiah: A New Translation*, Lowth notes how:

... from our constant use of close verbal Translations of both the Old and New Testaments; which has by degrees so moulded our language into such a conformity with that of the original Scriptures, that it can upon occasion assume the Hebrew character without appearing altogether forced and unnatural.[29]

Whatever one may think of the arguments of Diderot, Ferguson, and Peacock that increased linguistic sophistication inevitably brings with it a loss of poetic power, it certainly seems to be true that the Authorized Version of the Bible has played an incomparably bigger part in the development of English literature than any corresponding French or Spanish versions have in their literature, and, as a result, it has influenced the development of the English language in certain quite fundamental ways.

---

[27] See James C. McKusick, 'A New Poem by Samuel Taylor Coleridge', *Modern Philology*, 84 (1987), pp. 408–9.
[28] See Ina Lipkowitz, 'Inspiration and the Poetic Imagination: Samuel Taylor Coleridge', *Studies in Romanticism*, 30 (Winter 1991), pp. 607–9; and Tim Fulford, 'Coleridge and the Wisdom Tradition', *The Wordsworth Circle*, 22 (1991), pp. 77–8.
[29] *Isaiah: A New Translation* (1778), Vol. I, p. lxvii.

In particular, according to Coleridge, it had preserved a certain con-
creteness of expression in English that he clearly associates with the language's poetic vitality and which stands in sharp contrast with the spare
and classical elegance of (say) Louis Segond's famous French version of
the Bible. Moreover, whatever his later disagreements with Wordsworth
over the exact nature of poetic diction, Coleridge had been in 1798 a
co-author of the *Lyrical Ballads*, and as passionate a believer as his friend
and fellow-poet in the primitive sublimity of the language of ordinary
men. Now writing thirty years later, it is still self-evident to him that the
truly creative poetic language is that 'of natural objects'.

Among other things, we have here yet another illustration of one of
the most striking features of English eighteenth-century and Romantic
thought: its essential *conservatism*. It is worth reminding ourselves of the
historical irony that many of the major aesthetic and intellectual innovations during this period are as much the product of attempts to defend
an existing position or the *status quo* as of any conscious desire to pro-
mote change. Thus, for instance, it is clear that Lowth's revolutionary
stress on the meaning of biblical texts within their particular historical
context was not, in fact, so much an attempt to get rid of polysemous
typological and mystical interpretations of the Bible as to put them on
a sounder scholarly basis in order to resist Deist and Whig attacks on
their historical authenticity.[30] This goes some way at least to explain the
otherwise puzzling phenomenon that while British biblical scholars like
Lowth were quick to take up the new critical methods begun, and then
rapidly suppressed, in France, they were subsequently content to leave
the development of what was by then called the Higher Criticism almost
entirely to German scholars of the Lutheran tradition. Similarly Burke's
Reflections on the Revolution in France was presented to its readers in 1790
as no more than a commonsense restatement of traditional beliefs.[31] Yet
such features as its covertly mercantile assumptions about the economic
nature of freedom or the theory of the organic nature of the state were
innovative enough to set the agenda for debates on political theory for
most of the nineteenth century.

Coleridge is no exception to this trend. *On the Constitution of Church and
State*, was written in the late 1820s with the avowedly reactionary purpose
of preventing Catholic Emancipation by showing how it would violate

---

[30] This is particularly clear in the Preliminary Dissertation to his *Isaiah: A New Translation* (1778).
See, for instance, Vol. I, p. lxviii. For Whig attempts to undermine the biblical roots of Tory
ideology, see Henning Graf Reventlow, *The Authority of the Bible*, pp. 329 ff.

[31] See Prickett, *England and the French Revolution*, pp. 42–61.

what he called the 'blessed accidents' of the British Constitution. But through his highly original concept of the role of the Clerisy, it was to help set in motion unforeseen and far-reaching changes in British social and political life.[32] More fundamentally conservative, however, is the way in which his mental set belongs essentially to an undifferentiated world where literary criticism is *neither* a secular *nor* a religious activity, but one that unquestioningly partakes of both worlds. As a result, it is possible for him at one level to explore the structure of poetic metaphor in the Authorized Version, while at the same time being utterly confident of a divinely charged meaning underlying the text. Nor is this, I suspect, peculiar to his treatment of the Bible. Though it is necessarily for him the supreme example, it shows us, as it were by analogy, the meaning with which *all* language – and especially all *poetic* language – is informed.

In his Philosophical Lectures Coleridge had coined the word 'desynonymy' to suggest the process by which two new meanings can be drawn out of a single root word. But what is happening here is not so much a matter of separating particular meanings of words, as one of separating two entire *disciplines*, two different narratives, two ways of seeing the world. Moreover, as Coleridge himself would no doubt have been quick to point out, to use that word is to pre-judge the question of how different those two perspectives really are. There is a very real sense in which the secular study and criticism of literature has never really thrown off its religious origins, while the study of sacred texts has subsequently been bedevilled by its lack of contact with secular critical theory.[33] The separation, as much fortuitous as logical,[34] has arguably impoverished, even to some extent dismembered, both disciplines. But their situations are not quite mirror-images of one another. If it is true to say that Theology, like many amputees, has gradually become aware of an ache in its missing limb, the converse is rather more complicated. What has been amputated by the progressive secularization of literary studies is not so much a matter of intellectual structure as one of *meaning*. In invoking the relationship between the Authorized Version and the development of the English language, Coleridge is also tacitly appealing to what amounts almost to a theory of linguistic consubstantiation whereby the written word itself was felt to have a kind of divine force simply because it was the framework by which God had chosen to communicate with his people.

[32] See Stephen Prickett, 'Coleridge and the Idea of the Clerisy', in Walter B. Crawford (ed.), *Reading Coleridge: Approaches and Appreciations*, Ithaca and London: Cornell University Press, 1979, pp. 152–73.
[33] See Prickett, *Words and the Word*, pp. 196–9.   [34] Ibid. pp. 1–3.

Once we are conscious of it, there are hints of such a view in many of Coleridge's utterances, including the one with which we began. It is also present, for instance, in the famous passage in *The Statesman's Manual* where he describes the narratives of the Bible as

> ... The living *educts* of the imagination; of that reconciling and mediatory power, which incorporating the Reason in images of the Sense, and organising (as it were) the flux of the Senses, by the permanence and self-circling energies of the Reason, gives birth to a system of symbols, harmonious in themselves, and consubstantial with the truths, of which they are the *conductors* ... Hence ... The Sacred Book is worthily intitled *the* WORD OF GOD.[35]

The ostensible thrust of this passage would seem to be echoing Diderot in the claim that there is a self-authenticating quality to poetic language, which in the case of that supreme example, the Bible, offers a kind of inner conviction as a guarantee of truth. But that word 'consubstantial' carries further and stronger connotations implying that in some sense the famous gap between words and meaning can be bridged in poetic utterance. Though this passage was published in 1817 there are several suggestions of a similar view much earlier in his thinking. In an often-quoted letter to Godwin, for instance, in 1800, Coleridge is already running on from Horne Tooke's soon-to-be discarded etymology to the much larger and recurring question of the relation of words to what they purport to describe:

> Is thinking impossible without arbitrary signs? & – how far is the word 'arbitrary' a misnomer? Are not words etc. parts and germinations of the Plant? And what is the Law of their Growth?
> – In something of this order I would endeavour to destroy the old antithesis of Words & Things, elevating, as it were, words into Things, & living Things too.[36]

Once again, with hindsight, it is easy detect both a modern and a very traditional strain to this argument. Those favouring a modernist approach would point to how Coleridge, who may well be echoing Reid's famous metaphor of the development of language as a tree, might be said to be anticipating twentieth-century arguments about linguistic subjectivity and the way in which language so conditions consciousness as to create different ways of classifying and perceiving the same object. Those preferring to see a reactionary, even obscurantist Coleridge would no doubt stress instead the essentially religious basis of Hartley's psychology

---

[35] S.T. Coleridge, *Lay Sermons*, ed. R.J. White, Routledge, 1972, pp. 28–9.
[36] *Collected Letters*, ed. E.L. Griggs, Oxford University Press, 1956–9, Vol. I, pp. 625–6.

(which figures strongly in other parts of this letter) and the underlying assumption throughout this passage that there is a divinely appointed correspondence between language and the material world, which, however much it might have been dislocated and fractured by the Fall, nevertheless still endured as a kind of bedrock guarantee of reality. Both interpretations are, of course, distorted and partial. It is much more difficult for us, however, to register imaginatively what I believe to be the actual truth: namely that for Coleridge there was no contradiction between the two positions. Nor – confusingly – is this necessarily yet another example of Coleridge's essential conservatism being out of step with the more progressive thought of the age. One of the salutary effects of a book like Owen Barfield's fascinating study of Coleridge's relationship to *Naturphilosophie* and early nineteenth-century science, *What Coleridge Thought*,[37] was to remind us how much in Coleridge that is totally alien to modern ways of thinking nevertheless actually represented the most advanced scientific and philosophical theories of the day.

Before we dismiss Coleridge's linguistic theories, then, as yet another example of his so-called muddled thinking, it is worth recalling that such whispers of divinity within the machine of language persisted throughout the nineteenth and even into the late twentieth century.

NEWMAN: THE PHYSIOGNOMY OF DEVELOPMENT

John Henry Newman is not, perhaps, the most obvious Coleridgean of the Victorian age, but there is a sense in which he was by far the most lastingly influential.[38] For him, the Catholicism to which he had become a convert at the age of forty-five was to be distinguished from the Anglicanism which he had left by precisely the fact that it *was*, in his eyes, part of a universal narrative. But what made it universal was not its historical tradition, glorious as he believed that was, but its organic and living capacity to change and adapt to new circumstances. His word for this process was 'development'.

In a lecture on patterns of recognition in art, Professor E.H. Gombrich used to show two pairs of photographs, taken eighty years apart. One was of Emanuel Shinwell, the Labour politician, the other was of Bertrand Russell. In each case the rounded face of the baby was totally unlike that of the octogenarian in its shape, texture and creases – yet, extraor-

---

[37] Owen Barfield, *What Coleridge Thought*, Oxford University Press, 1972.

[38] For discussions of Coleridge's influence on Newman see John Coulson, *Newman and the Common Tradition*, Oxford: Clarendon Press, 1970, and Prickett, *Romanticism and Religion*.

dinarily enough, what came across in each case was not dissimilarity but recognizable likeness. There was no doubt at all which chubby baby was the proletarian Shinwell and which the latest addition to the aristocratic House of Russell. Recognition of both depended not so much on any particular shapes or configuration of lines as on that indefinable facial quality which we call 'expression'. With hindsight, we were left in no doubt that Mannie Shinwell was Shinwell even at the age of one; similarly Russell, surveying the world with, even then, a hint of aristocratic scepticism from his baby carriage, was nevertheless unmistakably Russell.

It is an example that would have delighted Newman, for it illustrates perfectly that quality of development which, however hard it might be to define or describe in the abstract, increasingly came to be seen by him as a fundamental organizing human principle. Indeed, much of his writing may be seen in terms of his attempt to find a satisfactory theoretical account of a phenomenon for which his reading of philosophy had left him inadequately tutored and whose practical importance he had discovered first in his own life.

If, on the one hand, it is as elusive and intangible as a facial expression, yet on the other, it is also as immediately recognizable. The idea of continuous narrative can be seen to lie at the heart of all Newman's thinking – whether on literature, education, theology or philosophy. Over and over again, at level after level, we find him returning to the question of what differentiates genuine organic life, with an internal dynamic and momentum of its own, from a mere mechanical ordering or arrangement. What distinguishes a work of genuine literature, for instance, is the relation of its parts to the whole, and the development of character and action so revealed. The development of the individual lies similarly at the centre of his notion of what constitutes a university. In theology, the idea of development – most famously, of course, in his book of that name – is present throughout his thinking, underlying his final critique of Liberalism as much as it does his early Anglican work on the Lives of the Saints. Perhaps most notably of all, it is central to the concept of the 'illative sense' in his last major work, *A Grammar of Assent*.

For Newman this idea of development was much more than merely a description of the way in which the human psyche works. What he called the 'illative sense' was nothing less than the power of the human mind to move from partial theoretical evidence to practical certainty. Certainty, Newman argues

...is the culmination of probabilities, independent of each other, arising out of the nature and circumstances of the particular case which is under review; probabilities too fine to avail separately, too subtle and circuitous to be convertible into syllogisms, too numerous and various for such conversion, even were they convertible. As a man's portrait differs from a sketch of him, in having, not merely a continuous outline, but all its details filled in, and shades and colours laid on and harmonized together, such is the multiform and intricate process of ratiocination, necessary for our reaching him as a concrete fact, compared with the rude operation of syllogistic logic.[39]

If this started as a version of the Romantic idea of the imagination, with its creative power, by the time we come to the *Grammar of Assent*, it resembles much more a Kierkegaardian 'leap of faith' by which the co-ordinated totality of the human personality is able, through the process of what he calls 'real' assent, to reach existentially towards levels of experience quite inaccessible to the 'notional' propositions of reason or dogma alone. In the best tradition of Christian theology what began as an observed phenomenon of contingent weakness ends by becoming the cornerstone of the whole edifice of faith.

The thesis that changed Newman's life, was set out in his *Essay on the Development of Doctrine* (1845). Traditional Catholic teaching, as expounded, for instance, by such eminent eighteenth-century theologians as J.B. Bossuet, had seen all movements in doctrine as unmistakable evidence for heresy. For Newman, such shifts, rightly understood, were on the contrary powerful evidence for the 'organic life' of Christian belief. What he calls the 'idea' of Christianity is not received passively by its adherents, 'but it becomes an active principle within them, leading them to an ever-new contemplation of itself, to an application of it in various directions, and a propagation of it on every side'.[40] This running narrative displays a common characteristic of all living organisms: it is in a continual process of growth and change. The true test of Catholicity is not just which Church is most like the supposed primitive form, but also which Church has demonstrated the greatest powers of organic development.

Not surprisingly, most of the debate about Newman's idea of development, then and since, has centred on the obvious religious conflict from which the book arose. Thus the seven tests by which we may distinguish what he calls 'genuine development' from its opposite, decay or 'corruption', are, in effect, ways of distinguishing between the changes

---

[39] *A Grammar of Assent*, ed. C.F. Harrold, new edn, Longman, 1957, p. 219.
[40] *Essay on the Development of Doctrine*, Sheed and Ward, 1960, p. 27.

inherent in contemporary Catholicism and those visible in Protestantism. As Owen Chadwick has pointed out in his book *From Bossuet to Newman*, the argument, though impressive, is nevertheless finally a circular one. How are we to know which are organic changes? Those that appear in Catholicism. But there is another part to Newman's argument whose polemical purpose is rather less clear: an argument for complexity rather than simplicity.

At first this is presented modestly enough. 'The more claim an idea has to be considered living', he notes, 'the more various will be its aspects; and the more social and political its nature, the more complicated and subtle will be its issues, and the longer and more eventful will be its course.'[41] This is especially true of something as ancient and complex as Christianity. No one aspect of it can be 'allowed to exclude or obscure another; . . . Christianity is dogmatical, devotional, practical all at once; it is esoteric and exoteric; it is indulgent and strict; it is light and dark; it is love and it is fear'.[42] Though this is a powerful celebration of the many strands that go to make up the Catholic tradition through the ages it is, as some of his critics noted at the time, not at first sight particularly relevant to the main thrust of his argument. Indeed, in some ways it actually makes his case marginally more difficult to demonstrate, since it prevents him at the outset from identifying a palpably Catholic 'leading idea' or core to Christianity by reference to which the truth or corruption of all the other accretions might be judged. Newman, however, has another final test up his sleeve much more dramatic and searching than the search for 'logical sequence' or 'chronic vigour' by which one might know particular doctrines or practices. We do not pick and choose our beliefs testing them one by one for their historic continuity, we accept or reject the Catholic Church *as a whole* – taking its many and varied parts on trust as we do so. And how do we know the Catholic Church itself? We *recognize* it in precisely the same way that we recognize the face of the little child in the wrinkles of the old man in the example with which we began. There can be no doubt in our minds when we encounter the true Church:

There is a religious communion claiming a divine commission, and holding all other bodies around it heretical or infidel; it is a well-organized well disciplined body; it is a sort of secret society, binding together its members by influences and by engagements which it is difficult for strangers to ascertain. It is spread over the known world; it may be weak or insignificant locally, but it is strong on the whole from its continuity; it may be smaller than all other religious

---

[41] Ibid. p. 41.   [42] Ibid. p. 27.

bodies together, but it is larger than each separately. It is a natural enemy to governments external to itself; it is intolerant and engrossing, and tends to a new modelling of society; it breaks laws, it divides families. It is a gross superstition: it is charged with the foulest crimes; it is despised by the intellect of the day; it is frightful to the imagination of many. And there is but one communion such.[43]

The passage is one of the most rhetorically splendid in Newman's entire output, but Newman's literary rhetoric always serves an end. It is as though his attempt to focus with minute verbal precision on something as indefinable yet persistent as total identity that survives the alteration of every constituent part also calls forth new powers of verbal expression. Thus here, anyone, pagan or Protestant, who stubs his toe against this rock, knows what he has encountered. 'Place this description before Pliny or Julian; place it before Frederick the Second or Guizot . . . Each knows at once, without asking a question, who is meant by it.'

The tactical leap from Pliny to Guizot makes the point: they see not the same organism – how could they after that passage of time? – but they recognize, as it were, the same stubborn expression on the face of the nineteen-hundred-year-old institution as was on the face of the unruly infant disrupter of the Roman Empire. It is this notion of the intangible unity of the whole that makes sense of the disparate parts and provides direction and meaning to change that is central to Newman's idea of the development of doctrine.

It is also, of course, central to Newman's sense of self. As I have argued at length elsewhere,[44] Newman, like Wordsworth, is always trying to tell us his own story. It is no accident that the *Essay on the Development of Doctrine* emerges from the four-year hiatus of 1841–5, when teetering between the Anglican Church that he knew and loved, and the unknown attractions of Roman Catholicism, he faced the greatest crisis of his life. In presenting this 'hypothesis to account for a difficulty', Newman specifically endows the Church with all the subtlety and complexity of a human psyche. Some changes to the individual are beneficial – even necessary if they are to adjust to new circumstances – others are retrograde and even damaging to the health of the whole. Implicit in the whole argument of the *Essay* is the unspoken question of the subtext: is Newman the Roman Catholic more or less John Henry Newman than was the Anglican fellow of Oriel? Is there a living organic development from one to the other? It was only when he felt able to answer *that* question in the affirmative that he felt able to take the final step. I believe we fail to understand the full

[43] Ibid. p. 150.   [44] Prickett, *Romanticism and Religion*, p. 174.

thrust of the *Essay* unless we see it as, in effect, the first draft of Newman's great and lifelong Apologia that was in the end to include nearly all his written output.

Certainly we quickly get a very clear answer to that question in institutional terms once Newman had finally taken the plunge. The delicately ironic title of the *Lectures on Certain Difficulties Felt by Anglicans in Submitting to the Catholic Church* conceals what is perhaps his most devastating attack on his old communion in terms of that final test of the overall life of the organism. And it is not merely any organism. This time the anthropomorphic nature of the metaphor (if metaphor it still is) which was implicit in the *Essay* of five years before is now made fully explicit. Images of sap or new shoots are discarded in favour of those of mummification. What it is now clear that the Church of England lacked above all is that basic condition of intelligent life: self-consciousness. It cannot tell its own story.

As a thing without a soul, it does not contemplate itself, define its intrinsic constitution, or ascertain its position. It has no traditions; it cannot be said to think; it does not know what it holds and what it does not; it is not even conscious of its own existence.[45]

It requires no great shift of focus to read all of the above as a negative statement of Newman's own vision of what individual consciousness *does* entail. For Newman now the true analogy of the Church is not a grain of mustard-seed, nor yet a vine, but a sentient human being – and preferably, indeed, one who had been educated at Oxford through the controversies of the 1820s and 1830s, and had held a fellowship at Oriel. But even as Newman begins to elaborate his metaphor there occurs a typically Romantic shift of perspective. Just as Wordsworth, in his Preface to the *Lyrical Ballads*, had answered his own question, What is a Poem? by defining the nature of a poet, so Newman answers his own question, What is the Church? by shifting from anthropomorphic imagery of the institution to the mind of the individual who is doing the imagining.

Thus it is that students of the Fathers, antiquarians, and poets, begin by assuming that the body to which they belong is that of which they read in time past, and then proceed to decorate it with that majesty and beauty of which history tells, or which their genius creates . . . But at length, either the force of circumstance or some unexpected accident dissipates it; and, as in fairy tales, the magic castle vanishes when the spell is broken, and nothing is seen but the wild heath, the barren rock, and the forlorn sheep-walk: so it is with us as regards the

---

45 *Lectures on Certain Difficulties Felt by Anglicans*, 2nd edn, 1850, p. 7.

Church of England, when we look in amazement on that which we thought so unearthly, and find so common-place or worthless. [46]

The description of the enquirers as 'students of the Fathers, antiquarians, and poets', leaves us in little doubt as to who these deluded Romantic figures are. Nor is the origin of this extended conceit in any way concealed. Those left 'alone and palely loitering' by La Belle Dame Sans Merci, thinly disguised as the Church of England, are Newman and the remnants of the Oxford Movement. Anglicanism is in reality less a Church than a *stage* in the growth of the individual's religious imagination, offering to those not yet ready for the real thing a simulacrum whose ultimate function is to awaken a longing in the soul for what it ultimately cannot satisfy – and so lead to the only Church that can meet these hitherto disappointed expectations. It is hard to think that Newman did not have in mind here Keats' comment, 'The Imagination may be compared to Adam's dream: he awoke, and found it true.'[47]

Once again the distinction is between genuine organic life and its febrile imitations. But a new element has crept in. How are we, finally, to distinguish between the living body and the vain enchantments of simulacra? the true story and the false? Beyond the application of rule-of-thumb tests, the final answer appears to be by means of the imagination. This is the reason for the apparent circularity of the argument of the *Essay*. It is only after our imaginations have intuitively grasped the whole picture that such tests will serve to convince us. Moreover it is the imagination, the very power that first led us to seek the Church in the wrong place, that will, eventually, also leave us dissatisfied with the insubstantiality of the false forms and guide us towards the one place where truth will be found. Those who know C.S. Lewis' early autobiographical allegory, *The Pilgrim's Regress*, will recognize here a surprising similarity between the conversion experiences of two very different kinds of Oxford men. It is perhaps the less surprising when we recall that the common link here is that particular English Romantic view of the imagination as the power that not merely responds to sense impressions, but actively shapes our apprehension of the world, not just in terms of sense-data, but also in our intellectual and spiritual existences. Once again, the stress lies on the wholeness of the individual person in contrast to those systems or ways of thinking that would fragment our experience and so, in the end, deny our humanity. As Newman writes in the *Grammar of Assent*, 'It is to the

---

[46] Ibid. pp. 6–7.

[47] Many of Keats' letters (including this one about 'Adam's dream') were known to the public through Richard Monkton Milnes, 1848 Life of Keats.

living mind that we must look for the means of using correctly principles of whatever kind.'[48] And again:

We are what we are, and we use, not trust our faculties. To debate about trusting in a case like this, is parallel to the confusion implied in wishing I had a choice if I would be created or no, or speculating what I should be like, if I were born of other parents . . . We are as little able to accept or reject our mental constitution as our being . . . We do not confront or bargain with ourselves. [49]

Whether individually or ecclesiastically we must start from *where* we are – and will inevitably be guided by *what* we are.

But between the abstract theory of the *Essay on Development* and the profoundly psychological *Grammar* lay a key event. Twenty years after his conversion to Catholicism, Newman was a largely forgotten figure. Many even thought he had died. Yet in 1864 Charles Kingsley, in an anti-Catholic pamphlet, made a vicious side-swipe at Newman, suggesting that Catholicism (and, by implication therefore, Newman himself) sanctioned lying – if it were in a 'good' cause. It was a big mistake. What Kingsley had done, in effect, was to challenge the whole integrity of Newman's personal narrative to date. Once again it was a matter of the expression on the face. Was Newman the Catholic more fully John Henry Newman than the Protestant of twenty years before, or was he in some sense a shrunken, warped, in some way even a diminished figure? Was the development that had followed his journey to Rome a true unfolding of latent powers that had not found an outlet in his previous existence, or was he in some way perverted and contaminated by the principles of his new spiritual environment?

Ironically, in what we have seen to be the terms set by the *Essay on Development*, Kingsley's challenge amounted to nothing less than a charge of 'corruption', or in other words what in an institution rather than an individual would amount to 'Protestantism'. It is small wonder that Newman reacted so vehemently – and rather than by rebutting the specific charges, by telling the story of his own life. Only in that way, by seeing the picture as a whole, could he put the specific points into context. 'There is', wrote Newman in the *Grammar of Assent*, 'no ultimate test of truth besides the testimony borne to truth by the mind itself.' Man's 'progress is a living growth, not a mechanism'.[50]

The *Grammar* is the culminating work of Newman's theory of development – by which, with hindsight, we can understand better the significance of the two earlier works, where, first on the macrocosmic and

---

[48] *Grammar of Assent*, p. 274.   [49] Ibid. p. 47.   [50] Ibid. p. 266.

then on the microcosmic scale, he had attempted to explore the differ-ence between living development and mechanism. What in the *Essay on Development* he had perceived primarily as a historical mode of growth, and in the *Apologia* had been linked with personal integrity, by 1870 he had come to see as a fundamental law of the mind's operation. For Newman the human psyche was neither logical nor a-logical, but, as befitted a story-telling animal, possessed of powers that made it rather 'super-logical' – capable of reaching beyond the powers of reason and proof to conclusions that we nevertheless act upon as certainties. At first sight this looks like a form of German idealism, but in fact Newman's argument here stems directly from a bold inversion of Locke, and seems to owe almost nothing to Kant or his repudiated followers such as Fichte or Jacobi. Whereas the Kantian 'reason' applies only to a limited range of innate ideas, the whole point of Newman's account of what he calls the 'illative sense' is that it applies equally to the entire range of mundane sense-experience. Religious assent is not therefore a peculiar and isolated phenomenon of human experience – of 'believing where we cannot prove' as Newman's contemporary, Tennyson, suggests in *In Memoriam* – but only the extreme end of a spectrum that begins in sim-ple sense-perception, and includes in its scope all our normal intercourse with the external world. Newman had read Hume as a teenager, and had been lastingly impressed by his so-called 'scepticism' – the demonstration of that yawning gulf between probabilities so strong that we stake every aspect of our lives upon them, and real 'proof'. It is this very Humean scepticism, based in turn upon logical extensions of Locke, that Newman now turns so effectively in the service of faith to produce a Copernican revolution of his own.

So far from being the *tabula rasa* assumed by Locke, the human mind is active and assimilating, stepping beyond evidence to create for itself wholes that are greater than the constituent parts. It is so much an accepted characteristic of our normal behaviour, moreover, that it occurs at an unconscious level in every act of sense-perception, and even when it occurs at a conscious level we scarcely notice what it is that we are doing.

This, the central argument of the *Grammar of Assent*, has always seemed to me Newman's most powerful contribution to philosophical theology. It is not the case that religious faith demands a peculiar kind of existential leap, but rather that it represents the most extreme, and therefore the most clearly visible example of a process that is constantly going on in every part of our lives without our normally being aware of it. The stress now is no longer on the truth or falsehood of specific propositions, but on the wholeness of our personal narrative. We do not perceive in terms of propositions; our schemata come from the life of the whole personality, and, beyond that, from the no less organic life of the cultural and linguistic community in which we live, and move, and have our being.

It is this organic continuity too, of course, between the culture and the individual that provides Newman with the link between the macrocosm and the microcosm, between the idea of development in the doctrine of the Church and the personal Apologia for his own life. It was also, I suspect, one of the main reasons why he was as frequently misunderstood by his new communion as by his old. Though he was to return over and over again throughout his life to the evils of 'liberalism', in the sense of putting the judgement of a private individual before the teachings of the Catholic Church, as Karl Rahner has pointed out, he was equally resolute in his insistence that to accept those teachings in the first place inescapably involved a prior act of the individual conscience – a point that was not so much anathema as simply incomprehensible to many of those on the continent, especially in Rome, who continued to feel that there was something dangerously liberal about even Newman's critique of liberalism. Or to put it another way, to us, 100 years later, the something indefinable in the expression on the face of the old Cardinal in those faded photographs looks remarkably like that on those paintings of the young Oxford don ardently embarking on the task of awakening the Church of England to its Catholic and Apostolic development.

POLANYI: THE ORIGINS OF MEANING

Dominant twentieth-century views of language have on the whole been severely functionalist. Lyotard, for instance, follows Wittgenstein in seeing language as a kind of 'game' between players under an agreed set of rules.

each of the various categories of utterance can be defined in terms of rules specifying the properties and the uses to which they can be put – in exactly the same way as the game of chess is defined by a set of rules determining the properties of each of the pieces...[51]

Following Foucault's interest not in content, but in the rules permitting content, Lyotard observes that in a game rules are part of an explicit

---

[51] *Postmodern Condition*, p. 10.

contract between players – without such rules there can be no game. Every utterance, he insists, should therefore be thought of as a 'move' in a game.

This idea that language operates as a kind of rule-bound game is one that was briefly popular among certain linguistic philosophers such as A. J. Ayer in the 1950s,[52] but which rapidly lost ground in the English-speaking world thereafter, and it is surprising to find it reappearing in the 1980s in France with no reference to the vigorous debate it then provoked. The problem is akin to that of the 'social contract' theory of government proposed by such Romantics as Rousseau. Just as no citizen is ever in practice invited to agree to such a 'contract', let alone sign it, so no user of language is ever in practice invited to agree to the rules of language before speaking it.

Nevertheless, such an essentialist view of language is still found among many scientists – especially those committed to a unified, or consilient, Theory-of-Everything, and who see languages in terms of computer codes. A. O. Wilson, for instance, sees the common property of science and art as 'the transmission of information', and proposes as a 'thought experiment' what he calls a 'mind-script' that would automatically transcribe 'information' into words. I know nothing of Wilson's knowledge of other languages, but this sounds like the proposal of a monoglot who speaks only English. Anyone with a sense of how differently languages divide up the world would be unlikely to see 'information' in such a clear-cut and abstract way. Languages, moreover, are used not just for transmission of information, but for concealment, evasion and lies. Umberto Eco, in *The Search for the Perfect Language*, has traced the progress and successive failures of this dream of a mind-script over the past 2,000 years, and it has, of course, gained currency once again with the quest for artificial intelligence. From at least the time of Dante onwards there have been consistent attempts to create a universal artificial and regular language – often with the declared ideal of eliminating the vagaries of metaphor. A variety of invented languages were proposed at the end of the nineteenth century, including Volapük (1879), Spelin (1886), Bopal (1887), Dil (1887), Balta (1893) and Veltparl (1896), of which only Esperanto (1887) has survived.[53] None have succeeded in becoming the universal medium that was hoped for. Computer codes such as BASIC are not, of course, languages in the full sense at all, but the use of the word 'language'

---

[52] See, for instance, Ayer, *Language, Truth and Logic*, Gollancz, 1946; also Prickett, *Words and the 'Word'*, pp. 220–1.

[53] See Umberto Eco, *The Search for the Perfect Language*, Blackwell, 1995, Ch. 15.

for such systems has led to considerable semantic confusion. Here, for instance, is David Deutsch:

...not all languages are equal. *Languages are theories.* In their vocabulary and grammar they embody substantial assertions about the world. Whenever we state a theory, only a small part of its content is explicit: the rest is carried by the language. Like all theories, languages are invented and selected for their ability to solve certain problems.[54]

For someone who believes in the multiverse, the appropriate question might be, 'what universe are *you* from?' While, as we shall see, it is certainly true that languages embody unconscious assertions about the world, these are neither necessarily consistent nor cumulative. Real languages are not selected for their problem-solving powers. We are inducted into language as tiny children, and come to consciousness within it, which is a very different kind of experience. Moreover, whereas the game of chess has scarcely altered in two millennia, all ordinary languages are in a constant process of change and evolution. New words are created for new objects and new kinds of experience; other words are constantly imported from foreign languages; rapid shifts of fashion and slang alter the entire flavour of a language in a very short period; and finally, and from our point of view, most importantly, expression is constantly altered by the great masters of language through works of art. English is the creation not merely of a long historical process, but of specific writers: Spenser, Shakespeare, Donne, Milton, Johnson, Coleridge, Keats and a host of other playwrights, poets and novelists. Whereas the mark of the chess Grand Master is to know how to use the rules of his game; the mark of the linguistic master is to know how to *break* the rules, to alter expression and to modify consciousness.

There are, however, two apparent exceptions to this general proposition. It is true that when we first start to learn a second language, as an adult, after our first childish language acquisition capacity has been 'switched off',[55] we have to learn by rules. But of course, if we persevere with that second language to the point of being bi-lingual, it is possible, though extremely difficult, to achieve the same mastery as a native speaker, and to 'break' the rules we have so painfully acquired. This is obviously a rare event, but Joseph Conrad, an exiled Pole who only learned English as an adult, went on to become one of the masters of twentieth-century English prose, while Samuel Beckett, a native English

[54] Deutsch, *Fabric of Reality*, 1997, p. 153.
[55] For a graphic description of this process, see Steven Pinker, *The Language Instinct*, Penguin, 1995.

speaker, by finding in French the perfect medium for his spare and witty play, *Waiting for Godot*, left his own indelible mark upon that language. But if these examples only turn out on inspection to support the general rule, the same cannot be said for the second case, that of technical language. In contrast with the language of ordinary speech, whose words are in a constant state of evolution and change, and which come to us complete with a massive historical freight, a specialist vocabulary is created for a limited pre-determined purpose. It is, in effect, the equivalent of the 'language-game' mentioned above. Whereas the word 'electricity' has a long history relating to a highly predictable, yet mysterious, natural force, the terms of its technical measurement, 'volt', 'watt', and 'amp', have a clearly fixed and unambiguous meaning. Unlike ordinary words, they have an exhaustive definition, and cannot evolve or change – though even here, the endless human capacity for creating metaphors has also leaked them into ordinary speech. A recent well-known biographer rather disparagingly described Walter Scott, the novelist, as being of 'low sexual voltage'.

Perhaps the most thorough-going theory of the way in which an 'open' as distinct from a 'closed' or technical language operates, however, was put forward by the philosopher Michael Polanyi – who though he is usually thought of as 'English', was born Hungarian, and is another example of that select band referred to above who have made a second language their own. Moreover, in keeping with his belief that a particular language is inseparable from a whole tradition of thought, Polanyi's approach to language seems to start with the English tradition we have been examining. Although I know of no mention of either Coleridge or Newman by name in any of his writings, anyone familiar with their work will have little difficulty in recognizing in Polanyi one of the twentieth century's most distinguished exponents of that same 'fiduciary tradition' of thought that came through the English Romantic movement into Victorian Anglicanism – and, as we have just seen, inspired one of the most powerful philosophical apologies for the Roman Catholic Church to appear since the Counter-Reformation.[56] Indeed, if it is really true that Polanyi was unaware of Newman's *Grammar of Assent* when he wrote *Personal Knowledge*, the similarities are quite uncanny. Both, for example, share a common epistemology, believing that commitment is an essential part of knowing, and that such knowledge, if expressed through language, cannot stand by itself but belongs to and is inescapably a part of a linguistic community.

---

[56] See Coulson, *Newman and the Common Tradition*, and Prickett, *Romanticism and Religion*.

What makes Polanyi so fascinating to anyone who has studied Newman, however, is the way in which he develops from these premises conclusions that not even the most committed of Victorian fideists would have contemplated. The most striking difference between his argument and Polanyi's is that whereas Newman finds his linguistic community in the 'community of faith', the Catholic Church itself, standing in contradistinction to the World which surrounds it, Polanyi sees no reason at all to cordon off the life and language of the Church from that of the rest of human existence and seems to imply that *all* language is of its intrinsic nature 'fiduciary', and ultimately therefore pointing towards the existence of God. We need, I think, to recognize how big a leap this is. If the general resemblances between Newman's *Grammar of Assent*, first published in 1870, and Polanyi's *Personal Knowledge* of 1958, are striking, this fundamental difference between them is little short of breathtaking in its implications – especially when we consider the historical context in which it took place. After almost a century of unparalleled growth in the physical sciences; after the triple assaults of Marx, Darwin and Freud upon the traditional human certainties; after the destruction of two World Wars; after a massive and seemingly irreversible ebbing of what Matthew Arnold had called the 'sea of Faith'; we have the extraordinary spectacle of a scientist and a philosopher trained in the then current traditions of mechanism and linguistic scepticism, advancing the argument that language itself is a crypto-theological device.

Though it is tempting to label such an argument 'anachronistic' it is, I think, worth pausing here to notice that this is not in fact the case. Not merely did Newman never go this far, but I can find no previous point in European history where it has ever been argued that language *per se* constituted a kind of evidence for God. Ever since Augustine, discussions of the religious nature of language had started with the idea of the Fall. For post-lapsarian humanity, after the catastrophe of Babel, language could never be more than a most imperfect and muddied medium for understanding either ourselves or the world around us. By the seventeenth century we find a widespread belief, common to such very different figures as Leibniz and Boehme, that underlying all known human languages was the original language of Adam.[57] For him alone, when before the Fall he had named the beasts, did words fully correspond to things by divinely delegated authority. In Boehme's words 'as Adam spoke for the first time, he gave names to all the creatures according to their qualities

---

[57] See Hans Aarsleff, 'Leibniz on Locke and Language', in *Locke to Saussure*, pp. 58–60.

and inherent effects'.[58] Though it was generally agreed that that first totalizing language was now irretrievably lost to mankind, something of its radical authority lingered, however distortedly, in all languages that descended from it. Many for instance believed that Hebrew, which was widely accepted as the oldest known language, was therefore the nearest to the Adamic root – though the matter was hotly enough debated for there to be a wide variety of dissident opinions. What all these linguistic theories had in common, however, was the grossly fallen nature of current living languages. They were neither held to be underpinned by God, nor could they in any way constitute an argument for the existence of Him. The first claim that the structure of language itself might have a hidden metaphysical agenda was made not by a theologian, but by someone who wanted to get rid of what he regarded as covert and illegitimate theology. 'I fear we are not getting rid of God', wrote Nietzsche, only partly tongue-in-cheek, 'because we still believe in grammar.'[59] So far as I know, his offer of a new proof of God was not taken up.

Polanyi's thesis, therefore, constitutes such a radical and original extension of the nineteenth-century tradition of Coleridge and Newman that we need to look closely at how he achieves this seemingly improbable feat. As has been said, 'language', for Polanyi, comprises not merely verbal systems but all forms of symbolic description and measurement – including, of course, mathematics.[60] For him, as for the Augustinian tradition that preceded him, there is of course no question of words or symbols corresponding directly to things as they were supposed to in the hypothetical language of Adam. Nor does he imagine that languages differ merely in having alternative words and grammars to describe an essentially interchangeable vision of the world. On the contrary, translation presents a real problem: even at times a theoretical impossibility.

Different languages are alternative conclusions, arrived at by the secular gropings of different groups of people at different periods of history. They sustain alternative conceptual frameworks, interpreting all things that can be talked about in terms of somewhat different allegedly recurrent features.[61]

If this were not difficult enough, Polanyi's insistence on the personalness and inwardness of knowledge also means that something of that same

---

[58] *Aurora, oder Morgenröthe im Aufgang*, Ch. 20, para. 91, in *Sämtliche Schriften (Faksimile-Neudruck der Ausgabe von 1730*, ed. Will-Erich Peukert), Vol. I, Stuttgart, 1955, p. 296.

[59] *Twilight of the Idols and the Anti-Christ*, trs and ed. R.J. Hollingdale, Penguin, 1968, p. 38.

[60] Polanyi, *Personal Knowledge*, p. 78.   [61] Ibid. p. 112.

disjunction between languages persists even at an individual level: we none of us see the world from quite the same viewpoint, and, consequently, we none of us use words in precisely the same sense. One might add also, as recent computer studies of authorship have made very clear, we each of us have a personal vocabulary that is as individual and unique as a fingerprint. In other words, Polanyi's theory of language starts from a philosophical subjectivism as radical as anything the twentieth century has to offer.

What makes this subjectivism truly radical, however, and fundamentally different from that of Newman, is that Polanyi uses the very personal quality of language as a springboard towards the possibility of universal communication. Writing on the logic of discovery, for instance, he suggests that 'even though we have never met the solution, we have a conception of it in the same sense as we have a conception of a forgotten name'[62] so that in some mysterious sense we will 'recognize' the outcome as right when we finally arrive at it. 'Our heuristic cravings imply, like our bodily appetites, the existence of something which has the properties required to satisfy us, and . . . the intuitions which guide our striving express this belief. But the satisfier of our cravings has in this case no bodily existence . . .' When it comes we will believe it because: 'It arrives accredited in advance by the heuristic craving which evoked it.'[63] In this context he quotes the mathematician Polya: 'When you have satisfied yourself that the theorem is true, you start proving it.'[64]

Though this may at first glance seem to resemble a stronger version of Newman's illative sense, I suspect that it has a diametrically different source. Newman's philosophy is rooted in the intellectual climate of early nineteenth-century Oxford, and, as David Newsome among others has pointed out,[65] is fundamentally Aristotelian in cast. The illative sense builds up its structures from what is in the end externally derived evidence. Polanyi's conviction that knowledge involves some kind of personal 'recognition' has, I suspect, its origins in a very different continental Platonic tradition. We need to remember, too, E. A. Burtt's now widely accepted thesis that the foundations of modern science and mathematics lie not in the Aristotelian tradition of observation and experiment, but in Platonic mysticism.[66] Certainly Polanyi is fully aware that the

---

[62] Ibid. p. 127.   [63] Ibid. p. 129.
[64] G. Polya, *Mathematics and Plausible Reasoning*, Oxford University Press, 1954, Vol. II, p. 76, quoted in Polanyi, *Personal Knowledge*, p. 131.
[65] David Newsome, *Two Classes of Men*, John Murray, 1974.
[66] Burtt, *Metaphysical Foundations of Modern Science*.

process of knowing as he describes it is both intuitional and, in the end, circular.[67]

But this circularity of intuition is only one side of the picture. We do not exist as individuals, but as members of a linguistic community in a state of what Polanyi calls – in what amounts almost to a re-coinage – 'conviviality'. We recall how that word was later borrowed by Illych, and then, from him by Lyotard.[68] For Polanyi a 'tacit sharing of knowing underlies every single act of articulate communication' so that 'our adherence to the truth can be seen to imply our adherence to a society which respects the truth, and which we trust to respect it'.[69] Now it is clear from the way in which he shapes the argument, as well as from the examples he gives, that his model here is that of the scientific community – and it is a group that, as he describes it, has more in common with the Catholic Church of Newman than one might suppose at first glance. So far from being the home of objective verified reason, as the commonly accepted nominalist rhetoric might suggest, he sees it as being the clearest example of an engaged, convivial, subjective and fideistic community. In reality, he points out, scientists do *not* try to verify every new fact or theory that is announced, they take the vast majority of their ideas from their peers on trust. They do, however, examine the credentials of each new piece of information, asking of it both its scientific provenance (does it come from a known and respected research team or institution?) and its place in the wider theoretical scheme of things (can this be seen as supporting or making nonsense of other known scientific laws or information?). Only when it passes these two accreditation tests does a new idea or information gain widespread acceptance – and therefore begin to be tested by further research and experiment. 'We must now recognise belief once more as the source of all knowledge', writes Polanyi, 'no intelligence, however critical or original, can operate outside a fiduciary framework.'[70]

As we have seen, this was an idea that was to play a key part in Kuhn's thinking – and in a wider, non-scientific context, in that of Derrida also.[71] The echoes of Plato are obvious enough here in this conception of 'truth', and Polanyi is refreshingly quick to acknowledge the metaphysical underpinnings of his epistemological system. Nevertheless, it is clear that this is intended as much as a descriptive psychological account as it is a prescriptive one. Though this may sound as if it is a portrait of a

---

[67] e.g. Polanyi, *Personal Knowledge*, p. 289.   [68] See Ch. 1. pp. 14–15.
[69] Polanyi, *Personal Knowledge*, p. 203.   [70] Ibid. p. 266.
[71] See *Religion*, Jacques Derrida and Gianni Vattimo (eds.), Cambridge: Polity Press, 1998.

community that has lost all touch with reality, this is not, he argues, the case. 'Truth' may, in the end, have a metaphysical as well as a physical reality, but that physical reality is a constant check on all our activities. 'Reality' in this very practical sense, is not 'out-there', the unknowable ultimate Kantian 'thing-in-itself', but, as we have seen, a construct in which we are active and cooperative partners. It is neither a matter of passive reception of external stimuli, nor of our own invention, but of a combination of the two. In this context Polanyi actually considers in some detail the example of the Azande tribe in Africa, as described by Evans-Pritchard, whose tribal and linguistic belief-structure did, by our standards, constitute a totally closed reasoning circle, impervious to all evidence that might undermine it.[72] His point is that while such hermetically sealed systems are always possible, they are in fact counter-examples, exceptions which prove the general rule. Though a Stalinist bureaucratic tyranny can always throw up a Lysenko, with a new socialist biology to suit the purposes of the prevailing ideology, in the end science has to remain in touch with reality. What was wrong with Soviet biology in the 1930s, like Soviet economics in the 1980s, was not that it formed part of a consistent theoretical framework – everybody's does that – but that in practice it didn't work. We might add to that a very important rider, and that is the fact that in the last resort, inflexible and mis-conceived as it was, Soviet biology and economics proved to be 'open' and not 'closed' systems. In other words, sooner or later everyone had to *concede* that they did not work. Unlike what we are told of the Azande, there was no way in which the linguistic community could go on for ever producing plausible and self-consistent explanations for the manifest failures of the system. As Abraham Lincoln is supposed to have said at Clinton in 1858, 'You can fool all of the people some of the time, and some of the people all of the time, but you can not fool all the people all of the time.'

That final inability of living ordinary human language to maintain itself as a totally closed system is what Polanyi means by 'indeterminacy'. It is here that we find what might be called his 'scientific subjectivism' pointing towards conclusions that are inescapably theological rather than merely linguistic. As Gödel, we recall, showed in relation to mathematical proofs and Tarki in language, 'the assertion that any theorem of a given formal language is true, can be made only by a sentence that is meaningless within that language'.[73] In so far as formal languages work with terms that are totally defined in advance, they are incapable of

[72] Polanyi, *Personal Knowledge*, pp. 288–94.   [73] Ibid. p. 259.

describing anything not so defined. Perhaps even more important is the converse, that 'only words of indeterminate meaning can have a bearing on reality'.[74] Just as perception is an active process of what Gombrich has called the 'making and matching of schemata',[75] so language too involves a continual open-ended process of comparing words with meanings. 'To speak a language', he writes, 'is to commit ourselves to the double indeterminacy due to our reliance both on its formalism and on our continual reconsideration of this formalism in its bearing on our experience.'[76] It is this openness and indeterminacy of living everyday language that divides it from formal technical languages in which the outcome is determined by initial terms of reference.

But there is another side to this notion of indeterminacy that is even more important. As we have seen, it is theoretically possible to construct a 'closed' fiduciary language which is based upon unsound premises, and which therefore lies. It is central to Polanyi's case that this is simply not possible with the open-endedness of living language, which is constantly subject to the disconcerting and unpredictable check of reality. It is presumably possible to tell lies in any language; what is not possible, he believed, is to imagine a living language so constituted that lies could not be detected and shown to be lies if the appropriate evidence were brought forward. Indeed, the concept of a lie can only exist in a context where we also know what truth means. In other words, however languages may differ (as they clearly do) in their ways of describing the world, all languages are ultimately subject to the idea of truth in some ultimate and therefore theological sense. Language thus bears witness to the existence of God.[77]

Though Polanyi never actually says this in so many words in *Personal Knowledge*, it appears to be the inescapable conclusion of his whole argument. But the very fact that he never states this thesis explicitly suggests that he himself may have had doubts as to whether it was a strictly legitimate inference to draw from his psycho-biological premises. Proving the existence of God from nature has at various points in history seemed like an entirely respectable exercise but it was not one that was likely to appeal to a majority of either his fellow scientists or philosophers in 1958. Indeed, it may well help to account for the relative eclipse of his reputation in the years following his death.

---

[74] Ibid. p. 251.   [75] E.H. Gombrich, *Art and Illusion*.

[76] Polanyi, *Personal Knowledge*, p. 95.

[77] See also Levinas' idea that 'Saying' bears witness to the existence of God. Emmanuel Levinas, *Otherwise than Being*, The Hague and London: Nijhoff, 1981.

STEINER, DERRIDA AND HART: PRESENCE AND ABSENCE

George Steiner's *Real Presences* was published in 1989. Partly because it proclaims itself to be a traditional, even a reactionary, book, its original-ity has not been widely noted, and it was not on the whole well-received by the critics. Yet what Steiner has to say about language seems to me an important contribution to the debate over meaning, language and story. Like Polanyi and Barthes he is overwhelmed by the limitless pos-sibility of language, and, in particular, by the formal indeterminacy of any sentence. In Saussurian terminology he allows that 'There is al-ways . . . "excess" of the signified beyond the signifier.'[78] For him, the greater the gap between what is said and what can be said about it, the greater the literary value of the text in question.[79] This notion of 'litera-ture' as a text inviting further comment and elucidation echoes Clifford Geertz' designation of 'thick descriptions', for those whose language is richer and more culturally dense, because they articulate the signifi-cance that particular actions or feelings have within a certain culture.[80] Such a definition of literature, of course, works equally well for scrip-tural texts, and reinforces the impression that Steiner, like Coleridge and Polanyi, resists the post-Romantic separation of literature and theology.

Thus it comes as no surprise to find Steiner differing sharply from Barthes, Derrida and Saussure over the question of 'meaning' – whether words have an innate historical stability in addition to their power of creating new meaning, or whether they are no more than algebraic terms, unrooted in the things they stand for and totally charged with meaning by their context. The theoretical epitome of this position he finds, not surprisingly, in 'the deconstructionist post-structuralist counter-theology of absence'.[81]

Steiner's theme is in direct contrast to this 'theology of absence'; in his own words,

It proposes that any coherent understanding of what language is and how lan-guage performs, that any coherent account of the capacity of human speech to communicate meaning and feeling is, in the final analysis, underwritten by the assumption of God's presence. I will put forward the argument that the

---

[78] George Steiner, *Real Presences*, Faber, 1989, p. 84.   [79] Ibid. p. 83.
[80] The term was originally coined by Gilbert Ryle, in *Concept of Mind*, Hutchinson, 1949, but its present resonance comes from Clifford Geertz, *The Interpretation of Cultures*, New York: Basic Books, 1973, Ch. 1.
[81] Steiner, *Real Presences*, p. 122.

experience of aesthetic meaning in particular, that of literature, of the arts, of musical form, infers the necessary possibility of this 'real presence'.[82]

Like Polanyi, he wishes to place himself within a fiduciary tradition, but at the centre of this tradition is neither the philosophic tradition of any believing community, nor that of the community of science. He offers instead what he calls (after Pascal's famous wager on the existence of God) 'a wager on transcendence', arguing that there is in the aesthetic, in a genuinely great work of art and in its reception, 'a presumption of presence'.[83] The word 'presence' is here used, almost defiantly, in a sense made popular by Derridean deconstructionists. It is the word for that unattainable post-lapsarian condition in which a text or word stands fully and completely for what it symbolically represents. In other words, Steiner is asserting with a boldness not hitherto attempted, the confluence of the aesthetic and the religious. All art is ultimately religious art. It is not in grammatology, but in poetry that we encounter God.

Kevin Hart's *The Trespass of the Sign* was published in 1989 – the same year as Steiner's book. Because it was by a lesser-known author it achieved much less widespread publicity, but is arguably the best book on deconstruction and theology yet to appear in the English-speaking world.[84] For Hart, Derrida presents at once a major threat to traditional theological speculation and an opportunity – perhaps the most important for several hundred years – for the development of a genuine negative theology. Like Polanyi he insists that it is one of the conditions of language that no text can be totalized; there will always be an ambiguity, an uncertainty, a gap between what can be said about it and the text itself.[85] Though he does not cite Polanyi, he does, like him, quote Gödel's theorem on formally undecidable propositions, and argues that Derrida achieves substantially the same result in philosophy.[86] For this reason, though he is familiar with the argument that God is, as it were, embedded in the nature of grammar, he is unimpressed by it. Hart thus sees himself as being at odds with both the conventional atheistic *and* theological appropriations of deconstruction, in that he does not believe that it has anything significant to say about God. What it challenges are the conventional notions of hermeneutics on which much of our idea of

---

[82] Ibid. p. 3.   [83] Ibid. p. 214.

[84] Hart is an Australian scholar with a rapidly growing reputation whose Ph.D. on Derrida from Melbourne University comes not from the Department of English Literature but the Department of Philosophy.

[85] Kevin Hart, *The Trespass of the Sign: Deconstruction, Theology and Philosophy*, Cambridge University Press, 1989, p. ix.

[86] Ibid. p. 83.

God still depends. What we need to recognise, he contends, is that 'far from being an object of deconstruction, Christian theology . . . is part of a process of deconstruction'.[87]

Behind this assertion there are, as he recognizes, two very different models of theology. One, as we have seen, stresses order, rationality and the workings of natural law; the other is concerned with the unpredictable, disconcerting and disruptive nature of the encounter with the divine. It is the former, embedded in the nature of grammar, that is destabilized by deconstruction; in so doing it creates and gives a new theoretical space for the latter. Here Hart quotes a very significant passage from Derrida:

There are thus two interpretations of interpretation, of structure, of sign, of play. The one seeks to decipher, dreams of deciphering a truth or an origin which escapes play and the order of the sign, and which lives the necessity of interpretation as an exile. The other, which is no longer turned toward the origin, affirms play and tries to pass beyond man and humanism, the name of man being the name of that being who, throughout the history of metaphysics or of onto-theology – in other words, throughout his entire history – has dreamed of full presence, the reassuring foundation, the origin and the end of play.[88]

The former system of interpretation is that of traditional philosophy and theology; the latter is the way used by literature – the telling of a story rather than the analysis of its meaning. Given the inability of language ever to be fully patient of interpretation, the former, the way of rationality, of order, and of law, is foredoomed never to achieve more than partial success. It is the poetic, the telling of a story, that, in the name of what Derrida here calls 'play', can sometimes come closest to full presence. Nevertheless, argues Derida, these two interpretations of interpretation cannot be absolutely separated from one another. They exist always in relationship – in an economy. The point is not so much that literature is using a different route towards presence, but that according to him, it is using the *only* route open to us, and philosophy and theology, without abandoning their roles of rationality, must now try to come to terms with what that means for the structures of their own ways of knowing.

I am citing Hart rather than Derrida here because Derrida himself has resisted the idea that his work has these kinds of theological implications. For Derrida, most traditional criticism has assumed that meaning is ultimately underwritten by presence – even to its extreme case,

[87] Ibid. p. 93.
[88] Ibid. p. 118; quoted from Derrida, *Writing and Difference*, trs and introduction by Alan Bass, Routledge, 1978, p. 292.

the presence of God who underwrites all meaning, even down to the seventy-seven meanings of the Torah, or the elaborate allegories of the Alexandrian Fathers. But, he contends, one can get exactly the same range of meanings by assuming an absence, rather than presence. In that sense, *Of Grammatology* concludes the long history of trying to find, or reconstruct philosophically, the divine language of Adam with which we began this chapter.[89] Despite Steiner's accusations, Derrida would deny that he prizes absence over presence. What he is primarily concerned to establish is that signification (i.e. meaning) occurs regardless of presence – a point popularized by Roland Barthes' phrase the 'death of the author'.

Hart is not a 'Derridean' in the normal sense of being a disciple. What he is doing is, rather, demonstrating that Derrida's arguments have implications that Derrida himself has not hitherto been aware of. From our point of view, Hart has done something else of importance. He has helped us to distinguish beween two very different – even totally antithetical – ways in which one might deduce the presence of God within the structure of language itself. One, the traditional way, looks to the nature of order and rationality, and sees God the supreme Lawgiver in action; the other, what in Hart's terminology is the deconstructionist path, sees the presence of God in terms of the openness of a text, the irruption of the new – what in traditional theology would be called 'the prophetic'.

Now it is true that neither Steiner nor Hart give any sign of ever having read Polanyi, and it is improbable that either would be in total agreement with him if they did so. Nevertheless, they are useful to us in this discussion because it seems to me that what they are struggling to articulate about the nature of language, its indeterminacy and its fiduciary nature, bear a strong family resembance to Polanyi's work, and suggest that the struggle against the denial of personal meaning has not merely not died out, but continues right at the heart of the contemporary debate over literary theory.

Polanyi's work was reacting to a very different intellectual world picture from that which faces us in the early twenty-first century. For better or worse, structuralism, post-structuralism and deconstruction have changed the face of debates about language. The kind of radical subjectivism envisaged by Polanyi appears cautious and conservative in relation to the fluidity of meaning taken for granted by, say, Derrida. When

---

[89] Jacques Derrida, *Of Grammatology*, trs Gayatri Spivak, Baltimore: Johns Hopkins Press, 1976.

Personal Knowledge was published, it was not the possibility of knowledge, but its personal quality that seemed to be the problem; today we take the *personal* for granted, it is *knowledge* itself that seems problematic. What is fascinating from a historical point of view is that in this unlikely context the idea of God has come to haunt the contemporary language-debate like a ghost within the mechanism of grammar.

There are two further points that follow from this. The first is that such a 'presence', such an idea of 'God', is strictly *regulative*. Like Kant's 'noumena', it can have no content in itself. We will each give it our own kind of meaning according to the ideas (not necessarily even beliefs) which we bring to it. Such a guarantor of meaning might range from the 'God' of the mathematicians,[90] who is no more than a theoretical absolute, to the kind of intensely felt divine presence of the advanced mystic. The second point follows from this, and that is that such a 'presence', however it be conceived, is the signal for a more heavily charged *irony* than any yet suggested. By stressing the essentially literary and poetic nature of biblical language, Coleridge was also, in effect, stressing its inherent irony. A string of later commentators, from Kierkegaard to Auerbach (using different translations from the Authorized Version favoured by Coleridge) have similarly pointed out how starkly devoid of 'foreground' detail are the great biblical narratives of the Old Testament.[91] What is left out of the story of Abraham and Isaac makes it one of the most mysterious and inaccessible narratives of our culture. For Kierkegaard it could not be told in any other way. Every reading we make of it opens the way for yet other readings, other problems, other glimpsed insights. Once seen, even though it is not really 'there', the figure over the tomb of Napoleon refuses to go away. Just as all modern science is essentially ironic, in that we are increasingly conscious of the provisional nature of its constructs, and of how obliquely its discoveries related to reality, so all modern readings of the Bible are also provisional, problematic and oblique. Not least of the ironies of the post-Enlightenment critical revolution in biblical studies is that it has produced not a greater understanding of the texts in question, but only a greater understanding of the problems in reading those texts. Indeed, the greater our understanding of language and narrative, the greater our sense of the unspoken gap between words and meaning.

[90] Stephen Hawking's famous phrase, 'the mind of God', at the end of *A Brief History of Time*, was taken up and used by Paul Davies as the title of his book, *The Mind of God: Science and the Search for Ultimate Meaning*, Simon and Schuster, 1992.

[91] See, for instance, Søren Kierkegaard, *Fear and Trembling*; Erich Auerbach, *Mimesis*, Ch. 1.

From that point of view the differences between Steiner and Hart are probably immaterial – though, incidentally, it does not seem to me that they are as far apart in their positions as might be suggested by their opposing reactions to Derridean deconstruction. Neither is prescriptive. There is in what they have to say none of the exclusivity and *hubris* of the academic system-builder. Both, on the contrary, start with the difficult and problematic nature of human experience and attempt that most delicate of feats: to understand how language might even partially describe what is essentially undescribable. Further, neither sees 'presence' as a natural or normal quality of language, but rather as something fleeting, rare and occasional. When it does occur it is totally disruptive and transforming. In science, art or theology alike it changes the apprehension of reality. It can suggest, point towards and reflect upon the unspeakable in ways that we can, whatever our very different private vocabularies, all recognize and be moved by. Whether such a linguistic phenomenon should be accounted a purely natural occurrence – paralleling the way that consciousness itself seems to arise in a seamless development from inanimate matter – or whether it should be seen as a new source of natural theology, or even a direct miracle, will be the subject of our next chapter.

CHAPTER 6

Twentieth-century fundamentalisms: Theology, truth and irony

RORTY: LANGUAGE AND REALITY

The relationship between words and things has always been problematic. Even if the most simple-minded attempt at translation quickly dispels any naive realist illusions that words stand simply for things, actions or thoughts, with a one-to-one correspondence between one language and another, the precise function of language in describing our material and mental experience was, and still is, deeply mysterious. Though, contrary to popular mythology, it seems that Eskimo languages have no more words for snow than English, there are huge variations in the ways various languages describe the world.[1] As we all know, French has two words for knowledge where English has only one; according to Benjamin Lee Whorf, Hopi Indians have different verbs for motion towards and away from the observer; the Japanese have different vocabularies for men and for women.[2] Until recently, however, few scholars were tempted to sever completely the Gordian knot tying words to the world, and argue that there is no *necessary relation at all* between our material surroundings and the stories we tell ourselves about them. Only with the advent of postmodernism has there appeared what we might call 'a linguistics of absence', rather than presence, and the idea of a theology and even a science based not on observation of phenomena, but simply on other, previous, stories about the world.

In his book *Contingency, Irony and Solidarity* (1989), Rorty suggests that there is now a quite fundamental split between those who see language as a secondary medium, describing in words objective truths about the universe, and those who, on the contrary, see language as a primary activity.

[1] Steven Pinker, *The Language Instinct*, p. 64.
[2] Benjamin Lee Whorf, *Language, Thought and Reality*, ed. J.B. Carroll, Cambridge, Mass.: MIT Press, 1956.

Some philosophers have remained faithful to the Enlightenment and have continued to identify themselves with the cause of science. They see the old struggle between science and religion, reason and unreason, as still going on ... These philosophers take science as the paradigmatic activity, and insist that natural science discovers truth rather than makes it. They regard 'making truth' as a merely metaphorical, and thoroughly misleading, phrase. They think of politics and art as spheres in which the notion of 'truth' is out of place ... [For the second kind of philosopher] great scientists invent descriptions of the world which are useful for the purposes of predicting and controlling what happens, just as poets and political thinkers invent other descriptions of it for other purposes. But there is no sense in which *any* of these descriptions is an accurate representation of the way the world is in itself.[3]

As the tone of his account suggests, Rorty supports this second position. To develop his case he invokes the linguistic ideas of Donald Davidson. For Davidson, language is not *a medium* at all. It neither represents the world as we find it, nor expresses our ideas about it. Abandoning the traditional assumption that language mediates between us and the world, or between our thoughts and ideas and other people, Rorty argues, should also help us to abandon many of the traditional questions of philosophy.

If we avoid this assumption, we shall not be inclined to ask questions like 'What is the place of consciousness in a world of molecules?'... 'What is the place of value in a world of fact?'... 'What is the relation between the solid table of common sense and the unsolid table of microphysics? We should not try to answer such questions ... We should restrict ourselves to questions like 'Does our use of these words get in the way of our use of those other words?' This is a question about whether our use of tools is inefficient, not a question about whether our philosophical beliefs are contradictory.[4]

Such a radical re-positioning of language as a primary human activity has no less radical implications, not merely for science, but for history, philosophy, language, aesthetics and, finally, not least, for human beings themselves. Thus intellectual history, so far from being a progressive development of ideas, becomes primarily a record of changes in vocabulary.

What Hegel describes as the process of spirit gradually becoming self-conscious of its intrinsic nature is better described as the process of European linguistic practices changing at a faster and faster rate ... What the Romantics expressed as the claim that imagination, rather than reason, is the central human faculty

[3] Richard Rorty, *Contingency, Irony and Solidarity*, Cambridge University Press, 1989, pp. 3–4.
[4] Ibid. pp. 11–12.

was the realization that a talent for speaking differently, rather than for arguing well, is the chief instrument for cultural change.[5]

Even what were previously seen as great intellectual debates of the past must be redescribed in terms of a more or less arbitrary shift in terminology.

As Kuhn argues in *The Copernican Revolution*, we did not decide on the basis of some telescopic observations, or on the basis of anything else, that the earth was not the centre of the universe, that macroscopic behaviour could be explained on the basis of microstructural motion, and that prediction and control should be the principal aim of scientific theorizing. Rather, after a hundred years of inconclusive muddle, the Europeans found themselves speaking in a way which took these interlocked theses for granted.[6]

Following from this, it comes as little surprise that for Rorty, philosophical history is also primarily a matter of linguistic change rather than of better arguments prevailing over weaker ones.

Interesting philosophy is rarely an examination of the pros and cons of a thesis. Usually it is, implicitly or explicitly, a contest between an entrenched vocabulary which has become a nuisance and a half-formed new vocabulary which vaguely promises great things.[7]

This is not necessarily a denial of progress, but it is a progress of language only, not a progressive discovery of how things really are. Thus, for instance,

The German idealists, the French revolutionaries, and the Romantic poets had in common a dim sense that human beings whose language changed so that they no longer spoke of themselves as responsible to nonhuman powers would thereby become a new kind of human beings.

Rorty continues,

The difficulty faced by a philosopher who, like myself, is sympathetic to this suggestion – one who thinks of himself as auxiliary to the poet rather than to the physicist – is to avoid hinting that this suggestion gets something right, that my sort of philosophy corresponds to the way things really are. For this talk of correspondence brings back just the sort of idea my sort of philosopher wants to get rid of, the idea that the world itself has an intrinsic nature.[8]

We must eliminate altogether the idea that these linguistic shifts represent the successful fitting together of pieces of a puzzle.

---

[5] Ibid. p. 8.   [6] Ibid. p. 6.   [7] Ibid. p. 8.   [8] Ibid. p. 7.

They are not the discovery of a reality behind the appearances, of an undistorted view of the whole picture with which to replace myopic views of its parts. The proper analogy is with the invention of new tools to take the place of old tools. To come up with such a vocabulary is more like discarding the lever and chock because one has envisaged the pulley, or like discarding gesso and tempera because one has figured out how to size canvas properly.[9]

But the process of redescribing language as a 'tool' rather than a 'medium' has, according to Davidson, inescapable consequences for our view of language itself.

We should realize that we have abandoned not only the ordinary notion of a language, but we have erased the boundary between knowing a language and knowing our way around the world generally. For there are no rules for arriving at passing theories that work . . . There is no more chance of regularizing, or teaching, this process than there is of regularizing or teaching the process of creating new theories to cope with new data – for that is what this process involves . . .

There is no such thing as language, not if a language is anything like what philosophers, at least, have supposed. There is therefore no such thing to be learned or mastered. We must give up the idea of a clearly defined shared structure which language users master and then apply to cases . . . We should give up the attempt to illuminate how we communicate by appeal to conventions.[10]

Finally, of course, we must also abandon the traditional, and very deeply rooted, notion of human beings as autonomous and unified individuals.

the traditional picture of the human situation has been one in which human beings are not simply networks of beliefs and desires but rather beings which *have* those beliefs and desires. The traditional view is that there is a core self which can look at, decide among, use, and express itself by means of, such beliefs and desires.[11]

Rather, we must think the human self as 'created by the use of a vocabulary rather than being adequately expressed in a vocabulary'.[12] At one level Rorty's conception of language is little more than an extension of what he calls the 'linguistic turn' affecting both philosophy and science in the later twentieth century. Nor is Rorty himself shy of drawing the connections between language and literature in this context. For him, Hegel is 'a poet' in his 'wide sense of the term', because he is 'one who makes

9 Ibid. p. 12.
10 Donald Davidson, 'A Nice Derangement of Epitaphs', in *Truth and Interpretation: Perspectives on the Philosophy of Donald Davidson*, ed. Ernest LePore, Oxford: Blackwell, 1984, p. 446. (Italics added by Rorty.)
11 Rorty, *Contingency, Irony and Solidarity*, p. 10.   12 Ibid. p. 7.

things new'.[13] Other modern 'poets' in this sense include not merely Proust, Nabokov and Orwell, but Nietzsche, Heidegger and Derrida. Once again, such an appropriation of all those who have changed our vocabulary into the ranks of literature is hardly new. For Friedrich Schlegel, philosophy was constantly striving to turn itself into poetry.[14] For Shelley, Plato, Jesus and Bacon were all to be included among the ranks of the poets. For T.S. Eliot, *only* those who had significantly altered expression could be considered as poets in the great European tradition at all.

More important, from our point of view today, we can see that Rorty's theory of language (one is tempted to call it the Rorty Theory of Everything) solves the problem of pluralism with which we began by cutting at a stroke the Gordian knot. If there is no truth, but only description; if there is no human centre, but only linguistic self-construction; if there is no argument, but only progressive shifts of vocabulary; there is no pluralism either. Above all, it is useless to ask the obvious question, 'Is this true?', since truth, and even rational investigation, have been conveniently dispensed with. We simply have a number of linguistic 'tools' at our disposal, and we are free to select whichever one which, for reasons of culture, need, aesthetics or fashion appeal to us most. We recall Screwtape's ominous words to Wormwood: 'Jargon, not argument, is your best ally.'

There is, nevertheless, one useful test that can be applied even to theories of irrationality, and that is what is sometimes known as the *tu quoque* ['you also'] argument. If, by your argument, there is no such thing as truth, then your argument *itself* cannot be true. Why, therefore, should we be persuaded by it in the first place? Rorty, we notice, has already tried to deflect some of the force of this reply by stressing that his theory does not correspond to the way things are, because there is no such underlying reality with which it can be compared. His historical analogies seem to suggest that persuasion is irrelevant, and that people in a century's time will have come round to holding these beliefs for no particular reason beyond the fact that a paradigm shift has mysteriously occurred.

There are two problems with such an inference, however. The first is that we live not merely in a literate society but in a print culture. We have written records. Even if there is no underlying reality to correspond to our descriptions, we can nevertheless check one written description against another. We can, for instance, observe that despite what Rorty

---

[13] Ibid. pp. 12–13.   [14] See, for instance, *Athenaeum* Fragments 116 and 304.

claims, Kuhn *never* entirely severs the link between changes in science and evidence. However much Newton's mechanics may have been hindered by French national pride and the suspicion of the scientific community towards what looked like a retrogressive revival of mediaeval theories of forces operating at a distance, Newton's ideas were eventually accepted not just because they became fashionable, but also because *they worked*.[15] Despite Rorty's attempts to appropriate Kuhn's arguments for himself, they actually support Polanyi's fiduciary view of science more than they do Rorty's nominalist one.

Something of the same slipperiness occurs with the citation of Donald Davidson. Anyone who takes the trouble to look up the passage cited from 'A Nice Derangement of Epitaphs' rapidly discovers that the sentences in question arise from a specific discussion of how we deal with misused words – in this case, Mrs Malaprop's language in *The Rivals*, the eighteenth-century play by Sheridan. Mrs Malaprop comically mangles her words, so that what was intended as 'a nice arrangement of epithets' emerges as Davidson's title. What Davidson is interested in is how we hear what she actually says and somehow adjust our mental set so that we re-interpret it correctly as meaning something quite different – *and* do it quickly enough to laugh at the joke. His point, therefore, is not that language doesn't exist at all, but that it works in a much more holistic way than conventional linguists have tended to assume.[16]

The second objection is logical: even if Kuhn's and Davidson's arguments *had* been exactly as Rorty interprets them, in the end Rorty's interpretation depends for its force on a truth-claim – two truth-claims in fact. The first is the mere fact that we *can* check his claims against his stated sources. The second brings us back to the now-familiar 'Cretan paradox'. To argue for the existence of arbitrary historical paradigm shifts in the past is a verifiable claim about historical processes. If it is true, then Rorty's case is both strengthened (this is indeed the way people change their minds . . .) but at the same time utterly destroyed, since verifiable truth, rather than mysterious shifts of language, has been made an integral part of the argument. If, on the other hand, Kuhn's argument can be shown to be false (on the whole a culture changes its world-picture for rational reasons) then Rorty's case also collapses. The best that he can do is to claim that so long as enough people *believe* in the Kuhnian theory of arbitrary paradigm changes (never mind the evidence . . .) then

---

[15] See above, pp. 54–62.
[16] See the ensuing debate between Ian Hacking and Michael Dummet; Davidson, *Truth and Interpretation*, pp. 459–76.

a shift of mental 'tools' has occurred. But even here there is a concealed truth-claim, *how are we to know* if such a shift has actually happened? Somewhere in this process verification always sneaks back in.[17]

It occurs most obviously in that metaphor of language as a 'tool', which is at once central to Rorty's argument, and, at the same time, curiously unexplored. Tools do not operate in a vacuum. They are for doing something specific.[18] If there is no 'way things really are', what is this tool of language supposed to be engaging with? Other, previous, and now to be discarded vocabularies? It is significant that the two examples of tools that he gives: the pulley, and sizing of a canvas, are both what one might call 'secondary' technologies. They do not engage directly with a new physical problem; they replace earlier, less efficient, ways of engaging with one. The question of the tool's material is thus by-passed. These tools belong in a sequence to which the beginning is conveniently over the horizon.

Moreover, if our choice of vocabularies is really so arbitrary, what about all those people who persist in feeling that they *do* have a centre; that language *does* mediate with their worlds; that there *is* such a thing as reality. What about those who, like Edward Said, believe that 'In human history there is always something beyond the reach of dominating systems no matter how deeply they saturate society.'[19] We cannot even label them 'misguided', or 'ignorant', because such terms again rely on tacit claims about truth. Since there seems no reason why one vocabulary should prevail over another, there also seems no reason why Rorty's own thesis should prevail either. In cutting the Gordian knot of pluralism, it seems, Rorty has cast himself adrift in a shoreless sea of relativity.

And this brings us to perhaps the most surprising point about Rorty. *He is a fundamentalist.* His argument is consistently presented within the framework of a stark either/or choice. There are those who 'see language as a secondary medium, describing in words objective truths about the universe', and 'those who, on the contrary, see language as a primary activity'. Yet this is, of course, a gross over-simplification. The implication that those who do not see language in Rorty's terms as 'a primary activity' will necessarily hold that it describes objective truths about the universe

---

[17] A point made in various forms by many of his critics. See Paul A. Boghossian, 'What is Social Construction', *Times Literary Supplement*, February 23, 2001. Also Thomas Nagel, *The Last Word*, Oxford University Press, 1997 and Bernard Williams' review of it in *The New York Review of Books*, 1998.

[18] A point which he accepts elsewhere in his writing. See 'Universality and Truth', in *Contingency, Irony and Solidarity*, p. 13.

[19] *The World, the Text and the Critic*, Cambridge, Mass.: Harvard University Press, 1983, pp. 246–7.

is nonsense. There are, as we have seen, many alternatives between what amount to two opposite fundamentalisms. Though there are no doubt those who, for religious reasons, believe every word of the Bible to be inspired by God, and therefore represent absolute truth, nobody who knows anything of the linguistics of the last two hundred years (to go back no further) would believe that all words correspond to things, relations between things, or to pre-existing abstractions. People can lie, make mistakes, and misuse words. As we have seen, the post-Romantic world has had to come to terms with the fact that truth can be created as well as discovered. Meaning is always a complex web of historical usage, clichés and metaphors, appropriation and misappropriation – and many other things. Increasingly, moreover, it is ironic rather than literal in tone.

This leads us to the prime sleight-of-hand behind Rorty's invocation of irony. Despite the prominent use of the word in his text, his argument is in fact totally un-ironic – and has to be so, because his definition of the word has, of course, to be consistent with his general argument about language. He writes:

I shall define an 'ironist' as someone who fulfills three conditions: (1) She has radical and continuing doubts about the final vocabuary she currently uses, because she has been impressed by other vocabularies, vocabularies taken as final by people or books she has encountered; (2) she realizes that argument phrased in her present vocabulary can neither underwrite nor dissolve these doubts; (3) insofar as she philosophizes about her situation, she does not think that her vocabulary is closer to reality than others...[20]

Now, of course, this looks very like the argument I have been using all along to justify the claim that in the fragmented post-Romantic world, all genuine knowledge must necessarily be ironic. But the differences are vital. For Rorty the ironic gap cannot be between language and reality, language and truth, or language and the world it purports to describe, because reality, truth and the world do not exist outside language. The ironic 'gap', therefore, has to be between one linguistic formulation, one vocabulary, and another. This is made very expicit:

...I call people of this sort 'ironists' because their realization that anything can be made to look good or bad by being redescribed... puts them in the position which Sartre called 'meta-stable', never quite able to take themselves seriously because always aware that the terms in which they describe themselves are

[20] Rorty, *Contingency, Irony and Solidarity*, p. 73.

subject to change, always aware of the contingency and fragility of their final vocabularies, and thus of their selves.[21]

The contrast between this and Kierkegaardian irony is absolute. Here surface is not being set in relation to depth; one kind of surface texture is simply being compared with another. There is no reality-check involved. 'Anything can be made to look good or bad by being redescribed...' This is not simply a matter of different metaphors. What is meant by the traditional metaphor of 'depth' in this context is the very factor that Rorty so resolutely seeks to deny: bedrock reality which is not subject to linguistic formulation. Thus, in the end, Lysenko's 'socialist biology' was *not* just a matter of opinion: it didn't work – and thousands, if not millions, died as a result. Similarly Rorty's use of Kuhn to support his own view of paradigm changes is *not* a matter of opinion: we can all read Kuhn and see for ourselves how Rorty has misused his source on this point. The traditional meaning of the word 'irony' places particular verbal statements in relation to some kind of 'other' truth: either something that is known to some or all of the recipients present (or, in the case of dramatic irony, the theatre audience); something that will become apparent later, something even that may not be known to anyone, but must be allowed for. Thus statements by astronomers about the size, age or structure of the cosmos tend to be ironic in the sense that they represent 'today's truth'. Any such statement contains the recognition that tomorrow we may know differently. The fundamentalist, by contrast, is the person who claims to *know* the final, fundamental truth about the cosmos – usually because of what he (or, as Rorty carefully says, 'she') takes to be divine revelation.

Rorty, of course, does not claim divine revelation. Far from it. But his own argument involves reference to what he calls 'final vocabulary'.

All human beings carry about a set of words which they employ to justify their actions, their beliefs, and their lives... They are the words in which we tell, sometimes prospectively and sometimes retrospectively, the story of our lives. I shall call these words a person's 'final vocabulary'.[22]

'A metaphysician' (not a good word in Rorty's vocabulary) is someone who assumes 'that the presence of a term in his own final vocabulary ensures that it refers to something which *has* a real essence.' This, of course, is in contrast with the 'liberal ironist' who, we recall, is characterized by 'radical and continuing doubts about the final vocabulary she currently

---

[21] Ibid. pp. 73–4.   [22] Ibid. p. 73.

uses'. This is modest enough. But, as we have seen, not merely with Rorty, but with Foucault as well, there is (and has to be) a claim to reality in any such nominalist argument. Just as Foucault's categorical denial of grand narratives itself falls into the trap of constituting a covert grand narrative, so Rorty's claim that there is nothing 'beyond' or 'beneath' language *itself* constitutes a metaphysic, a claim to truth – which, of course, like all metaphysics, is finally unverifiable.

Thus Rorty's liberal ironist also falls victim to the now-familiar Cretan paradox. If her claim that all vocabularies and descriptions are equally relative is true, then that claim to unverifiable relativity may itself also be false; if, on the other hand, her claim to unverifiable relativity is true, then the various conflicting vocabularies are not equally relative. The millions of biblical fundamentalists in America invoked earlier, for instance, must be *wrong*. But is a sense of final relativity irony at all? As we have seen, 'irony' in the sense in which I have been using the word (following, among others, Kierkegaard and Bloom) involves the contrast between two orders of reality: one which is thought, or at least, *claimed* to be true; the other, a different one, which is eventually *shown* to be so. Irony depends at some level on a hidden reality, whose presence must always be assumed, even if it cannot always be necessarily disclosed.

My claim that Rorty is a fundamentalist rather than an ironist is because he does not recognize the possibility that his own final vocabulary may be wrong. I am not, of course, referring to the so-called 'final vocabulary' of his supposed 'liberal ironist', but to his *real* final vocabulary which states the principle of linguistic relativity.

Thus despite the title, *Contingency, Irony and Solidarity*, there is little use, discussion or understanding of irony in the text of his book – and it is difficult to see how there could be. There is no hidden meaning to be implicitly drawn on, because there is, in his view, nothing to be hidden. There can be no implicit conflict between various versions of reality; there can be no gap between what is asserted and what we all know to be true; all is surface, there is no depth. Jürgen Habermas, the German philosopher, has acutely suggested that Rorty's 'irony' actually depends upon 'a kind of *nostalgie de la vérité*' (a nostalgia for the truth).[23] In other words, that ultimately it legitimizes itself by a distant hands-off reference to the very thing it explicitly denies. Once again, we are reminded of the claims of Barthes and Steiner, coming as they do from very different

[23] Jürgen Habermas, 'Richard Rorty's Pragmatic Turn', in Brandom (ed.), *Rorty and his Critics*, p. 33.

positions, that God is the supreme logothete, the ultimate guarantor of meaning.

Michael Polanyi, we recall, insisted that any linguistic system is in the end open to the checks of reality. Polanyi starts from a subjectivism as radical as that of Rorty or any deconstructionst.[24] But for him, though it is possible to create 'closed' systems in which verification is either impossible or irrelevant, they are, of their nature, short-lived. Rorty's vision of endless, anchorless, redescription is, of course, a 'closed system' in Polanyi's sense in that there is no external reality-check on it. And there are other forms of reality-check, less dramatic but no less finally compelling, than the Soviet crop-failures which undid Lysenko.

Perhaps the greatest irony about Rorty's nominalism – and we can legitimately, according to our definition, observe such 'ironies' – is his claim to give new status and value to literature, as one of the prime sources of verbal re-description. Of such authors as Swift, Hegel, Proust and Trilling, he writes:

We do not care whether these writers managed to live up to their own self-images. (Alexander Nehamas says he is not concerned with 'the miserable little man who wrote [Nietzsche's books]' *Nietzsche: Life as Literature* p. 234.) What we want to know is whether to adopt those images – to re-create ourselves, in whole or in part, in these people's image ... We re-describe ourselves, our situation, our past, in those terms and compare the results with alternative redescriptions which use the vocabularies of alternative figures ... Literary criticism does for ironists what the search for universal moral principles is supposed to do for metaphysicians.[25]

This, I would contend, betrays a fundamental lack of understanding of what literature is and how it works. The novel may indeed be the natural art form of pluralism, but a novel that is unrelated to any recognizable truth at all is boring, if not downright unreadable. And this, surely, is where traditional literary criticism has a legitimate and distinctive voice in this paradoxical debate. On the one hand, we find scientists, historians, theologians and linguistic philosophers, not necessarily all postmodernists, but all responding to the aesthetic and linguistic turn of late twentieth-century thought by redescribing their own professional activities not in terms of truth, but in terms of stories of one form or another. On the other, we find creative writers and critics, the very people who, according to Plato, were the makers of fiction, the liars to be excluded from his ideal state, struggling to ground their aesthetic creations in terms of 'truth'.

---

[24] See above, pp. 183–8.   [25] Ibid. pp. 79–80.

This does not have to be 'truth' in a sense which an earlier generation of historians, scientists and theologians would necessarily have either recognized or readily endorsed. As the German Romantics were among the first to recognize, truth may be made as well as found. To claim that our stories about the world must be grounded in truth, is neither to claim that human nature is constant and unchanging, nor that it is an ephemeral and purely linguistic invention. There is good evidence to suggest that people *have* changed very considerably over the few thousand years for which we have written records, and the source of that evidence is largely from the way we construct our fictions. There is also considerable evidence for the kind of massive historical redescriptions, or paradigm-shifts, that Kuhn and Rorty both point to. Similarly Davidson's insistence on a holistic approach to the complexity of language, and the human capacity to deal with linguistic redescription is immensely valuable. But if this were purely a question of linguistic description, it is hard to know why the narrative relics of earlier periods, other vocabularies, and other languages should move us as they so evidently do.

Why *should* the great linguistic constructs of the past, the Bible, Homer, Plato, Virgil, Dante or Shakespeare not merely affect us in the ways they do, but affect us directly *through translation*? This is not because the receptor languages already contained the concepts necessary to assimilate new works. Quite the contrary, in fact. When the Vulgate was translated into English in the early sixteenth century it was to reshape the English language in totally unpredictable ways.[26] Similarly, modern German is effectively the creation of Luther's translation of the Bible. The impact of Shakespeare on Chinese and Japanese is not because those languages were peculiarly receptive to the cadences and conventions of sixteenth-century English. It is hard to avoid the conclusion that in all these cases language draws on and speaks to that something human and extra-linguistic referred to by Said. We must remind ourselves that what differentiates the great literary narratives of the past from their scientific, historical or philosophic contemporaries is their sheer durability. We still read them. (And in case anyone should object that neither the Bible nor Plato should be so quickly appropriated as 'literary narrative', I reply that here – at least – I stand with Schlegel, Shelley and Rorty. As twentieth-century readers, we cannot help reading them in the Romantic sense of creating, rather than revealing truth.)

[26] See Prickett, *Words and the Word* and *Origins of Narrative*.

But this returns us to the original problem of fragmentation and pluralism to which Davidson and Rorty seemed, at least, to be offering a solution. Certainly it signally fails to release us from the Gordian knot. But if we accept, with Cupitt, Derrida, Feynman, Gribbin, Gould, Rorty or Schlegel that literature offers us the paradigm narrative form by which we may better understand the narratives of other disciplines, we do not have to accept what seems to me the somewhat naive model of what constitutes a 'story' such arguments are often taken to imply. Literary narratives are very far from being the free-floating fictions, or arbitrary redescriptions. As we have seen in the course of this book, stories come in many forms, and achieve many ends. Moreover, as Douglas Adams' old pole-squatting sage reminds us, we all have different stories to tell. Seen thus, pluralism itself takes on a somewhat different complexion. To assert that there is more to the universe than our descriptions of it, does not imply that there is a single verifiable truth, or that our descriptions are not themselves an integral part of the universe. It is that very suggestion, implied by Niels Bohr's quantum theory, and explicitly argued by Eugene Wigner, that mind is part of the apparently objective nature of things, which has caused such fierce debate in the twentieth-century scientific community. What some have denounced as heresy has been seen by others as the engine of yet another imminent paradigm-shift.[27]

POSTMODERNISM AND POETIC LANGUAGE: RELIGION AS AESTHETICS

Despite the logical problems inherent in his linguistic philosophy, however, Rorty's belief that there is nothing 'behind' language represents a persistent and strongly held, if minority view. In a recent book, *After God: The Future of Religion* (1997), the Cambridge theologian Don Cupitt echoes Rorty's extreme nominalism, returning again and again to this theme:

the magical supernatural world of religion was, all along, a mythical representation of the world of language . . . Language is the supernatural power that has called us out of nature . . .

the entire supernatural world of religion is a mythical representation of the creative – and also demonic – powers of language; [which explains why] the

---

[27] See *The Ghost in the Atom*, eds. P.C.W. Davies and J.R. Brown, Canto: Cambridge University Press, 1993.

turn to language in late modern and postmodern philosophy is having such a great impact upon religious thought.

The history of human thought has been the history of our discovery of what was all along implicit in our language, our first and greatest invention; and the supernatural world of religion turns out all along to have been in various ways a mythical representation of the truly magical world of linguistic meaning.[28]

As the reference to 'postmodern philosophy' indicates, Cupitt identifies his own demythologizing of theology with what he sees as parallel deconstructive and fragmenting moves in history, literature and philosophy by such figures as Foucault, Derrida and Rorty. Like them, he believes there are no grand narratives.

Today, however, the whole cosmological or grand narrative side of religion has totally collapsed. We know, if we know anything, that there is no rationally ordered scheme of things out there, no grand-narrative meaning-of-life already laid on for our lives to be fitted into. We know, if we know anything, that there isn't literally any supernatural order, and there is not literally any life after death. This is all there is, and, as everyone knows, when you're dead you're dead.[29]

Like the postmodernists, Cupitt wants a new and central place for literature, and calls for the creation (or, rather, a return) to what he calls 'poetical theology', which had been, he believes, lost in the literalism of the Reformation and Enlightenment. For him, the dense poetic allegory and symbolism of the mediaeval world were superseded at the Reformation by a legalistic literalism. Under the new cultural regimes instituted by the Reformation and Counter-Reformation:

The propositions of faith were to be accepted as realistically or literally true descriptions of supernatural states of affairs and goings-on, and were to be believed as a matter of legal and moral duty simply upon the authority of the Revealer . . . These doctrines effectively destroyed theology as an epic subject and a subject of major cultural importance, because they left the theologian with no important job to do except advocacy.[30]

This, Cupitt argues, was not an accidental development. Christianity has always been hostile to poetical theology because it was too deeply enmeshed in Graeco-Roman paganism.

Augustine quotes the late-Roman writer Varro as distinguishing among the *philosophical theology*, which is simply the truth as it is known to philosophers

---

[28] Don Cupitt, *After God: The Future of Religion*, Weidenfeld and Nicolson, 1997, pp. xv; 16; 18; 46–7.
[29] Ibid. p. 103.   [30] Ibid. p. 113.

and is taught by them in their schools; the *civil theology*, which is the established state religion whose rites are performed in the temples; and the *poetical theology* displayed in the work of poets and dramatists as they rework the old myths about the gods . . . Augustine's own purpose is of course to drive the poetical theology underground, and to keep it firmly repressed for the next thousand years. Having invented his own epic narrative theology, Augustine does not want it to have any rivals.[31]

After Augustine, poetical theology could not easily re-enter Christianity directly.

But it could and did enter indirectly, by way of the very strikingly effective Renaissance revival and exploitation of classical mythology . . . Using this vocabulary [Renaissance artists] built a new order – a new way of seeing, a new attitude to the senses and to this world, a new vision of landscape and of the human body, a new awareness of the passions and of role play, a new sense of human life as theatre – in short, the early modern world. They showed that a poetical theology can be the instrument by which a culture transforms and rejuvenates itself.[32]

For Cupitt, moreover, postmodernism is the direct descendant of the old poetical theology – diverse, fragmented, ironic and playful.

In retrospect it is now possible to recognise a postmodernist and poetical strand already within Western Christianity going back as far as the later Middle Ages. It shows up whenever a religious theme is treated with a touch, or more than a touch, of irony, satire, self-mockery, or playfulness . . .

Such a playful type of poetical theology was tolerable and tolerated precisely because it does not undermine but rather confirms the authority of the normality that it mocks. In the period of the great theological crisis (1780–1840), however, it became clear to the leading spirits in Germany and neighbouring lands that Christianity really *had* died as dogma. Kant and Hegel, the French Revolution, and the Young Hegelians D.F. Strauss, Feuerbach and Karl Marx between them had seen to that. In which case Christianity might now be available for transformation by a thoroughgoing poetical theology. It could perhaps be reborn as and in art.[33]

For Cupitt, religion – true poetical religion – has always been a form of art, and it is the privilege of our own time to understand and exploit the full significance of this fact. But before we are too carried away by this literal apotheosis of aesthetics, we should perhaps check a little more closely the theory of history and the actual evidence that underpins it.

---

[31] Ibid. pp. 114–15.   [32] Ibid. p. 115.   [33] Ibid. p. 116.

First of all we should note that Cupitt distinguishes right at the outset between Classical pagan 'poetical theology' and the rival Christian 'epic narrative theology' of Augustine. Yet, of course, the distinction here is not between poetry on the one side, and legal and moral literalism on the other, but between two different mythological systems – both in their own way equally 'poetic'. Are the stories of Hercules, Perseus or Theseus, any more 'poetic' than those of Jacob, Moses or Samson? Is the story of the fall of Troy or the wanderings of Odysseus more or less an 'epic' than the story of the conquest and occupation of the Promised Land, or that of David?

Though Augustine did indeed seek to foreground the mythology of the Bible over that of the Classical world, this was a theological, not an aesthetic choice. There is ample evidence that Augustine, like the other classically educated Church Fathers, Ambrose, Jerome, Gregory or Tertullian, found the Hebrew of the Old Testament, and, more especially, the *koinē* Greek of the New, a continual aesthetic barrier. *Koinē* is not a literary language at all, but a low-staus common patois spoken amongst non-native Greek speakers in the trading communities of the eastern Mediterranean. For the classically trained scholars who were to lead the Church in the second, third and fourth centuries, this bastard New Testament Greek was a continual aesthetic barrier. Unless the whole wealth of the classical literary tradition was to be rejected out of hand, some way had to be found of explaining why the Holy Spirit, which was believed to have inspired the New Testament writers, had such a poor prose style.

For Tertullian (writing c. 200 CE) the answer was to avoid comparison. 'What has Athens to do with Jerusalem? . . . We must seek the Lord in purity of heart . . . Since Christ Jesus, there is no room for further curiosity, since the gospel no need for further research.[34] Similarly, for Gregory, 'the same lips cannot sound the praises of both Jupiter and Christ'. At first sight Ambrose too seemed to agree, arguing like Tertullian that the scriptures contained all necessary instruction,[35] yet he clearly saw nothing wrong in openly structuring his *De officiis ministrorum*, written for the clergy of Milan, on Cicero's *De officiis*. Ambrose's pupil, Augustine, likewise admits in his *Confessions* that it was Cicero's philosophy that had set him on the road to conversion by giving him a passion for true wisdom.

---

[34] *De praescriptione hereticorum*, 7.
[35] See the 'Epilogue' by P.G. Walsh to J.G. Kenney (eds.), *The Cambridge History of Classical Literature*, Vol. II, part 5: 'The Later Principate', Cambridge University Press, 1982, pp. 107–8. I am greatly indebted to Professor Walsh's guidance in this area.

Perhaps the most agonizing conflict of aesthetic loyalties is recorded by Jerome, another avid Ciceronian. Compared with the classics, the 'uncultivated language' of the Old Latin Bible was so offensive that, he wrote, it made his 'skin crawl'.[36] Soon after he fell ill and dreamed that he had died. Asked before the judgement seat what manner of man he was, he replied that he was a Christian. 'Thou liest,' came the reply, 'thou art a Ciceronian, not a Christian.'[37]

So reluctant, in fact, were the Church Fathers to abandon the pagan grand narratives, that, as has been mentioned, a massive and sustained attempt was made over the succeeding centuries to incorporate the classical myths into the Christian one. By the time of Augustine this process was already well advanced. Cupitt's suggestion that the theology of the Author of *The City of God* was not 'poetic', therefore, is extraordinary.

More to the point, Augustine's was a 'theology' in the sense that the classical myths were not – and probably never had been. One of the fascinating mysteries of European history is the disappearance of the classical myths as a belief-system, even while they were retained as cultural heritage. As Richard Jenkyns has pointed out, the total death of a religion is one of the rarest events in history.

Once any new system of belief has commended itself to a considerable body of people it is seldom altogether eradicated; Zoroastrianism, founded more than two and a half thousand years ago, has survived for the past millennium or so with less than 150,000 adherents . . . Religions do not die; they become cataleptic . . . To this general rule there is one enormous exception. The growth of Christianity completely destroyed the great Indo-European pantheons, Norse, German, and Graeco-Roman. Some time in the sixth century A.D. the last man died who believed in the existence of Juno and Venus and Apollo, and in the succeeding centuries Asgard and Niflheim went the way of Olympus.[38]

What is equally extraordinary is the way in which, having collapsed like a pack of cards under the onslaught of Christianity, the old European religions did not disappear, but were retained culturally as 'mythology'. Noting the extraordinary persistence of this fundamental European mythological dualism (especially between Christian and classical mythology) it has been suggested that the European pagan systems *never were* 'religions' at all in the sense that the semitic ones (Judaism, Christianity and Islam) were.[39]

---

[36] See David Norton, *A History of the Bible as Literature*, Vol. I, p. 32.   [37] Ibid.
[38] Richard Jenkyns, *The Victorians and Ancient Greece*, Oxford: Blackwell, 1980, pp. 174–5.
[39] This may also be true of the one great surviving Indo-European religion, Hinduism.

Christian condemnation of the Graeco-Roman pantheon has always centred on the scandalous behaviour of the gods themselves, who were very obviously no more than humans writ large, with the same vices, lusts and appetites as their votaries. For someone reared in the Judeo-Christian tradition, the notion that such figures as Apollo, Mars or Venus were 'divine' was almost a contradiction in terms. Direct competition between the Olympus set and the mysterious and righteous God of the Hebrews was always going to be a case of 'no contest'. Plutarch's story of the sailors off the Greek island of Praxi, that first Christmas night, hearing a voice crying 'great Pan is dead!' says it all – incidentally, in what must be one of the great historical moments of poetical theology.

> And that dismal cry rose slowly
> And sank slowly through the air,
> Full of spirit's melancholy
> And eternity's despair !
> And they heard the words it said –
> Pan is dead ! great Pan is dead!
> Pan, Pan is dead![40]

However, if we look at works where both pagan and Christian systems exist side-by-side, such as Chaucer's *Troilus and Crysede*, we can see at once that, so far from representing competing systems, they are actually performing different and complementary functions in the story.

Here, the Greek gods provide what is, in effect, *a language of psychology*: a way of describing the interior worlds of people who, as we have seen, had no such interior space at all in the original Greek epic.[41] Chaucer was writing 2,000 years after Homer, in a Christian culture which, as Chateaubriand saw, had provided a quite new and un-classical way of experiencing individuality. The utter desolation of Chaucer's Troilus at losing Crysede is not the public shame of classical antiquity, but an interiorized personal grief at the loss of the woman he loves in a mediaeval culture still lacking an adequate vocabulary of emotion to describe the newly interiorized self.

What is less easy to discover, of course, is whether the classical pantheon was *always*, in our terms, more a system of exteriorized psychology than of religion in the Judeo-Christian sense, but it would certainly go a long way to explain the speed and finality of the Christian victory – as well as the way in which the new religion could absorb

---

[40] Elizabeth Barrett Browning, 'The Dead Pan'.   [41] See above, pp. 98–9.

and re-cycle the appropriated culture of pagan mythology for its own uses afterwards. But it seems arguable that, though the pagan religion of classical antiquity occupied the same social and cultural function that Christianity was later to do, whatever – perhaps unrecoverable – religious function it may have had, it was never a 'theology' in our sense at all. 'Poetical theology', in the sense in which Varro uses it, was always a Christian rather than a pagan possession. Once the interior space of the modern post-Renaissance, or better, post-Romantic, consciousness has been experienced, the modern ego, whether or not it may reject the Christianity that liberated it, cannot go back to the dark and stuffy room of the pre-Christian classical world. Even the mannered aesthetic late nineteenth-century neo-paganism of Pater and Swinburne cannot shake off Christianity, which it is then forced to parody, rather than returning to anything like genuine paganism. However splendid the 'poetic' of the ancient world, declared Chateaubriand, it is totally outshone by what he calls 'the Poetic of Christianity': that 'whatever may be the genius of Homer and the majesty of his gods, his *marvellous* and all his grandeur are nevertheless eclipsed by the *marvellous* of Christianity'.[42] With every allowance for the parochialism of a Eurocentric viewpoint, the Christian story, as told in 2,000 years of European art, literature and music, surely constitutes the greatest poetical theology there has ever been.

Cupitt, however, has other, more curious gods. 'When people cease to believe in God', G.K. Chesterton once remarked, 'they do not believe in nothing; they begin to believe in everything.' Still an ordained Anglican priest, Cupitt has ceased to believe in God, and now believes in the *Zeitgeist* instead. He is a fundamentalist not in the sense of having a revealed and unquestioned religious dogma, but in the opposite sense that he has unquestioningly embraced the spirit of the age. He now seeks not an eternal Rock of Ages, defying the flux of human existence, but a religion expressing our times, where moral values 'swim or sink, in our daily converse, exactly like and along with economic values' where everything floats on a free global market – 'not only money and prices but also linguistic meanings, religious truths, and moral and aesthetic values'. As with values, so with people.

People are becoming de-traditionalized, nomadized, 'casualized', as the old fixed points of reference disappear. Instead of marriage, a series of relationships, instead of a home, a series of addresses; instead of a career, freelancing; instead

---

[42] Chateaubriand, *The Genius of Christianity* (1802) trs Charles White, Baltimore, 1856, p. 330.

of a church, the irregularly mushrooming politics of protest; instead of a faith, whatever one is currently 'into'; instead of stable identities, pluralism and flux; instead of society, the market and one's own circle.[43]

Difficult as it is to read such passages without suspecting satire, Cupitt is apparently serious. This is clearly not a message for the deserted; the homeless; the unemployed; the devout, the resolute or the visionary. Francis of Assisi, Vincent de Paul, Bunyan, Wesley and Mother Teresa must look elsewhere. 'It is very postmodern suddenly to realise that we no longer actually need roots, identity, stability, or a provenance' insists Cupitt. 'We can do without all these things . . . '[44] (Especially, one might add, from the safe and well-heeled confines of a Cambridge college.) We remember Dean Inge's warning: 'whoever marries the spirit of the age will find himself a widower in the next'.

Yet it is too easy simply to mock the unintended ironies of Cupitt's theme. Goethe and Nietzsche, rather than Swift, are his mentors: we must immerse ourselves in the destructive element. 'If we can't beat postmodernity,' he writes, 'we should embrace it. I am proposing a very considerable redefinition of religion, a redefinition that (to adopt the Christian vocabulary) will bring religion closer to the Kingdom than to the Church, closer to the Sermon on the Mount than to any sort of orthodox theology, and will make it very short termist in outlook. Unlike the secular theologies of the 1960s, it will "aestheticise" religion, in the sense that it sees religious living in terms of artistic practice and symbolic expression.'[45]

Though he does not believe in 'an infinite and eternal super Being, who transcends the world and is the ultimate ground of all existence and value', he wants to retain a 'religion' that is poetic, mystical and subjective. Central to this aestheticization of religion are the linguistic arts – poetry, drama and narrative take precedence over the visual, the tactile and the musical. Yet our opinion of Cupitt's historical and aesthetic sense is unlikely to be strengthened by other historical references. For instance, his claim that during 'the great theological crisis (1780–1840) . . . it became clear that Kant and Hegel, the French Revolution, and the Young Hegelians D.F. Strauss, Feuerbach, and Karl Marx' had between them killed off Christianity as dogma, is curiously one-sided. Even if one were to agree with the premise (and a lot hangs on that word 'dogma'), the omission of Schleiermacher from the list of leading spirits in Germany (not to mention other Europeans like Chateaubriand or

---

[43] Cupitt, *After God*, p. 74.   [44] Ibid. p. 99.   [45] Ibid. p. xiv.

Coleridge) means that, with the exception of a reference to Blake, he never seriously considers the reconstructions of Christianity also offered by the Romantics. His conclusion that 'Christianity might now be available for transformation by a thoroughgoing poetical theology' ignores 200 years of precisely that process.

Indeed, history is not Cupitt's strong point. The Enlightenment, he informs us 'had been as damaging to art as to religion, and for much the same reasons.'

> Since Descartes, the demand had been all for a thoroughly demystified world view, expressed in the strongest possible terms. True sentences must either report empirical facts or precisely state the logical relations between clear and distinct ideas. In the older culture the world had been held together by language, that is, by a complex symbolic network of analogies, correspondences, and great narratives. But the triumph of the newer ideal meant that there was no longer any room for the strong, world-building uses of language. Tragic drama, epic poetry, and the great tradition in religious art simply ceased.[46]

So much for the descent from historicizing to actual history. This kind of generalization demands facts. As I have been at pains to show throughout this book, eighteenth-century England was already a highly pluralistic society, and overall generalities about the absence (or presence) of particular qualities of art and literature is dubious activity at the best of times. In England, we recall, the eighteenth century was not merely the time of the Enlightenment, but also of the Wesleys, of Methodism, millenarianism, enthusiasm and sentiment. Periods of great tragic drama are always brief, and far between – England had not seen one since Shakespeare's time – and in France Racine manages to miss the eighteenth century by a year. But as for epic poetry, and religious art, so far from lacking them, the eighteenth century is peculiarly rich in both. It was arguably the greatest age of hymn-writing, and perhaps also of Church music. The age of Newton and Locke was also that of Handel and Bach – to be followed by Haydn and Mozart. Though painting *was* notably less devotional than in the seventeenth century, there is still the genius of Tiepolo – and at the end of the century even Goya, Blake's contemporary, was to achieve a new and contemporary spirituality with his paintings in the Church of San Antonio de la Florida. Nor can we draw sharp distinctions between Enlightenment and religious figures. Which was Goya? Both, or neither? The Wesleys were in many ways typical Enlightenment men in their

---

[46] Ibid. p. 111.

attitudes, but Charles Wesley is also one of the finest poets in the English language – and, as anyone who has ever sung *Hark the Herald Angels Sing* will acknowledge, certainly a major religious writer. By any stretch of imagination Dryden, Pope, Johnson and Thomson were all major epic poets.

But Cupitt is not just mistaken historically. He also has no feeling for, or knowledge of, literature. It is not that *despite* the superficial rationalism of the Enlightenment, eighteenth-century society was nevertheless sufficently pluralist for there to be many more 'poetic' counter-currents than Cupitt supposes. On the contrary, it has long been argued that much of the peculiar artistic richness of the period from the Restoration to Jane Austen (what is sometimes called the 'long eighteenth century') is directly related to the prevailing rationalist temper. Not for nothing was it the great age of satire. One suspects that at the back of Cupitt's mind is the idea that satire is inimical to 'great art'; that one could discount such works as Dryden's *Absolom and Achitophel*, Pope's *Rape of the Lock*, or Johnson's *Vanity of Human Wishes*, as 'epic poetry' because because they are also 'satires'. No poet would hold such a view. Moreover, I would argue, irony (the key element in most satire), though not essential to great art, especially before 1700, is *increasingly* central to post-1800 art. And, of course, in reality epic poetry constitutes only a fraction of the poetic outpouring of the period – I am deliberately using the word 'poetic' in Cupitt's own broad post-Lowthian, or Shelleyan sense of aesthetic literature in verse or prose. As well as poets, such as Rochester, Prior, Gay and even Crabbe, there were a host of satiric prose-writers, including Addison, Swift, Fielding, Sterne, and, of course, Jane Austen herself.

But irony is a strange quality. Simply because it relates, however obliquely, to what I am going to insist on calling reality (without inverted commas) it floats like something seen out of the corner of one's eye: focus too closely on it, try to make it the basis of some postmodern fundamentalism, and it eludes us. But things glimpsed out of the corner of the eye are nonetheless real. There are excellent evolutionary reasons why our peripheral vision is many times more sensitive to both light and motion than head-on sharp focus. Tunnel vision is dangerous alike to prehistoric hunter–gatherers and to modern motorway drivers; it is perhaps most dangerous of all in fundamentalist postmodernist theoreticians who want to appropriate 'literature' and 'irony' as models for relativity. It is to those haunting mirages that we must now turn.

LOGOS AND LOGOTHETE: READING REALITY

There are three conditions which often look alike
Yet differ completely, flourish in the same hedgerow:
Attachment to self and to things and to persons, detachment
From self and from things and from persons; and, growing
 between them, indifference
Which resembles the others as death resembles life,
Being between two lives – unflowering, between
The live and the dead nettle.

        (T.S. Eliot, *Little Gidding*, 150–6)

Our problem is not quite that of Eliot, but the similarities are instructive; we, too, are concerned with things that look alike, yet differ completely. We have suggested there is little alternative in modern humanity's approach to knowledge between fundamentalism (defined as a belief in a 'given' immutable truth, whether by divine revelation, political dogma, or linguistic or psychological theory) and irony, where two orders of reality are contrasted, one assumed or claimed, the other hidden, undisclosed. Yet, as we have seen, some of those with the most sweeping and all-embracing fundamentalist systems have been the quickest to appropriate for themselves a language of literary and poetic forms with such associated techniques as polyvalency, fragmentation and irony. For Rorty, it is the poets who have re-shaped language, and so enriched our experience by re-describing the world; for Cupitt, the manifest historic failure of all Christian dogmas necessitates a return to the poetic theology of our pagan ancestors, re-clothed in the art-forms of our own time. Both claim for their views a postmodernist and artistic licence that permits them to dispense theoretically with close argument, probability and evidence. Above all, both have embraced the idea of 'irony' as a catch-all explanation for confusions, inconsistency and contradiction, while doing away with the notion of 'presence' which more traditional critics (including Eliot himself) had seen as central to art.

For Eliot, both attachment to things, and detachment from them were valid paths to spiritual experience. Elsewhere he calls them 'the way up' and 'the 'way down'.[47] Both eventually attain the same goal – presence. Neither is easy. Both involve, in their own ways, 'grasping the nettle'. What is a sterile void is the third way, growing between them: 'indifference'. The appeal to what one might call 'nominalistic irony' by

---

[47] See Northrop Frye, *T.S. Eliot*, Writers and Critics Series, Oliver and Boyd, 1968.

Rorty and Cupitt is a similar sterile indifference. Its easy and indifferent relativism allows for any kind of position – so long, that is, as it is relative. Once the framework of relativism is in place, all the stubborn difficulty, the problems of what Maurice, that great opponent of systems, called 'method', can easily be accommodated. Knowledge will always be incomplete and fragmented; language will be in a state of flux; poetic irony is the only possible attitude in a world with no final answers.

The trouble is, I believe they are very nearly right in every one of these assumptions. Yet in contrast with the *real* ironists (such as Eliot himself) such borrowed literary clothes merely call attention to their nakedness. As we have seen, 'postmodernism' is not, and never has been, a single coherent aesthetic or philosophical creed. It is not even clear who is, or is not, a postmodernist. If, for instance, Foucault seems to be laying claim to the territory in his influential essay, 'What of Derrida?' The Derrida invoked by Rorty to shore up his own position is very much a postmodernist; but Hart's Derrida, seemingly opening the possibility of negative theology for the first time in half a millennium, almost against his will, is a very different kind of philosopher.

Interpretation, as Schleiermacher noted, is endless – or, as the French critic Roland Barthes, has remarked, 'textual analysis is founded on *reading* rather than on the objective structure of the text'.[48] Elsewhere, in his famous essay on 'The Death of the Author', he adds:

> . . . a text is not a line of words releasing a single 'theological' meaning (the 'message' of the Author-God) but a multi-dimensional space in which a variety of writings, none of them original, blend and clash. The text is a tissue of quotations drawn from the innumerable centres of culture.[49]

For Barthes, the indeterminate nature of language, and, much more, the correspondingly indeterminacy of a written text has incalculable hermeneutical consequences:

> Once the author is removed, the claim to decipher a text becomes quite futile. To give a text an Author is to impose a limit on that text, to furnish it with a final signified, to close the writing . . . literature (it would be better from now on to say *writing*), by refusing to assign a 'secret', an ultimate meaning, to the text (and to the world as text), liberates what may be called an anti-theological activity, an activity that is truly revolutionary since to refuse to fix meaning is, in the end, to refuse God and his hypostases – reason, science, law.[50]

---

[48] Roland Barthes, 'The Struggle with the Angel', *Image–Music–Text*, trs Stephen Heath, New York: Hill & Wang, 1997.
[49] 'The Death of the Author', in Barthes, *Image–Music–Text*, p. 146.   [50] Ibid. p. 147.

This is a highly pregnant passage, replete with precisely the 'tissue of quotations drawn from the innumerable centres of culture' that we have been alerted to, and we must look as closely at the implications of its imagery as at what it is actually saying. To begin with he seems to be using the idea of 'openness' and 'closure' in a text in a way that is totally opposed to, say, Polanyi's. For Barthes, such symbols of hermeneutic order as reason, science and law are products not of openness and indeterminacy but of closure and fixity of meaning. Yet on closer inspection it is clear that what is being contrasted here is not the closure of a formal technical language versus the openness of a living one, but language with an 'ultimate meaning' (known or not) as against one that refuses to fix meaning at all. The terminology may be different, but the point is in fact astonishingly similar to Polanyi's: meaning is the product of an author and of authorial intention, and belongs to a world where things can be shown to be true or false.

For historical reasons that word 'revolutionary' is in French both stronger and more positive in tone than it appears in English translation. For similar historical reasons, the description of an ultimate meaning to a text as 'theological' carries a much more sharply hostile freight than the English translation might suggest. According to this view of history, it was the Revolution that in 1789 freed France from the burden of Catholic clerical dogma. But there is more to that word 'theological' than mere Gallic anti-clericalism. Schleiermacher's hermeneutics, for all its stress on the terminal incompleteness of human interpretation, *was* ultimately a theological activity. Barthes' terminal relativity has no such anchor. His (unspoken) rejection of Schleiermacher is, therefore, at two levels: ostensibly he is denying the implicit theological bias of previous hermeneutics; at another level, as a twentieth-century Frenchman who had lived under the German occupation of his country in Second World War, he is also denying the historical debt that French post-war criticism undoubtedly owes to the German Romanticism of Schleiermacher and his Jena associates.[51]

However, there is still more to that word 'theological' in this context than the national politics of twentieth-century scholarship. It stands here apparently for *any* externally imposed reading. The corollary seems to be that without such externally imposed principles of interpretation, 'meaning' itself becomes so elusive and problematic as to slide into a welter of perpetual possibility. For Barthes, meaning does not reside in

[51] See, for instance, Andrew Bowie, *From Romanticism to Critical Theory: The Philosophy of German Literary Theory*, Routledge, 1997.

the text itself, but in what we bring to it. It is important to notice that this can only be expressed negatively: as 'an *anti-theological* activity'. To put it positively is to give the game away. Hence that curiously arcane word 'hypostases'. The original Greek meaning is, literally, 'that which stands under' something. In French, as in English, it is a theological term, meaning 'essence', or 'personal existence', as in the three 'hypostases of the Godhead' in the doctrine of the Trinity. Reason, science and law, three of the most commonly imposed external disciplines in reading a text are thus seen not just as aspects of God, but specifically 'personalities' of God in the sense of being like the persons of the Trinity.

Though his negative formulation conceals the obvious corollary, what Barthes is doing, in effect, is defining 'theology' as first and foremost the *creation of meaning*. Meaning is created when a text is interpreted in the light of a particular system of thought – originally a theological system, but, by extension, all the principles of modern interpretation. Reason and logic, the scientific community, and the legal system are seen as expressions of the Judeo-Christian heritage. The idea that 'the death of the author' has the effect of 'liberating' what he calls 'an anti-theological activity' suggests that Barthes himself is opposed to reason, science and law alike – though, as usual in such defences of irrationality, it is hard to see how we could interpret such a passage without the use of the kind of (reasoned) analysis I have just been offering. In this case, however, it may be permissible to suspect a very real sense of irony at work.

Certainly it would be hard to offer a more powerful defence of theology, in its very simplest signification of 'a sense of God'. If, so the argument seems to run, we push meaning back far enough, even beyond the practical everyday dictates of reason, science or law, we encounter only Humean scepticism or metaphysics – in other words, God. If, as both Steiner and Hart seem to concur, meaning is ultimately guaranteed by God, we do not need that theologians' holy grail, a 'proof' of God. The concept of 'proof' itself is meaningless without God.

There is, however, an important caveat here: the 'God' so invoked is a logical figment only. In Kantian terms he is 'regulative' not 'constitutive'. Though such a hypothetical god of the grammarians is certainly not inconsistent with the Judeo-Christian God of the Bible, we cannot deduce such a figure from this argument. Nor, in my opinion, should we try. Though, I agree with Polanyi that an open linguistic system makes it impossible to tell lies indefinitely, we can, I believe, go no further than Hart's argument that it is possible once again perhaps to think in terms of negative theology. But for anyone who knows the tradition of negative theology, that is a very long way indeed. Moreover, we note that such a hidden presence guaranteeing meaning seems to draw on a chain of historical ideas of irony going back at least as far as Plato. If we accept the Barthesian proposition: 'without God, no meaning', all the evidence we have been looking at suggests the inevitable corollary: 'without God, no irony'.

Indeed, irony and meaning are like the opposite poles of a magnet: negative and positive. One automatically implies the other. Conversely, of course, language unrelated to any meaning, any reality (however 'hidden' or 'veiled'), is incapable of irony either. Though it is perfectly possible to be both liberal and ironic, Rorty's 'liberal ironist' is a chimera. Just as Rorty and Cupitt could not even present their arguments in language if their idea of language were actually correct, so their notion of irony is an ironic impossibility, a simulacrum that takes whatever life and credibility it has from our dim recognition (or Habermas' 'nostalgia for truth') that there is something very like what they are describing which *could* be true.

However, the fact that such ultimate irony is impossible for them, does not mean that functional colloquial irony is not *as* possible for them, as for any other person in the street. What, for instance, of the Rortean sceptic who greets the pamphlet-selling doorstep fundamentalist with the mild response that there might be more things in heaven and earth than dreamed of in her philosophy? Is this not as truly ironic as a very similar exchange I once heard between an eminent evolutionary scientist and an embarrassingly misguided clergyman who had tried to debate the status of Darwinian theory with him? The answer, of course, has to be yes. In the latter case, the scientist was very gently alluding to the possibility of a scientific reality to which *neither* of them had any kind of final knowledge – though it goes without saying that the speaker had a far better understanding of his ignorance than this particular clergyman. In the former case, our Rortean sceptic is alluding to another kind of hidden knowledge – the relativity of knowledge and the finality of language, in the sense that there is in the end no hidden reality behind the words themselves. The fact that I do not believe that this is true, does not surely prevent her own answer being one of irony. Similarly, there is nothing to stop the most rabid fundamentalist being ironic against the hidden bedrock of her beliefs (however temperamentally unlikely). We don't know what Father Brown, G.K. Chesterton's priestly detective, thought about the theory of evolution, but we do know that he was in all things to do with his Church, entirely orthodox. Whether or not that makes him a fundamentalist or an ironist in our terms depends on our view of Chesterton's Catholicism;[52] but certainly Father Brown saw the world in profoundly ironic terms.

It is no accident that in discussing twentieth-century religion, we take our examples less from theological tomes than from contemporary art and literature. Religion has indeed been as much subject to the aesthetic turn of twentieth-century thought as mathematics, philosophy or any other branch of knowledge. Nor is it accidental that to make the necessary distinctions between ideas that look alike but differ profoundly we have used an example from that profoundly religious, but no less profoundly ironic poet, T.S. Eliot. *Little Gidding* is about many things, but one of them is the ironic nature of modern religious experience.

> If you came this way,
> Taking the route you would be likely to take
> From the place you would be likely to come from,
> ... If you came at night like a broken king,
> If you came by day not knowing what you came for,
> It would be the same, when you leave the rough road
> And turn behind the pig-sty to the dull façade
> And the tombstone. And what you thought you came for
> Is only a shell, a husk of meaning
> From which the purpose breaks only when it is fulfilled
> If at all. Either you had no purpose
> Or the purpose is beyond the end you figured
> And is altered in fulfilment. There are other places
> Which also are the world's end, some at the sea jaws,
> Or over a dark lake, in a desert or a city –
> But this is the nearest, in place and time,
> Now and in England.

The elusiveness of the place described here is as elusive as the experience described. Of the manor house at Little Gidding, once the home of Nicholas Ferrar and of the small (married) religious community he founded there, nothing now remains. Ferrar's community was broken up and scattered by the Cromwellians in 1646 because it had sheltered Charles I fleeing from his catastrophic defeat at the battle of Naseby. After his death (in 1637) the house itself was destroyed. All that is left beside the later brick farmhouse (and the pig-sty, still there when I first

---

[52] The evidence of Chesterton's brilliantly provocative book, *Orthodoxy*, Bodley Head, 1908, is a hermeneutic exercise in itself, but certainly *The Man Who Was Thursday*, puts Chesterton firmly on the side of the ironists.

made my own pilgrimage) is the tiny chapel of the community,[53] and, in front of it, Ferrar's own tombstone.

What Eliot does not mention, however, is the inscription carved on the stone lintel of the chapel door: 'This is none other than the gate of heaven.' The irony lies not so much in the uninformed reader's ignorance of this, though everything in the passage refers obliquely to it, as in the fact that no reader, no pilgrim, however well-informed, *is* in a position to understand what it does mean. For the experience to have any real religious meaning, our intentions, our understandings, are alike transformed by the nature of that experience into something other than what we set out with.

For Eliot himself, the context was unique and particular. The young American philosophy graduate had come to England, the land of his ancestors, to find not merely his personal roots, but also, unexpectedly, to find roots in a Christianity that all his education had trained him initially to reject. The poem itself, the last of the *Four Quartets*, grew from both his own years of personal crisis over the ending of his first marriage from 1936 onwards and from his sense of the much wider crisis of the Second World War going on around him. *Little Gidding* had been begun in the early part of 1941, before either America or Russia had entered the War, and when Britain, it seemed, was all that stood against the barbarism of Hitler's Germany.[54] Whatever the experience to be found at Little Gidding at that moment of spiritual crisis, it had to be understood against the backdrop of a far larger drama whose outcome was then unknown.

But for us, the experience of reading the poem has to be one of a very different kind of irony. Eliot himself, and all the protagonists of that very personal drama which underpinned the public poem are now as dead as the two sides of the English Civil War whose actions created and destroyed the original community.

> We cannot revive old factions
> We cannot restore old policies
> Or follow an antique drum.
> Those men, and those who opposed them
> And those whom they opposed
> Accept the constitution of silence
> And are folded in a single party.

[53] Rebuilt in the eighteenth century, and added to again in the nineteenth.
[54] See Lyndall Gordon, *Eliot's New Life*, Oxford University Press, 1998, pp. 124–45.

The real irony of the poem's theme concerns not any particular historical outcome whose end was 'hidden' from the characters involved, however seriously it had to be taken at the time, but the perpetual irony of religious experience, whose purpose is always 'beyond the end you figured/And is altered in fulfilment'.

When we describe such experiences as 'poetic', we mean not merely that we most commonly turn to poetry to try to put our most complex and intimate feelings into words, but also that *only* an aesthetic medium can begin to convey something of the innate quality of such religious experiences. What we do *not* mean, unlike Rorty, is that the language of poetry is primary, referring not to some other 'hidden' quality of experience, but to something it has itself created. *Nor* do we mean, unlike Cupitt, that religion and aesthetics are alike the reified creation of language itself. Ironist and fundamentalist alike reject the third condition, which resembles theirs only as death resembles life.

It is now the task of twenty-first-century theology to make conscious and explicit the inescapably aesthetic nature of its own historic tradition. That is, for the modern, not to say the postmodern consciousness, meaning and irony are henceforward inseparable companions. Not merely is meaning inexhaustible; not merely can we never say enough; we are more and more conscious of what must be hidden, what is unsaid, what may never be finally put into words. 'Whereof one cannot speak, thereon one must remain silent' wrote Wittgenstein famously (*Wovon man nicht sprechen kann, darüber muss man schweigen*). It might be more accurate to say, 'whereof one cannot speak, thereof must one for ever continue to speak with irony'. Wittgenstein's dictum was, at best, a palpable half-truth – but, of course, he was being ironic. Wasn't he?[55]

---

[55] See Marie McGinn's review of Laurence Goldstein's *Clear and Queer Thinking: Wittgenstein's Development and his Relevance to Modern Thought*, *Times Literary Supplement*, May 26, 2000, p. 24.

CHAPTER 7

Science and religion: Language, metaphor and consilience

ETCHING WITH UNIVERSAL ACID

For a period that is supposed to have rejected grand narratives, our current interest in them verges on the obsessive. If literal belief in the old biblical grand narrative of Genesis has waned (at least in educated circles) it has been replaced by the scarcely less all-encompassing narrative of evolution. For Daniel Dennett, the mechanism Darwin attempted to describe in his *Origin of Species* can now be used (as Darwin never did) to explain almost every feature of the universe from the Big Bang onwards.[1] That mechanism, or 'algorithm', is natural selection.[2]

For Dennett and his militantly atheist sociobiological allies, such as Richard Dawkins, or A.O. Wilson, the triumphant narrative of natural selection has not merely obliterated, but replaced the Judeo-Christian narrative of the creation and destiny of humanity. In his metaphorical terminology, there are many 'cranes' but no 'skyhooks' in the ascent of man. Life has pulled itself up from primordial slime with no aids from above. Science has displaced religion, not just conceptually, but rhetorically as well.

For Dennett that Darwinian algorithm of natural selection constitutes a 'universal acid' – a fantasy common to many schoolchildren when they begin to study chemistry. Once invented, universal acid is, by definition, uncontainable.

---

[1] *Darwin's Dangerous Idea*, pp. 48–60.

[2] But see Gould's comment on Dennett's choice of this word: 'I am perfectly happy to allow – indeed I do not see how anyone could deny – that natural selection, operating by its bare-bones mechanics, is algorithmic: variation proposes and selection disposes. So if natural selection builds all of evolution without the interposition of auxiliary processes or intermediate complexities, then I suppose that evolution is algorithmic too. But – and here we encounter Dennett's disabling error once again – evolution includes so much in addition to natural selection that it cannot be algorithmic in Dennett's simple calculational sense.' Stephen Jay Gould, 'More Things in Heaven and Earth', in Hilary and Steven Rose (eds.), *Alas Poor Darwin: Arguments Against Evolutionary Psychology*, Cape, 2000, p. 93.

Universal acid is a liquid so corrosive that it will eat through *anything*! The problem is: what do you keep it in? It dissolves glass bottles and stainless-steel canisters as readily as paper bags. What would happen if you somehow came upon or created a dollop of universal acid? Would the whole planet eventually be destroyed? What would it leave in its wake? After everything had been transformed by its encounter with universal acid, what would the world look like? Little did I realise that in a few years I would encounter an idea – Darwin's idea – bearing an unmistakable likeness to universal acid: it eats through just about every traditional concept, and leaves in its wake a revolutionized world-view, with most of the old landmarks still recognizable, but transformed in fundamental ways.[3]

Dennett's metaphor is an engaging one – and not just because it draws on a fantasy re-invented by generations of schoolboys (including myself!). So engaging is it, in fact, that it is easy for us to miss the actual logical process involved. 'Universal acid' is a myth in the sense we explored in the first chapter: a genuine and observable phenomenon (certain acids will dissolve particular solids) is taken, and projected to the point where it extends to everything – and is therefore meaningless. It is also, as Dennett rightly says, unimaginable. Part of the attraction of the fantasy, of course, is that we *cannot* imagine an acid that would eat up the whole world. But, at another metaphorical level, we *can* of course imagine the corrosive power of the acid to eat into traditional (and especially traditional Christian) beliefs about the world.[4] Dennett is only too well aware of the suggestive secondary power of words. But, having verbalized the visually unimaginable, he then goes on to use this metaphor for an idea, a 'universal narrative', whose consequences are, he claims, equally unimaginable for most of us.

As I have suggested, the analogy is so engaging that it is easy to miss how it actually operates. The workings of the universal acid are unimaginable because they are impossible and absurd – indeed, it is its very absurdity that delights us. The implied universal narrative, however, is no less unimaginable but, we are asked to believe, in contrast, essentially true. Now there is nothing intrinsically illegitimate about this style of rhetoric. After all, there are plenty of aspects of the world which we have to accept as true, even if we cannot imagine them. As we shall see, quantum theory is one such example; multiple universes is another; for Christians, the Doctrine of the Trinity or belief in an afterlife would probably also qualify. In each case, the magic of language allows us to

---

3 Dennett, *Darwin's Dangerous Idea*, p. 63.
4 See Gould, 'More Things in Heaven and Earth', in Rose (eds.), *Alas Poor Darwin*, p. 91.

formulate metaphors for aspects of reality that cannot, and never will be, either perceived or directly approached. Indeed, this is not so much a special function of language, as an extreme example of something that goes on every day. Descriptions of something we have not seen rest on analogies with things we have seen: the first atom bomb was 'brighter than a thousand suns'. We have already seen how Owen Barfield traces the historical movement from outward observable events to metaphors of invisible 'inner' ones: we 'see', or do not 'see', what others mean; we can 'grasp' what they are trying to say, 'touch their hearts', or 'hurt their feelings' by failing to do either. Every metaphor we use – and many, like the ones just cited, have ceased to be conscious metaphors, and so have become 'literal' again – is founded on just such a process. They are all of them, in effect, little narratives.

But behind the main, conscious, metaphor of Dennett's principle of universal acid are other metaphors, of which he may or may not be so aware. Why, for instance, that curiously mixed metaphor of the acid 'eating' and then 'leaving' things 'in its wake'? Things that are 'eaten' are commonly 'excreted'. But Dennett's choice of words is not, I suspect, transatlantic prudery. The reference to 'landmarks' in the next sentence suggests we are in some sense navigating, going on a sea-voyage, which would naturally leave such a wake. The word 'eating' harks back thematically, if not grammatically, to a few sentences earlier where we learn that the acid cannot be contained by 'glass bottles', 'stainless-steel canisters' or 'paper bags' – a sequence that slides imperceptibly from memories of the equipment of the school chemistry laboratory to the boys' packed lunches. These are also the things, unfortunately, that are all too often thrown overboard from ships when they have served their purpose, and pollute beaches the world over.

But beneath this level of associative metaphors lurks yet another level of probably unconsious but culturally potent imagery. In the tradition of thought Dennett has long-since discarded, but was doubtless indoctrinated with at the same time as chemistry lessons, what is it that cannot be 'contained' by any material or barrier on earth? That other famous schoolboy liquid: the Holy Spirit. No wonder that our journey through Dennett's book has become a voyage (he actually uses the phrase a 'missionary voyage' of his enterprise elsewhere) and no wonder he is anticipating as a result 'a revolutionized word-view', whose landmarks, though 'still recognizable', are fundamentally 'transformed'. Richard Dawkins, one of Dennett's heroes, actually uses the word 'transfiguration' to describe the way in which he hopes to bring about changes in our perception of the world.[5] This is all the language of the Christian apocalypse, now pressed into service in the cause of the religion of sociobiology, and its son, evolutionary psychology. The universal acid, it seems, so far from eating away the foundations of religion, works more like a silver dip.

This is actually neither surprising nor original. Several of the recent biographies of Darwin have noted how Darwin's supporters, Hooker, Huxley, Lubbock, Spencer, Tyndall, and the other members of what they called the 'X Club', set themselves as early as 1864 deliberately to counter what was felt to be the stifling influence of Anglican orthodoxy both inside the Royal Society, and in the country as a whole, by turning natural selection into what amounted to an alternative religious creed.[6] Darwinism had its own grand narrative, with its creation story, scientist clergy, saints and martyrs, goal for humanity, and even (as we have seen above) its own apocalypse of enlightenment. They talked of their movement in terms of a 'new reformation' within the scientific establishment. Little has changed in the period since then. As Dorothy Nelkin has argued, Richard Dawkins' *The Selfish Gene* (1976) offers us what is essentially a substitute 'theological narrative: the things of this world (the body) do not matter, while the soul (DNA) lasts for ever'.[7] For E.O. Wilson, 'you get a sense of immortality' as genes move on to future generations. Elsewhere Dennett himself has no difficulty with the idea that Darwinism might offer a substitute religion.

Whereas biologists like Gould are suitably cautious about extrapolating from natural selection into the complexities of human society, as one might expect from modern purveyors of grand narratives, neither Dennett nor Wilson have been able to resist the seemingly obligatory final chapters dealing with culture, moral values and religion. Indeed, what has infuriated many of their critics is the ease with which they move from biological experiments to pontificating about some of the most complex and difficult problems of human culture, from theories of rape to the 'meaning' of great art.[8] Similarly, the title of Matt Ridley's book, *The Origins of Virtue* (note the confidence of that opening definite article) suggests the scale of ambition, if not the quality of the achievement.[9] The problem, however, is the feebleness of the religion which is being advocated, which so conspicuously lacks the transformational and

---

[5] See Gabriel Dover, 'Anti-Dawkins', in H. and S. Rose (eds.), *Alas Poor Darwin*, p. 55.
[6] Adrian Desmond and James Moore, *Darwin*, pp. 525 ff.
[7] Dorothy Nelkin, 'Less Selfish than Sacred? Genes and the Religious Impulse in Evolutionary Psychology', in H. and S. Rose (eds.), *Alas Poor Darwin*, p. 19.
[8] Ibid.   [9] Matt Ridley, *The Origins of Virtue*, Viking, 1996.

apocalyptic qualities to which the imagery of its apostles hopefully aspires.

Indeed, Ridley's book may be taken to epitomize a problem that has dogged all attempts to move from generalizations about the supposed evolution of the human brain during the Pleistocene period (an area of much conjecture and little evidence!) to questions of morals and modern social organization. Much of the book is taken up with discussions of how we might re-design society to make 'moral' (i.e. socially acceptable) modes of behaviour pay, and discourage anti-social behaviour. This is obviously an important and indeed fascinating topic that concerns us all. Who would not be willing to work for quite radical re-structuring of our socety if we could really eliminate, or even drastically cut violence and fraud in the world? Equally, however, it demonstrates the almost messianic beliefs that lie behind attempts to bring hard science (biology) to bear on problems that have hitherto defeated woolly-minded economists, sociologists, political scientists, moralists and theologians. Marx, after all, believed he was doing exactly the same thing; so did Herbert Spencer, with social Darwinism; so did Durkheim and the early sociologists. In Hilary Rose's neat phrase, 'the rhetoric of arrival' has been a recurring phenomenon of the story of 'biology-as-destiny' as it has been repeatedly presented over the past 150 years.[10]

Much of Ridley's book, however, is taken up with accounts of increasingly complex versions of 'prisoner's dilemma' games, in which the opportunity to gain by cheating is supposedly offset by the much greater gains possible to those who refrain from cheating – provided everyone else does the same! Clearly the 'scientific' study of 'virtue' along these lines has some way to go before it can be used as the basis of a political programme . . . One only has to look at a text from the real world of crime, James Gilligan's book, *Violence*, to see the almost boundless naivety of those who would start to deal with any of our social problems from an *a priori* standpoint. Gilligan, now of the Harvard Medical School, was director of mental health for the Massachussetts prison system from 1981 to 1991. During his time of office there, in one of the most violent prison systems in the world, he was able to reduce lethal violence, both homicidal and (more common) suicidal, nearly to zero, while some other types of individual and collective violence, such as riots and hostage taking, both common during the 1970s, had disappeared throughout the entire state system by the late 1980s.[11]

[10] Hilary Rose, 'Colonizing the Social Sciences?', H. and S. Rose (eds.), *Alas Poor Darwin*, p. 114.
[11] James Gilligan, *Violence: Reflections on our Deadliest Epidemic*, N.Y.: Putnam's Sons (1996) and London: Jessica Kingsley, 2000, p. 26.

If Gilligan is inspired by an other-worldly religion, he gives no evidence of it in his book, but he begins with and constantly returns to those age-old metaphysical problems of tragedy and justice central to the biblical and classical literary views of the world, and so absent from those of economists, political scientists and sociologists.[12] Turning to the disappearance of his own grandmother, a halfbreed and much abused Indian who killed her son before vanishing for ever, Gilligan contemplates his own family story.

Listening to these endless tellings and retellings of family tragedies, one can hear the interminable reworking of disasters too painful to be let go, yet too scandalous to acknowledge. So generation after generation tells the same story over and over again, in hushed tones, with this variation or that of one detail or another, but always with the same horrifying denouement. Why keep telling the story? In the effort to make sense of a 'senseless' tragedy? To follow the old formula and see if there might finally be a catharsis of the pity and fear this story arouses? To reach the end of a collective mourning for a lost mother and child and the amputated family they left behind? In the hope that in the latest retelling the story will by some magic, end differently, that the act of telling and retelling might undo the past and make it not have happened? Or in the hope that even if the story does remain the same, the process of telling it might change what happened from reality to fiction, to 'nothing but' a story, a 'myth'? But, of course, that never occurs, since nothing reflects reality more pitilessly and relentlessly than so-called myth and fiction. So our stories go on and on, as they have since we humans first began sitting around fires, in caves, acquiring the language with which to tell our stories. For it is in telling stories that we originally acquired our humanness; and we are not so much rational animals, as Aristotle said, or tool-making ones, as Ben Franklin put it, but first and foremost story-telling ones.[13]

A number of very different things strike the reader about this account. The first is how superficially similar it is to the mythical 'Pleistocene', cave-man culture invented by the evolutionary psychologists. But its similarity is that of the satiric resemblance between William Golding's tortured and superstitious people in *The Inheritors*, and H.G. Wells' portrait of our happy, guilt-free, 'primitive' ancestors. As Hilary Rose says, the evolutionary psychologists' view of our stone-age past looks 'embarrassingly like the Flintstones'.[14] Gilligan's convicts are certainly one with their cave-dwelling ancestors, but, like their descendants, those early cave-dwellers are already a troubled, haunted people, whose language

---

[12] Ibid. pp. 11–12.   [13] Ibid. p. 4.
[14] Hilary Rose, 'Colonising the Social Sciences', in H. and S. Rose (eds.), *Alas Poor Darwin*, p. 118.

has evolved not to let them cope with the marginalities of their outward life, but to tell stories, and create myths, to exorcise their inner demons.

And this brings into focus the most glaring gap of all in the evolutionary psychologists' portrait of our Flintstone past. There is in their account no conflict of values, no original sin to contend with. How could there be? If there are no skyhooks, all values *must be* emergent. Some, like human sacrifice, we have now discarded; others, like blood-feuding, the subjugation of women, torture and slavery we hope we are slowly but surely getting rid of. Yet if all values are equally emergent, whence this apparent *hierarchy* of values? – for all those mentioned have been, and some still are, given value-laden justifications. Good and evil are terms we play with at our peril in the one-dimensional consilient universe. Dualism is not so much a hangover from a dark and outmoded religious past, but an existential description. William Golding again:

> All day long the trains run on rails. Eclipses are predictable. Penicillin cures pneumonia and the atom splits to order. All day long, year in, year out, the daylight explanation drives back the mystery and reveals a reality usable, understandable and detached. The scalpel and the microscope fail, the oscilloscope moves closer to behaviour. The gorgeous dance is self-contained, then; does not need the music which in my mad moments I have heard . . .
>
> All day long action is weighed in the balance and found not opportune nor fortunate or ill-advised, but good or evil. For this mode which we must call the spirit breathes through the universe and does not touch it; touches only the dark things, held prisoner, incommunicado, touches, judges, sentences and passes on. Her world was real, both worlds are real. There is no bridge.[15]

Despite its Flintstone trappings, Gilligan's view of language is oddly Judeo/classical. Language is not so much the vehicle of progress as the means by which we struggle to understand humanity's tragic fate, the injustice and cruelty of the gods – or God, for the Old Testament is as replete with tragedy as the Greek theatre. Language is for telling stories, but, mysteriously, in every culture so far studied, and not least our own, the stories our ancestors told were *not* about how better to hunt cave-bears (a favourite with what we might call the 'practical Lascaux' school of thought) but about metaphysics: rainbow serpents, gods and demons, ancestral tragedies of women and men. Hunting, I suspect, they understood very well, and, however physically dangerous, it was not very verbally taxing; life was more complex, and needed words and stories.

---

[15] William Golding, *Free Fall*, Faber, 1959, pp. 252–3.

And here, of course, we encounter the real crux in this dialogue of the deaf over grand narratives. For twentieth-century sociobiologists and evolutionary psychologists, like their nineteenth-century Darwinian fore-bears of the X Club, there is no doubt about the particular Christian grand narrative that must be overthrown and replaced by that of natural selection. It is the story of Creation – the Book of Genesis. The obvi-ousness of this target has obligingly been confirmed by a noisy minority of fundamentalist Christians, mostly nowadays in the US, who have frantically tried to defend this version of the Hebrew Creation myth by a variety of dubious means, including something called 'Creation Science'. Yet, as we have seen, even in 1859, when the *Origin of Species* appeared, the leading theologians of the day, such as Maurice and Newman, failed even to become excited. There were, indeed, others, such as J.A. Froude, who lost their faith as a direct consequence of Darwin. It was left to the much more pedestrian and oleaginous 'Soapy' Sam Wilberforce to lead a somewhat confused attack. Not least of the ironies of this convoluted story is the fact that the biblical fundamentalism that gave historical sta-tus to Genesis was not a strong tradition in the pre-Reformation Church, but was itself a product of the same seventeenth-century intellectual rev-olution that gave rise to science.[16]

If one were to ask a contemporary Christian, or, better still, ask a contemporary Christian *convert*, what was for them the central narra-tive of their religion, I suspect none would name the Genesis story. The record of 'conversion narratives' (suspect as they may be in other ways) is convincingly unanimous on this point. From John Wesley feeling his heart 'strangely warmed' in a little chapel in Aldersgate Street, to the Clapham Sect, Mark Rutherford, the later disillusioned Edmund Gosse, the numerous converts of Billy Graham, or even the do-it-yourself Mal-colm Muggeridge, what has led them to Christianity has been a sense that here might be found the key to the great haunting mysteries of good and evil described by Gilligan that were not merely part of their existential world, but *internal* to their sense of being. Neither Paul nor Augustine would have demurred. If the language varies according to the sect and sub-culture, for most it has been described as a sense of Christ as their personal saviour, with an accompanying belief that their sins were forgiven. All however would have agreed with Coleridge's disdain for Paley's *Evidences of Christianity*, and the idea that a 'proof of God' lay somehow in verifying the biblical story of Creation.

---

[16] See Prickett, *Words and the Word*, p. 200.

Hence, I more than fear . . . the prevailing taste for Books of Natural Theology, Physico-Theology, Demonstrations of God from Nature, Evidences of Christianity, &c., &c. *Evidences* of Christianity! I am weary of the Word. Make a man feel the *want* of it; rouse him, if you can, to the self-knowledge of his *need* for it; and you may safely trust it to its own Evidence . . .[17]

Whatever Christianity offered in the late Roman Empire (and there is considerable evidence of change over the centuries) the grand narrative of post-Romantic Christianity has centred not around the Creation, but the Crucifixion – around metaphors of 'sin' and 'redemption', good and evil, tragedy and loss, restoration and forgiveness. It has been an inward, not an outward story – peculiarly resistant to the depredations of universal acid.

The problem with evolutionary psychology lies not with what is probably an over-simplified view of evolution, but with what is certainly an over-simplified psychology, and, above all, a naive sense of the inevitability of contemporary Western values. We should perhaps revive what T.E. Hulme, the early twentieth-century philosopher, called his 'critique of satisfaction'. In what amounted to a devastating attack on some of the leading cultural theorists of his day, he argued that those who wished to project their vision on to society, to correct or reform it, should be asked first to submit their ultimate goal: their vision of the 'good life', 'great art', or the 'good society'.

The philosophers share a view of what would be a *satisfying* destiny for man, which they take over from the Renaissance. They are all satisfied with certain conceptions of the relation of man to the world. These *conclusions* are never questioned in this respect. Their truth may be questioned, but never their *satisfactoriness*. This ought to be questioned. This is what I mean by a *critique of satisfaction*. When Croce, for example, finishes up with the final world-picture of the 'legitimate' mystery of infinite progress and the infinite perfectability of man – I at once want to point out that not only is this not true, but, what is even more important, if true, such a shallow conception would be quite unworthy of the emotion he feels towards it.[18]

By their visions shall ye know them.

LANGUAGE AS CHANGE

There is nothing new in the idea that language can convey multiple narratives, telling more than one story at any time. The multi-layered

[17] S.T. Coleridge, *Aids to Reflection* (1825), Edinburgh: Grant, 1905, p. 363.
[18] T.E. Hulme, *Speculations*, Kegan Paul, 1924, pp. 16–17.

narrative of Dennett's universal acid is the rule, rather than the exception. Both the consensus of the authorities we have so far cited, and the evidence we have been looking at, would seem to support Gilligan's argument that language is *primarily* a story-telling medium. Though we should, I think, be very wary of arguing that language is 'for' anything at all, *if* we were to apply the Dennett principle of 'reverse engineering', and ask how it was primarily used, I suspect that Gilligan would be shown to be right. We might even construct a speculative theory that those Flintstone families who told the best stories around the fireside evolved wider vocabularies, showed more solidarity, or in other ways gained crucial survival advantages.

What we can say, is that as we have seen, David Deutsch's functionalist view of language is clearly *wrong*. Languages are not 'theories', and they are neither 'invented' nor 'selected for their ability to solve certain problems'.[19] Gödel's theorem would predict that it is impossible to give a satisfactorily comprehensive definition of language because we are attempting to use language to define language. We may be ignorant of most actual languages, but we can never stand outside *language* itself. Like St Augustine's view of time: we all know what language is until we come to try and describe it. Nevertheless, many of our common assumptions about it have recently been challenged by cognitive scientists, such as Noam Chomsky. Here, for instance, is Steven Pinker, a sociobiologist heavily influenced by Chomsky:

Language is not a cultural artifact that we learn the way we learn to tell the time or how the federal government works. Instead it is a distinct piece of the biological makeup of our brains. Language is a complex, specialized skill, which develops in the child spontaneously, without conscious effort or formal instruction, is deployed without awareness of its underlying logic, is quantitatively the same in every individual, and is distinct from more general abilities to process information or behave intelligently.[20]

If Pinker is right, and Donald Davidson's suggestions about our instinctive capacity to sort out malapropisms would seem to support him, language may well prove to be *even less* accessible to study than many earlier linguists had supposed.[21] However, our concern here is only tangentially connected with the supposed innate capacities of the brain to process language. It concerns, rather, its *emergent* properties. Just as we can

---

[19] Deutsch, *Fabric of Reality*, 1997, p. 153.
[20] Pinker, *The Language Instinct*, p. 18.
[21] Hence perhaps the charge sometimes laid against Chomskian linguistics, that it has failed to offer a satisfactory programme of prediction, experiment and research.

observe that equally indefinable quality, consciousness, to have *emerged* – somehow, it matters not – from unconscious matter, so we can observe that language, as we find ourselves coming to consciousness within it, has itself certain important emergent qualities. And here, perforce, we move inexorably from speculative biology to written history. We have a another story to try and understand.

Though description and narrative are clearly among their prime functions, as we have seen, languages are much *more* than systems of description. As Newman argued, in many ways anticipating Saussure, and even, more distantly, Chomsky, language creates a whole that is greater than the sum of its parts. Words, like our perceptions, take on meaning from the contextual totality, permitting us to construct wholes from scattered fragments, certainty from partial and incomplete evidence. Indeed, just as our sense-perceptions are not passively received, but the product of an active interplay between ourselves and the raw sense-data, so our reception of language involves a similar personal interpretation. A whole twentieth-century theory of reading, 'reader-response' theory, predicates just such a process.

The important thing about such processes is that they are essentially *creative*, rather than either passive or repetitive. Pinker again:

> . . . virtually every sentence that a person utters or understands is a brand-new combination of words, appearing for the first time in the history of the universe. Therefore a language cannot be a repertoire of responses; the brain must contain a recipe or programme that can build an unlimited set of sentences out of a finite list of words. That programme may be called a mental grammar (not to be confused with pedagogical or stylistic 'grammars', which are just guides to the etiquette of written prose). The second fundamental fact is that children develop these complex grammars rapidly and without formal instruction and grow up to give consistent interpretations to novel sentence constructions that they have never before encountered.[22]

No two people speak or use language in precisely the same way. A whole new science of computer stylistics has grown up in recent years. If you analyse the ten commonest words used, there will not be much variation between most people. Words like 'a', 'an', 'and', 'the', 'here' and 'there', will predominate. But the commonest *fifty* words in a person's vocabulary will be as unique to that individual as a fingerprint. Such analysis has been used to weed out forged passages in police statements or so-called 'confessions'. More interestingly it has been applied to the authorship

---

[22] Pinker, *The Language Instinct*, p. 22.

of literature with fascinating results. Biblical scholars had long suspected the Epistle to the Hebrews was not by Paul, but computer analysis confirmed it. In the year that Henry Fielding, the eighteenth-century English novelist, died, his sister Sarah, who was also a novelist, published two novels – an unusual increase on her usual rate of output. Computer analysis reveals that the novels in question fall stylistically half-way between her usual style and her brother's – circumstantial evidence for critics' suspicions that she had inherited unfinished novels among her brother's papers, and had completed and published them as her own work. This was a period when (unlike today) men and women had distinctively different vocabularies – possibly because boys tended to have a classical education not shared by their sisters. Be that as it may, not merely do the characters in Jane Austen's novels have their own distinctively different vocabularies, like real people, but men and women show precisely this group difference in vocabulary. More startling is the fact that her heroes and villians also have characteristically different vocabularies – enabling modern critics to solve the long-standing puzzle as to whether the mysterious Edward Denham, one of the central figures of her unfinished novel, *Sanditon*, would turn out to be hero or villain (he *is* the villain!).[23]

In real life, however, sometimes characters are less obliging. Moreover, the innately personal and creative aspect of language means that it is also in a constant process of change. Each generation, each decade uses its language slightly differently. Indeed, not merely is change innate to language; there is a sense in which we can say that language is *about* the new. In his brilliantly suggestive book, *Orality and Literacy*, the Japanese-American Jesuit, J. Walter Ong, stresses the differences between the unchanging nature of oral societies, and the rapid changes that we have come to take for granted in literate ones.[24] What also comes across, however, is the difficulty traditional oral societies have in *preventing* change. Tribal memory-men, songlines, and proverbial wisdom are not a dead hand, giving primacy to ways of attempting to remember the past, they are also part of a very necessary attempt to slow down useless changes that could only destabilize and weaken proven recipes for survival in the harsh and unforgiving environments of many traditional societies.

In the literate history of modern Europe we know how markedly different eighteenth-century English (or French, or German) is from nineteenth-, or twentieth-century English (French or German). Even

[23] John Burrows, *Computation into Criticism*, Oxford: Clarendon Press, 1987.
[24] J. Walter Ong, *Orality and Literacy: The Technologising of the Word*, Routledge, 1982.

without a computer, a little training can enable any student to 'date' a passage of prose (or verse) of more than, say, 250 words, to within a decade with reasonable confidence. Some of this change is merely a matter of fashion – in particular sub-groups' slang often changes from month to month, rather than year to year – but, as we have seen, other changes in language and syntax reflect much more deep-seated shifts in human consciousness.

But 'reflect' may be the wrong word here. Trying to decide whether the word 'sentimental' was coined to describe a new emotional attitude to others and to the world for which people previously had no name, or whether the word intrigued and propelled people towards the attitude is like asking which came first, the chicken or the egg. What seems certain is that if you had tried out the word 'sentimental' on Attila the Hun, the Vikings or twelfth-century Crusaders, you would have been unlikely to have found a sympathetic response. The word is part of a particular historical and cultural package. Late eighteenth-century Russia was in many ways quite as brutal a society as that of the Huns or the Crusaders, but it *was* captivated by a spate of translations of Sterne's *Sentimental Journey* – often via versions in German or French – which most educated Russians spoke anyway, often as their first language. Everybody who was anybody among the tiny literate population ('the chattering classes' of the day) was reading (or pretending to read) him. When Baroness Dimsdale, wife of Henry Dimsdale, the doctor who inoculated Catherine the Great against smallpox, was introduced to the Empress, her 'gratitude' we are told, 'so far got the better of her good breeding that, when her majesty entered the saloon, instead of half kneeling to kiss the hand held out with so much grace, she flew towards her like a tiger, and almost smothered the poor Empress with hugging and kissing. As soon as the suffering sovereign could disengage herself, and shake her feathers, after so rude and boisterous an embrace, she walked on smiling and told the baron that *madame son épouse* was *très aimable*...'[25] It has been suggested that the Empress' remarkable restraint was due to her impression that this was the new English 'sentimental' fashion of greeting.[26] It is *also* true, of course, that the Russian notion of sentimentality was never quite the same as the English (or French or German) – and that people were tortured and put to death in much the same brutal and arbitrary ways as

---

[25] James Walker, *Paramythia* (1821) cited in *An English Lady at the Court of Catherine the Great: The Journal of Baroness Elizabeth Dimsdale* (1781), ed. A.G. Cross, Cambridge: Crest Publications, 1989, p. 51.

[26] A view not entirely supported by her alleged remark to her attendants, *Ces choses arrivent quelque fois*.

before. Sentimentality did not lead automatically to greater humanity. In eighteenth-century England you could, notoriously, be hanged for stealing a handkerchief – and the law was eventually changed less for humanitarian reasons than because juries were increasingly refusing to convict in open-and-shut cases. In France, the Reign of Terror was yet to come.

Just as in evolution there are irrelevant and also profoundly significant mutations, so in the evolution of cultures and languages, there are both arbitrary swings of fashion and real, long-term, shifts of thought and feeling of enormous importance. Though – contra Rorty and Cupitt – words do not necessarily create their own reality, under certain conditions they may help to influence perception. As we have seen in the course of this investigation, English has evolved and changed in certain very distinct ways in the past 300 years. Some of these changes, like the movement from outer to inner consciousness (Chapter Three), are common to most other major European languages; others are arguably peculiar to the development of English, and only spread, if at all, to other languages at a later stage. We have already seen Peter Harrison's argument that the word 'religion', with its associated concepts of pluralism, emerged first in late seventeenth-century England (Chapter Four). The evidence suggests that the words 'sentiment' and 'sentimentality' are another example – though it is typical of the irony never absent from the word that Sterne begins his *Sentimental Journey* with a (deliberate?) cultural *mis*-reading: 'They do these things better in France", I said.' We recall, similarly, Coleridge's argument from Diderot that English was a less abstract, more poetical language than French (Chapter Five).

Thus it is not merely literature, or 'high art', that opens up new ways of thinking, feeling and understanding the world. Though these are the most common and visible 'stories' that change the world, as we have seen, there are other narratives – most obviously in politics, history and science – that have had quite as powerful an effect on the evolution of our culture. All these various narratives have opened up new ways of seeing and experiencing the world. All have modified perception. This is not just a matter of the external world, however. As we have seen, they have also opened up quite new areas of 'internal space', and created new possibilities of introspection that have irrevocably changed our sense of self. Jane Eyre's emotional confrontation with Rochester ('*I* care for myself!') marks both a psychological and a religious transformation. A seventeenth-century governess *could not* have answered as she did; an eighteenth-century one would have been most unlikely to – and it is, of course, vital to the plot to understand that Rochester himself could neither have anticipated nor understood such a sense of self from a woman, let alone a woman with neither money nor status. His subsequent blinding, and (it is hinted) possible return to sight, uses the metaphors of King Lear to tell a new, essentially nineteenth-century story, of knowledge and redemption through suffering. Even as Darwin was contemplating his momentous new theory, the religion that his followers were to proclaim he had displaced had been turning inwards, away from proofs of God and evidences of creation towards moral and spiritual self-discovery.

Even Charlotte Brontë, however, would have been surprised by the strange pirouette performed by language-theories themselves over the next century. As we have seen, the origins of language had generally been held to be divine until almost the end of the eighteenth century; this was displaced by totally secular theories in the nineteenth; by the twentieth century we find language being proclaimed by Polanyi and Steiner as a vehicle, if not of immanence, at least of self-correcting truth (Chapter Five), and by Rorty and Cupitt as something nearer a free-standing creator of worlds (Chapter Six). None of these grand narratives, it must be stressed, however internally self-contradictory they may turn out to be, are necessarily in conflict with that other hotly debated area of Chomskian linguistics. What sociobiology, and its later offshoot, evolutionary psychology, has so far had to offer in concrete terms (rather than rhetoric) has been largely confined to the evolutionary and neural bases of language while philosophers of language, literary critics and historians have been more interested in its *emergent* qualities.

A REBIRTH OF IMAGES

What this study has, I hope, shown is that emergence is as much a cultural as a biological quality. For a variety of reasons, some already discussed, some of which we may not be aware of for generations, our ways of discussing, describing and comprehending the world have been in a process of much more radical change than has generally been assumed. In *The Origins of Consciousness with the Breakdown of the Bi-Cameral Mind*, (1982) Julian Jaynes argued that up until sometime around two and a half thousand years ago people actually *heard* their own thoughts as external voices – which accounts for way in which Hebrew prophets or Greek heroes believed they were the direct recipients of divine inspiration. Extraordinary as such a hypothesis may seem, it is certainly in line with what we know about later processes of internalization,[27] but, of course, it is hard to think of what might constitute conclusive evidence one way or the other. Over the last 300 years, however, where we are dealing with texts closer to ourselves, as we have seen, we *do* have conclusive written evidence for no less radical shifts of consciousness.

Not merely has one grand narrative of origins and destiny largely replaced another, but many (and not just the postmodernists) have come to distrust *any* such over-arching narratives. If some think we are on the verge of some kind of theory of everything, and that knowledge is approaching a point of consilience, others are quick to point out that there is not even agreement as to what a theory-of-everything should include,[28] and that the real state of knowledge is more fragmented (and more *fundamentally* fragmented) than it has ever been. Nor are the battle-lines clearly drawn. Those who believe in an achievable unity include religious fundamentalists, both Islamic and Christian, together with some of their bitterest opponents, ranging from sociobiologists like Wilson, applied physicists like Deutsch, to philosophers such as Rorty and theologians like Cupitt. The fact that I would argue that all of these are 'fundamentalists' in the sense we have outlined in earlier chapters would be unlikely to gain much agreement of any of those named.[29] Nor would the label appeal to those postmodernists, including Foucault himself, who are theoretically committed to the idea that *no* comprehensive unified theory is ever possible, or should ever be sought after.

Those, on the the other hand, who suspect that fragmentation is here to stay (at least for the foreseeable future) but keep an open mind about what is, or is not, ultimately possible, *also* include biologists (Gould) theoretical physicists (D'Espagnat) and theologians (Lash). What these have in common with most novelists, poets and creative writers of the post-Romantic era is a feeling that the world seems increasingly complex, elusive, subjective and ironic. For all these irony was the only possible response to what the German Romantics saw as 'the sense of the human situation hovering and oscillating between the indefinable limits

---

[27] Until relatively recently, reading was always vocal. It is said that St Ambrose was the first person to read silently. St Augustine records his first meeting with the great man: 'When he read, his eyes scanned the page and his heart sought out the meaning, but his voice was silent and his tongue was still. Anyone could approach him freely and guests were not commonly announced, so that often, when we came to visit him, we found him reading like this in silence, for he never read aloud.' (*Confessions*, VI. 3) See also Alberto Manguel, *A History of Reading*, HarperCollins, 1996, p. 42.

[28] See, for instance, Deutsch, *Fabric of Reality*, Ch. 1.

[29] Though the term is not just mine: see, for instance, Hilary Rose, 'Colonising the Social Sciences', in H. and S. Rose (eds.), *Alas Poor Darwin*, pp. 106–28.

of absolute unity or absolute diversity or chaos'.[30] For such there is a growing awareness that even the language they use is shifting beneath their feet, and that the kinds of description of the physical world, of culture, and of their society once possible, are no longer so – that the relationship of language to the world and therefore the nature of human consciousness itself is undergoing profound changes.

Psycho-science is probably an even less respectable field than psycho-history, yet it hardly seems accidental that the discovery of the unpredictable behaviour of quantum particles should have coincided with modernist challenges to traditional ways of seeing the world. The sometimes uncanny parallels between art and physics have been discussed by Leonard Shlan, who notes how the need for a single favoured point of view came to dominate art, music and physics at almost the same time in the sixteenth century:

A single favoured point of view became fundamental to all three disciplines. In perspectivist art, the entire canvas was designed to be seen by a passive spectator, standing in the favoured location several feet in front of the painting. In physics, an external reality could be measured because the observer was peering at it through a telescope from a favoured position of absolute rest. In music, the principle of a single point of view became manifest in the form of key ... [31]

... Key became the favoured and privileged tonal centre of a composition, corresponding to the perspectivist viewpoint in art and absolute rest in science. One of the founding fathers of the Camerata was the peppery theorist–composer Vincenzo Galilei, the father of Galileo – who played an important part in introducing the concept of *basso continuo*, which contributed to the acceptance of home key. 'A single key corresponds in principle to the inertial rest frame in science coincidentally discovered by his son.'[32]

The implications for all three activities were profound.

The single home key, like the focal point in perspective and the concept of absolute rest, represents a world whose point of view is monocular and mathematically organized. This principle allowed each discipline to order the parts of any of its compositions into a hierarchical and coherent set of relationships. Alberti's perspective,[33] Newton's *Principia*, and J.S. Bach's *Art of the Fugue* each

---

[30] Jack Forstman, *A Romantic Triangle: Schleiermacher and Early German Romanticism*, Missoula Montana: Scholars Press, 1977, p. 9.

[31] Leonard Shlan, *Art and Physics: Parallel Visions in Space, Time and Light*, N.Y.: William Morrow, 1991.

[32] H.W. Janson and Joseph Kernan, *A History of Art and Music*, Englewood Cliffs, N.J.: Prentice-Hall, 1960. Cited by Shlan, *Art and Physics*, p. 279.

[33] Leone Battista Alberti, *On Painting*, trs John R. Spencer, New Haven: Yale University Press, 1956.

manifests this singular notion, and all represent nothing less than the re-ordering of thought itself.[34]

The point stands, I think, even if we note that only Alberti's treatise, *On Painting*, is actually sixteenth-century, whereas Newton's *Principia* belongs to the late seventeenth century and Bach's *Art of the Fugue* was only published after his death in the middle of the eighteenth. What Shlan does not call attention to, however, is the degree to which this revolution in thought and perception is a *metaphorical* one. To use a phrase originally coined by Austin Farrer for the book of Revelation, this triple shift of viewpoint was part of a 'rebirth of images'.[35] The musical term 'key' is a direct translation of Guido Aretino's metaphor, from the Latin 'clavis'. But, of course, a 'key' in English, Italian or Latin, unlocks something, both physically, as in a lock, and also metaphorically, as in a problem or puzzle. In this case what the key controls – or gives us entry to – is a 'point of view': a phrase which significantly makes its appearance in English (from the French) very early in the eighteenth century, shortly after the publication of Newton's *Principia*, and about the same time as Bach was writing his *Art of the Fugue*. Within a few years Samuel Richardson, Laurence Sterne and Jane Austen were all to make keys pivotal sexual images in novels. What had changed was not merely a way of seeing the world, but a way of telling stories about it.[36]

Significantly, all three notions, of perspective, of absolute rest and of musical key, began to break down almost simultaneously in the early twentieth century. In the period up to the First World War, Picasso and Braque continued the experiments with perspective begun as early as Cézanne, and in Cubism formalized a new perspectiveless and simultaneous way of painting that was profoundly to affect all future art. At the same time, the primacy of the musical key was being challeged by Schönberg, and his pupils, Berg and Webern, while the idea of the fixed and independent observer was definitively undermined by Einstein's General Theory of Relativity. Meanwhile, the writers we now call 'modernist', such as James Joyce, Franz Kafka, Virginia Woolf – too diffuse and too international a group to call a 'movement' – were no longer satisfied with the traditional stabilities of realism: character, plot and authorial standpoint. Irony was so much a part of this new way of

---

[34] Shlan, *Art and Physics*, p. 279.

[35] Austin Farrer, *A Rebirth of Images*, Dacre Press, 1944.

[36] See *Clarissa*, *Tristram Shandy*, Ch. 1, and *Mansfield Park*, Book 1, Ch. 10; also Alastair Duckworth, *The Improvement of the Estate*, Baltimore, Md.: Johns Hopkins University Press, 1971, p. 18; and Prickett, *Origins of Narrative*, pp. 132–4.

reading the world that little or nothing could be taken at face value. Events were told and retold from a variety of standpoints, with no omniscient master-narrative to give the 'correct' version.

It was, however, quantum theory that was to change the nature of description so radically as to prevent any return to the relative certainties of the nineteenth century. The problem presented by the new physics was not so much the bizarre behaviour of matter at the level of sub-atomic particles, but that it made description – whether verbal or mathematical – *a crucial part* of that behaviour. The effectiveness of the theory in terms of its powers of prediction has never been in question. Indeed, it has permitted a level of experimental precision unprecedented in science, and no known experiment has ever contradicted the predictions of quantum mechanics in the last fifty years. The difficulty which was already becoming clear in the late 1920s and early 1930s, was not over technical aspects of the theory but its interpretation.[37] Here, for instance, is John Gribbin:

> All the things I have talked about as making up an atom . . . are part of a self-consistent story which both explains past observations and makes it possible to predict what will happen in future experiments. But our understanding of what an atom 'is' has changed several times in the last hundred years or so, and different images, (different models) are still useful in different contexts today.
>
> . . . not only do we not know what an atom is 'really', we *cannot* ever know what an atom is 'really'. We can only know what an atom is *like*. By probing it in certain ways, we find that, under those circumstances, it is 'like' a billiard ball. Probe it another way, and we find that it is 'like' the Solar System. Ask a third set of questions, and the answer we get is that it is 'like' a positively charged nucleus surrounded by a fuzzy cloud of electrons. These are all images that we carry over from the everyday world to build a picture of what the atom 'is'. We construct a model, or an image; but then, all too often, we forget what we have done, and we confuse the image with reality. So when one particular model turns out not to apply in all circumstances, even a respectable physicist like Nick Herbert can fall into the trap of calling it 'a lie'.[38]

But this is still only an extreme example of the familiar problem of metaphor. As we have seen, we can only understand our world by the

---

[37] There are many excellent accounts of quantum theory for the layman now easily available. My main debts are to *The Ghost in the Atom*, ed. Paul Davies and J.R. Brown, Cambridge University Press, 1986; Paul Davies', *The Mind of God: Science and the Search for Ultimate Meaning*, Simon & Schuster, 1992; and John Gribbin, *Schrödinger's Kittens and the Search for Reality*, Weidenfeld & Nicolson, 1995.

[38] Herbert, *Quantum Reality*, Rider, 1985, p. 197; Gribbin, *Schrödinger's Kittens*, pp. 185; 186.

'making and matching' of metaphor and simile. The difficulty with quantum theory, however, is that, according to the Danish physicist, Niels Bohr, founder of what is now the most widely accepted ('Copenhagen') interpretation, it is impossible to describe what goes on at a sub-atomic level without making *that description a part of the process itself.*

An example of this has been given by the physicist John Wheeler to illustrate how intimate is the connection between description and 'reality' in quantum physics. He was, he tells us, once invited to play an after-dinner round of Twenty Questions. The questioner, of course, had to leave the room while the other guests decided on the word. On finally being readmitted, he found a smile on everyone's face, indicating a joke or a plot. He nevertheless started his attempt to find the word. 'Is it animal?' 'No.' 'Is it mineral?' 'Yes.' 'Is it green?' 'No.' 'Is it white?' 'Yes.' The first answers came quickly enough, but then the pace mysteriously slowed as the respondents had to think longer and longer about replies to even the simplest questions. Finally, when he guessed 'cloud', and was told 'yes', everyone burst out laughing.

They explained to me that . . . they had agreed not to agree on a word. Each one questioned could answer as he pleased – with one requirement that he should have a word in mind compatible with his own response and all that had gone before. Otherwise, if I challenged, he lost. The surprise version of the game of twenty questions was therefore as difficult for my colleagues as it was for me.

What is the symbolism of this story? The world, we once believed, exists 'out there' independent of any act of observation. The electron in the atom we once considered to have each moment a definite position and a definite momentum. I, entering, thought the room contained a definite word. In actuality the word was developed step by step through the questions I raised, as the information about the electron is brought into being by the experiment that the observer chooses to make; that is, by the kind of registering equipment that he puts into place. Had I asked different questions or the same questions in a different order I would have ended up with a different word as the experimenter would have ended up with a different story for the doings of the electron. However, the power I had in bringing the particular word 'cloud' into being was partial only. A major part of the selection lay in the 'yes' and 'no' replies of the colleagues around the room. Similarly, the experimenter has some substantial influence on what will happen to the electron by the choice of experiments he will do on it, 'questions he will put to nature'; but he knows there is a certain unpredictability about what any one of his measurements will disclose, about what 'answers nature will give', about what will happen when 'God plays dice'. This comparison between the world of quantum observations and the surprise party version of twenty questions misses much, but it makes the central point. In the game, no word is a word until that word is promoted to reality by the choice of questions asked and answers given. In the real world of quantum physics, *no elementary phenomenon is a phenomenon until it is a recorded phenomenon.*[39]

It is this element of participation by the observer's description that makes the Copenhagen interpretation so hard to imagine. Some, indeed, have found it *so* hard to imagine that they have attempted other models of reality. David Deutsch, for instance, believes in the 'multiverse' – parallel universes – insisting that it is the *only* tenable explanation of what he calls, with considerable understatement, 'a remarkable and counter-intuitive reality'.[40] Others have found his 'solution' even more difficult to accept than the problem it was meant to solve, especially when he claims that 'Shor's algorithm' (discovered in 1994) has enabled him to perform calculations harnessing computers *in other universes* to the power of 10^{500} – a considerable number, if we recall that there are only about 10^{80} atoms in the entire visible universe.[41]

Nevertheless, one should not underestimate the sheer difficulty of grasping the Copenhagen interpretation. Einstein himself never accepted it.[42] Richard Feynman famously wrote 'nobody understands quantum mechanics':

Do not keep saying to yourself, if you can possibly avoid it, 'But how can it be like that?' because you will go 'down the drain' into a blind alley from which nobody has yet escaped. Nobody knows how it can be like that.[43]

Nor does Bohr try to make it easy for the layman, used to a world where description and object described are separable. It is, he insists, meaningless to ask what an electron 'really' is. Or at least, if you ask the question, physics cannot supply the answer. Physics, he famously declared, tells us not about what is, but what we can *say* to each other concerning the world.[44] Similarly, as Davies and Brown put it, energy is not a thing, but a form of description:

Energy is a purely abstract quantity, introduced into physics as a useful model with which we can short-cut complex calculations. You cannot see or touch energy, yet the word is now so much part of daily conversation that people think of energy as a tangible entity with an existence of its own. In reality,

---

39 Davies and Brown (eds.), *Ghost in the Atom*, pp. 23–4.
40 *The Fabric of Reality*, p. 51.   41 Ibid. p. 215.
42 See the discussion with Sir Rudolf Peierls in Paul Davies and J.R. Brown (eds.), *The Ghost in the Atom*, pp. 75–6.
43 *The Character of Physical Law*, p. 129.
44 Davies and Brown (eds.), *The Ghost in the Atom*, p. 11.

energy is merely part of a set of mathematical relationships that connect together observations of mechanical processes in a simple way.[45]

Description is not merely indivisible from interpretation in the ways in which we have seen in chapter one. With quantum physics, description and interpretation are, as it were, part of the thing-in-itself. It is, moreover, whether in mathematical or verbal terms, inescapably part of a wider narrative, from which it takes (and contributes to) its meaning. This intermixture of metaphor, narrative and description is repeatedly stressed by physicists as *what their discipline is about*. The Nobel Prizewinning physicist, Eugene Wigner, has famously insisted that the solution to the problem is that 'mind' must be seen as part of the physical composition of the universe – and therefore that the transition from a quantum phenomenon to knowledge or meaning depends on the existence of conscious observers.[46] Rudolf Peierls, the Oxford physicist, actually addresses the obvious (if mind-bending) question: if observation actually constitutes part of the universe itself, in what sense could it have existed before there were observers?

Q: Can we think that in some sense the universe was unreal or undecided before there were any human beings around to exorcise the ghost worlds of quantum theory?

Peierls: No. Because we have some information about the origins of the world. We can see around us in the universe many traces of what happened there before. We haven't understood all of it clearly, but the information is there. We can therefore set up a description of the universe in terms of the information available to us.

You're saying that in a sense our existence as observers here and now, 15 billion years after the big bang, is in some sense responsible for the reality of that big bang because we are looking back and seeing the traces of it . . .

Again I object to your saying reality. I don't know what that is. The point is I'm not saying that our thinking about the universe creates it as such; only that it creates a description. If physics consists of a description of what we see or what we might see and what we will see, and if there is nobody available to observe this system, then there can be no description.[47]

One can see how Jung's sense of humanity completing the world, Rorty's idea of there being nothing 'behind' language, and D'Espagnat's belief in a 'veiled' reality would resonate with such an essentially linguistic and metaphorical definition of physics. The point is that even if the

45 Ibid. p. 26.   46 Ibid. p. 63.   47 Ibid. p. 75.

Copenhagen interpretation of quantum theory is wrong – and a number of theoretical physicists including Bell, Deutsch and Gribbin have all argued for alternatives[48] – such replacements, whether they be expressed both linguistically and mathematically, or only in mathematical terms, *are still only metaphorical descriptions.* Moreover irony is not just present, but – and to a degree still largely unrecognized – as theoretically implicit in modern physics as it is in verbal descriptions.

We have come full circle from the ideal of Bacon, Hobbes and Locke of a 'perfect' scientific language, purged of the misleading impurity of metaphor, and giving in some almost mystical sense direct access to reality.[49] Instead image and metaphor are not merely a central part of physics, they seem also – in a sense no one quite understands – to be part of the universe itself. The question for us, however, is not so much the outcome of what is clearly going to be a very protracted debate about the 'fabric' or 'meaning' of the universe – if indeed there is an outcome, and not endless further fragmentation – but how far what has happened in physics reflects in an extreme form the state of our knowledge as a whole?

THE FABRIC OF THE UNIVERSE

'Fabric': from the Latin, *fabrica*, adapted from *faber*, worker in metal, stone, wood, etc. See 'forge'.

1. A product of skilled workmanship:

    i An edifice or building (1483)

    ii A contrivance; an engine or appliance *obs.* (1596)

    iii 'Any body formed by the conjunction of dissimilar parts'; a frame, a structure (1633)

    iv A manufactured material; now only a 'textile fabric', a woven stuff (1753)

2.   v The action or process of framing or constructing; erection (of a building); formation (of an animal body of its parts); now only *spec.* The construction and maintenance (of a Church) (1611)

    vi Kind or method of construction or formation

        a of things in general, buildings, instruments etc. Also style (of architecture) *obs.* (1644)

        b of manufactured materials. Chiefly of textile materials: Texture (1758)

---

[48] See interviews with John Bell and David Deutsch in Davies and Brown (eds.), *The Ghost in the Atom*; Deutsch, *The Fabric of Reality*; and John Gribbin, *Schrödinger's Kittens.*

[49] Umberto Eco, *The Search for the Perfect Language*, esp. Ch. 10.

vii Of a textile article: The woven substance; tissue, fibre (1823)
viii A building erected for purposes of manufacture; a place where work
  is carried on; a factory, manufactory. *rare.* (1656)

Some words are narratives in themselves. Whether this was the story that
David Deutsch wanted to tell when he chose the word 'fabric' for the title
of his book, *The Fabric of Reality*, or whether he simply had in mind what
is in fact the newest meaning of all, 'a textile article', is immaterial. As we
have seen, languages change; words notoriously do not mean the same as
their roots. Nonetheless, the evolutionary story of this word is peculiarly
apt to our purpose. From an orginal idea of craftsmanship, we move to
the grander scale of architecture – especially of a Church – and thence to
the idea of and assemblage of any complex structure, whether building
or organism, before turning finally to the weave, the warp and the weft,
of a piece of cloth. In so doing we have, accidentally perhaps, traced
the metaphorical outline of almost every historical grand narrative of
the universe. The Hebrew Genesis gives way to the great architectronic
system of the mediaeval church, only to be superseded by Newtonian
mechanism, and then Darwinian biology . . . But cloth? Where does that
fit in?

Well . . . there's always 'a man of the cloth' – our source, the *OED*,
reveals that that curious euphemism for a parson is a relatively late and
particular form of the more general idea that a servant should wear
his master's uniform. Its first recorded use, c.1685, coincides with the
foundation of the Royal Society and what we now, with hindsight, see as
the beginning of the scientific revolution. Maybe it is appropriate that
the association of priests and cloth should only begin with the decline of
ecclesiastical power. But the priestly element is nonetheless important.
And those whose metaphorical master is the suffering servant can only
be proud of their humble livery. If Wilson's consilience is like PVC – an
artificial plastic sheet, the same in all directions, inorganic, inert and non-
biodegradable – the fabric of our dualistic universe is of old-fashioned
cloth, with a warp and weft running at right angles to each other, woven
from organic material, and subject to change, rot and decay. 'Warp' and
'weft', incidentally, are among the most ancient words in our language,
used as early as the eighth century (c.725) and derived from the Old
Norse terms for fish netting.

If the weft (the short cross threads) of our fabric be knowledge (that
is metaphors) of the external world, the domain of the sciences and
associated disciplines, the warp is the moral, intuitive, internalized world,

that of introspection, the arts – and of sin, heroism, joy and tragedy. These are the long threads, running the length of the weave thoughout recorded history, and doubtless beyond. What begins as only a collection of loose, disjointed organic fibres is spun and then woven together, by hand or loom, to form the finished textile. The materials are natural, but the gathering, the assembly, the spinning, weaving, pattern, and all the skill of the workmanship are human.

The image also reminds us of Clifford Geertz' idea of culturally 'thick' and 'thin' descriptions (Chapter Five). One of the interesting lessons of the past 300 years has been in the failure of Christianity to 'modernize' itself by shedding excess metaphysical baggage. From eighteenth-century deism, to Matthew Arnold's desire to ditch the *Aberglaube* of traditional supernatural Christian belief,[50] to Bultmann's 'demythologizing' of the Gospels, to Cupitt's linguistic turn, all attempts to thin down the dense metaphorical structure of traditional (Vincentian) Christianity has rapidly and repeatedly failed, however defensible the particular prunings suggested might seem. This is not so much evidence for the literal truth of the original package, however, as evidence for the metaphorical nature of *any* such truth. The surprising thing about the controversy over John Robinson's *Honest to God* in the 1960s was not what he had to say, but how many people seemed incapable of admitting that their religion was as metaphorical as their science. In both cases, the fabric of the universe weaves tighter with the threads of thick descriptions.

Like all metaphors, however, the image of a fabric (even perhaps now a tweed) will only take us so far. It may perhaps differentiate this traditional dualistic 'fabric' from the extruded PVC or vinyl favoured by Deutsch or Wilson. But like all metaphors, all analogies, it is as subject to incompleteness as any set in Gödel's theorem. In Dante's *Divine Comedy*, Virgil, who personifies human wisdom, learning and skill, can take Dante through Hell and Purgatory as far as the meeting with Beatrice, the divine vision. There he unexpectedly disappears, leaving Dante bereft of support, to find that everything he has so far learned, and which has got him to the Earthly Paradise, is valueless.[51] As Northrop Frye once observed, metaphors are like a psychopomp, a spirit of classical mythology who conducted the dead to the underworld, pointing ahead to indicate, '*there* you must go, where I cannot take you'. Can we frame a metaphor for a participation in the natural world so intimate that description actually

---

[50] See Prickett, *Romanticism and Religion*, pp. 211–23.
[51] *Purgatorio*, Stanzas XXVII–XXXII. See also Prickett, *Words and the Word*, pp. 149–73.

forms part of the structure of matter itself? If it is the role of language to allow us to imagine the unimaginable, then maybe there is just a chance.

One such is John Wheeler's story of playing Twenty Questions without a particular word in *anyone's* mind. Part of its irony lies in the oblique reference (familiar enought to any physicist) to Einstein's dismissal of quantum theory with the remark 'God does not play at dice'. Like most physicists of the generation after Einstein, Wheeler is not sure *what* God is playing at, but he obviously thought it looked suspiciously like a game of chance of some sort. But Einstein's remark, whether or not reputable science, was prescient in its imagery. With the collapse of classical Newtonian physics God had made at least a metaphorical comeback. Stephen Hawking's reference to 'the mind of God' at the end of his best-selling *Brief History of Time* may have been little more than a rhetorical flourish, but it illustrates how difficult it is to keep God *out* of at least the rhetoric of the mysterious new physics. It was enough for Paul Davies to make the phrase into the title of his 1992 book, *The Mind of God: Science and the Search for Ultimate Meaning*. The result, though fascinating reading, is, as one might expect, hardly a work of theology.

However, Davies does summarize an argument which has gained some currency in twentieth-century science and religion debates: the so-called 'anthropic principle'. This rests on the idea that had conditions not merely on earth, but thoughout the entire universe, been only marginally different from the way they are, life could never have existed. All life, for instance, depends on certain properties of carbon atoms, and these cannot be formed within our solar system, but only within some of the largest stars. We are all of us running on star-dust.

Carbon nuclei are made by rather a tricky process involving the simultaneous encounter of three high-speed helium nuclei, which then stick together. Because of the rarity of triple-nucleus encounters, the reaction can proceed at a significant rate only at certain well-defined energies (termed 'resonances'), where the reaction rate is substantially amplified by quantum effects. By good fortune, one of these resonances is positioned just about right to correspond to the sort of energies that helium nuclei have inside large stars . . . A detailed study also revealed other 'coincidences' without which carbon would not be both produced and preserved inside stars.[52]

The astronomer Fred Hoyle was so impressed by this 'monstrous series of accidents', he commented that it was as if 'the laws of nuclear physics have been deliberately designed with regard to the consequences they

---

[52] *The Mind of God*, p. 199.

produce inside the stars.[53] He was later to say that the universe looks like a 'put-up job', as though somebody had been 'monkeying' with the laws of physics.[54] Others such as the mathematician turned theologian, John Polkinghorne, have cited this anthropic principle with qualified approval.

This seemingly uncanny principle of coincidence operates also at another level: that of human interpretation. Eugene Wigner notes what he calls the unreasonable effectiveness of mathematics in the natural sciences. It was Pythagoras who first referred to the God who was always doing mathematics, and the correspondence of mathematical theory and experimental data in physics, in particular, has fascinated and baffled generations of scientists and philosophers alike. For some it is so close as to compel the belief that mathematics is in some deep sense the natural language of science.[55] Wigner writes:

> The enormous usefulness of mathematics in the natural sciences is something bordering on the mysterious and there is no rational explanation for it. It is not at all natural that 'laws of nature' exist, much less that man is able to discover them. The miracle of the appropriateness of the language of mathematics for the formulation of the laws of physics is a wonderful gift which we neither understand nor deserve.[56]

Though neither the anthropic principle, nor the uncanny ability of mathematics to describe the natural world, amount to 'proofs of God' likely to give a confirmed atheist sleepless nights, they are both what one might expect in a universe where our descriptive metaphors are in some sense part of the fabric of reality itself.

A universe described in terms of symbol and metaphor is, in any case, not one that is *ever* going to provide proofs of God, though it may, in Peter Berger's memorable phrase, occasionally whisper 'rumours of angels'.[57] What is surely interesting is that the word 'God' re-entered scientific description, however figuratively, at the same time as the idea of science-as-narrative. The struggle of the Darwinian X Club to provide an alternative scientific narrative to the traditional Christian one seems to have come full circle. That attempt to provide an alternative narrative to Christianity has come to look, in retrospect, fatally like trying to take

---

53 *Religion and the Scientists*, ed. Mervyn Stockwood, SCM Press, 1959, p. 82.
54 Fred Hoyle, *The Intelligent Universe*, Michael Joseph, 1983, p. 218.
55 Wilson, *Consilience*, p. 52.
56 'The Unreasonable Effectiveness of Mathematics in the Natural Sciences', *Communications on Pure and Applied Mathematics*, 13:1–14, 1960. Cited by Wilson, *Consilience*.
57 Peter Berger, *A Rumour of Angels* (1969), Pelican, Penguin Books, 1971.

on Christianity on what neither side realized was religion's own home ground: the art of story-telling.

Science as a series of stories seems irresistibly to invoke the God whose own book consists of a collection of enigmatic and scandalous stories. It also suggests closer parallels between the symbols and metaphors of science and those of other textual discourses, whether literature or theology. In the Jewish tradition the world was created from the alphabet, and, ever since it seems, description and reality have been inseparably linked.

The real message of the anthropic principle is thus not that God may (or may not) be proved by science. Kant's principle that God cannot be an object *in* the world seems sound. The point is, rather, that if we are to regard science as primarily a process of telling stories about the world, we should expect such stories, like other narratives, to be multi-valent, ambiguous – and ironic. This is not a matter of the mindless relativism of the patronizing 'this is true for me/them'. There is no open non-judgemental relativism about finding different layers of meaning in a literary narrative. Evidence plays as strong a part here as it does in any other rational debate. But readers of literature are accustomed to find many kinds of stories wrapped around each other in any major narrative, and the short strands of our 'woven' fabric of the universe are made up of many fibres, just as the long ones are. The anthropic narrative is 'there' – and can be demonstrated. Similarly, the metaphors that compose Daniel Dennett's myth of the universal acid tell several stories – and not necessarily just the ones that he was conscious of. Nor should we glibly attach the label 'Freudian' to such detailed readings. They were around a long time before Sigmund Freud. As Leo Salingar once remarked to me, 'Freud may not have known much about human beings, but he was a damn good traditional critic.' We have already seen the origins of such polyvalent readings in biblical criticism, and how such ways of reading were incorporated into the novel just at the time when a rising literalism and fundamentalism were making such readings of the Bible less popular. Freud and his followers were the heirs of the German Romantic movement. What they did do very successfully, was to assist in the expansion of interior worlds by making such literary, and ultimately biblical, ways of reading much more available in the social sciences.

Finally, we should expect to find the stories told by post-Romantic science to be ambiguous and ironic – as indeed they are. No one who has read so far will need convincing of the sense of what is 'hidden' behind the baffling intricacies of quantum mechanics, nor that physicists like D'Espagnat or biologists like Gould are unaware of such ironies. Two important things follow from this, however. The first is that this is historically a *new* way of seeing the world. As we have seen, while irony is at least as old as the book of Genesis, it was very slow to be recognized critically as a separate narrative quality. Kierkegaard (following Friedrich Schlegel) was the first modern writer to produce a specific treatise on it. Similarly, though Newton had indeed a sense of what was hidden in nature – the 'discoverer' of gravity could hardly fail to – it would be incorrect to see Newtonian mechanics or optics as in any sense ironic. Darwin's work, on the other hand, is suffused with a sense of the ironic implications of his theory, as well as by a sense of how much lay below the surface of his argument.

Confirmation of our increasing cultural awareness of irony in the twentieth century comes also from an unexpected quarter. When I attended lectures by C.S. Lewis at Cambridge in the late 1950s he warned us specifically against discovering irony in sixteenth- and seventeenth-century works where, he maintained, often none was intended. Without going into the problems of individual texts, or the intentional fallacy, he was in general probably right. The author of the profoundly ironic *Screwtape Letters* did not, however, discuss what was to me (even then) the much more interesting question of *why* twentieth-century students should instinctively read earlier texts in terms of presumed irony.

The second point that follows from this is that the nature of the stories we tell about ourselves and the world around us changes significantly over time. The history of science is not so much that of an aggregated body of knowledge, as a fluid changing body, constantly re-interpreting its own structure in the light of new discoveries. We know that many creatures' eyes (including our own) are better equipped to detect change rather than continuities in the surrounding environment. As we have seen, our languages have something of the same quality. An ever-expanding inner world and a growing sense of irony are both hallmarks of post-Romantic narrative. Simply from a stylistic point of view the changes in the stories told by science, not to mention those told by philosophers and theologians over the past 200 years have shown much of the same development. That is not to say, of course, that this is a 'literary' development, or that science has been (however unconsciously) driven by literary or even cultural programmes. On the contrary, as Gillian Beer, among others, has shown, Darwin helped to set the agenda for a multitude of subsequent novels and other related narratives. The way in which cultures develop is subject to a large number of variables, some of which are parts of long-term historical movements, others entirely contingent. Such processes are immensely complex and (to judge by the success of past predictions by experts) still little understood.

These cultural intertextualities are not, however, an argument for consilience in Wilson's sense, any more than they give grounds for hope that the kind of Theory-of-Everything envisaged by Deutsch will be achieved. Indeed, like Fukuyama's dangerous prediction of the 'end of history', all such omega-points (in Teilhard de Chardin's phrase) are profoundly a-historical. What does Wilson envisage would happen the year *after* consilience has been officially proclaimed? Would we tidy up the few loose ends, then stop doing science, and all go home? Even if we understand 'consilience' not as the arrival of a final theory-of-everything, but more modestly in terms of an end to the current fragmentation of knowledge, such grand narratives have usually proved temporary and inherently unstable. It is probably a safe prediction that, like dreams of a perfect universal language, such ideas will continue to be aired at regular intervals, and no doubt earn their authors a welcome supplement to their academic salaries, but the eventual postponement of that millennium, like other millenarian prophecies of the past, is also safely predictable. Just as events and their afterlife are inexhaustibly interpretable, we live in a world geared less to unity than to fragmentation. Small-scale consiliences will occur; new rifts and divergencies will appear in seemingly rock-solid foundations. The fabric of what we may call the 'narrative universe' is not hospitable to fundamentalists of any hue.

Nevertheless, the recognition that science, like philosophy, and like theology, tells us ever-changing stories about the nature of our world *is* consilience of a kind – and a particularly important kind. It suggests, among other things, that Newman may have been prophetic in arguing that religious experience was part of a continuum, of a kind with our intellectual and our perceptual experience, in that in all cases we create for ourselves 'illative' unities from otherwise hopelessly incoherent fragments. The warp and the weft of our fabric will always be distinct, always pulling at right angles to one another, and the pattern of narrative will always be constantly in the process of change. This is certainly not a proof of the God who entered the world through stories, but as long as there are stories He will probably figure in them. As Wallace Stevens writes,

Description is revelation. It is not
The thing described, nor false facsimile.

It is an artificial thing that exists,
In its own seeming, plainly visible,

Yet not too closely the double of our lives,
Intenser than any actual life could be,

A text should be born that we might read,
More explicit than the experience of sun

And moon, the book of reconciliation,
Book of a concept only possible

In description[58]

Our quest here has concerned not the Bible, but what the mediaevals saw as that *other* book of God, the book of nature. In the early nineteenth century Coleridge proclaimed that we must read the Bible 'as any other book'. Our evidence suggests that in the early twenty-first century it is now time for us to read the book of nature in precisely the same way.[59]

---

[58] 'Description Without Place', from *The Collected Poems of Wallace Stevens*, Faber, 1955, pp. 344–5.

[59] See Coleridge on the Bible: 'I take up this work with the purpose to read it for the first time as I should any other work...' *Confessions of an Inquiring Spirit*, ed. Henry Nelson, 2nd edn, Pickering, 1840, p. 9.

Concluding conversational postscript: The tomb of Napoleon

We began from the now popular idea that science, like theology, and indeed like most other ways of knowing, is really in the business of telling stories about the world. As we have seen, such a notion has passed from shocking to respectable, and finally to cliché, in a relatively short period in the last quarter of the twentieth century. A millennium article by the veteran Jesuit, Walter J. Ong, cites a whole clutch of recent publications dealing with science and religion as 'stories' of the universe.[1] There are, however, dangers in such a dramatic reinstatement of narrative as, if not 'queen of the sciences', at least a kind of quasi-omniscient Jeeves-like lab assistant.[2]

It is not the danger of reducing all knowledge to a single medium. That term 'reducing' is a weasel-word. Anyone who has read so far should be aware that so far from there being any *reduction* in such a highly unlikely consilience, there is a considerable enhancement of our understanding of the world in recognizing the part played by narrative in every description of it – and no less in analysing such narratives with the techniques and insights created by the professionals: literary critics and their ilk. Nor is it the danger of claiming (like Rorty) that narrative is *all* there is. Such an over-simplification is as crude as the assumption that all words correspond to real entities; both are patently self-defeating. The fundamental problem of the relationship between language and the material world remains deeply mysterious – and the corollary of Gödel's theorem would suggest that it is likely to remain so as long as we have to use words to discuss the problem.

---

[1] For example, Diarmuid O'Murchu, *Quantum Theology: Spiritual Implications of the New Physics*; Brian Swimme and Thomas Berry, *The Universe Story: From the Primordial Flaring Forth to the Ecozoic Era – A Celebration of the Unfolding of the Cosmos*; Kevin Bradt, *Story as a Way of Knowing*. See Walter J. Ong, 'Where Are We Now?: Some Elemental Cosmological Considerations', *Christianity and Literature*, Vol. 50, No. 1 (Autumn 2000), pp. 7–13.

[2] A former member of Glasgow University, however, cannot but be aware of the example of James Watt, who worked his way from lab assistant to Professor of Mechanical Engineering.

The principal danger is rather that of assuming that narratives all tell the *same kind* of story: that if science and religion both consist of telling stories about the world, then they are both parallel activities of somehow equal and comparable status, rather than being totally incommensurable. But not merely are our stories of the world partial, incomplete and fragmentary, *no* amount of scientific progress will settle political, philosophic, moral or religious questions. For William Golding, 'both worlds are real. There is no bridge.'[3] Attempts to produce hybrids of such unassimilable things smack of sociobiological ethics, Christian Science, Spiritualism, Creation Science, the Aetherius Society and a whole host of other dubious narratives based on illigitimate premises and evidence ranging from the flimsy to the non-existent.

Nor has the basic problem of pluralism, with which we began, been resolved by stressing that this is more a matter of competing human narratives than a basic instability of the universe itself. We are still obliged to sift evidence, assess probabilities, and check our sources. Our problem with the quantum theory is that our own current, peculiarly well-attested, narrative is scarcely comprehensible. Moreover, there is even less unity over moral and religious questions than over science. Cultures clash. Muslims are likely to continue to see many aspects of society quite differently from Christians or Jews. This is not, I suspect, a matter of the temporary and incomplete nature of our present knowledge. As has been suggested, consilience is not just *not* around the corner. It is a chimera. If past experience is anything to go on (and, for those of us not mystics, seers and visionaries, we have nothing else) finding the ultimate particle, the unification of forces, even the grand final Theory of Everything, however unlikely, will only reveal further, yet more interesting and compelling questions to be answered.

In other words, knowledge, if not theoretically infinite (and we can have little concept of what that might mean), is in practical terms impossible to complete. There is always more to be said, further questions to be asked, more of the story to be told. Words, as Coleridge came to see, cannot correspond to things, because the relationship between the two is neither constant, nor contingent, but *essentially* unstable. Moreover, the narratives we tell operate simultaneously at many different levels. To pretend that what Stephen Jay Gould calls 'the story of the horse' (Chapter One) is a strictly 'scientific' account of a particular evolutionary process is not merely scientifically naïve, it is also morally and aesthetically

---

[3] See above, p. 231.

naïve to ignore what it tells us about nineteenth-century Anglo-American culture, and its intellectual, social and religious conflicts. Yet even this is a multi-layered meta-narrative, woven both on the warp and the weft. If that story performed one function in the society that constructed it (and, in fact, it performed several) it has, in addition, another for us, in that it reveals aspects of that society (its desire, for instance, to produce a coherent and hierarchical evolutionary 'ladder') of which it was unlikely to have been explicitly conscious. No doubt a future historian of late twentieth-century biological theory will find in Gould's discussion of the case revealing aspects of our own time – not to mention of Gould's involvement in particular controversies with his contemporary scientific peers.

The more we recognize such instabilities, the more we must come to recognize what Bloom has seen as the irony of incommensurables, or what Kierkegaard saw as the fundamental irony at the centre of all our narratives. Kierkegaard, moreover, went further than any of his contemporaries in seeing irony not merely as present within our narratives of the world, but actually as characteristic of them, and, indeed, *essential* to them. Within two years of completing his doctoral dissertation on *The Concept of Irony*, he had published the two volumes of *Either/Or* (in February 1843), his *Three Edifying Discourses* (May 1843), and what has perhaps become his best-known book, *Fear and Trembling* together with *Repetition* (October 1843).[4] In the course of this astonishing burst of creativity, he was to elaborate the complex and dialectical triad that was to lie at the heart of much of his subsequent thinking on irony.

For him there were three levels, or stages, in the development of Abraham as what he called the 'knight of faith'. These were the aesthetic, the ethical and, finally, the religious. The point about these stages is that each is good in itself, but is fatally (and ironically) undermined by the next. Thus what he calls 'the beautiful story' of Abraham and his son Isaac on Mount Moriah must stand criticism from the ethical standpoint (is it *ever* right to practise human sacrifice? – *even* more of the firstborn child, after he has reached an age to understand what is happening?). But, in turn, the ethical is undermined by the religious, in which God's will (however mysterious) is seen to prevail. Each level is wholly incommensurable with the others, yet as each higher stage is reached, the earlier stages, which originally looked like ultimate values in themselves, are re-interpreted and revalued. But, for Kierkegaard, the

---

[4] See Walter Lowrie's Introduction to *Fear and Trembling*, pp. 9 ff.

aesthetic cannot ever be subsumed into the ethical, nor the ethical into the religious. Their values are not overturned or denied; they are, in Bloom's word, *incommensurable*. Plurality and irony are not so much the result of imperfect understanding, or incomplete knowledge, they are, as we saw in the final chapter, part of the very fabric of existence.

If this is a difficult doctrine, Kierkegaard was well aware of its difficulties. The whole point of his telling and re-telling the story of Abraham and Isaac is to highlight its insolubly problematic status, and if the reader is not troubled by the feeling that this story is neither beautiful, nor ethical, nor religious, then he or she has not yet begun to struggle with its meaning. 'Though Abraham arouses my admiration', writes Kierkegaard, 'he at the same time appals me.' Any easy account of the story, that sidesteps the impossibility of grasping his actions, would 'leave out the distress, the dread, the paradox'.[5]

But for us, there are further problems with this schema. Words slip, slide, and change their meanings. As we have seen, the aesthetic turn of twentieth-century thought means that the appeal and meaning of the aesthetic is likely to be greater for us than for Kierkegaard's bourgeois Danish contemporaries, for whom 'art' was less likely to have been experienced as a form of inner expression than as an externally prescribed, circumscribed, and even commodified form of decoration – and the 'aesthetic' an abstract quality enmeshed in the less-than-elegant prose of Kant, Fichte and Schelling. At the same time, the word 'religious' has declined in relative status. Movements like 'the religious right' in the US have given the English word at least associations of narrowness and rigidity that are clearly foreign to Kierkegaard's idea of openness and absolute submission in an act of faith. The idea of a higher obedience than that of the ethical – especially one that incites to murder – has, for the twentieth century, echoes of Himmler's exhortations to his SS brigades. At one level this may simply enhance Kierkegaard's sense of the paradox of the Abraham story, but at another, it may also illustrate how context can destabilize meaning.

Since this is a re-reading of his ideas for a different age and context, rather than a commentary on Kierkegaard, we are perhaps justified in offering here our own creative *mis*reading, by *reversing* his triad of faith, to give us, in ascending order, the religious, the ethical and the aesthetic. We thus start with (what is now) the externally controlled and bounded, and move through the inner-directed limitations of the ethical, before arriving

---

[5] Kierkegaard, *Fear and Trembling*, Problem 1, pp. 71; 75.

(like Dante in the Earthly Paradise[6]) at the terrifying non-choice of the truly free, to respond to the transcendent Other. If we find this better expressed in our time by the arts than in what is now popularly meant by 'religion', we would not be alone. Hans Urs von Balthasar's attempt to approach God by way of Kant's Third Critique, on beauty, was startlingly at odds with the conventional Thomism of Catholic thought when it first appeared in mid-century, but it was to prove prophetic.[7] 'Great works of art', he wrote, 'appear like inexplicable eruptions on the stage of history. Sociologists are as unable to calculate the precise day of their origin as they are to explain in retrospect why they appeared when they did ... [Art's] unique utterance becomes a universal language; and the greater a work of art, the more extensive the cultural sphere it dominates will be.'[8] We recall also Steiner's claim that 'the experience of aesthetic meaning in particular, that of literature, of the arts, of musical form, infers the necessary possibility of this 'real presence'.[9] Such a meaning of 'aesthetic' as replacing the 'religious' is, of course, only possible if we take it in the modern sense of permitting (if only theoretically) full presence – in other words, giving it much the same force as Kierkegaard wants to give to the 'religious'. Or, better still, in reading Kierkegaard, we have to understand the 'religious' as subsuming the 'aesthetic' in our sense. This means that our understanding of the aesthetics of narrative changes the way in which we understand religion just as much as it changes the way in which we read science, or history – or any other discipline.

As with Dante's own movement from Hell, through Purgatory to Paradise, Kierkegaard's original triad is not a staircase, still less an escalator. Indeed, it may only be those who have traversed all three who have the right to speak of it as an 'ascent' at all. The final stage may even be better spoken of as a matter of 'assent'. Each stage is separate, and seemingly complete in itself. As with sight for someone who is blind, or sound for the totally deaf, there is no understanding of the next stage(s) until reached. Only then is a revaluation possible of what has gone before. Only looking backwards is the irony of incommensurables apparent – and that is an irony that, by definition, can never be fully articulated.

What is valuable about Kierkegaard's trinity is that it makes pluralism not an accidental or contingent phenomenon of modern society, but a

[6] See Prickett, *Words and the Word*, Ch. 4. pp. 149–73.

[7] See in particular his massive, seven-volume, theological aesthetics, *The Glory of the Lord*, ed. John Riches, Edinburgh: T & T Clark, 1982–9.

[8] *Two Say Why*, trs. John Griffiths, Search Press, 1973, pp. 20–1.   [9] Ibid. p. 3.

normal and indeed essential ingredient of experience. If the aesthetic, the ethical, and the religious can be described as occupying *the same* inner space, they tell utterly different narratives about it. All three narratives are, however, properly ironic in that they share an awareness not necessarily of *what* is concealed, but that there *is* a concealed; that there is more that can be said; that there are many different and conflicting descriptions of what it is like at the Back of the North Wind.[10]

Other narratives, other metaphors, intervene – interrupt. 'The shortest definition of religion: interruption' writes Johann Baptist Metz.[11] In reply to the objection of the German theologian, Jürgen Moltmann, that this definition is inadequate, because a single interruption can always be deflected or absorbed, thereby allowing things to continue as usual, Kevin Hart proposes 'the second shortest definition of religion': 'absolute interruption'.[12] The phrase, as Hart points out, comes originally from the French critic, Maurice Blanchot, though a similar idea is to be found in the work of his Jewish compatriot, the philosopher Emmanuel Levinas.[13] Whatever its modern sources, however, narratives of absolute interruption abound in the Old Testament – as in the New – from Moses and the burning bush to Elijah's encounter with the 'still small voice' on Horeb.[14]

But, as both Blanchot and Levinas make clear, there is nothing exclusively, or, indeed, *intrinsically* religious about such interruptions. The full title of Blanchot's meditation is 'Interruption (as on a Reimann Surface)'. Although it is not entirely clear whether he understood all the implications of his choice of the mathematical curvature of space as a metaphor of communication, his main point concerns 'a change in the form or structure of language (when speaking is first of all writing) – a change metaphorically comparable to that which made Euclid's geometry into that of Reimann'.[15] Theoretical physics, too, has its interruptions. But that metaphor of 'interruption' has further connotations in the light

---

[10] See George MacDonald, *At the Back of the North Wind*, 1871.

[11] Johann Baptist Metz, *Faith in History and Society: Towards a Practical Fundamental Theology*, trs David Smith, Burns & Oates, 1980, p. 171. I owe this quotation, and much of what follows to Kevin Hart's paper, 'Absolute Interruption: On Faith' in *Questioning God*, ed. John D. Caputo, Indiana University Press, 2001.

[12] Moltmann writes: 'Interruption is not an eschatological category. The eschatological category is conversion.' *The Coming of God: Christian Eschatology*, trs Margaret Kohl, Minneapolis: Fortress Press, 1996, p. 22.

[13] Hart, 'Absolute Interruption'; Maurice Blanchot, 'L'Interruption', *Nouvelle Revue Française*, 142, octobre 1964, pp. 674–85; Emmanuel Levinas, 'Enigme et phénomène,' *Esprit* 33, juin 1965, pp. 1128–42.

[14] See Prickett, *Words and the Word*, Ch. 1.

[15] Maurice Blanchot, *The Infinite Conversation*, trs Susan Hanson, Minneapolis: University of Minnesota Press, 1993, p. 77.

of the title of the book where Blanchot expands this ideas: *The Infinite Conversation*. What, for instance, is the difference between 'narrative' and 'conversation'? What is the difference between interrupting a narrative and interrupting a conversation? Is the 'aesthetic' conversation, or narration?

'In the beginning', Erasmus translated the opening of John's Gospel, 'was the conversation.' Whether the Greek *logos* or 'word' originally included the idea of conversation is, in a sense, immaterial. Like many Greek words used in the *koinē* of the New Testament, that word *logos* was already in the process of being given a new connotation and meaning through its context. Erasmus was re-reading, re-interrogating his source. He was, as it were, entering into a conversation with it, as his Christianity had always traditionally conversed with its own and with the Hebrew scriptures.

But it will not have escaped the reader who has read so far that Kierkegaard is, as so often, there before us once again. The narrative of Abraham that he so painstakingly works and re-works in *Fear and Trembling* is, famously, a conversation – Abraham converses with God and even, desperately, also with Isaac. Kierkegaard converses with his text – and, directly addressing us, the readers. As every reader of fiction well knows, the difference between narrative and conversation is not one of genre, but of *response*. The difference between passively absorbing a narrative, and questioning, puzzling over it, interrogating it is crucial to how we understand any narrative, whether of literature, art, music, history, mathematics, science or religion. It is central to Newman's distinction between the passive 'notional assent' and the active 'real assent' – and as Newman, in some moods, one of the most ironic of writers, knew well, irony is a quality inherent in the latter, not the former.

An analysis of Kierkegaard's own metaphor of irony, that of the anonymous print of *The Tomb of Napoleon*, now in the Royal Library in Copenhagen, is similarly 'conversational'. A reading of it will, of course, involve all the interpretative layers that we have already noted in the case of Gould's story of the horse. What, for instance, was its original purpose? Against whom (if anyone) was the irony originally directed? What does that tell *us* about Danish society of the immediate post-Napoleonic era? But equally significant, in this case, is that it demands an interactive response from the viewer. A passive, unresponsive glance is not an option. It can *only* be 'understood' by seeing what is, at first glance, completely hidden. This, in other words, is a picture that demands 'conversation' with those who encounter it.

Between the two trees there is an empty space; as the eye follows the outline, suddenly Napoleon himself emerges from this nothing, and now it is impossible to have him disappear again. Once the eye has seen him, it goes on seeing him with almost alarming necessity.

Nor will it have escaped the reader that this picture is, of course, *also* a metaphor of presence. That 'alarming necessity' is, in effect, the traditional hallmark of presence. Somebody else may see nothing at all, except – literally – 'an empty space', but once that space has been interrupted it is impossible *not* to see the figure that haunts the picture. It would, no doubt, have delighted Napoleon hugely to be taken as the form, not merely of irony, but of interruption and presence as well. That radical re-reading by a disillusioned Danish Romantic of an anonymous popular print may yet turn out to have given the unwitting French Emperor one of his most lasting contributions to human thought.

Bibliography

Unless stated otherwise, place of publication is London.

Aarsleff, Hans, *From Locke to Saussure: Essays on the Study of Language and Intellectual History*, Minneapolis: University of Minnesota Press, 1982.

Abrams, M.H., *The Mirror and the Lamp*, N.Y.: Oxford University Press, 1953; reprinted N.Y.: Norton, 1958.

Adams, Douglas, *Mostly Harmless*, Oxford: Heinemann, 1992.

Adams, Hazard, *Philosophy of the Literary Symbolic*, Tallahassee: Florida State University Press, 1983.

Addison, Joseph, 'The Pleasures of the Imagination' (1712), *Spectator* 413.

Akenside, Mark, *Pleasures of the Imagination* (1744).

Alberti, Leone Battista, *On Painting*, trs John R. Spencer, New Haven: Yale University Press, 1956.

Allison, Henry E., *Kant's Transcendental Idealism*, New Haven: Yale University Press, 1983.

Aristotle, *The Poetics*, trs L. J. Potts, Cambridge University Press, 1959.

Armstrong, A.H. (ed.), *Cambridge History of Later Greek and Early Mediaeval Philosophy*, Cambridge University Press, 1967.

Ashton, John, *Understanding the Fourth Gospel*, Oxford: Clarendon Press, 1991.

Athenaeum 1798–1800, Stuttgart: J.G. Cotta'sche Buchhandlung Nachf.

Auerbach, Erich, *Mimesis*, Princeton University Press, 1953.

Ayer, A. J., *Language, Truth and Logic*, Gollancz, 1946.

Balthasar, Hans Urs von, *The Glory of the Lord*, ed. John Riches, Edinburgh: T & T Clark, 1982–9.

——*Two Say Why*, trs John Griffiths, Search Press, 1973.

Barfield, Owen, 'The Nature of Meaning', *Seven*, Vol. II, 1981.

——*Saving the Appearances*, N.Y.: Harcourt Brace, 1957.

——*What Coleridge Thought*, Oxford University Press, 1972.

Barthes, Roland, *Image–Music–Text*, trs Stephen Heath, N.Y.: Hill & Wang, 1997.

Bartlett, F.C., *Memory*, Cambridge University Press, 1932.

Beer, Gillian, *[Darwin's Plots]: Evolutionary Narrative in Darwin, George Eliot and Nineteenth Century Fiction*, Routledge, 1983.

Berger, Peter, *A Rumour of Angels* (1969), Pelican, Harmondsworth: Penguin, 1971.

Berlin, Isaiah, *Four Essays on Liberty*, Oxford University Press, 1969.

_____ *Vico and Herder: Two Studies in the History of Ideas*, Hogarth Press, 1976.

Black, Max (ed.), *The Importance of Language*, Eaglewood Cliffs, N.J.: Prentice-Hall, 1962.

Blair, Hugh, *Lectures on Rhetoric and Belles Lettres* (1783), 2 vols., Edinburgh, 1820.

Blake, William, *Complete Writings*, ed. Geoffrey Keynes, Oxford University Press, 1966.

Blanchot, Maurice, 'L'Interruption', *Nouvelle Revue Française*, 142, octobre, 1964.

_____ *The Infinite Conversation*, trs Susan Hanson, Minneapolis: University of Minnesota Press, 1993.

Bloom, Harold, *Anxiety of Influence*, N.Y.: Oxford University Press, 1973.

_____ *The Book of J*, N.Y.: Vintage, 1991.

Boehme, Jakob, *Mysterium Magnum: or An Exposition of the First Book of Moses Called Genesis*, 1623.

Boghossian, Paul A., 'What is Social Construction?' *Times Literary Supplement*, February 23, 2001.

Borges, Jorge Luis, *Selected Non-Fictions*, trs Esther Allen, Suzanne Jill Levine and Eliot Weinberger, ed. Eliot Weinberger, N.Y.: Viking, 1999.

Bowie, Andrew, *From Romanticism to Critical Theory: The Philosophy of German Literary Theory*, Routledge, 1997.

Brandom, Robert B. (ed.), *Rorty and his Critics*, Oxford: Blackwell, 2000.

Brantley, Richard E., *Locke, Wesley, and the Method of English Romanticism*, Gainsville: University of Florida Press, 1984.

Burdon, Christopher, *The Apocalypse in England: Revelation Unravelling, 1700–1834*, Macmillan, 1997.

Burrows, John, *Computation into Criticism*, Oxford: Clarendon Press, 1987.

Burtt, E.A., *Metaphysical Foundations of Modern Science*, Routledge, 1932.

Butler, Marilyn, *Peacock Displayed*, Routledge & Kegan Paul, 1979.

Cajori, Florian (ed.), *Sir Isaac Newton's Mathematical Principles of Natural Philosophy and his System of the World*, Berkeley, Calif.: University of California Press, 1946.

Carroll, J., Review of three biographies of Charles Darwin, *Times Literary Supplement*, February 20, 1998, pp. 7–8.

Cave, Terrence, *Recognitions: A Study in Poetics*, Oxford: Clarendon Press, 1988.

Chardin, Pierre Teilhard de, *The Phenomenon of Man*, trs Bernard Wall, Collins, 1959.

Chateaubriand, René François Auguste de, *The Genius of Christianity* (1802), trs Charles White, Baltimore, 1856.

Chesterton, G.K., *Orthodoxy*, Bodley Head, 1908.

Church, R.W., *The Gifts of Civilization*, new edn, Macmillan, 1890.

Clark, J.C.D., *English Society 1688–1832*, Cambridge University Press, 1985.

Coleridge, J.T., *Memoir of the Rev. John Keble* (1869).

Coleridge, Samuel Taylor, *Aids to Reflection* (1825), Edinburgh: Grant, 1905.

_____ *Collected Letters*, ed. E.L. Griggs, Oxford University Press, 1956–9.

_____ *Confessions of an Inquiring Spirit*, ed. Henry Nelson, 2nd edn, Pickering, 1840.

＿＿*Lay Sermons*, ed. R.J. White, Routledge, 1972.

＿＿*Notebooks*, ed. Kathleen Coburn and Merton Christensen, Routledge, 1990.

＿＿*Table Talk*, ed. H.N. Coleridge, 1852.

Coulson, John, *Newman and the Common Tradition*, Oxford: Clarendon Press, 1970.

Cox, Murray and Theilgaard, Alice, *Mutative Metaphors in Psychotherapy: The Aeolian Mode*, Tavistock, 1987.

Creed, J.M., *The Divinity of Jesus Christ*, Cambridge University Press, 1938.

Cross, A.G., (ed.), *An English Lady at the Court of Catherine the Great: The Journal of Baroness Elizabeth Dimsdale* (1781), Cambridge: Crest Publications, 1989.

Cupitt, Don, *After God: The Future of Religion*, Weidenfeld and Nicolson, 1997.

Currie, Robert, Gilbert, Alan, and Horsley, Lee (eds.), *Churches and Churchgoers: Patterns of Church Growth in the British Isles since 1700*, Oxford: Clarendon Press, 1977.

Curtius, Ernst, *Essays on European Literature*, trs Michael Kowal, Princeton University Press, 1973.

Daniell, David, *Tyndale's New Testament*, New Haven, 1989.

Darwin, Charles, *The Autobiography of Charles Darwin*, Watts & Co., 1929.

＿＿*The Origin of Species*, ed. John Burrow, Harmondsworth: Penguin, 1968.

＿＿*The Variation of Animals and Plants Under Domestication*, John Murray, 1875.

Davidson, Donald, *Truth and Interpretation: Perspectives on the Philosophy of Donald Davidson*, ed. Ernest LePore, Oxford: Blackwell, 1984.

Davies, Paul, *The Mind of God: Science and the Search for Ultimate Meaning*, Simon & Schuster, 1992.

＿＿*Superforce*, Oxford: Heinemann, 1984.

Davies, Paul, and Brown, J.R. (eds.), *The Ghost in the Atom*, Canto, Cambridge University Press, 1993.

Davis, P.J., and Hersh, R., *The Mathematical Experience*, Harmondsworth: Penguin, 1983.

Davis, Walter, *Inwardness and Existence: Subjectivity in/and Hegel, Heidegger, Marx and Freud*, Madison, Wis.: University of Wisconsin Press, 1989.

de Man, Paul, *Blindness and Insight: Essays on the Rhetoric of Contemporary Criticism* (1983), 2nd edn, Routledge, 1989.

Deconinck-Brossard, Françoise, 'England and France in the Eighteenth Century', in *Reading the Text*, ed. S. Prickett, Oxford: Blackwell, 1991.

Dennett, Daniel, *Darwin's Dangerous Idea: Evolution and the Meanings of Life*, Harmondsworth: Penguin, 1996.

Derrida Jacques, *Of Grammatology*, trs Gayatri Spivak, Baltimore: Johns Hopkins Press, 1976.

＿＿*Religion*, ed. Jacques Derrida and Gianni Vattimo, Cambridge: Polity Press, 1998.

＿＿'Remarks on Deconstruction and Pragmatism', in *Deconstruction and Pragmatism*, ed. Chantal Mouffe, Routledge, 1996.

＿＿*Writing and Difference*, trs and introduction by Alan Bass, Routledge, 1978.

Desmond, Adrian and Moore, James, *Charles Darwin*, Michael Joseph, 1991.

D'Espagnat, Bernard, *Reality and the Physicist: Knowledge, Duration and the Quantum World*, trs J.C. Whitehouse and Bernard D'Espagnat, Cambridge University Press, 1989.

Deutsch, David, *The Fabric of Reality*, Harmondsworth: Penguin, 1997.

Docherty, Thomas (ed.), *Postmodernism: A Reader*, Harvester Wheatsheaf, 1993.

Duckworth, Alastair, *The Improvement of the Estate*, Baltimore, Md.: Johns Hopkins University Press, 1971.

Eco, Umberto, *The Search for the Perfect Language*, trs James Fentress, Oxford: Blackwell, 1995.

Eichner, Hans, *Friedrich Schlegel*, New York: Twaine, 1970.

Ellis, Markman, *The Politics of Sensibility: Race, Gender and Commerce in the Sentimental Novel*, Cambridge University Press, 1998.

Faber, Geoffrey, *Oxford Apostles*, Faber, 1933.

Farrar, Austen, *A Rebirth of Images*, Dacre Press, 1944.

Faverty, Frederic E., *Matthew Arnold the Ethnologist*, Evanston, Ill.: Northwestern University Press, 1951.

Feynman, Richard, *The Character of Physical Law*, BBC, 1965.

Forstman, Jack, *A Romantic Triangle: Schleiermacher and Early German Romanticism*, Missoula, Mont.: Scholars Press, 1977.

Foucault, Michel, *The Foucault Reader*, ed. Paul Rabinow, N.Y.: Pantheon Books, 1984.

——*Power/Knowledge: Selected Interviews and Other Writings 1972–1977*, ed. Colin Gordon, Harvester, 1980.

Freud, Sigmund, *Introductory Lectures on Psychoanalysis*, Harmondsworth: Penguin, 1973.

Frye, Northrop, *Anatomy of Criticism*, Princeton University Press, 1957.

——*T.S. Eliot*, Writers and Critics Series, Oliver and Boyd, 1968.

Fukuyama, Francis, 'The End of History?', *The National Interest*, Summer, 1989.

Fulford, Tim, 'Coleridge and the Wisdom Tradition,' *The Wordsworth Circle*, 22, 1991, pp. 77–8.

Gablik, S., *Progress in Art*, N.Y.: Rizzoli, 1977.

Gadamer, Hans Georg, *Philosophical Hermeneutics*, trs and ed. David E. Linge, University of California Press, 1976.

Galileo, *Dialogues Concerning Two New Sciences*, trs H. Crew and A. de Salvio, Evanston, Ill.: Northwestern University Press, 1946.

Geertz, Clifford, *The Interpretation of Cultures*, N.Y.: Basic Books, 1973.

Gilligan, James, *Violence: Reflections on our Deadliest Epidemic*, N.Y.: Putnam's Sons, 1996 and London: Jessica Kingsley, 2000.

Golding, William, *Free Fall*, Faber, 1959.

Gombrich, E.H., *Art and Illusion: A Study in the Psychology of Pictorial Representation* (1960), revised edn, Princeton University Press, 1961.

Goodenough, E.R., *Introduction to Philo Judaeus*, 2nd edn, Oxford: Basil Blackwell, 1962 (1st edn, New Haven, Conn.: Yale University Press, 1940).

Gordon, Lyndall, *Eliot's New Life*, Oxford University Press, 1998.

Gould, Stephen Jay, *Bully for Brontosaurus: Reflections in Natural History*, Hutchinson Radius, 1991.

———*Life's Grandeur: The Spread of Excellence from Plato to Darwin*, Cape, 1996.

Gould, Warwick, and Reeves, Marjorie, *Joachim of Fiore and the Myth of the Eternal Evangel in the Nineteenth Century*, Oxford: Clarendon Press, 1987.

Gribbin, John, *Schrödinger's Kittens, and the Search for Reality*, Weidenfeld and Nicolson, 1995.

Hampshire, Stuart, *Innocence and Experience*, Harvard University Press, 1989.

———*Morality and Conflict*, Harvard University Press, 1983.

Hare, Augustus and Julius, *Guesses at Truth by Two Brothers*, 1827.

———*Guesses at Truth*, 2 vols., Macmillan, 1871.

Harrison, J.F.C., *The Second Coming: Popular Millenarianism 1780–1850*, Routledge, 1979.

Harrison, Peter, *'Religion' and the Religions in the English Enlightenment*, Cambridge University Press, 1990.

Hart, Kevin, 'Absolute Interruption', in *Questioning God*, ed. John D. Caputo, Indiana University Press, 2001.

———*Samuel Johnson and the Culture of Property*, Cambridge University Press, 1999.

———*The Trespass of the Sign: Deconstruction, Theology and Philosophy*, Cambridge University Press, 1989.

Heidegger, Martin, *Existence and Being*, trs Douglas Scott, Vision Press, 1949.

Heilbut, Anthony, *Thomas Mann: Eros and Literature*, N.Y.: Knopf, 1995.

Herder, Johann Gottfried, 'Essay on the Origin of Language' (1772), in *Herder on Social and Political Culture*, trs and ed. F.M. Barnard, Cambridge University Press, 1969.

———*The Spirit of Hebrew Poetry*, (1782–3), trs James Marsh, Burlington, Vt., 1833.

Holland, Lady Saba, *Memoir of the Rev. Sydney Smith*, 2 vols., 1855.

Hoyle, Fred, *The Intelligent Universe*, Michael Joseph, 1983.

Hulme, T.E., *Speculations*, Kegan Paul, 1924.

Humboldt, Wilhelm von, *On Language* (1836), trs Peter Heath, introduction by Hans Aarsleff, Cambridge University Press, 1988.

Hunt, John Dixon, and Willis, Peter (eds.), *The Genius of the Place: The English Landscape Garden 1620–1820*, 2nd edn, Cambridge, Mass.: MIT Press, 1988.

Hussey, Christopher, *English Gardens and Landscapes 1700–1750*, London, 1967.

Jay, Elisabeth, *The Religion of the Heart*, Oxford: Clarendon Press, 1979.

Jenkyns, Richard, *The Victorians and Ancient Greece*, Oxford: Blackwell, 1980.

Jung, C.G., *Collected Works*, ed. H. Read, M. Fordham and G. Adler, Routledge, 1953–78, Vol. XVI.

———*Memories, Dreams, Reflections*, ed. Aniela Jaffé, trs Richard and Clara Winston, Collins, 1963.

Kant, Immanuel, *Critique of Judgement*, trs J.H. Bernard, N.Y.: Hafner, 1951.

Keble, John, *Lectures on Poetry*, trs E.K. Francis, 2 vols., Oxford University Press, 1912.

———Review of *Life of Scott* (1838), in *Occasional Papers and Reviews*, Oxford University Press, 1877.

Kekes, John, *The Morality of Pluralism*, Princeton University Press, 1993.

——*Multiculturalism*, Princeton University Press, 1994.

Kelsall, Malcolm, 'The Iconography of Stourhead', *Journal of the Warbury and Courtauld Institutes*, Vol. 46, 1983, pp. 133–43.

Kenny, J.F., *The Sources for the Early History of Ireland* (1929), reprinted, Irish University Press, 1968.

Kierkegaard, Søren, *The Concept of Irony, with Continual Reference to Socrates* (1841), ed. and trs Howard V. Hong and Edna H. Hong, Princeton University Press, 1989.

——*Fear and Trembling*, trs and introduction Walter Lowrie (1941), Princeton University Press, 1954.

Kissinger, Henry, *American Foreign Policy*, N.Y.: Norton, 1974.

Kort, Wesley A., *Take Read: Scripture, Textuality and Cultural Practice*, Pennsylvania State University Press, 1996.

Kugel, James L., *The Idea of Biblical Poetry: Parallelism and its History*, Yale University Press, 1981.

Kuhn, Thomas, *The Structure of Scientific Revolutions*, University of Chicago Press, 1962.

Lacoue-Labarthe, Philippe, and Nancy, Jean-Luc, *The Literary Absolute: The Theory of Literature in German Romanticism* (1978), trs Philip Barnard and Cheryl Lester, Albany: State University of New York Press, 1988.

Lash, Nicholas, *The Beginning and End of Religion*, Cambridge University Press, 1996.

Levinas, Emmanuel, 'Enigme et phénomène,' *Esprit* 33, juin 1965.

——*Otherwise than Being*, The Hague and London: Nijhoff, 1981.

Lewis, C.S., *Pilgrim's Regress*, Geoffrey Bles, 1943.

——*The Screwtape Letters*, Geoffrey Bles, 1942.

——*They Asked for a Paper*, Geoffrey Bles, 1962.

Lindsay, Jack, *William Blake*, Constable, 1978.

Lipkowitz, Ina, 'Inspiration and the Poetic Imagination: Samuel Taylor Coleridge', *Studies in Romanticism*, 30, Winter, 1991, pp. 607–9.

Locke, John, *Essay Concerning Human Understanding* (1690).

——*A Letter Concerning Toleration*, in *Treatise of Civil Government and A Letter Concerning Toleration*, ed. Charles L. Sherman, N.Y.: Appleton–Century–Crofts, 1965.

Lovejoy, A.O., *The Great Chain of Being*, Harvard University Press, 1936.

Lowth, Robert, *Isaiah: A New Translation*, 5th edn, 2 vols., Edinburgh, 1807.

——*The Sacred Poetry of the Hebrews* (1753), trs G. Gregory, 2 vols., London, 1787; facsimile edition N.Y.: Gailand, 1971.

Lyotard, Jean-François, *The Postmodern Condition: A Report on Knowledge*, trs Geoff Bennington and Brain Massumi, foreword by Fredric Jameson, Manchester University Press, 1984.

MacDonald, George, *At the Back of the North Wind*, 1871.

McFarland, Thomas, *Coleridge and the Pantheist Tradition*, Oxford: Clarendon Press, 1969.

——*Romanticism and the Forms of Ruin*, Princeton University Press, 1981.

Mackenzie, John M., *Orientalism: History, Theory and the Arts*, Manchester University Press, 1995.

McKusick, James C., 'A New Poem by Samuel Taylor Coleridge', *Modern Philology*, 84 (1987), pp. 408–9.

Malins, Edward, *English Landscape and Literature 1660–1840*, 1966.

Manguel, Alberto, *A History of Reading*, HarperCollins, 1996.

Maurice, F.D., *The Kingdom of Christ*, 4th edn, 2 vols., Macmillan, 1891.

_____*Lectures in Ecclesiastical History of the First and Second Centuries*, Macmillan, 1854.

Maurice, Frederick (ed.), *The Life of F.D. Maurice*, 4th edn, 2 vols., Macmillan, 1885.

Medawar, P.B., *The Art of the Soluble*, 6th edn, Methuen, 1967.

Metz, Johann Baptist, *Faith in History and Society: Towards a Practical Fundamental Theology*, trs David Smith, Burns & Oates, 1980.

Milbank, John, *The Word Made Strange: Theology, Language, Culture*, Oxford: Blackwell, 1997.

Milbank, John, Pickstock, Catherine, and Ward, Graham, *Radical Orthodoxy: A New Theology*, Routledge, 1999.

Mills, C. Wright, *The Sociological Imagination*, N.Y.: Oxford University Press, 1959.

Milton, John, *Poems*, ed. John Carey and Alastair Fowler, Longman, 1968.

Mitchell, W. J.T., *Picture Theory*, University of Chicago Press, 1994.

Moltmann, Jürgen, *The Coming of God: Christian Eschatology*, trs Margaret Kohl, Minneapolis: Fortress Press, 1996.

Montaigne, Michel de, *Essays*, trs John Florio, N.Y.: Modern Library, 1933.

Mosser, Monique, and Teyssot, Georges (eds.), *The History of Garden Design: The Western Tradition from the Renaissance to the Present Day*, Thames and Hudson, 1991.

Mozley, Thomas, *Reminiscences: Chiefly of Oriel College and the Oxford Movement*, 2 vols., 1882.

Nagel, Thomas, *The Last Word*, Oxford University Press, 1997.

Needham, Joseph, *Human Law and the Laws of Nature in China and the West*, L.T. Hobhouse Memorial Trust Lecture, Cambridge University Press, 1951.

_____*The Shorter Science and Civilization in China: An Abridgement of Joseph Needham's Original Text*, Vol. I, prepared by Colin A. Ronan, Cambridge University Press, 1978.

Newman, John Henry, *Essay on the Development of Doctrine*, Sheed and Ward, 1960.

_____*Essays*, ed. Henry Nettleship, Oxford, 2 vols., 1889.

_____*A Grammar of Assent*, ed. C.F. Harrold, new edn, Longman, 1957.

_____*Lectures on Certain Difficulties Felt by Anglicans*, 2nd edn, 1850.

Newsome, David, *The Parting of Friends*, John Murray, 1966.

_____*Two Classes of Men*, London: Murray, 1974.

Nicolson, Marjorie Hope, *Newton Demands the Muse*, Archon Books, 1963.

Nietzsche, Friedrich, *Twilight of the Idols and the Anti-Christ*, trs and ed. R.J. Hollingdale, Harmondsworth: Penguin, 1968.

Norton, David, *History of the Bible as Literature*, 2 vols., Cambridge University Press, 1993.

Nussbaum, Martha, *The Fragility of Goodness*, Cambridge University Press, 1986.

Nuttall, A.D., *The Alternative Trinity: Gnostic Heresy in Marlowe, Milton, and Blake*, Oxford: Clarendon Press, 1998.

_____ *A Common Sky*, Sussex University Press, Chatto, 1974.

Oakshott, Michael, *Rationalism in Politics*, London: Methuen, 1962.

_____ *On Human Conduct*, Oxford: Clarendon Press, 1975.

Ong, Walter J., *Orality and Literacy: The Technologising of the Word*, Routledge, 1982.

_____ 'Where Are We Now?: Some Elemental Cosmological Considerations', *Christianity and Literature*, Vol. 50, No. 1. Autumn, 2000.

Paley, William, *Natural Theology: or Evidences of the Existence and Attributes of the Deity, Collected from the Appearances of Nature*, 3rd edn, 1803.

Palmer, R.R., *The World of the French Revolution*, Allen & Unwin, 1971.

Pattison, George, *Kierkegaard: The Aesthetic and the Religious*, Macmillan, 1992.

Paulson, Ronald, *Emblem and Expression: Meaning in English Art of the Eighteenth Century*, Cambridge, Mass.: Harvard University Press and London: Thames and Hudson, 1975.

Peacock, Thomas Love, *The Four Ages of Poetry*, ed. H.F.B. Brett-Smith, Percy Reprints, No. 3, Oxford, Blackwell, 1953.

Pearson, Hesketh, *The Smith of Smiths*, Harmondsworth: Penguin, 1948.

Penrose, Roger, 'Ingenious Ingénue', *Times Higher Education Supplement*, April 3, 1998.

Perkins, William, *The Art of Prophecying*, 1592.

Pinker, Steven, *The Language Instinct*, Harmondsworth: Penguin, 1995.

Polanyi, Michael, *Personal Knowledge*, Routledge, 1958.

Polya, G., *Mathematics and Plausible Reasoning*, 2 vols., Oxford University Press, 1954.

Popper, Karl, *The Logic of Scientific Discovery*, Hutchinson, 1959.

Porter, H.C., 'The Nose of Wax: Scripture and the Spirit from Erasmus to Milton', *Transactions of the Royal Historical Society*, 5th Series, Vol. 14, 1964.

Prickett, Stephen, 'Coleridge and the Idea of the Clerisy', in Walter B. Crawford (ed.), *Reading Coleridge: Approaches and Appreciations*, Ithaca and London: Cornell University Press, 1979.

_____ *Coleridge and Wordsworth: The Poetry of Growth*, Cambridge University Press, 1970.

_____ *England and the French Revolution*, Macmillan, 1988.

_____ 'Fictions and Metafictions: *Phantastes, Wilhelm Meister* and the idea of the Bildungsroman', in *The Gold Thread: Essays on George MacDonald*, ed. William Raeper, Edinburgh University Press, 1991.

_____ *Origins of Narrative: The Romantic Appropriation of the Bible*, Cambridge University Press, 1996.

_____ 'Peacock's Four Ages Recycled', *British Journal of Aesthetics*, Spring, 1982.

_____*Romanticism and Religion: The Tradition of Coleridge and Wordsworth in the Victorian Church*, Cambridge University Press, 1976.

_____*Victorian Fantasy*, Brighton: Harvester Press/Indiana University Press, 1979.

_____*Words and the Word: Language, Poetics and Biblical Interpretation*, Cambridge University Press, 1986.

Prickett, Stephen (ed.), *Reading the Text: Biblical Criticism and Literary Theory*, Oxford: Blackwell, 1991.

Rawls, John, *A Theory of Justice*, Harvard University Press, 1971.

Reventlow, Henning Graf, *The Authority of the Bible and the Rise of the Modern World*, trs John Bowden, SCM Press, 1984.

Ridley, Matt, *The Origins of Virtue*, Viking, 1996.

Rorty, Richard, *Contingency, Irony and Solidarity*, Cambridge University Press, 1989.

_____*Philosophy and the Mirror of Nature*, Princeton University Press, 1979.

Rose, Hilary and Steven, (eds.), *Alas Poor Darwin: Arguments Against Evolutionary Psychology*, Cape, 2000.

Ryle, Gilbert, *Concept of Mind*, Hutchinson, 1949.

Sahlins, Marshall, *How 'Natives' Think: About Captain Cook, For Example*, University of Chicago Press, 1995.

Said, Edward, *Orientalism: Western Conceptions of the Orient*, Harmondsworth: Penguin, 1991.

_____*The World, the Text and the Critic*, Cambridge, Mass.: Harvard University Press, 1983.

Schlegel, Friedrich von, *Friedrich Schlegel's Lucinde and the Fragments*, trs and introduction Peter Firchow, Minneapolis: University of Minnesota Press and Oxford University Press, 1971.

Schweitzer, Albert, *The Quest of the Historical Jesus*, 3rd edn, A. and C. Black, 1954.

Sheldrake, Rupert, *The Presence of the Past: Morphic Resonance and the Habits of Nature*, Collins, 1988.

Shlan, Leonard, *Art and Physics: Parallel Visions in Space, Time and Light*, N.Y.: William Morrow, 1991.

Skinner, Quentin (ed.), *The Return of Grand Theory in the Human Sciences*, Cambridge University Press, 1985.

Smiles, Samuel, *Character*, John Murray, 1884.

Steiner, George, *After Babel: Aspects of Language and Translation*, Oxford University Press, 1976.

_____*Real Presences*, Faber, 1989.

Stephenson, Roger, *Goethe's Conception of Knowledge and Science*, Edinburgh University Press, 1995.

Stevens, Anthony, *Private Myths: Dreams and Dreaming*, Harmondsworth: Penguin, 1966.

Stevens, Wallace, *Collected Poems*, Faber, 1955.

Stewart, Dugald, *Philosophical Lectures* (1816).

Stockwood, Mervyn (ed.), *Religion and the Scientists*, SCM Press, 1959.

Stove, D.C., *Popper and After: Four Modern Irrationalists*, Oxford: Pergamon Press, 1982.

Strawson, Peter, 'Social Morality and Individual Ideal', In *Freedom and Resentment*, Methuen, 1974.

Taylor, Charles, *Multiculturalism*, Princeton University Press, 1994.

——*Sources of the Self: The Making of the Modern Identity*, Cambridge University Press, 1989.

Templeton, Douglas, *The New Testament as True Fiction*, Sheffield Academic Press, 1999.

Thagard, Paul, *Conceptual Revolutions*, Princeton University Press, 1992.

Thirlwall, Connop, *Essays, Speeches and Sermons*, ed. Stewart Perowne, Bentley & Son, 1880.

Thomson, James, *The Seasons* (1726–30).

Vico, Giambattista, *The New Science* (1744), trs Thomas Goddard Bergin and Max Harrold Frisch, Ithaca, N.Y.: Cornell University Press, 1968.

Vidler, Alec, *F.D. Maurice and Company*, SCM Press, 1966.

Walsh, P.G., and Kenney, J.G. (eds.), The Cambridge History of Classical Literature, Vol. II, Cambridge University Press, 1982.

Wellek, René, *Immanuel Kant in England*, Princeton University Press, 1931.

Whalley, George, 'The Bristol Library Borrowings of Southey and Coleridge, 1793–8', *The Library*, 5th Series, 4 (1949), 11–32.

Whorf, Benjamin Lee, *Language, Thought and Reality*, ed. J.B. Carroll, Cambridge, Mass.: M.I.T. Press, 1956.

Willey, Basil, *The Eighteenth-Century Background: Studies in the Idea of Nature in the Thought of the Period*, Chatto, 1940.

Williams, Bernard, *Ethics and the Limits of Philosophy*, Fontana, 1985.

Williams, Rowan, *Lost Icons: Reflections on Cultural Bereavement*, Edinburgh: T. & T. Clark, 2000.

Williamson, John, *A Brief Memoir of the Rev. Charles Simeon, M.A.*, 1848.

Wilson, Edward O., *Consilience: The Unity of Knowledge*, Little, Brown, 1998.

Woodbridge, Kenneth, 'The Sacred Landscape: Painters and the Lake Garden at Stowhead', *Apollo*, 88, 1968.

Young, Edward, *Conjectures on Original Composition in a Letter to the Author of Sir Charles Grandison*, 1759.

Index